No Stopping
Us Now

ALSO BY Gail Collins

When Everything Changed: The Amazing Journey of American Women from 1960 to the Present

America's Women: Four Hundred Years of Dolls, Drudges, Helpmates, and Heroines

As Texas Goes . . . : How the Lone Star State Hijacked the American Agenda

Scorpion Tongues: Gossip, Celebrity, and American Politics

No Stopping Us Now

-◄- -►-

THE ADVENTURES OF OLDER WOMEN IN AMERICAN HISTORY

-◄- -►-

Gail Collins

LITTLE, BROWN AND COMPANY

NEW YORK BOSTON LONDON

Little, Brown and Company
Hachette Book Group
1290 Avenue of the Americas, New York, NY 10104
littlebrown.com

First Edition: October 2019

Little, Brown and Company is a division of Hachette Book Group, Inc. The Little,
Brown name and logo are trademarks of Hachette Book Group, Inc.

The publisher is not responsible for websites (or their content) that are not owned by
the publisher.

The Hachette Speakers Bureau provides a wide range of authors for speaking events.
To find out more, go to hachettespeakersbureau.com or call (866) 376-6591.

ISBN 978-0-316-28654-1 (hc) / 978-0-316-42608-4 (large print)
LCCN 2019940322

10 9 8 7 6 5 4 3 2 1

LSC-C

Printed in the United States of America

To Dan, as always

CONTENTS

➤➤ ◀◀

No Stopping
Us Now

INTRODUCTION

➤ ◄

In this youth-made world, when a woman's over 25, she's considered old. Or on the way," began a 1971 ad for hair coloring. It went on to assure the reader—after quite a bit of depressing verbiage—that all was not lost. With Loving Care on your side, "You're not getting older. You're getting better!"

Well, that was a relief.

The ad became a classic. For years the "You're not getting older" slogan would pop up all over the place—at one point in a heavily orchestrated song with a melody so triumphant you'd have thought it was celebrating a moon landing, or the evacuation of Dunkirk.

We're a lot more sophisticated now. Nobody thinks 25 is old. But virtually nobody who spots her first gray hairs is going to sigh virtuously and let nature take its course, either. "There's a reason why forty, fifty, and sixty don't look the way they used to," Nora Ephron once wrote, "and it's not because of feminism, or better living through exercise. It's because of hair dye."

We've expanded our vision of what women can do at any age—Ruth Bader Ginsburg working out with her personal trainer at 86 before a day at the Supreme Court sounds perfectly reasonable, not to mention deeply desirable. But that doesn't mean our prejudice against growing older has been erased. If it had, the 7,000 or so cosmetic surgeons in America would be way underemployed.

This is the story of women and age in America, from the colonies to the twenty-first century, from Martha Washington to Hillary Clinton. There were definitely some points when getting older was easier than others. That's always been the case, throughout history, around the planet. "Herodotus tells us of some tribes who worshipped their elders as gods and of others who ate them," wrote historian David Hackett Fischer. The extremes in America, fortunately, have been somewhat less dire.

Who counts as an "older" woman? Well, there have been some pretty dramatic swings in opinion. In the early colonial south, any woman short of menopause counted as a hot young marriage prospect. But after the American Revolution, in female-laden northern cities, turning 30 without a husband meant entering the realm of old maid-hood. This is not going to be a tale of steady progress toward an age-indifferent tomorrow. However, we can definitely pick out some eras that look more enticing than others. And then decide whether the one we're living in now is a moment of real transition.

Traveling through American history, we'll see how attitudes toward women in their middle and later years shifted. There are some very clear patterns. One is that matter of scarcity. A 50-year-old widow could start her own business while choosing from among a dozen eager suitors if she happened to be one of a handful of females in a gold rush town in the middle of the nineteenth century.

The second, inevitably, is economic. Eras in which older women were able to earn money or increase their family's assets were eras in which they were . . . popular. In colonial times, a widowed grandmother who was a skilled spinner or sausage maker got plenty of respect. Jump ahead 100 years, move to a city, and your middle-class housewife had only one job to do: have babies and rear them. When the kids were grown, she was consigned to a rocking chair in the corner—metaphorically and frequently literally.

Our first generation of great female public figures came into their political prime in the mid-nineteenth century, when they were in their 50s or 60s. Their America still believed a woman's place was in the home. But some canny strategists—like Elizabeth Cady Stanton— came up with a pseudo compromise. They stayed home, raised the kids, and then took off on their lecture tours, bearing their gray hair as the proud proof that they'd followed the rules. Now it was time to raise hell and fight for abolition and women's rights.

Suddenly women were composing odes to menopause. One mid-nineteenth-century reformer announced that the end of fertility was a time for "super-exaltation." On the other hand, that was also a time when some doctors were beginning to theorize that postmenopausal women who engaged in sex were risking their lives and their sanity. There are no periods in American history when all the news is good.

During the period between the Civil War and the end of World War I, female entertainment celebrities tended to be older. You could be a glamorous singer at 50 and a famous beauty on the stage at 60 or 70. That was the age when "popular entertainment" meant lectures and theater. Then came the movies, with their unforgiving close-ups, at the same time that an enormous economic boom put outrageous new consuming power into the hands of the young. Older women were no longer in vogue or in view. In popular films of the day, they were usually busty dowagers sternly disapproving of their male counterparts, who swanned around speakeasies with showgirls.

The national mood got serious during the Depression and World War II—and Eleanor Roosevelt was the most admired woman in the country. Then, after another postwar obsession with the consumer power of the younger generation, came the women's liberation movement, whose heroines included middle-aged women like Betty Friedan and Ella Baker. At about the same time, the New Left was preaching, "Don't trust anyone over 30."

The biggest changes for older women were sparked when the booming post–World War II economy sputtered and families found it harder and harder to live a middle-class life on just the husband's salary. Suddenly women who had always been raised to aspire to domestic bliss began to be valued for their moneymaking potential. I have a vivid memory of talking with a group of male college students in the 1980s, all of whom agreed that the most important qualities in a wife were personality and "good earning capacity." They were probably downplaying physical attractiveness for the benefit of the visiting feminist. But it was still a sea change—after a national history in which men remained in their "prime" decades after women were judged old and on the shelf, things were evening out a little. (Yeah, you say, but what about female movie stars who get put out to pasture at 35? Yeah, I say, well, what about Meryl Streep? We'll talk.)

Besides the social challenges aging women face, there are, of course, physical problems. The body deteriorates with time, but the process was a lot faster if you happened to be getting older in an era when there were no antibiotics, sanitation was bad, and even relatively simple injuries during childbirth could cause a lifetime of misery. It's no wonder that colonial Americans regarded a healthy old age as a sign of God's special favor—though not even a benevolent deity seemed capable of guaranteeing a healthy set of teeth. Back then, women who got sick or became invalids were counseled to regard their disabilities as divine will, and a welcome opportunity to demonstrate the virtue of suffering with a smile. That philosophy reigned for some time, until health reformers popped up and started arguing that a hearty old age was less about God and more about proper diet and exercise. (And, in some quarters, avoidance of sex.) Popular ministers in the late nineteenth century mixed the two themes and argued that virtuous behavior would win you a long life span, while bad thoughts and deeds meant a miserable decline starting around 50.

Now middle-aged women looking at census projections may start thinking about what kind of career they'll want in their 80s. We've lived through an era of such extraordinary change and expanding possibility that it sometimes seems as if nothing, including age, can slow us down.

Imagining the future is easier if we look back on where we've been so far. Whether it's a 77-year-old midwife riding out in the middle of the night to help a patient in 1800 or an 80-year-old riveter making planes during World War II or an 86-year-old justice getting in shape for another Supreme Court session, the heroines are the women who fight back age by living for something more than just survival.

And we'll raise a glass, to toast whatever comes next.

1. The Colonies

"IF THEY BE BUT CIVIL, AND UNDER 50 YEARS OF AGE"

Legend has it that in 1630, a "romping girl" named Anne Pollard was the first colonial woman to set foot in the new settlement of Boston. Whether Anne was first or not, she definitely stayed for quite a while— she died there in 1725 at the age of 104, leaving behind 130 descendants. In the years between, she married, opened a tavern with her husband, and later ran it herself as a widow. As Anne grew older and older, she became a local celebrity, and a lucky visitor who dropped into the tavern might be invited to share a "social pipe" with the city's most famous matriarch. If you visit Boston Common today, you can find a young Anne depicted on the Founders Memorial.

Her story is a useful reminder that while early American settlers did not generally live as long as we do now, some of them did get to be very old. Of the women who managed to reach 21 in the late-seventeenth-century Plymouth Colony, about 7 percent made it past 90. You just had to be very, very lucky. Today, aging tends to be a rather confident progression through childhood, young adulthood, and into middle age, at which point we might begin to seriously contemplate our own mortality. In the colonial period, death could come at any time—infants died, children died, teenagers died. Young women died in childbirth; young men were lost at sea. Houses—and towns—caught fire. Plagues and epidemic diseases appeared and whisked away hundreds of people of all ages.

In 1632, the 19-year-old Massachusetts poet Anne Bradstreet wrote "Upon a Fit of Sickness":

Twice ten years old, not fully told
Since nature gave me breath
My race is run, my thread is spun
Lo here is fatal Death.

Bradstreet lived to be 60, but clearly she took her era's worldview to heart.

If New Englanders had a shaky life expectancy, it was absolutely nothing compared to the situation in the early southern colonies, where, thanks to the malarial swamps, mortality rates before 1624 ran as high as 37 percent. The upside was that women who did manage to survive had a raft of opportunities. Their tenure as prime marriage candidates could stretch out until menopause. "If any Maid or single Woman have a desire to go over, they will think themselves in the Golden Age, when Men paid a Dowry for their Wives: for if they be but Civil, and under 50 years of Age, some honest Man or other, will purchase them for their Wives," wrote one English promoter who was trying to encourage emigration. This open attitude toward age on the part of the male population had a lot to do with the fact that there was only one woman for every six men.

SAFER "IN HER HANDS THAN IN ANY MAN[']S"

The southern colonies were an excellent example of an important rule in American history: when there aren't enough people, outsiders who wouldn't normally get a chance to shine are suddenly in demand. If you were a middle-aged black woman in nineteenth-century Massachusetts, your work options were probably limited to doing laundry or somebody else's household chores. However, if you were a black pioneer in the West, you could own the only bar in town or be the stagecoach driver.

If you were Margaret Brent in seventeenth-century Maryland, you could step up and save your colony. Brent was described as a large woman with red hair, and that's all the help we're going to get in imagining her. The fact that she never married was so unusual for the time and place that many scholars have concluded she had taken a religious vow of celibacy. But she certainly did not seem to shun all worldly goods. She threw herself into the business of lending money to the newer settlers and spent much of her middle age in court, suing her fellow colonists 134 times, mainly for debt repayment. She generally won. That's why she's referred to—rather loosely—as America's first female lawyer. Maryland's governor was so impressed that he made her executrix of his estate. Later, when mercenary soldiers were threatening to level the colony, the dying governor put her in charge of restoring the peace. She did—by raising enough money to bribe everybody to go away.

Since Brent was a unique figure, it's tricky to give her story any universal meaning—other than the one about desperate times breeding desperate measures. (The Maryland Assembly said that during its crisis the colony was safer "in her hands than in any man[']s." But they still refused to allow her to have a vote.) Most women who came to the early south had less dramatic stories. Mainly they were just hoping to make a good marriage. Given the bad water, bad air, and overall miasma of the place, the chances were slim that they'd live long enough to enjoy it. But the matrimonial odds were so favorable that a woman in good health could just keep marrying up. Frances Culpeper wed a large landowner in what is now North Carolina when she was 18. He died, and Frances inherited most of his property. The now-wealthy widow was soon remarried—this time to Sir William Berkeley, the governor of Virginia. Frances, 36, was now Lady Berkeley and equipped with a sizable guaranteed income for life. About a decade and many adventures later, Lord Berkeley died from the effects of a bout with malaria. Frances was married again, at 46, to a younger man who became governor of the Carolinas. But she was always known as Lady Berkeley.

"IN THE DARK ALL CATS ARE GREY"

Life for women in the northern colonies was much…calmer. New arrivals found the climate and living conditions healthier than in the crowded, sewage-swamped cities of Europe they'd left behind. And the women who did make it to middle age and beyond sometimes concluded that older was better. "I have often thought that women who live to get over the time of Child-bareing, if other things are favourable to them, experience more comfort and satisfaction than at any other period of their lives," wrote Elizabeth Drinker in her diary. She was 61 at the time, and she had lived an action-packed life. Her husband, Henry, a

Philadelphia businessman, had been exiled during the Revolutionary War as a suspected Tory sympathizer. Elizabeth made her way to Valley Forge in 1778 to plead his case to George Washington — who offered a good dinner but not much assistance. Eventually reunited with Henry, she later nursed her household through a terrible yellow fever epidemic that took nearly 10 percent of Philadelphia's population.

Drinker was wealthier than most colonial women of her time, but the rhythms of her life were typical. She married in her 20s, bore children until middle age, and was still raising her brood when her oldest offspring began to have families of their own. Even when the children left the house, most of them continued to live nearby, and her life was full of domestic duties and babies. There was no real empty nest, just a slightly calmer one. And you could see how, after nine deliveries and two miscarriages, she might have regarded aging as something of a picnic.

Elizabeth Drinker would live into her 70s, but like everyone in the colonies, she understood how quickly death could strike people of any age — only four of her nine children would survive her. Given the poor chances of living for a very long time, old people were often regarded as having been singled out by the Creator as particularly worthy. "If a man is favored with long life... it is God that has lengthened his days," said Boston minister Increase Mather, who made it to 84 himself. One Massachusetts congregation, whose 1682 seating plan still exists, made the status of seniority perfectly clear. The best seat, next to the pulpit, went to the minister's wife, and the one next to her was reserved for the widow of the previous minister. Then came the elders, and the elders' wives, and the widows of elders. (A woman could be old in Massachusetts, but she couldn't be an elder.) Then came the congregation, which was divided by gender and seated according to age, with the youngest members consigned to the rear. The church was the center of life in those communities. If you were an older woman wondering if you still had a place in the scheme of things, it must have been hugely reassuring to walk into Sunday service and stride up the aisle, past your younger relatives and neighbors, and take an honored seat near the front.

As we've seen, a woman of 50 might count as an extremely desirable marriage prospect if she happened to live in a very high-mortality region. Even in the healthier north, when it came to sex in general, male opinions on the perfect age for a partner varied. Benjamin Franklin, the ultimate pragmatist, wrote a famous letter to a young friend, counseling him that if he intended to have affairs, he should prefer "old Women to young ones." They were more interesting, Franklin argued, and anyway "in the dark all Cats are grey."

We will pause for a moment to consider whether that was a compliment.

"I BELIEVE I NEVER HAD A GOWN BETTER MADE"

No specific milestone signified passage into old age among colonial women. By 40, many had already lost a husband and offspring. Many 60-year-olds were still raising their children—the average housewife was 63 when her youngest left home. Every woman who was capable of lifting a finger was expected to take part in household chores. And nobody was going to tell you to slow down because your hair was getting white.

Martha Ballard, a Maine midwife, spent her life balancing her job delivering babies with a mind-boggling list of domestic duties: spinning, knitting, sewing, preparing the family food, tending chickens and sheep. Around 1800, as she approached her 70s, she began to cut back; but then the other local midwife died and Ballard stepped up. At 77 she was still answering late-night calls that could drag on well into the next day. ("The patient was safe delivered at 3 hour pm of her fifth son. I tarried all night.") On another occasion, after mother and child had been cared for, Ballard took a nap, had some breakfast with the family, rode on to visit another patient, and then came home to do "my ironing and some mending." Besides delivering babies, she prepared bodies for burial and visited the sick, sometimes dispensing medicines of her own making. She reached her clients mainly by horse, crossing rivers and traversing bad or nonexistent roads in Maine weather. She wrote about climbing "mountains of ice" on one expedition and falling from her horse into the mud during another. There were other midwives who probably performed just as heroically. On Long Island, Lucretia Lester was said to have delivered 1,300 babies and lost only two. We really don't know if Ballard was particularly unusual. She just happened to be the one who kept a diary.

As long as midwives were needed, nobody objected to their riding around the countryside in the middle of the night at any age. The same was true of every occupation where competent workers were in short supply. Elizabeth Drinker was fitted for a new dress by a seamstress named Susannah Swett and wrote happily: "I believe I never had a gown better made in my life and she is now within seven weeks of 73 years of age." But just because the colonists were ready to hire the elderly for a job that needed doing, it didn't mean that prejudices didn't exist. Drinker added that the surprise of seeing someone "work so neatly at such an age is the cause of my making the memorandum."

"be in Behaviour as becometh Holiness"

Ministers urged their aging female parishioners to achieve serenity by contemplating death as the passage to a far happier life in heaven. (When the clergyman Mather Byles passed away, his daughter announced she was "in rapture" over his good fortune.) While they waited, women were supposed to gradually withdraw from the world, spending more and more time in prayer and contemplation while enjoying earthly pleasures less and less—but still, of course, continuing to perform the household chores. In Boston, Rev. Benjamin Colman preached that it was the duty of "aged women" to repress their discontents and "be in Behaviour as becometh Holiness." This was especially important, he said, when it came to "Publick Appearance & Conversation; Garb, Dress, Gate, Countenance, Speech, Silence, Gesture"—a list that pretty much swept the board except for the aforementioned housework.

Plenty of reports from colonial days make it clear that women of every age ignored the ministers when it came to staying silent. But they did adapt their dress to their time of life. Most women lived on farms, wearing simple, loose dresses that were easy to work in. As they aged, they generally began to avoid bright colors and don close-fitting caps. The public message was pretty clear: the cap wearers were out of the marriage market and putting away their plumage. But they were also covering the signs of graying hair. It was stage one in an ongoing struggle that would proceed, over the next few centuries, through false curls, turbans, wigs, and every other method of concealment women could concoct. When we look at portraits of them wearing their dark dresses and caps, they often seem to be nothing but somber faces floating in the dark.

Things were a lot less dreary in the fashionable world of high society. Gray hair was actually in — it was a symbol of dignity and importance. But the idea was not to flaunt your own gray locks. You wore a large, dramatic gray wig. Maria and Harriet Trumbull, teenage sisters who reported back to their Connecticut family on the fashions of New York in 1801, sent their mother a white wig, telling her that the women in society "wear white *hair* altogather now." There could be nothing less fashionable, they warned, "than a black wig."

Women applied bacon to their faces to avoid wrinkles, or used a paste made from eggs and alum boiled in rosewater. Tactics of that kind were socially acceptable, as long as the family could spare the bacon and eggs. But the revolutionary era regarded cosmetics as ... un-American — a sinister trick to trap unwary males into marriage with women who were older, or less attractive, than they appeared. When Americans were under British rule, some people apparently believed that cosmetics were illegal and that women who "impose upon, seduce or betray into matrimony any of his Majesty's subjects by virtue of scents, cosmetics, washes, paints, artificial teeth, false hair or high-heeled shoes, shall incur the penalty of the law now in force against witchcraft." Stories about "Hoops and Heels" laws pop up all over our early history. It's not clear that one was ever passed, and none ever seems to have been enforced. But the sentiment certainly existed.

"THE WOMEN ARE PITIFULLY TOOTH-SHAKEN"

Teeth were a problem for older colonists of both sexes — although there's no record of any legislature trying to punish men for wearing artificial dentures when they were courting. There was no dentistry as we know it. Barbers and mechanics were sometimes called in to treat rotten teeth, but their only remedy was to pull them. (Paul Revere, a goldsmith, also practiced a little dental work on the side.) The toothbrush had been invented, but the early versions were generally made of hog bristles, which were very expensive. Toothpaste didn't become widely used until the late 1800s, and if a colonial woman did try to clean her teeth, the process involved a coarse linen cloth and, occasionally, a mixture of honey and sugar to theoretically wipe away decay.

If you lived into adulthood in colonial America you probably would not, alas, have all your teeth. And the number you could hang on to obviously dropped with age. Researchers excavating the site of the Jamestown settlement in Virginia discovered the body of a woman in early middle age who had only five teeth. Some of the others had been gone so long by the time of her death that the tooth sockets had completely closed over. Jamestown was notoriously a tough place to live — malnutrition was so bad that legend had it one settler was tried for having eaten his wife. But even when times got easier and food was plentiful, the dental situation didn't much improve. "The women are pitifully tooth-shaken, whether through the coldness of the climate or by sweet-meats, of which they have a score, I am not able to affirm," a visitor reported.

George Washington had famously bad teeth and ill-fitting dentures. Martha seemed to be in better shape. She had lost some of hers by the White House years and was wearing a kind of bridge, but it must have worked — Abigail Adams reported that the First Lady's teeth were "beautiful." Very few people were wealthy enough to acquire false teeth of any type, and the average colonial woman was forced to live with a premature look of toothless old age. Eyeglasses were expensive, too — and a luxury that women doing close sewing by candle at night must have yearned for. Both George and Martha Washington wore glasses by the end of their lives. But when Dolley Madison needed help reading or sewing, she shared a pair with her husband the president.

Women talked a lot about their ailments and physical disorders, which were legion. "To be old in early America was to be wracked by illness. It was to live in physical misery, with pain as a constant companion," writes David Hackett Fischer. Anne Bradstreet was subject to fainting spells that could leave her unconscious for hours — one of her later poems was titled "Deliverance from a Fitt of Fainting." Elizabeth Drinker's diary is a veritable catalogue of symptoms, from fevers to "giddiness in my head, occasion'd by the obstruction in my bowels." When she was 60, Drinker wrote that since she was feeling poorly almost all the time, she wasn't going to mention health matters. If she were being less discreet, she added, "I should daily say I was unwell."

"Dyspepsia"—an umbrella term for the many varieties of indigestion—was a near-universal complaint, and it's no wonder, given the unsanitary conditions under which food was slaughtered and cooked. It was almost always accompanied by "peevishness, doubts, fears, wandering thoughts and ridiculous fancies," claimed Benjamin Waterhouse, a late-eighteenth-century physician who was among the first faculty members at Harvard Medical School.

Elizabeth Drinker's ideas about remedies sound more hair-raising than her symptoms. She attempted to cure her daughter of what Drinker described as "worms" by dosing her with "Venice Treacle," a concoction whose five dozen ingredients included alcohol, opium, and honey. Bleeding was a favorite prescription. It was based on an ancient theory that physical distress was produced by too much blood in the system. Or the wrong kind. The real attraction was probably just that it was something the doctor could do, to look as if he had a plan. If a patient was complaining of back pain from rheumatism, for instance, the doctor might use a "scarificator" that pushed 15 or 20 small blades into her back to reduce the amount of blood. Drinker, when she was troubled with constipation, mused that "loosing blood might be a temporary relief" and later reported feeling "very languid" after having "lost, at least 12 ounces blood." Unlike most of her contemporaries, she had recourse to a physician, although it's hard to say if that did her much good, given all that bloodletting.

In an age without aspirin, let alone antibiotics, people of both sexes suffered from many ailments we can cure today with a pill or at least simple surgery. Benjamin Franklin, who had a bladder stone, said that only the use of opium made life "tolerable." Women were also tormented by damage from childbirth that would be easily repairable today. In the nineteenth century, the famous abolitionist orator Angelina Grimké had what her husband called "injuries" that "shattered incurably her nervous system." The problems apparently included a hernia and a prolapsed uterus—the latter so dire that her uterus sometimes protruded from her body, causing intense pain. Perhaps the worst nonfatal childbirth damage involved a tear in the wall between the vagina and the bladder or rectum, leaving victims unable to control a constant leakage of urine or feces. They were usually doomed to live confined to their rooms, permanently uncomfortable and treated like pariahs because of the stench.

No one in the eighteenth century could cure those problems, but when it came to the ordinary ailments of day-to-day life, it was usually the oldest woman in the family who had the remedy. A newlywed bride would probably arrive at her first home knowing the basics. But when the baby had a cough or her husband was tortured by those ever-present bowel issues, she would seek advice from her mother or an older neighbor. The same thing was true if a chicken failed to produce eggs or the bread didn't rise. Women who had spent their lives as homemakers retained influence as they aged because they knew things. The list of skills a farm wife had to master was endless: spinning thread, weaving cloth, churning butter, making everything from candles to cheese to soap to sausage.

Women produced so many valuable products that they could run a parallel economic universe, bartering and trading their goods. They also had their own informal social system in which the older women were expected to advise their juniors. In 1664 in Massachusetts, Elizabeth Perkins and Agnes Ewens were called to court to testify in a case involving a younger woman they knew. But they declined to appear, arguing that they had counseled the person in question and did not want to break the confidence, since she had followed their advice and done well ever since. They were asking for a kind of "professional immunity," and they received it.

Esther Lewis, who was widowed at 42, was an excellent — if somewhat over-the-top — example of older women's influence and power. In the early nineteenth century, she ran the family's 150-acre Pennsylvania farm by herself until she was in her 60s, and in her diary she records churning 288 pounds of butter in one year, with a plan to increase production the next. She supervised the drying of apples, making of applesauce, rendering of lard, and the production of about 1,000 candles a year for the household. She also educated her four daughters, sheltered runaway slaves, and — when she happened to notice some unusual stones on the ground — figured out that her land contained iron ore and established a successful mining operation. Esther apparently inherited this gift for overachievement. Her mother, Rebecca, moved to her daughter's farm at 79 and took on the job of spinning yarn. She produced about 33,000 yards a year.

"GOOD MOTHER, FAREWELL"

We don't know nearly enough about black women of any age in the colonies. Almost all of them first arrived as slaves or indentured servants, who could eventually work out their term of service and become free. Children of mixed race born in the colonies usually took their status from their mothers. That was the story for Jenny Slew, who was born in 1719, the daughter of a free white woman and a male slave. Her parents were apparently able to live as husband and wife, and Jenny was raised free. As far as we know, she lived her life in quiet anonymity. (There was undoubtedly some private domestic drama since she went through several husbands.) Then, when she was 46, a white man named John Whipple kidnapped her "with force and arms" and tried to keep her as his slave. Jenny filed suit and demanded her freedom. Whipple's defense was that Jenny, as a married woman, had no right to go to court on her own. A husband was supposed to represent her. The judge found that argument perfectly reasonable and Whipple won the case, giving us an excellent insight into why so many of the women who would fight for abolition in the next century also added their own rights to the agenda.

Undeterred, Jenny appealed. This time she got a trial by jury and she won, gaining both her freedom and a financial judgment against Whipple. She then left the courtroom and walked out of history — sort of. One of the lawyers present in the Salem courthouse when the verdict came down was John Adams. "Attended Court," he wrote later. "Heard the trial of an action of trespass, brought by a mulatto woman, for damages, for restoring her liberty. This is called suing for liberty; the first action that ever I knew of the sort, though I have heard there have been many." This was in 1765. Fourteen years later, Adams would begin work on the Massachusetts State Constitution, drafting a declaration of rights that stated "all men are born free and equal." In 1780, it became state law.

In 1781, the new constitution caught the attention of Mum Bett, a slave of about 35 who was living in Massachusetts under an abusive mistress—Bett had once stopped the woman from hitting her younger sister with a shovel and wound up getting hit herself, with a deep wound to her arm. Bett got a young lawyer named Theodore Sedgwick, who filed suit, arguing that her enslavement was unconstitutional. They won, paving the way for the state's official abolition of slavery in 1783. After her victory, Bett took a new name and became, appropriately enough, Elizabeth Freeman. She took a job with the Sedgwick family, serving as a surrogate mother for the children when Sedgwick's wife plunged into illness and depression. She saved her wages, bought land, and built a home of her own, where she lived in retirement. When she died, at 85, she was buried in the Sedgwick family plot under a tombstone that noted: "She could neither read nor write, yet in her own sphere she had no superior or equal. She neither wasted time nor property. She never violated a trust, nor failed to perform a duty. In every situation of domestic trial, she was the most efficient helper and the tenderest friend. Good mother, farewell."

"THE TENDENCY OF OLD WOMEN TO BREED MISCHIEF"

All the roads to power and prestige we've looked at were private—older women got to sit near the minister but not *be* the minister. They might be consulted for advice, but they were never elected to office. There were, of course, exceptions—the one rule to which there is no exception is that there will always be exceptions. A few early colonial women did become preachers and theologians, like the famous Anne Hutchinson of Massachusetts, who one observer said "preaches better Gospell than any of your black-coates that have been at the Ninneversity." But Hutchinson was probably not a role model for many younger women unless they were prepared to be jailed, tried on multiple charges, convicted, and banished to Rhode Island while still in their 40s. And then to be widowed, moved to what is now the Bronx, and massacred in an Indian attack at 52.

A more optimistic example might have been the Quakers, who did manage some division of authority between the sexes. But if people really wanted to see older women triumph in a public role, they needed to look at Native Americans—which, unfortunately, very few of them ever did. In 1789, a young woman named Ann Powell kept a diary of an adventurous trip she and some relatives undertook from Montreal to Detroit. After stopping at Niagara Falls, Powell and her party were invited to watch an Iroquois council meeting, in which the participants included "some old squaws." She was struck by the women's influence. When a man in her own culture grew infirm and senile, she mused, people described him as an "old woman." With the Iroquois, things seemed to be different. "On the banks of Lake Erie a woman becomes respectable as she grows old, and I suppose the greatest compliment you can pay a young hero is that he is as wise as an old woman," she wrote.

The Iroquois, like many other eastern tribes, divided their labor: women grew most of the food while men hunted for protein. The basic form of government was the clan—an extended family in which the older women chose which man would be chief, and had the power to remove him if he failed to meet with their approval. "Nothing is more real than this superiority of women," one French visitor wrote.

While older women continued to have an active part in tribal life long after the arrival of the Europeans, they were as affected as everyone else by the newcomers. By the time Ann Powell visited the Iroquois council and recorded her impressions, their way of living was already under attack. Native hunting land had been usurped by colonial farmers, and many of the tribes found themselves confined to reservations. Missionaries were uncomfortable with the traditional division of labor because it did not reflect their conviction that men were meant to enjoy the status of provider while women performed backup jobs like cooking and sewing and making cloth. Over the years, the American government would make repeated attempts to foist spinning wheels on the tribes, the better to nudge the women toward a proper place.

White incursion was catastrophic, not least because it also often meant the introduction of liquor. Handsome Lake, a Seneca leader, went into an alcoholic delirium in 1799 and had a vision in which the Creator revealed he was angry about four evils: whiskey, witchcraft, love magic, and abortions. All but the first appeared to be the doing of women, particularly the senior women. Handsome Lake declared that God wanted the Seneca to live in nuclear families, not matrilineal clans, and was also unhappy that the women taught their daughters how to use birth control: "The Creator is sad because of the tendency of old women to breed mischief." Most of his targets were allowed to repent. But one refused to cooperate and demanded that Handsome Lake tell her exactly what she had done wrong. He ordered his followers to kill her, and they did. The witch hunt continued, but the rest of the alleged witches figured out that a quick request for his absolution would get them off the hook, and they successfully begged forgiveness.

Handsome Lake was not the only person who connected older women with witchcraft. In 1646, an English writer had deplored the way in which "every old woman with a wrinkled face, a furr'd brow, a hairy lip, a gobber tooth, a squint eye, a squeaking voice, or a scolding tongue, having a ragged coate on her back, a skull cap on her head, a spindle in her hand, and a Dog or Cat by her side, is not only suspected but pronounced for a witch." That was actually a lot of specificity — in the colonies, people seemed prepared to act on a far shorter checklist. During the last half of the seventeenth century, as many as 200 people were officially accused as witches in New England, and they ranged from Ann Hibbins, a wealthy Boston widow who had a history of fighting with workmen over their bills, to a number of cranky beggar women. Many of the victims had less than cherubic personalities, although in Salem the witch-hunters accused 71-year-old Rebecca Nurse, a respected member of the community, pulling her out of her sickbed and off to jail, trial, and hanging, all within four months. Most of the accused were older women, and the accusers were often in their teens. "Must the younger Women, do yee say, hearken to the Elder?" one of the Salem girls demanded of a "spectre" she claimed was torturing her.

"PUTRID ABOMINATION TO THE DEITY"

Both the colonists and the Indians seemed to agree that one sign of possible witch-like tendencies was an older woman who lived alone. This was no short-term prejudice — in 1820, the census of Shrewsbury, Massachusetts, reported only two households with a single inhabitant. One, a spinster, was "old Moll Garfield the witch." The other, a man, was just listed as "an insane person." If a widow wanted to avoid solitude, she generally wound up living with her adult children, and in the colonies, where many farmhouses consisted of a single dark room, that must have been less than convenient. Most early homes also had only one chair, which was reserved for the head of the household. The widowed mother would presumably have been confined to a stool. Even as time went on and houses got bigger, the chances were that in all but the wealthiest families the only real bedroom would belong to the parents. Grand-mothers would likely sleep in a chamber with the children. Or with other female relatives who might have come to live for a while and help with the chores. Or maybe with everybody. Frequently families just set aside one large room where everyone slept, piled up on various mats.

Life in an average colonial home wasn't all that comfortable for any-one, but it must have been particularly tough on older people. Even if a family was wealthy enough to avoid sleeping on the floor, the bedding situation wasn't designed for back support. Feather beds were regarded as the height of luxury, but they were terrible in hot weather. They were also so high that they required stairs to mount them. One Massachusetts woman remembered dreading the arrival of morning and the necessity of climbing down from her huge, fluffy feather bed. And at night, unless she happened to hit the mattress just right, she "passed my night in roll-ing down hill, or in vain efforts to scramble to the top, to avoid falling out on the floor."

Women who still had their husbands in old age usually continued to live independently, able to make their own choices on issues like floor versus feathers. But the story of the colonial era is frequently about wid-ows. Nearly every woman married sooner or later—particularly in the 1600s and particularly in the south, where that shortage of females made spinsterhood almost an affront. "An old maid is one of the most cranky, ill-natured, maggoty, peevish, conceited, disagreeable, hypocritical, fretful, noisy, gibing, canting, censorious, out-of-the-way, never-to-be-pleased, good for nothing creatures," hyperventilated a North Carolina paper. The antipathy was not so intense in the north, where the balance of the sexes was more even. (This is not to say it was nonexistent. A newspaper in 1790 called a spinster a "putrid abomination to the deity.")

At any rate, the vast majority of women did marry, and a very large proportion of them went on to survive their husbands. One eighteenth-century census in Massachusetts found widows outnumbering widowers seven to one.

Colonial widows had a public image of fragility. This may be because women who found themselves in need of assistance knew they were more likely to get it if they depicted themselves as rather pathetic creatures. After the Revolution, when Tory sympathizers in America appealed to the king of England for restoration of some of their confiscated properties, men described themselves as "unfortunate," while women tended to say they were "poor, helpless" widows. The distinctly nonpathetic writer Judith Sargent Murray yearned for the day when "the term, *helpless widow,* might be rendered as unfrequent and inapplicable as that of *helpless widower.*"

Many widows were the furthest thing from miserable or needy. Some took new husbands — in the early south, it became a kind of career. But there were definite advantages to avoiding remarriage. Most of the colonies followed English law, under which married women had virtually no legal rights. Their husbands controlled their property, their income if they had any, and — at least in theory — their behavior. As the British jurist William Blackstone famously put it, under the law a married couple was one person, and that person was the husband. A widow, on the other hand, could do what she pleased, if she had the income with which to do it. Some, like Anne Pollard, wound up running the family business. While innkeeping and tailoring were both regarded as offshoots of housewives' natural duties, colonial women showed up in less expected places, too. Ann Franklin, Ben Franklin's sister-in-law, became the first woman printer in New England when she took over the family business after her husband's death. Ann, about 39 at the time, had five children to support, and she built a prosperous establishment, which produced everything from books to election ballots. Her son, James, eventually came on as her business partner. But when he died, Ann, at 66, continued on her own. Lydia Bailey, a Philadelphia widow, had a 53-year publishing career during which she trained 42 men in the trade.

Some male colonists complained about a "widowarchy" of women who'd taken over their husbands' estates and trading businesses. "And now her Husband is deceas'd, she thinks that upon the Setting of the Sun, the Moon is to govern," grumbled Cotton Mather, another famous Puritan minister, who estimated that 20 percent of his congregation were widows.

If a husband failed to leave a will, a widow automatically got the use of one-third of his property during her lifetime. But she didn't have the right to sell anything, and the situation probably got uncomfortable if there was an eager male heir or two watching her every move. The specificity of some wills did seem to foretell a generational clash in the making. Thomas King of Plymouth Colony willed his house to his son but decreed that his wife would have "the East End" along with "a liberty to make some use of the Cellars and and [*sic*] leantoos." Beatrice Plummer of Newbury got "the new room, half the orchard, half the apples," and a list of other items down to "a pewter pint pott, a paire of old curtaines & vallens." One hopes there weren't family fights over exactly how many apples constituted half.

We're talking here about older women who had property. It seemed that nobody wanted the ones who didn't. The deference and respect that elders received was frequently connected to the presumption that they came attached to a certain amount of wealth. There was nothing the colonials disliked more than a person who couldn't make a contribution. In New Jersey, officials were instructed to search arriving ships to make sure there were no undesirables waiting to come ashore, like lunatics, vagabonds, or "old persons." Indigent women were sometimes boarded off with members of the community, who might use them as housekeepers or farmworkers. If they were unable to work, there was usually some form of shelter available, like community almshouses. It might sound better than being driven homeless from town to town, but "to me a cave or a wigwam would be far preferable," wrote one visitor to the Friends' Widows Asylum in Pennsylvania. A Gloucester woman named Judith Stevens discovered her old tutor living in an almshouse in 1775 and described it as a "last resort of wretchedness."

"like a Spartan mother"

All this talk about widows brings us to Martha Washington, who went from wealthy widow to the first First Lady. In all of American history, she is perhaps the American who was most admired without ever being seriously discussed. She was first married at 18 to Daniel Parke Custis, whose father was one of the richest men in the colonies, and one of the most difficult. Martha managed to persuade the elder Custis — who had vetoed the marriage — that she was just what he needed in a daughter-in-law. She won the day with "a prudent speech," a family friend reported.

By the time she was in her mid-20s, Martha was a widow — and an extremely rich one, running the vast Custis estates herself, and better than many of her male counterparts. (Colonial planters were often totally at sea when it came to turning a profit.) Many years later, she would urge her newly widowed niece to do everything possible "to keep all your matters in order yourself without depending on others as that is the only way to be happy to have all your business in your one [*sic*] hands." Dependence, she added, was a "wrached" state. But when it came to her own life, Martha, like many other eighteenth-century American widows, ditched independence as soon as possible. She entertained suitors and decided that George Washington was the one. Despite the fact that George brought very little wealth into the union, her new husband instantly assumed full control over her property.

George was by many accounts a devoted mate, although he was deeply disappointed that the marriage was childless. Given the fact that Martha was still in her 20s when they wed and had already given birth to four babies, it's likely that only George imagined fertility was her problem, and not his.

Only one of Martha's children lived to adulthood, and when he, too, died, the Washingtons took over raising his young daughter and son. (This is an excellent opportunity to note that she nicknamed one grandchild, George Washington Parke Custis, both "Washy" and "Tub.") When the Revolutionary War came, she was a loyal supporter of the cause — one of George's colleagues reported that Martha talked to him and another man "like a Spartan mother to her son on going to battle."

During the winter months, she was always with her husband at Valley Forge or whatever other cold encampment the soldiers were hunkered down in. Unlike the rank and file, the officers and their families had fairly comfortable quarters, so Martha didn't suffer from the weather. But she made herself useful, leading the other wives in projects like nursing the sick, sock knitting for the troops, and entertaining the staff and guests. One of the visitors was Elizabeth Drinker, attempting to get support for her exiled husband. Drinker found Martha "a sociable pretty kind of Woman" but referred to her dismissively as "Wife."

Martha had definitely become the Wife. Visitors always praised her sociability and good conversation, but the public world hardly regarded her as a person to be reckoned with. Perhaps it was in part her stature. A short woman, Martha often had to get the attention of her rather lofty husband by tugging at his sleeve. Did she regret giving up her independence? She never said. She had reverted to a life of pure domestic responsibilities, which were many: they hosted several hundred guests a year, some of whom lingered for months. There were lots of servants to help with the housework when people arrived. But Martha was completely in charge of their entertainment. After dinner, George would retire to his ease in the library, leaving his wife to chat up the visitors in the drawing room. Almost everyone found her an agreeable conversationalist— except Thomas Jefferson, who thought Martha "rather weak" and possibly a little dim. This would be more notable if Thomas Jefferson had not been a terrible male chauvinist. He was the Founding Father who once warned his daughter not to go out without a bonnet "because it will make you very ugly and then we should not love you so much."

By the time her husband became president, Martha was in her 50s and had graduated to the role of Older Woman. Even entertaining guests was no longer done on her terms. In an effort to show impartiality, George wanted social life limited to official events, like mass receptions and formal state dinners, which were universally described as soul deadening. There were also assemblies, when George danced but Martha didn't. After one of the dinners, a senator from North Carolina reported that he had "the honor of drinking coffee with his Lady, a most amiable woman." (George was apparently still fleeing to his study.) "If I live much longer," the senator continued, "I believe I shall at last be reconciled to the company of old women . . . a circumstance which I once thought impossible." At the time, Martha was 58 and the senator was 56. It was probably men like that who goaded the First Lady into saying, repeatedly, that the job of presidential wife should really go to someone "younger and gayer."

The Washingtons' retirement from public life was brief—George, whom Martha had begun calling "Old Man," died at 67, less than three years after he left the presidency. The end came after a brief illness during which his doctors' enthusiastic treatment deprived him of up to half of his body's blood. Martha controlled the income from his estate, but this time she had no heart for business. She followed him soon after, dying at 70. Perhaps she was worn out from offering hospitality to the hordes of visitors who came to offer their condolences. "She speaks of death as a pleasant journey," said a friend.

"The fewer women the better"

By the end of the colonial period there was no shortage of women, even in the south. "The fewer women the better," wrote a Maryland man who hoped to import a boatload of indentured servants. Being older meant losing stature, too. The Revolutionary War seemed to embolden younger Americans to cast off the bounds of elder power as well as royal tyranny. While in the pre-revolutionary era people had tended to represent themselves as being older than they were, the tide turned and they veered toward pretending they were younger.

The idea that older people deserved the highest veneration may not always have been honored in practice during colonial times, but at least it was a general ideal. After independence, even the principle was questioned. Followers of the theologian John Wesley were warned that grandmothers needed to be reined in when it came to child-rearing. "Your mother, or your husband's mother, may live with you; and you will do well to show her all possible respect. But let her on no account have the least share in the management of your children," Wesley advised. "She would undo all that you had done; she would give them their own will in all things. She would humour them to the destruction of their souls if not their bodies."

It was a change of attitude that had been coming on for some time. A new country that was founded by throwing off the yoke of authority was naturally going to be less enthusiastic about deferring to the older generation. Even the church seating arrangements stopped reflecting the idea that senior congregants deserved to sit in the front. By the end of the eighteenth century, the best seats were going to the richest members.

2. The 1800s Arrive

In a well-furnished drawing room, "through the long half-opened windows of which might be seen the receding avenues of a park filled with stately trees, sat two ladies," began a short story in an issue of a popular women's magazine in 1837. They were sisters — one of whom, we learn rather quickly, is a "radiant beauty of seventeen." The other, who is thirty-two, has, um, a nice smile. "The brilliant colours of youth were faded on her less rounded cheek, upon which was left but an undecided tint," the author reported sadly. The older sister was still wearing ribbons on her dress and in her hair, but instead of mere decoration, they were there "to conceal with taste the ravages of years."

Welcome to the nineteenth century. You have probably gathered that we are a long way from the days in the Chesapeake when being 45 and in decent health was enough to make you a great marriage candidate.

Colonial America had been, in a way, a good place to age — lack of doctors, dentists, and medication excepted. In a raw, underpopulated, and frequently disorganized new country, anybody was welcome if she was useful. Older women who no longer had the distractions of child-rearing had plenty of opportunities to offer their services — as counselors, midwives, tavern keepers, or even printers. If they were housewives who knew more about cheese making or botany or fine sewing than their juniors, then they were respected teachers. And if there was a shortage of wives, nobody was going to complain about a little gray hair.

But in the decades between the Revolutionary War and 1820, the attitude toward older women gradually became something close to downright hostility. People were moving to the cities, where farmwife skills were no longer in demand, and men were encouraged to confine their courting to the youngest candidates. A Currier & Ives lithograph from 1850 depicts *The Life and Age of Woman,* and the high point seems to be stage 3, when our heroine is 15: "Now glorious as a full-blown flower, the heart of manhood feels her power." Five years later, at stage 4, she's already a matron, and hardly a self-reliant one. "A husband now her arms entwine, she clings around him like a vine," explained the caption.

The Revolution had brought a spirit of out-with-the-old that extended to more than governments. But the most important reason older women lost status was purely pragmatic: they had no economic purpose. As the country got more crowded, men stepped up — or, depending on your perspective, elbowed their way in — and began to provide services that had been women's jobs before. Male physicians took over the delivery of babies. Male merchants ran the family stores. On the farm, housewives still held a position that combined hard work with prestige and power, thanks to their skill in making things for the family to eat or wear or sell. But by the 1800s, although most Americans still lived in farming communities, the focus had shifted to the new urban class, which was eager to dictate the way things were supposed to be.

In the cities, few middle-class women did anything that increased the family wealth. They still sewed, but the cloth they used came from a store, as did the candles and the food on the table. Many didn't even cook, since it was easy to afford help in the kitchen. They were almost exclusively defined as mothers, and motherhood was glorified to make up for all the other things that had been cut out of their portfolio. You'll remember that in the late 1700s, First Lady Martha Washington was the most famous woman in the nation. But in the nineteenth century, essay writers began penning tributes instead to...George Washington's mother. "There is no fame in the world more pure than that of the mother of Washington, and no woman since the Mother of Christ has left a better claim to the affectionate reverence of mankind," wrote a poet-intellectual named Rufus Griswold in 1854. It stood to reason. The greatest woman had to be the mother of the greatest man. The fact that Washington had found his mother supremely irritating never came up in the national conversation.

The role of mother was the only show in town, but it had a very limited run. The size of a middle-class family was shrinking. Urban parents quickly realized that children were very expensive in a world in which there were no fields for the youngsters to till, eggs to collect, or vegetable gardens to weed. Instead, they had to be educated, set up in careers, or given dowries to attract good husbands. At the beginning of the 1800s, American mothers averaged around seven children. By the end of the century, it was half that. Women were being restricted to maternal careers at the very time their years of active motherhood were growing shorter. And once the last child was gone, they were literally put into a corner—the one with a rocking chair. It was, one writer remembered, an era when "our grandmothers took to caps, false teeth and knitting before they were forty." (That would have been for the privileged, who could afford the teeth.)

It was certainly a bad time to be older. The Revolution had diminished the whole idea that senior citizens deserved special respect. The skills for which they had been valued were no longer in much demand— at least in the cities, where the new social attitudes were being forged. As a sign of how things had changed, the 1842 report of the Indigent Widows' and Single Women's Society concluded: "with the aged, we have few sympathies. They belong to a generation that has passed away; they can promise us neither reciprocation nor reward. Our reverence for them is rarely an active principle."

"It is only on emergencies"

To understand what happened in the nineteenth century, let's consider the career of Sarah Josepha Hale. She was one of the most influential people in the United States—editor of the most popular magazine, author of well-read essays, stories, and poems, one of which happened to be "Mary Had a Little Lamb." Hale started working in the public world when she was 18 and retired when she was 89. Yet she spent her life marketing the vision of the American woman as a domestic goddess, confined to home and hearth. That way, she assured her readers, they could "enjoy the luxuries of wealth without enduring the labors to acquire it; and the honors of office, without feeling its cares, and the glory of victory without suffering the dangers of the battle." She wrote a novel in which the heroine ruins her life and dies a pathetic pauper because she insisted on delivering lectures about women's rights.

You may be wondering how Hale came to justify her own extremely active engagement in the outside world. It was, she said, because her husband had died at a young age, leaving her with five children to raise and support. "It is only on emergencies, in cases where duty demands the sacrifice of female sensitiveness, that a lady of sense and delicacy will come before the public in a manner to make herself conspicuous," she wrote. "There is little danger that such an one will be arrogant in her pretensions. These remarks may be considered as allusions to our own case." Apparently no one was hard-hearted enough to point out that Hale's own "emergency" lasted until her youngest child was 55.

The mass media had arrived. In the colonial era, most families only had access to a few books—or perhaps just the Bible. They got their coaching in social attitudes mainly from their minister. In the New England colonies, the average churchgoer listened to about 7,000 sermons over her lifetime. But the new city population spent less time in church, and people no longer clustered together in close-knit communities where everyone heard and shared exactly the same opinions. Meanwhile, new printing technologies and widespread literacy created a publishing boom, most of it directed at women. And they were reading magazines like the one Hale edited: *Godey's Lady's Book.*

Godey's told its readers what to think, what to wear, what to cook, and what sort of pictures to hang on the dining room walls. It had a plan for the perfect life of the middle-class American woman, and everybody wanted to hear about it—even if they were still far from middle-class themselves. The industrial economy was booming, and while the average housewife still didn't have a dining room to decorate, much less a five-bedroom "dream house," she could imagine that such good things might be just around the corner: heating that covered more than the area right in front of the fireplace. Real windows with panes of glass, not oiled paper. Oil lamps, curtains, clocks, carpets.

The queens of this new world of comfort were those young mothers, providing moral uplift to the husbands who would venture out to do battle in the grubby, amoral outside world. *Godey's* didn't have a whole lot of suggestions for what older women could contribute. If you were Sarah Josepha Hale, you could become the most influential magazine editor in the country. But she had that emergency.

Besides magazines, American women were also reading novels written by their fellow countrywomen and featuring a new breed of wholesome but spunky female heroines. The stories offered up a variety of plots: sometimes the lead character was a penniless orphan, sometimes a wealthy social butterfly who loses everything due to the fecklessness of her male guardians. (Susan Warner, one of the most popular writers of the period, specialized in these crises. Her own father's bad investments devoured the family estate, plus most of the income from her books.) Sometimes the heroine was an adventurer who survived shipwrecks and outwitted murderers. Sometimes she was saintly beyond belief. Catharine Sedgwick got the ball rolling in 1822 with *A New-England Tale*, starring a paragon named Jane, an orphan who lives with what may be some of the worst relatives in American fiction but never complains or loses her temper. In another early women's novel, *Two Pictures,* the heroine dedicates herself to nursing a dying woman who had ruined her life, robbed her of her inheritance, and kept her from marrying the man she loved. Some readers must have yearned to get back to the shipwrecks.

The adventures varied, but not the age of the heroine. As a women's magazine essayist explained the rules of the genre: "She was always beautiful seventeen; and her antithesis and foil was the snubbed, spinster governess invariably described as nine-and-twenty, with lines of age and grief graven deep in her face."

"LIKE A TRUNK WITHOUT A LABEL"

The high-status job for most older women had always been domestic adviser—showing the younger generation how to cook, sew, and make decisions about running their homes. But that was fading a bit, too. Daughters and nieces often didn't even live in the same city as their mothers and aunts. And if they did, their advice might not always seem as valuable as the instruction from the new experts in books and magazines.

That brings us to Lydia Maria Child, who's later going to be an important character in our story—the first woman who had both a national voice and an obsession with what it means to age. She was the product of an intellectual family, and she never followed the traditional gender path. She taught school and published her first novel, *Hobomok,* in 1824, when she was in her early 20s. It's the tale of Mary, a lovely young thing whose "sylph-like figure afforded a fine contrast to the decaying elegance of her mother" who, by the generational arithmetic of the era, was possibly still in her 30s. Although Child kept to the lovely-young-thing-in-distress model of the era, her actual plot went on a completely different track. Mary weds Hobomok, a noble Indian, and has his son. But then Mary's true love, Charles, who was thought to have drowned at sea, makes a miraculous reappearance. Hobomok gallantly vanishes into the forest, leaving behind a divorce decree that allows the two to live happily ever after. Little Hobomok is renamed Charles and in the last chapter goes off to finish his studies in England.

Even though the Anglo-Saxons triumph in the end, all that interracial love and divorce made the book controversial, and it was not a financial success. Child needed to make money—she had married another intellectual, a man of high principles but no earning capacity whatsoever. She searched for a new, nonfictional literary route and struck gold with a how-to manual for young marrieds, *The Frugal Housewife*. It was hardly the first domestic advice book, but it was perhaps the most down-to-earth—full of tips on how to restore a stained shirt or rescue "injured" meat. Child, who would spend her entire life pinching pennies, felt each member of the family should be dedicated to either "earning or saving money." Sarah Josepha Hale hated that kind of thinking. Men were supposed to worry about finances, she wrote. "Let us keep our women and children from the contagion as long as possible." But despite Hale's indignation, *The Frugal Housewife* was a huge hit.

Another very different advice book that made an impact was Catharine Beecher's *A Treatise on Domestic Economy*. Beecher was part of a celebrity family led by the famous minister Lyman Beecher, and she never worried about the actual economics of household management. In fact, she never married or had a home to manage. Her sister, Harriet Beecher Stowe, once said Catharine spent her life "wandering like a trunk without a label." She was an educator and lecturer, self-consciously high-minded, whose vision was all about raising the status of women's domestic role. The housewife was the moral beacon of the nation, she argued, and young women needed the best possible education so they'd be ready to mold the future generations of the republic. Beecher would devote her career to that crusade, but she also needed money, and after her *Treatise* was a smash success, she followed up with a book of recipes.

"THE MISERABLE CANT THAT MATRIMONY IS ESSENTIAL"

Young women certainly were getting plenty of advice on how to become a good housewife. But first they had to get married. And there weren't enough potential husbands in the new urban American world to accommodate everybody who wanted one. A lot of the ambitious young men were going west—Catharine Beecher liked to remind audiences in the Northeast that the region had a surplus of 14,000 unmarried women. Trying to put the most positive light on the situation, women's magazines dutifully preached that it was better to live alone than marry the "wrong man." The authors of all the romantic stories and novels never seemed to believe that was really a happy ending. They invariably held out hope that a prince would come, even if his stagecoach seemed overdue.

Catharine Sedgwick became one of the most famous writers of the period. (She was also one of the children raised by Mum Bett—or Elizabeth Freeman—after Sedgwick's father served as Bett's lawyer in that historic anti-slavery case.) Her last novel, *Married or Single?*, started with a preface that assured readers that not having a husband was fine: "we raise our voice with all our might against the miserable cant that matrimony is essential to the feebler sex." Sedgwick's heroine, Grace, does indeed reject a morally compromised suitor, choosing instead to live with her married sister, giving music lessons and embracing serene singlehood. Then, after everything seems settled, a perfect man suddenly appears on the scene and pops the question. It was not much of a moral—unless Sedgwick's single readers were supposed to be impressed that Grace didn't make her match until she was in her 20s.

"OLD PEOPLE OF THE BEST BREEDING"

Youthfulness had never been more desirable, but older women were most definitely not allowed to attempt to look younger. Nobody was pushing the idea that wearing cosmetics should be a crime anymore, but the respectable world still regarded any effort to disguise one's age through makeup or costume or hair color as appalling. "No devices to give a deceitful appearance of youth can be justified by the sense of fitness and good taste," counseled Robert Tomes, nineteenth-century author of *The Bazar Book of Decorum*. Wigs and other "false hair" came in for special denunciation. "Old people of the best breeding now seldom resort to the hair-dresser to refurbish their shattered and decaying frames," Tomes reported, in what was apparently supposed to be encouragement.

The era when people of fashion wore elaborate wigs or powdered their hair to try to look older and more dignified was over. Gray was out, but America was still a long way from the time when women could casually wash it away. Some women did dye their hair—one guidebook recommended a mixture of equal parts oxide of bismuth, spermaceti, and hog lard. However that worked out, it was probably better than the artificial dyes that were beginning to come on the market, bearing no resemblance whatsoever to any actual hair color. In 1831, *Ladies' Magazine and Literary Gazette* told the story of one "young lady ... not twenty-eight" who used a bottle of Imperial Hair Restorer and discovered that she had given her tresses "a near resemblance to the dark changeable green of the peacock's feather." *Godey's* magazine was firm about coloring or cosmetics—"Whatever is false or artificial is as reprehensible in dress as in morals"—but it did concede to offer its older readers one nonartificial tip on restoring hair loss: "rub the bald places frequently with an onion." The universally accepted way for a woman to hide gray was still tucking all the hair beneath those close-fitting caps. Some women tried to extend the deception by putting phony hair along the edges—Dolley Madison, a social star until the end of her life, posed for a photograph when she was eighty, wearing one of her signature turbans, with artificial dark curls cascading down around her ears.

The new magazines with their hand-colored prints of the latest dresses created the nation's first mass fashion craze. But the styles were meant mainly for young women, and wearing them at the wrong age was another one of the era's post-thirty sins. "I was one day walking the streets of a city, when I perceived just before me an exceedingly juvenile figure enveloped in a cloud of rose-coloured drapery, with towering plumes in her wide spread bonnet," wrote an essayist with great distaste. "I followed her elastic movements some distance down the street, when she suddenly turned and disclosed to me, not the bloom and dimples of fifteen as I had anticipated, but a face that I well know had reckoned more than fifty winters....Had I seen this lady suitably dressed, in grave colours, without flounces and feathers, with a matronly cap surmounted honestly by a pair of spectacles, I should have felt much more respect for her character."

The one advantage older women did retain was a general expectation that they look rather well padded. The pre–Civil War era was one of those periods in American history when women of marriageable age were supposed to be not just slender but so thin as to be virtually asexual. "You must dismiss all ideas of voluptuousness...and the like, and summon up all such associations as you have been accustomed to connect with the words sylph and fairy," decreed one dean of New York society. It must have been a relief for women to reach the status of matron and relax a little. But then, in return, they were expected to stick their hair under a cap.

"FEELING THEMSELVES TO BE MERE FURNITURE"

In 1833, Catharine Sedgwick, who was then in her 40s, described the social life of New York, which was dominated by large evening parties. While people of all ages attended the galas, she said, they were "only adapted to the young, gay and dancing part of the population. The fathers and mothers are mere spectators, driven to the wall and feeling themselves to be mere furniture." It was natural, Sedgwick wrote, for older women to look for an excuse to stay home. "Our poor married lady has played out the play, and what [is] so dull as a theatre when the curtain has fallen!"

Sedgwick herself never married, so her sense of ostracism must have been even worse than that of friends who got to watch their children have fun while they lingered on the sidelines. But it wasn't easy for anyone. The writer Caroline Kirkland, herself a married woman of 50, protested that society was painting her and her contemporaries into a corner: "To dress cheerfully and becomingly is considered as an attempt to affect youth; to converse gaily an unsuitable effort to attract admirers. There is really no limit to the ungracious things said."

It was a change that had been coming since the late colonial days. Older women—and married women in general—had very little role in the lighthearted side of society. "No sooner are they married than they begin to lead a life of comparative seclusion; and once mothers, they are actually buried to the world," reported Francis Grund, a German émigré who wrote several books about life in America in the 1830s. Anyone who was non-young generally refrained from dancing at parties. Back in earlier times, men and women didn't necessarily come in close contact on the dance floor—there was a lot of bobbing around in opposing lines. But the waltz had arrived; things had gotten more intimate, and the idea of watching your mother dance with a man's arm around her waist was...icky. There was also that all-purpose inclination to keep the older folk on the sidelines. "The elderly part of the company were *spectators only,*" a guest reported after a lively gathering in Boston. We can assume that some of the elderly people in question were still in their 30s.

People who felt left behind in old age had always taken comfort from the idea of a heavenly afterlife. That continued to be the case in the nineteenth century—Ralph Waldo Emerson said his aunt Mary Moody Emerson, who died in 1863, slept for years "in a bed made in the form of a coffin" and wore a shroud day and night to get herself into the proper state of mind for her inevitable end. The idea that older people were finding solace in contemplation of their eternal reward was particularly popular with the non-old, who seemed to feel that was pretty much all their seniors were good for. That lithograph on the stages of a woman's life had the 70-year-old "always to church and in her place." That was a rather cheerful stage compared to the ones that came after—"second childhood" at 80, and by 90 "a useless cumberer on the Earth" who really would do everyone a favor if she left as soon as possible. Any way you looked at it, the last thing expected of a woman of later years was being the life of a party.

But once again, we have to acknowledge the exceptions. When it came to the rule that women should note their advancing age by behaving in the most discreet and depressing manner possible, one rebel was

Madame Eliza Jumel, a glamorous widow with a lively past who married former vice president Aaron Burr when she was in her 50s and he was in his 70s. The press reports seemed more interested in his age than hers. "Col. Burr is an old man, manifestly sliding down to the grave in the vigor of mental manhood," reported a Hartford paper, which described his new wife as "a lady of fifty or fifty-five, rather comely, and we should think well fitted to sustain an old gentleman under the infirmities of age. We really hope she will prove an *Aaron's* rod, and not a rod to Aaron."

The marriage wasn't a success — Eliza sued for divorce and reclaimed the name of "Madame Jumel." But she still referred to herself frequently as the widow of the famous revolutionary-era figure, which was literally true, given that the divorce went through a few hours after Burr's death. People might have gossiped in private, but in public Madame Jumel traveled in high society in both Europe and America. When she was in her 80s, a Saratoga paper ran a profile that said she "seems to enjoy, the festivities of this gay watering place with as much delight as if she was the reigning belle of the season." True, the very respectable set looked down on her. But she went almost everywhere and had a good time. The secret of her success was probably twofold: she was extremely rich and she was the widow of Aaron Burr, who despite his own checkered career was, after all, one of the Founding Fathers. Her social profile seemed to grow as she aged, and as the number of living Americans with personal connections to the Founders diminished. Perhaps the moral here is that if you have money, you can afford to ignore social rules. Or maybe the trick is to marry a former vice president. Either way, it wasn't something that could work for your average widow.

"Do not know one healthy woman"

When it came to physical problems, things hadn't improved much since the early days. Catharine Beecher visited friends in Illinois and reported: "Mrs. H. an invalid. Mrs. G. scrofula. Mrs. W. liver complaint. Mrs. K. pelvic disorders. Mrs. S. pelvic diseases. Mrs. B. pelvic diseases very badly. Mrs. B. not healthy. Mrs. T. very feeble. Mrs. G. cancer. Mrs. N. liver complaint. Do not know one healthy woman in the place."

It's hard to tell how many of these complaints reflected genuine sickness. There were certainly multitudinous reasons for women to become ill — from injuries relating to childbirth to the epidemics of diseases like cholera, which, until the second half of the century, medical science didn't recognize was connected to contaminated water. People who moved from farms to cities continued to eat heavy, meat-centered breakfasts even after they had adopted a more sedentary lifestyle. And in a city, there was a very good chance that a lot of the food products that came into the house carried the potential for diarrhea or gastric upset.

Working women undoubtedly suffered most — the strains of sewing in rooms with terrible lighting left seamstresses with strained eyes and permanently cramped necks and backs. But naturally the complaints that got attention were mainly from the upper classes. And being ill did seem to be sort of fashionable among wealthier families. Josephine DeMott, a circus performer who married a wealthy Ohio man and learned how to behave in his social circle, diligently visited with doctors and developed fainting attacks. "It was a thrilling game and in order to compete with any ability you had to be ready with illnesses," she said. "The worse they were, the more operations you had to your name, the higher you ranked."

Doctors were playing a major role in American life, and they were becoming more and more expansive in their ideas about women's health. Unfortunately, that sometimes made things worse — particularly when it came to menopause. In the colonial era, doctors' attitude, to the degree that they had one, seemed to be that menopause was a dangerous time in a woman's life but not necessarily the start of a downhill slide. By the nineteenth century, things had changed. One of the most influential medical books of the post-revolutionary period said that an end to menstruation "is sufficient to disorder the whole frame and often to destroy life itself."

Besides menopause, the other all-purpose diagnosis was "nervous disorder." Problems with "nerves" were not limited to women. Many Americans of both sexes — including members of the always intellectual and frequently neurotic Beecher family — read *American Nervousness*, a book by physician George Beard, who believed his countrymen were having their nerves wrecked by the effects of modern civilization.

Beard blamed pressures like "steam-power, the periodical press, the telegraph, the sciences." He also added "the mental activity of women" as one of the age's particular problems.

And the tooth issue continued to be a torment. Tomes—our *Bazar Book of Decorum* expert—warned that "the various painful face, head and ear aches, and disorders of the eye, as well as the fatal cancer and tedious ulcers of the tongue and lips, are often due to no other cause than a decayed and ragged tooth." He helpfully urged his readers to buy a toothbrush and refrain from cracking nuts with their teeth.

"AS SHE CRAWLED TO ME ALMOST HALF HER NAKED BODY WAS EXPOSED"

The hysteria over finding a husband before you got too old was less intense in the free black community. Outside the tiny elite, African American men had a difficult time finding work, and women did not necessarily see having a husband as a key to financial security. Elleanor Eldridge, who supported herself in trades like weaving and cheese making, said her aunt had warned her to avoid marriage as "A WASTE OF TIME!" and Eldridge followed her advice. During the time the white woman she worked for was courting and marrying, Eldridge said with satisfaction, "I knit five pairs of stockings!"

Still, the ideal of a stay-at-home wife was glorified by the black media—it represented a break with the traditions of slavery and a way men could nail down their role as head of the household. Martin Delany, a black leader in Pennsylvania in the pre–Civil War era, lashed out at married women who "voluntarily leave home and become chambermaids...in all probability, to enable them to obtain more fine or costly articles of dress or furniture."

Of course, until the Civil War most African American women lived in the South as slaves. Within the slave communities, the oldest women were relied upon as healers. The "old 'omans" looked after the sick, delivered babies, and made herbal remedies. And, at least in some cases, they specialized in conjuring. Ann Parker, a former slave in North Carolina, told an interviewer that she remembered her mother being both feared and respected for her magical powers: "Yes, she was a queen."

When the white folks were out of sight, Parker said, the other slaves bowed down to her mother "and does what she says." But for most slaves, getting old presented the danger of being regarded as useless. They were often simply given a plot of land and told to support themselves with what they could grow. Moses Grandy, a slave, recalled that when his mother became old she was "sent to live in a little lonely log-hut in the woods" without any food except whatever their relatives could squirrel away and take to her at night. Grandy's mother, who was blind, was unable to help herself. "Many a time, when I have drawn near to my mother's hut, I have heard her grieving and crying on these accounts," he said. But, he added, "she was not treated worse than others: it is the general practice."

Frances Kemble, a British actress who married a Georgia plantation owner, wrote about an elderly slave named Hannah "seamed with wrinkles and bowed and twisted with age and infirmity...as she crawled to me almost half her naked body was exposed through the miserable tatters that she held on with one hand." It was illegal for an owner to simply free a slave and kick her off the plantation when she got old, but Southern cities had a suspiciously large number of elderly black residents, which suggested the rule was widely ignored.

"USED TO LIFE'S REFINEMENTS"

Most Americans still grew old and died in their homes, with other members of their families around them. The very poor had to rely on the charity of their community—whether they and the community liked it or not. But it was a sign of the times that in the early nineteenth century charitable groups started to establish separate old-age homes for middle-class women—like St. Luke's Episcopal Home for Aged Women in New York, which was founded in 1852 for "needy gentlewomen" who were "used to life's refinements." While the new urban middle class had a lot of advantages, many families clearly did not feel they had enough room to accommodate old relatives.

Philadelphia's Indigent Widows' and Single Women's Society started in 1817, and the founders made it clear they only wanted to take care of formerly well-to-do women—the ones who always had been poor, they theorized, were "inured" to the condition. A little later the society decided to charge a $150 entrance fee under the theory that formerly comfortable women would still be able to raise it, while the requirement would screen out "unworthy objects." The entrance fee price tag continued to go up until by 1887 it hit $400 — the equivalent of at least $10,000 today. Also, the group's early portrait of their residents as cheerful workers, raising money by sewing and knitting, changed. The women, the management decided, were too infirm to be able "to contribute by their industry to their support." The infantilization of old age was everywhere. The Home for Aged and Infirm Colored People, which was founded by Quakers and wealthy black Philadelphians, reminded its workers that the residents were nothing more than "children of mature growth." It was, undoubtedly, a lot easier to boss your elders around if you regarded them as nothing more than wrinkled toddlers.

Whatever depressing things happened to old women, it's important to remember that life was almost always worse for indigent old men. They labored under a special stigma. Society assumed that women were dependent on men for support, and that if left on their own they might reasonably fall into penury. Men didn't seem to have any excuse. And relatives found elderly men less useful than women, who could at least help with childcare and sewing. "There is absolutely no class of humanity so sadly powerless to aid themselves, so useless in any of the ordinary duties of the household and so unwelcomed among strangers as destitute old men," noted a report from the Old Man's Home of Philadelphia.

3 . Before the Civil War

"FAT, FAIR AND FORTY"

Margaret Fuller was a pre–Civil War reformer and an intellectual, always ahead of her time. But in her mid-thirties, she seemed to accept the idea that her best days were over. "See a common woman at forty," she wrote in her landmark work *Woman in the Nineteenth Century*. "See her, who was, indeed, a lovely girl, in the coarse, full-blown dahlia flower of what is commonly matron-beauty, 'fat, fair and forty,' showily dressed, and with manners as broad and full as her frill or satin cloak." When people compliment such a lady, Fuller mused, she is "always spoken and thought of upholstery-wise." The version of woman-at-forty that Fuller claimed to admire was exactly the opposite, featuring a "careworn face, from which every soft line is blotted, those faded eyes, from which lonely tears have driven the flashes of fancy." It was a more noble vision, but not one most people would look forward to achieving.

As unattractive as she made older women sound — either the fat and frilly ones or the ravaged ones with faded eyes — Fuller was unhappy about the way not-young people were elbowed out of American social life. "It is the topic of jest and amazement with foreigners that what is called society is given up so much into the hands of boys and girls," she wrote angrily. "Accordingly it wants spirit, variety and depth of tone, and we find there no historical presences, none of the charms, infinite in variety, of Cleopatra, no heads of Julius Caesar, overflowing with meanings, as the sun with light." (She knew many of the great intellectuals and artists of her era, but when she envisioned good party guests, she had to reach back a few millennia.)

Fuller, who was thin, dark, and moving into the old-maid danger zone, was probably imagining her own future, unwelcome at the best gatherings while the "boys and girls" held center stage. She was prescient about a great many things but misread the tea leaves on that one. Not long after her book was published, the *New-York Daily Tribune* sent

Fuller — one of the first women to write for American newspapers — to Europe as a correspondent. She covered the Italian civil war and fell in love with a young marquis who was one of the leaders on the republican side. At age 40 she was sailing back to America with notes for a new book, her romantic husband, and their little son. Tragically, their ship ran aground off the coast of New York and all three of them were drowned. It was a terrible ending to her saga, but all the promise Fuller must have felt during the last part of her short life did come true for members of her generation. She died in 1850, when remarkable women were beginning to find new ways to have adventures and make an impact during middle age and later. Elizabeth Cady Stanton saw it coming.

"WE SHALL NOT BE IN OUR PRIME BEFORE FIFTY"

"Courage Susan, this is my last baby and she will be two years old in January," 40-year-old Elizabeth Cady Stanton wrote soothingly to Susan B. Anthony. Stanton had just given birth for the sixth time, deeply discouraging Anthony, who was waiting for the moment when her friend could leave housekeeping behind and help her organize the women's rights movement. "Two years more and — time will tell what! You and I have the prospect of a good long life," Stanton predicted confidently. "We shall not be in our prime before fifty, and after that we shall be good for twenty years at least."

This was in 1857, nearly 60 years after Elizabeth Drinker had theorized that the best time of a woman's life was when childbearing days were behind her. Since then, the general attitude toward aging had gotten gloomier. But there was Stanton, reviving the best-is-yet-to-come theory, and in a new way. Getting older, to her, meant more than leaving behind the burden of reproduction. Stanton saw middle age as a time when life would really open up — when she could travel and give lectures and write books and enjoy a big, successful career pursuing the causes she cared most about. Aging would be the key to achievement, excitement, and power. It was a radical vision, but then Stanton was a pretty radical person.

Every time you run into a period in American history in which the whole female side of the country seems housebound and downtrodden, amazing people pop up and remind you that this, too, shall pass. The women's world was already stirring around the edges in the early 1800s, but the new possibilities became more evident as time went on. While doctors were describing their menopausal patients in the bleakest terms possible, women who had gotten past that point in their lives were beginning to see its advantages. Perhaps it was true that motherhood was women's greatest role, and that to carry it out properly they had to remain pretty much chained to the hearth. But once the children were grown, surely there had to be another stage — something better than that lithograph of the 80-year-old in her second childhood. Eliza Farnham, a social reformer, announced that the time when women bemoaned their loss of youth was "long since past for enlightened women" and that she personally had a sense of "super-exaltation" about her postmenopausal prospects.

The great public issue was slavery, and it shattered the traditional middle-class division of labor in which men ruled in the dog-eat-dog outside world while women reigned in the home. White Americans were learning — particularly through Harriet Beecher Stowe's hugely popular novel *Uncle Tom's Cabin* — that slavery was all about *families*. Husbands and wives were separated, children torn away from their parents, innocent girls raped by their white overseers. So women, the guardians of the family, the keepers of the moral light, were drawn into the fight.

The more progressive side of the country warmed to the idea of letting abolitionist women into the public world — as long as the cause was high-minded and the women in question were older. Age opened some doors: young women were supposed to be home raising their children. And they certainly weren't meant to be making public appearances while they were still attractive to men — like the radical lecturer Fanny Wright, who drew crowds to her speeches about slavery, women's rights, and the plight of the American worker. But she also caused riots — and not many women yearned to be known as "The Great Red Harlot of Infidelity." Maria Stewart, an African American pioneer lecturer, tried making speeches in Boston when she was in her 20s but got a negative response even from the black community. "I find it is no use for me as an individual to try to make myself useful among my color in this city," she said in a farewell address after a three-year struggle to be heard.

The remarkable Angelina Grimké and her sister Sarah, abolition crusaders who were pioneers in giving speeches to audiences that included men, frequently ran into danger from angry mobs, sometimes carrying torches. Catharine Beecher, who had once been a friend, parted company with the sisters because of their speaking tours. Women, she said, should avoid politics and retire to domesticity, where they could triumph through "kindly, generous, peaceful and benevolent principles." This from a woman who, you will recall, never kept a home of her own.

Angelina, the star speaker, was rather gaunt and already regarded as an old maid when she was relatively young. Then she stunned everyone by marrying Theodore Weld, a prominent abolition crusader himself. She was one of the nation's first vocal advocates of women's rights, and a public speaker, and past 30 — and she found a husband! It was too much even for many reformers — one of Weld's abolitionist friends told him "nature recoiled" at the prospect of such a union.

If people were going to accept being lectured to by women, it was generally easier to start with speakers who looked warm and maternal, like Elizabeth Cady Stanton, well-dressed in a matronly sort of way, with her gray hair carefully arranged. Stanton — who had persuaded her husband, Henry, to ditch the word "obey" in their wedding ceremony — was a natural writer who could dash off a lecture or magazine article in the time most people would take to organize their desks. She had entered the reform movement when she was young, but she couldn't travel or work for her causes the way her friends wished. She was still overwhelmed with her duties as a wife and mother, and Henry Stanton was not all that liberated when it came to the question of men sharing in household chores. In the end, there would be yet another baby after number six. "Alas!! Alas!!!!" wrote Anthony. "I only scold now that for a moment's pleasure to herself or her husband, she should thus increase the load of cares under which she already groans."

Eventually Stanton was able to leave her children in the care of relatives and begin to lecture and campaign for a sort of middle-aged-women's liberation. Rather than question the popular conviction that a woman's place was in the home, Stanton argued for stages: "the same woman may have a different sphere at different times." You raised your family, and then you could take to the road. She pointed to her friend the reformer Lucretia Mott: "married early in life and brought up a large family of children.... Her children are now settled in their own homes.... Lucretia Mott has now no domestic cares.... Who shall tell us that this divinely inspired woman is out of her sphere in her public endeavors?"

"I GO STRAIGHT TO MY ROOMS . . . AND EAT A CRACKER"

Susan B. Anthony's entry into the women's rights movement was much like Stanton's — minus all those children. It was inevitable that the two of them would get together. They had complementary talents — Anthony was tireless as a behind-the-scenes organizer and Stanton could quickly provide the speeches, essays, and petitions. They were spiritual twins but physical polar opposites: the round, jolly mother of seven and the spare, austere spinster. Anthony claimed she had never suffered during her arduous travels because she eschewed the kind of late suppers Stanton adored. After a lecture, Anthony said rather proudly, "I go straight to my rooms, take a bath and drink a cup of hot milk and eat a cracker."

Much as the general public preferred a good meal to a cracker, Stanton got a more positive response on the lecture trail. Anthony tended to deliver rather boring speeches in a monotone. And her physical appearance also worked against her, thanks to the popular conviction that while young women couldn't be too slim, those who reached middle age were meant to be rather round. "Susan is lean, cadaverous and intellectual with the proportions of a file and the voice of a hurdy-gurdy," snarled the *New York World*. Unlike Stanton, she was also frequently indifferent to matters of dress. "That ancient daughter of Methuselah, Susan B. Anthony, passed through our city yesterday," announced a paper in Kalamazoo — Anthony was 54 at the time — "[w]ith a bonnet on her head looking as if she had recently descended from Noah's ark."

It was another example of the nation's Old Maid fixation. To people who did not know her personally — especially the ones who disagreed with her politics — Anthony appeared to be all the things young women were trained to avoid like the plague. Stanton, in an effort to combat the stereotype, wrote that "Miss Anthony's love-life" was expressed through her "steadfast, earnest labors for men in general. She has been a watchful and affectionate daughter, sister, friend, and those who have felt the pulsations of her great heart know how warmly it beats for all." While Stanton understood how unfair it was to play the old maid card, she used it herself on occasion. She claimed Catharine Beecher, a longtime rival, might have been more humane if Beecher had "loved with sufficient devotion, passion and abandon any of Adam's sons."

The people who knew Anthony understood that she in no way resembled the bitter, disappointed stereotype that every girl learned to fear as her future. When she turned 50, her friends threw a party to express their affection. "The comments of the leading journals, next day, were highly complimentary," Stanton later wrote, referring to articles like the one in the *New York Sun,* headlined "A Brave Old Maid." All the stories, she said, "dwelt on the fact that, at last, a woman had arisen brave enough to assert her right to grow old and openly declare that a half century had rolled over her head."

"I FEEL LIKE A SQUEEZED SPONGE"

Stanton believed that menopause had redirected her "vital forces" from her reproductive organs to her brain. And she needed all the forces she could muster once she embarked on her speaking tour. Lectures were the chief source of entertainment for many Americans in an age before radio or movies, and Stanton quickly became a popular attraction. While she pursued the cause of women's rights wherever she went, she used humor to win over the audience and often framed her talks around homely topics like "Our Boys" or "Our Girls." She dressed carefully, in black silk, and curled her gray hair every night. Journalists compared her to Queen Victoria and — yes! — George Washington's mother.

In an era when travel was still primitive and accommodations uncomfortable, the tours were grueling. Stanton claimed she needed the money to help support her family and pay for her children's college tuitions. While this sounds a lot like Sarah Josepha Hale's argument about feeding her fatherless babies, it was probably at least partly true — Henry Stanton had only fitful success in his work as a lawyer. But there must have been something in her that loved being on the road. She would hit 30 or 40 stops in a six-week stretch, speaking almost every day and twice on Sundays. She could sleep at will. In her 60s, Stanton could nap while sitting up on trains, or in hotel lobbies if emergency struck. It was a talent she attributed to all her experience with restless babies, and a gift that other famous older women, including Hillary Clinton, have enjoyed.

"Two months more containing sixty-one days still stretch their long length before me," she wrote a friend. "I must pack and unpack my trunk sixty-one times...rehearse 'Our Boys,' 'Our Girls' or 'Home Life' sixty-one times, eat 183 more miserable meals...shake hands with sixty-one more committees, smile, try to look intelligent and interested in everyone who approaches me, while I feel like a squeezed sponge." Still, she was having extraordinary experiences. She recalled speaking on behalf of a suffrage referendum in the Midwest, standing in a large mill one dark night with a single candle lighting her face, before an audience that was virtually invisible except for a vague glow from the whites of their eyes. She saw "all the wonders" of Yosemite Valley, even though she had to climb down a steep path after her horse turned out to be too weary to accommodate her. "The next day I was too stiff and sore to move a finger. However, in due time I awoke to the glory and grandeur of that wonderful valley, of which no descriptions nor paintings can give the slightest idea," Stanton wrote in her memoir.

What happened to Stanton was not just that getting older released her from family responsibilities. It allowed her to have adventures — adventures that, in the mid-nineteenth century, younger women couldn't enjoy. Her matronly appearance protected her from sexual predators, and the fact that she had seven children gave her audiences the reassurance that whatever she was saying must be respectable — even though Stanton was actually among the most radical voices of her era, particularly on hot-button issues like marriage, divorce, and sex. Both Stanton and Anthony were free to be themselves during their travels, living in ways a well-bred younger woman could never have gotten away with. Stanton killed the boredom on a train trip from Texas to New York by playing cards with some army officers. Anthony once delivered a talk from the top of a billiards table.

Stanton stayed on the lecture trail for up to eight months a year until she was 65, and Anthony traveled well into her 70s. During one stint, Stanton reported that after speaking in Iowa one evening she had an oyster supper, packed, took a short nap, and set off for Minnesota at two in the morning. She traveled through "a fearful snowstorm" on a small cart drawn by a mule. When she arrived at the station for the next leg of the trip, she discovered her train would be two hours late. So she "rolled my cloak up for a pillow, lay down on the bench and went to sleep." Anthony once made a six-hour, seventeen-mile trip over frozen mud in a lumber wagon. It was an era when transportation was reliably unreliable. Boats ran aground, trains derailed, wagons broke their wheels. Dorothea Dix, another older woman from the Northeast who became a national figure for her reform work, once found herself stranded in Pennsylvania and wound up being ferried to her destination by "an old waterman, astride upon a drift log half under water."

"DISCOVERED IN TIME TO PREVENT ANY INJURY TO LIFE OR LIMB"

Black women had been on the road, lecturing, from the beginning of the century. Mainly they spoke about racial improvement, religion, and — obviously — abolition. In her autobiography, Jarena Lee, a minister, recounted one day in which she traveled on foot from Philadelphia "thirty miles to Downingtown and gave ten sermons while there." Any difficulties a white woman might encounter were quadrupled for African Americans. The houses where they stayed were less comfortable, the transportation even less reliable. Frances Ellen Watkins Harper, the poet and anti-slavery orator, remembered when someone removed the linchpins from her wagon in the hopes of causing an accident. The sabotage was, happily, "discovered in time to prevent any injury to life or limb."

Sojourner Truth, a former slave to a Dutch family in New York who became a popular anti-slavery speaker, was regularly heckled and threatened — the fact that she was in her 60s inhibited the crowds not a whit. When a mob in Indiana threatened to burn down the building where she was talking, Truth famously said, "Then I will speak upon the ashes." On another occasion, hecklers claimed she was a man in disguise and demanded that she be physically examined by some of the ladies present. Truth bared her breasts to the crowd and, as an abolitionist paper reported, "told them that her breasts had suckled many a white babe, to the exclusion of her own offspring," and that "it was not to her shame that she uncovered her breast before them, but to their shame."

Harriet Tubman, at 43 a scout for the Union army, was traveling home to Auburn, New York, on a military pass when the conductor decided she didn't belong in a car with white passengers. It took four men to move her; she spent the rest of the trip imprisoned in the baggage car, nursing injuries that would trouble her for months. During the war, Tubman worked behind enemy lines, setting up a spy network to inform the Union soldiers where useful targets were located and leading Union boats to spots where fugitive slaves were waiting to be rescued. While she was hardly given proper credit by the white press, one report from a Boston newspaper described her commander, a white officer named James Montgomery, as dashing into enemy territory, destroying millions of dollars in military supplies and cotton, and striking terror into the hearts of the confederacy "under the guidance of a black woman."

While nobody else could do what Tubman was doing, there were lots of women helping move slaves north on the Underground Railroad. There was no particular age requirement for the job, but the volunteers tended to be older simply because they owned a farm or business or home where people could be sheltered. Henrietta Duterte, a Philadelphia undertaker, sometimes hid runaways in caskets or disguised them as part of a funeral procession when they had to make their escape. One elderly woman in the Midwest who was sheltering two escaped slaves in her barn threatened two bounty hunters with a knife, forcing them into a corncrib and holding them at bay while the fugitives made their getaway.

"HIS LAUNDRY BILL IS PAID"

Stanton and Anthony amazed contemporaries with their ability to withstand the rigors of travel. But their travails paled in comparison to those of the women who went west during the pioneer era. The whole concept of getting in a coach and driving across empty plains, deserts, and mountains, past Indians who quite reasonably tended to be hostile, was not something that generally appealed to older people of either sex. Once they reached their destinations, frontier life was so exhausting that it appeared to create an instant class of elderly women out of the young ones who took up the challenge. "I am a very old woman," wrote 29-year-old Sarah Everett from her family's farm in Kansas. "My face is thin sunken and wrinkled, my hands bony withered and hard."

Of course, the fact that life in the West was exhausting and often dangerous didn't dissuade adventurous spirits from giving it a try. Tabitha Moffat Brown headed for Oregon at 66 with her brother and two of her adult children. The little company wandered hundreds of miles off track into the Utah desert and ran out of food during a mountain crossing through the snow. When Brown did make it to her destination, she instantly took a six-and-a-quarter-cent piece she'd found and used it to start a small business sewing buckskin gloves. Within two years she'd managed to open a school for pioneer children and orphans, which eventually grew into today's Pacific University. It's an extraordinary story — in 1987, the state legislature named Brown "The Mother of Oregon." But it does also underline the fact that pioneering spirit did not come easy.

The early West was like the early South in the opportunities it offered women who would never have gotten them in more well-populated places. Older women worked at everything from taxidermy to running houses of prostitution — establishments that were arguably a necessary evil in a world where men could outnumber women 33 to 1. There were several legendary drivers, like "Stagecoach" Mary Fields, a six-foot-tall African American who was one of the first female U.S. mail carriers. Fields was past 50 when she moved to a Catholic mission in Montana, where she helped out by hauling supplies. She later got a job driving that coach and was legendary for her strength and endurance — when the snow was too deep for the horses, she delivered the mail on foot in snowshoes. At 69, she sort-of retired and opened a laundry. One of the stories about her holds that she was drinking in the local saloon at age 70 when one of her laundry customers walked in and declared he was refusing to pay his bill. Fields followed him out the saloon door, decked him with a single punch, then walked back in and announced, "His laundry bill is paid." She was extremely popular in her hometown of Cascade—when Montana passed a law barring women from saloons, the mayor granted her an exemption. And when her laundry was destroyed by a fire, the townspeople rallied together to build her a new one.

"LOOKING LIKE A USED-UP ARTICLE NOW"

By the time she hit her mid-40s—the age when women like Stanton were just beginning to take to the public stage—Fanny Wright, the sexy, riot-inducing lecturer of the early 1800s, was worn down. Still, she crossed the Atlantic seven times in her last 13 years, visited Haiti—where she had once helped relocate former slaves—and traveled continually up and down the Mississippi River. In 1852, when she was 56, Wright slipped on the ice and broke her hip, an injury that would lead to her death. She suffered terribly—but not too much to fail to notice the publication of *Uncle Tom's Cabin* and request a copy.

Uncle Tom's Cabin wouldn't thrill many African American readers if it came out today—there was a reason why, during the civil rights movement, black men who seemed overly deferential to white opinion were called "Uncle Toms." But it defined an era, particularly for the middle-class white women in the North who were drawn into the fight against slavery by the novel. None of the other female speakers or writers or magazine editors of the period could match the fame of Uncle Tom's creator, Harriet Beecher Stowe. The first publishers she had approached with the book proposal turned her down, theorizing that women novelists should be writing about shipwrecks and heartbreak, not something like slavery. They went down in the historical pantheon of bad guessers. It became a national and international sensation. Stowe made $10,000 for her share of the sales in the first three months alone— the equivalent of more than a quarter of a million dollars today and a literary record at the time.

Stowe was a long-married mother of seven who described herself in a letter to one of her admirers as "a little bit of a woman—somewhat more than forty—about as thin & dry as a pinch of snuff; never very much to look at in my best days—& looking like a used-up article now." Everybody wanted to hear her speak, but Stowe felt it was improper for a woman to address a mixed audience of men and women. In her equivalent of a book tour, she sat in a box in the audience while her husband, Calvin, read her remarks. Then things changed and women lecturers became so common that even 61-year-old Harriet Beecher Stowe felt comfortable taking to the road. She loved it. "So far my health has been better than any autumn for several years," she wrote to her family. "The fatigue of excitement & all lessens as I get accustomed to it & the fatigue of railroad travel seems to do me good I never sleep better than after a long day[']s ride." After a very rough rail trip from Chicago to Cincinnati, her daughter wrote that she was not sure she had ever seen her mother "so utterly used up worn out and exhausted." But Stowe fortified herself with a day of rest, a massage, and a pick-me-up of raw eggs beaten with sherry, then went on to do another successful performance.

4. The Mid-1800s

"TRAVEL CHEERFULLY TOWARD THE SUNSET!"

Lydia Maria Child, who had given so much advice to young women in her cookbooks, found another lucrative subject in older people. She had already cobbled together selected readings for children, and it seemed natural to move on to the other out-of-the-mainstream part of the population. *Looking Toward Sunset,* a collection of poems, short stories, and essays about aging, became a bestseller in 1865. That was particularly impressive given the size of the target audience — only about 3 percent of the country was over 65.

A modern reader would probably find the book treacly in the extreme. There are short stories about spunky Old Aunty and wise Old Uncle Tommy, both beloved by the little people in their neighborhood. ("Oh, Uncle Tommy, I believe we should always be good children if you could only be along with us all the time.") There were "moral hints" and "hints about health." ("Never step from your bed with the naked feet on an uncarpeted floor. I have known it to be the exciting cause of months of illness.") Plus many poems and essays about looking forward to a heavenly reward. ("Having arrived at this state of peacefulness and submission, I find the last few years the happiest of my life. To you, my dear friend, who are so much younger, I would say, Travel cheerfully toward the sunset!")

These were all familiar messages. But Child pushed things a bit further. Happiness in old age, she wrote, comes with thinking about something other than yourself — whether it was by fighting for political causes, knitting socks for the poor, or just memorizing a nursery rhyme to entertain the neighbors' kids. Child was clearly hoping her readers would "take an interest in some of the great questions of the age," listing possible topics from slavery to Indian rights to "improvements in architecture." Still, she needed every reader she could get, and she was willing to settle for just about anything, sock knitting included.

It was an important step. In the colonial era, women who were too old—or wealthy—to work were expected to spend their later years praying and contemplating the next life. Now they were warned that if they really wanted to be happy when their child-rearing years were over, they had better start getting beyond their sitting rooms.

Lydia Maria Child took her own advice. In 1833, she published the path-breaking *An Appeal in Favor of That Class of Americans Called Africans,* which not only called for the immediate liberation of all slaves in the South but also denounced the racism and discrimination the free black community encountered in the North. It was shocking to a public that was used to thinking of her as the nice lady who knew how to remove laundry stains.

Child was actually an important member of the Boston reform community, and while some of her intellectual friends sneered at her stories about wise Uncle Tommy, none of them had written anything nearly as daring as *An Appeal*. She might have been in the center of the public world—a civic star—as the nation marched toward abolition and women's rights. But the demands of her ailing and difficult father drew her away from everything she found bright or exciting. "All my dreams have settled into a stoical resignation to life as it comes," she wrote to a friend.

That was the catch: the world might be willing to accept older women taking greater roles in public life. But nobody thought they should dodge the responsibility of caring for aged relatives. So a lot of gifted, ambitious women wound up getting stuck. Child was hardly the only one who broke through the barriers to national achievement in midlife and then had to retreat to tend an ailing parent. Louisa May Alcott was famous in her 30s when her novel *Little Women* captured the hearts of generations of schoolgirls. When she went out in public, she would be rushed by her fans—at one event, when Alcott was too ill to speak, she agreed to stand and turn around on the stage so the hundreds of girls in the audience could at least look at her. Then things went downhill. She wrote *Little Women* sequels, which she loathed, but which provided money to help support her impecunious family. Then she went home to tend her mother, and later, already in bad health herself, she was caught up with the care of her father. Alcott wrote in her diary that she would "never live my own life."

Lydia Maria Child was stoically caring for her demanding family members when an old friend from the abolition movement, Senator Charles Sumner, was attacked on the floor of the Senate by a cane-wielding congressman from South Carolina. The crisis roused Child from her resigned torpor; she returned to writing essays and began meeting with her old associates at the Boston Female Anti-Slavery Society. Following her own advice, she was worrying about something much larger than her own life.

If Child never found the kind of happiness her *Looking Toward Sunset* readers might have imagined, it was probably because she was so much ahead of her time. After the war, she produced a book of poems and essays for former slaves, to help their transition into new lives. It was another version of her collections for children and old people, but this time there was no expectation of a bestseller. Just to get *The Freedmen's Book* published, Child used the profits she had saved from her other work. She also scrounged up another $200 toward the cause by foregoing new clothes and skimping on butter, sugar, and tea. "Her dress is usually plain, not even neat," complained Edgar Allan Poe, who visited Child in her later years. While she "has always been distinguished for her energetic and active philanthropy," he concluded, she was "anything but fashionable."

"WE ARE BUSY *OLD MAIDS*"

As much as they struggled financially throughout their lives, Child and Alcott were still among the very few middle-class women of their era who supported themselves. Writing was an acceptable calling, since it could be done within the confines of the home, but the number of writers who made money was tiny. There weren't really any nonliterary professions for women. Even in 1870, almost all the women who worked for wages outside the farm were either domestic servants or laborers in factories. We can presume that most of them weren't looking forward to continuing their employment into old age.

So the fate of older women depended mainly on whether they were married. If they were, and their husbands were good earners, they devoted themselves to the glorious sphere of domesticity that the magazines kept extolling. Some may have found it less than glorious, but it was at least a sphere, and it was theirs. Except for the lucky few with inherited wealth, women who weren't married were stuck. They were almost inevitably going to wind up living with a relative's family, staying in the background and performing all the chores no one else wanted to handle. Anna Bingham of Tennessee was just such a person, and her letters catalogue a rather monotonous life of spinning and weaving and nursing. "Between [caring for] old *people,* puny *children,* and clothing all, besides attending to other things, we are busy *old maids,*" she wrote with a marked lack of enthusiasm. Magazine readers could find a lot of paeans to these virtuous aunts or aging daughters, but nobody really looked forward to becoming one.

Teaching was the way out. "Generally speaking, there seems to be no very extensive sphere of usefulness for a single woman but that which can be found in the limits of a school-room," said Catharine Beecher. So far in our story, Beecher hasn't been all that inspiring a figure. But we're now going to talk about her as the woman who helped make teaching a socially acceptable profession. It was still regarded as a man's job in the early nineteenth century—colonial women had run "dames' schools" in their homes, but they made very little money. The real schools wanted male teachers, mainly because of the prejudice against working women.

That gradually changed as public schools expanded. Administrators realized women were better able to handle the children...and cheaper. *Much* cheaper. In the period between 1860 and 1880, a female teacher in a city made an average of $8.57 a week, which was lower than the salary of a male unskilled laborer. Beecher, for all her interest in promoting education as a career for unmarried women, was also a school owner and very keen on the idea that teachers would not get much money: "To make education universal," she decreed, "it must be moderate in expense." And the prestige wasn't necessarily higher than the salaries. In 1865, *Harper's New Monthly* published a short story told from the view of a teacher, Milly, whose brother Tom has flunked out of college. Milly suggests he might try tutoring some of her students to put some savings away. Tom tells her he'd rather commit suicide.

The people running the schools were almost invariably men. Susan

B. Anthony was a 28-year-old teacher in charge of girls' education at a private school in upstate New York when the supervisor retired and was replaced by a 19-year-old male who immediately started arguing with Anthony about discipline. It was this sort of thing that propelled her into a career in women's rights. Besides the tiny salaries and the bossy men, teachers also had to wrestle with huge classes—60 students wasn't at all unusual.

Cynics might conclude that Beecher and education reformers like her had merely opened the door to low-paying, low-prestige, stupendously stressful employment that might make sitting fireside at some relative's home mending the family's clothes seem kind of attractive. It doesn't sound like much of a leap forward. Yet historically speaking, it was. Single women now had a path toward economic independence—in a professional job they could pursue into old age. Granted, in the early days the salary wasn't enough to support them, unless they lived at the school or roomed with the families of their pupils. Who sometimes stuck them in a room with the children. Or skimped on their food. Or spied on them to make sure they weren't pursuing any forbidden activities like taking a ride with a young man or patronizing the local ice cream parlor. But you've got to start somewhere.

A few entrepreneurial women tried expanding their horizons by opening their own schools. It seemed like a perfect ambition—usefulness, control, and income all wrapped up into one respectable package. But the going was very, very rough. Catharine Beecher's Western Female Institute went bankrupt six years after it opened in Ohio. Sarah Mapps Douglass, a black educator in Philadelphia, opened an academy for African American girls that seemed to be going well at first. "The school numbers over 40, selected from our best families," a visitor reported. But in 1838, she had to admit that she couldn't make enough money to continue, and the Female Anti-Slavery Society agreed to take it over as a charity. Clara Barton opened the first public school in Bordentown, New Jersey, and ran it so well that the town voted to build a much larger schoolhouse. On the day it opened, Barton discovered that she was no longer principal—the job had been given to a man, at twice her salary.

"After I served the flag so faithfully"

After the Civil War, Harriet Tubman kept up some of her Underground Railroad skills — she could drop from her rocking chair and flatten herself against the ground, then quietly slither up behind an unsuspecting friend or relative. It was, as it turned out, an excellent way to entertain her granddaughter.

Tubman had returned to her farm in New York, which also became home to any number of needy relatives, orphans, and indigent old people. She married one of her boarders, a former slave and veteran named Nelson Davis, who may have been more than 20 years her junior. (His age was a little fuzzy, as was Tubman's; the critical thing was that they seemed to be a happy couple.) Always short on money, Tubman battled a long time to get a veteran's pension from the government. "You wouldn't think that after I served the flag so faithfully I should come to want under its folds," she said. After her husband died, she finally did get a pension — but it was as his widow, not for her own service.

Sojourner Truth was never very clear on her age, either, but she was probably in her early 70s when, after the war ended, she began a new battle with the streetcar system in Washington, DC. African Americans had the legal right to ride with the white passengers, but it was a rule the conductors usually ignored. She was dragged behind one car after the conductor refused to wait for her to board. On another occasion, when a streetcar was about to pass her by, Truth shouted, "I want to ride!" and stopped both the car and the surrounding traffic while she climbed on. The conductor threatened to throw her back off, but Truth stood firm and the other passengers began laughing and declaring her the winner of the encounter. Things didn't always end so well. One conductor twisted her arm when she resisted being evicted from his car. Truth did manage to get him convicted of assault and battery, but the incident left a pain in her shoulder that lingered for the rest of her life.

Then Truth moved north, back on the lecture circuit, raising money to resettle the newly freed slaves. "I have been hoping that somebody would print a little of what I am doing," she complained, "but the papers seem to be content simply in saying how old I am."

Like many women of both races, Truth was shocked when Congress marked the end of slavery by giving the right to vote to male blacks but not women. She had predicted that "if colored men get their rights and not colored women theirs, the colored men will be masters over the women and it will be just as bad as it was before." But the reaction of many white feminists went much further — Elizabeth Cady Stanton and others began complaining about well-educated white women being disenfranchised while "ignorant negroes and foreigners" got to vote.

This is a good time to point out that virtually all the nineteenth-century white heroines we've been applauding were also, undeniably, racists. When the first national gathering of women's anti-slavery societies convened in New York in 1837, there was a lengthy debate about whether black members could be admitted. After the war, the suffrage movement made seamy alliances with racist politicians who were trying to disenfranchise the new black voters. So did temperance leaders, who feared blacks would oppose outlawing the sale of alcohol.

That's why one of the best stories of the post–Civil War era involves the Grimké sisters, who were living in semiretirement when Angelina read a story about a young African American man named Archibald Grimké giving a lecture in Pennsylvania. She wrote to him, introducing herself and asking about his background. Archibald responded that he was the son of her brother, a South Carolina slaveholder. It was a sad but typical story: Archibald's mother, Nancy, had been a slave in the home of Henry Grimké and became his mistress after Grimké's wife died. They had three children, and Henry had asked they be provided for in his will. But his white son and heir had ignored the request and tried to take the family as his slaves.

"I am glad you have taken the name of Grimké — it was *once* one of the noblest names of Carolina," replied Angelina, in a long letter that expressed her intention to visit. It was probably more than Archibald had anticipated. As Grimké biographer Gerda Lerner pointed out, in that situation most white abolitionists would not have gone further than a pleasant, but brief, exchange. The sisters had other ideas. They instantly adopted their black nephews as part of the family. Although Angelina, Sarah, and Theodore Weld spent their lives teetering on the verge of penury, they provided financial support for their new relative's college education. To do it, Angelina directed all her earnings to the cause and Sarah gave up whatever very modest extras she had ever treated herself to. Archibald Henry Grimké became a nationally prominent leader, who told people it was his aunts who made him "a liberal in religion, a radical in the woman suffrage movement, in politics and on the race question." One of the last letters Sarah wrote before her death in 1873 concerned her efforts to raise money for "Archie," who was then studying at Harvard Law School and who, she noted proudly, seemed to "far exceed in talents" any of her white Grimké nephews.

"ACCIDENTS AND THE EVIL INFLUENCES OF OTHERS EXCEPTED"

The Grimkés were ahead of their time on dozens of fronts. Another was health reform. The sisters were followers of Sylvester Graham, who advocated a diet of no meat or spices and very sparse use of dairy products or stimulants like coffee and tea. Since the sisters also disliked cooking, their regimen often consisted of raw fruit for breakfast, stewed beans at lunch, and more fruit at the end of the day. Elizabeth Cady Stanton, who visited Angelina often, enjoyed every part of the get-togethers except the meals.

Most American women had been taught — with the help of all those magazines like *Godey's* and the self-help books that were pouring off the presses — that the keys to having a pleasant and rewarding old age were good works and trust in God. But in the mid-nineteenth century, people began to talk about more physical strategies. Mary Gove Nichols, a popular lecturer on health issues, told her mainly female audiences that they needed to stop regarding illness as a visitation of God's will: "Many seem to have no idea that there are established laws with respect to life and health, and that the transgression of these laws is followed by disease."

The victim of a bad marriage to an indolent husband, Nichols attempted to support her family by starting — what else? — a school. In her free time, she prowled through medical books, trying to understand why she suffered from such indifferent health. She saw the light when she attended a lecture by Sylvester Graham, who preached the glories of vegetarianism, temperance, and whole-grain crackers. She put her students on a strict Graham diet. The school didn't last much longer, nor did the marriage. But Nichols became nationally known for her health lectures to women—which included then-shocking descriptions of female anatomy—and for her writings in magazines like the omnipresent *Godey's*. Most of her recommendations were similar to other health reformers': a well-balanced, meat-free diet; frequent baths; clean air and good ventilation. Follow those rules, she said, and anyone with a normal constitution would live to a happy and healthy old age—"accidents and the evil influences of others excepted." Like Graham and many other health reformers, Nichols believed that "stimulants" were to be avoided, whether they were spices or sex. In 1839, she published a denunciation of masturbation titled *Solitary Vice: An Address to Parents and Those Who Have the Care of Children*.

The health reformers weren't exactly taking over the nation, but they did attract a following, mainly among the growing urban middle class. And they marked an important shift of thinking about aging—the idea that people were responsible for how long they lived and how robust they were during their later years. Decrepitude was no longer a misfortune to be endured patiently; it was a sign you had not made the proper effort. William Alcott, a relative of Louisa May and an influential writer on health issues, said that in the future, a child who was a good Christian would live to be 100, but the wicked would be lucky to make 50. The Rev. Henry Ward Beecher, Catharine and Harriet's famous brother, preached that every person was meant to live to be at least 80—unless that person screwed up. "You may sin at one end, but God takes it off at the other," he warned.

"UNENDING COMPLAINTS AGAINST HIS WIFE"

Beecher was the pastor of the big and very prominent Plymouth Church in Brooklyn, where thousands of people tried to cram into Sunday services to hear him speak. Rejecting the stern old theology of the Calvinist past, he offered the public a God who was kind, forgiving, and all about love—the heavenly kind. But in 1872, he was in trouble over another version. Victoria Woodhull, the women's rights advocate and proponent of "free love," announced that Beecher was having an adulterous affair with a parishioner, Elizabeth Tilton. One of Woodhull's arguments against monogamy was that when husbands and wives promised to be sexually faithful to each other, only the women ended up following the rules. Beecher, she said, was an excellent case to prove her point.

All this turned into a sex scandal that seemed to involve virtually every famous person in the country. (Elizabeth Cady Stanton was the one who first told Woodhull about the Beecher gossip.) It's of interest to us because it was the classic tale of an older married man — Beecher was in his 60s — betraying his aging wife with a younger woman.

Elizabeth Tilton was 40 herself but small and fragile. She looked, a newspaper reporter said, "more like a school-girl of 18." Her husband, Theodore, worked with Beecher on an abolitionist newspaper. The two men were great friends, and Henry spent a lot of time at the Tilton house, with one or both of the younger people. All three of them were extremely emotional, given to a lot of hugging and kissing. After Woodhull made her charges, Tilton claimed Beecher had indeed slept with his wife. Beecher denied it. Each man was badgering Elizabeth to tell the world that his story was right. The poor woman, who was clearly not the sturdiest possible character, confessed that she'd had sex with Beecher, then retracted the confession.

Theodore Tilton eventually sued Beecher for alienation of affection, and the ensuing trial was a long parade of front-page headlines. One New York newspaper claimed it was the biggest story since the Lincoln assassination. Crowds stood in line to get seats in the courtroom, and the rest of the nation talked about it over the dinner table. Catharine and Harriet took their brother's part, while their sister Isabella, a prominent women's rights advocate, sided with Theodore Tilton. (Like many women of the era, Isabella was a spiritualist who believed she could communicate with the dead, and much later, after her siblings had passed away, she revealed that she had conferred with them in the spirit world and they had forgiven her.)

But what about the betrayed wife? Eunice Beecher had been married to Henry 34 years at the time of the scandal. She was slightly older than her husband and definitely not a romantic figure. She was apparently never invited to those hug-heavy evenings; nobody seemed sure whether Eunice had resented the enormous amount of time her husband spent hanging around with the Tiltons, who were young enough to be his children. But she apparently never complained, and during the scandal she stood firmly behind Henry, whom she described to her family as simply a "dear guileless simple-hearted man." And since she maintained his innocence, she accepted Elizabeth's as well, talking to her in the courtroom and counseling her, at one point, to abandon Theodore because of his own admitted past affairs. One newspaper reported that Eunice said "she would not live a day with a man who was guilty of Tilton's crimes against marital fidelity."

The jury failed to reach a verdict. That seemed, at first, like a fatal blow to the minister, who couldn't convince 12 citizens that he was innocent. But he won in the court of public opinion—if this had been a normal small-town scandal we might have said that the neighborhood decided to stay friends with Henry Beecher and snub Theodore Tilton. In the process, the press turned Eunice Beecher into the heroine. Reporters noted that she came to the trial every single day, sitting stonily while Tilton reported that Henry "used to pour in my ears unending complaints against his wife.... He said to me one day: 'O Theodore, God might strip all other gifts from me if he would only give me a wife like Elizabeth and a home like yours.' "

"[A]nd there she remains," one paper said, admiring the way Mrs. Beecher stayed at her husband's side, "grimly, unflinchingly, inflexibly."

If the concept of grim, unflinching, and inflexible also seemed to fit Mrs. Beecher in life beyond the courtroom, the stories never hinted at it. "A Remarkable Woman," said the *St. Louis Globe-Democrat*. A Chicago paper noted that until the trial, Eunice had never appeared in the public eye, but the recent unfortunate events had "brought her prominently to the front, and in a light which, even her enemies must concede, is most favorable." It was the conclusion the world apparently wanted to hear. The charismatic celebrity survived, slightly humbled, and the faithful older woman won the day.

After the trial was over, Beecher went back to his adoring congregation.

He had to scramble to repair his ruined finances, but the church generously raised his salary to lend a hand. He also appeared in a Pears' Soap ad, announcing, "If CLEANLINESS is next to GODLINESS, soap must be considered as a means of GRACE, and a clergyman who recommends MORAL things should be willing to recommend soap." The Tilton marriage ended, and Theodore wandered off to Paris. Elizabeth remained in the congregation until she felt compelled to once again change her mind and announce that she really had committed adultery with the pastor. After that, she faded out of history.

Eunice, meanwhile, embarked on a post-trial career as the author of domestic help books. One was titled *All Around the House; or, How to Make Homes Happy*.

"There's a face that haunts me ever"

Given all the action in the Beecher family, it's no wonder that Catharine and Harriet needed a little relief. They'd become big fans of hydrotherapy — or "the water cure" — a middle-class answer to everything from nerves to dyspepsia to fainting fits. It was a respite that particularly appealed to older women, based on constant immersion in steam, baths, and wet compresses. Harriet's husband, Calvin, complained that when he visited her at a spa, he was denied sexual relations because she was swaddled in cold towels day and night.

Some of the therapy involved more stimulating liquids. When Harriet was trying to recover from a bout of cholera, she went to a spa in Brattleboro, Vermont, where the treatment included brandy — patients got up to five shots a day. You weren't supposed to think of this as drinking. Home remedies laced with alcohol were common around the country. Another popular medication that the Stowe family took frequently was calomel, a kind of mercury. It's possible that some of the ailments Harriet was trying to cure — headaches, loss of control of her hands, and confusion — were symptoms of mercury poisoning. There was a lot of that going around. Louisa May Alcott may have suffered from mercury poisoning after receiving calomel as a wartime volunteer at the Union Hotel Hospital. Her life was increasingly dominated by trembling, weakness, a fluttering pulse, and leg and arm pain so severe that she sometimes could not write. "The hospital experience was a costly one for me," she said. "Never well since."

Doctors had been drugging their patients since colonial days, prescribing opium for everything from diarrhea to painful menstruation. They were also still using leeches well into the nineteenth century, applying them everywhere, including inside the nose and in a woman's vagina. It was no wonder people complained of feeling terrible. Laudanum, a form of opium, was a popular cough medication, and it was easy to obtain even without a doctor's assistance.

Women self-medicated as a matter of course. One manual helpfully suggested that even while traveling, they keep a "small box" of health care aids, such as "absorbent cotton, sticking plaster, bandages of muslin or flannel, thread and needles, pins, Vaseline, aromatic spirits of ammonia, tincture of asafoetida, oil of cloves, Hoffman's Anodyne, syrup of ipecac, laudanum, magnesia, mustard, paregoric, spiced syrup of rhubarb, turpentine," adding that "to these may be added camphor-water, essence of ginger, lime-water and sweet spirits of nitre." God knows what was supposed to be stocked in the medicine cabinet at home.

The less creative simply turned to patent medicines, which were often largely alcohol. Somehow this also didn't seem to count as drinking—activist Abby Hopper Gibbons regarded herself as rather unique among the temperance reformers for refusing to medicate herself with brandy. Lydia Pinkham's tonic, which was enormously popular among women in the late nineteenth century, was a mixture of herbs, roots, and alcohol that came in a bottle bearing a portrait of the 60-year-old grandmother who, the company said, had created the recipe. She was, to her fans, the epitome of all those mothers, aunts, and grandmothers who knew just what to do when a member of the family had a health complaint.

"There's a face that haunts me ever," sang college students at Dartmouth in the 1880s.

There are eyes mine always meet
As I read the morning paper.
As I walk the crowded street.
Ah! She knows not what I suffer;

Hers is now a world-wide fame,
But till death that face shall greet me.
Lydia Pinkham is her name.

"TO FASHION'S SHRINE TO DIE"

One thing almost everyone, from physicians to health reformers to women's rights advocates, agreed on was that corsets were bad. They were so tight that many believed they literally rearranged the wearers' ribs and internal organs. "That pulmonary disease, affections of the heart and insanity are in its train, and that it leads some of our fairest and dearest to fashion's shrine to die, is placed beyond a doubt, by strong medical testimony," wrote the poet Lydia Sigourney in her advice book. Critics did tend to get carried away, but at minimum the corsets made life uncomfortable and limited women's movements, particularly when combined with petticoats and heavy skirts that trailed close to the ground. In wintertime, a woman might leave her house underneath about 37 pounds of clothing. And, of course, the discomfort was greatest for older — and often larger — women. Dr. John Harvey Kellogg, a dietary reformer and cornflakes inventor, once corseted his wife's collie to study the effect on the dog's breathing ability. The animal, taking advantage of Kellogg's belief in fresh air, jumped out an open window and ran home to take refuge with Mrs. Kellogg, unceremoniously concluding the experiment.

The recalcitrant collie was perhaps an omen that dress reform was going to be harder than some of its advocates imagined. The movement found its most famous remedy in bloomers, an outfit consisting of a tunic and pants that somewhat resembled a costume in a Turkish harem. It did allow the wearer to move around naturally and sit without gasping for breath. But the idea of women in pants drove the establishment crazy. Newspapers claimed bloomer advocates were plotting an end to the traditional family. Editor Sarah Hale was, perhaps unsurprisingly, not a fan. "Does it make any sense to sacrifice not only your social enjoyments but also your usefulness for the purpose of making an ineffectual attempt to change a fashion under which so many people have lived in health and comfort that it would be difficult to persuade them it is injurious?" *Godey's* asked, rather rhetorically.

Mary Gove Nichols, who was once hit by a rock when she wore bloomers in public, solved the problem by moving to a utopian commune in New York when she was in her 40s. There, a visiting reporter revealed in awe, the women not only wore pants; they asked men to dance at the commune parties. The Grimké sisters wore bloomers at their progressive school, and it's nice to think of them bustling around the dining room in their Turkish trousers, serving their students unseasoned vegetarian meals. But even Angelina and Sarah didn't stay with the costume indefinitely. Elizabeth Cady Stanton, who had been sure that she would wear bloomers forever, retreated when she got letters from her sons at school, denouncing them. The bloomer cause was certainly not helped by the fact that the billowy pants were unflattering to most figures. It would be a long time before women of all ages would feel comfortable wearing pants in public.

"TO DYE OR NOT TO DYE"

While etiquette books and women's magazines continued to warn women against hair dye, it appeared that men used it rather regularly. In the run-up to the Civil War, there were lots of jokes about men suddenly deciding to stop washing away gray when they realized a youthful appearance could lead to a summons from the draft board. A story from Tennessee described an older man who was coloring his hair in order to woo a "fair, fat and forty buxom widow." (Apparently some people found the description more favorable than Margaret Fuller did.) But, the paper reported, when the imposter found himself called up before the draft board, he quickly confessed he had been trying to trick the widow into thinking he was only thirty-eight: "I wanted to get married," he explained. Then, the paper claimed, "the widower's hair dye was washed away, his false teeth had been removed, his form was bent by the immense pressure of mental anxiety," and observers concluded he was closer to eighty.

Okay, possibly an apocryphal story. But the legend of men giving up their hair dye in order to avoid conscription was so popular, there must have been something behind it. The *New-York Tribune* claimed that the men's fashion industry was in a tailspin: "Nobody, except some ancient female, has used hair dye since the call was made for all men 'under 45 years of age.'"

It's hard to know if there were really all that many "ancient females" using dyes, either. There was a lot going against the practice: it was looked down upon socially, the results generally weren't convincing, and it was dangerous. Stories about people collapsing or being driven mad by the lead in their hair dyes showed up repeatedly in papers around the country. Neither health standards nor journalism standards were particularly high in the middle of the nineteenth century, so it's hard to tell how much of this was exaggerated, but a report to New York City's Board of Health in 1870 did find that all hair treatments it tested contained lead, or nitrate of silver.

Some of the reported victims were women, like "a lady in Fauquier county, Va.," who was "paralyzed a few days ago from excessive use of hair dye containing sugar of lead." But most of the alleged fatalities were male. In 1869, several news outlets reported an investigation into the death of one Dr. J. M. Witherwax, which concluded that the good doctor had perished from lead poisoning, thanks to a hair dye he had applied every day for four years. A few years later, a former governor of Pennsylvania, John Geary, died suddenly while he was fixing breakfast for his son. Some observers attributed his unexpected demise to an old war wound, but others thought Geary had been poisoned by a dye he used to cover his gray beard.

Once the war was over, the nation had a bit of a let's-party mentality, and it did appear that more and more members of both sexes used hair coloring to eliminate gray. Henry Ward Beecher wrote about whether "to dye or not to dye," giving men a pass while throwing all the blame on their women: "If his wife will love him the better, or if she will be made happier, in the name of love, let him dye." As for the wives themselves, Beecher preferred those who abstained but graciously added that "if her happiness may be promoted by hiding the early gray, we see no reason for criticism." Other parties were far more judgmental. A Boston paper in 1872 lashed out: "Ladies who are so unscrupulous as to heighten their natural charms by the use of paint and hair dye have a great deal to answer for. Not only do they sail under false colours, but they destroy that confidence which weak man is naturally disposed to extend to them without limitation, and they cause him frequently to mistrust complexions and heads of hair innocent of any paint but that bestowed by nature's brush."

"GROWING OLD! GROWING OLD!"

Sarah Josepha Hale was 89 when she retired from *Godey's* in 1877, after 50 years as editor. She apparently kept writing, at least in private. For her 90th birthday she read her family a poem she had composed for the occasion:

> *Growing old! Growing old! Do they say it of me?*
> *Do they hint my fine fancies are faded and fled?*
> *That my garden of life, like the winter-swept tree,*
> *Is frozen and dying, or fallen and dead?*
> *Is the heart growing old, when each beautiful thing,*
> *Like a landscape at eve, looks more tenderly bright*
> *And love sweeter seems, as the bird's wand'ring wing*
> *Draws nearer her nest at the coming of night?*

Three of her five children had predeceased her. That was an old story in American family life, but it was beginning to be more unusual. Infant mortality had been plunging, and it was no longer as common for young adults to be carried off by a sudden fever. Families in poor neighborhoods were still ravaged by the effects of bad sanitation, unpasteurized milk, and poor nutrition. But in the middle class, the newer generation was beginning to regard death less as an unpredictable bolt of lightning and more as something that happened to old people.

As for *Godey's Lady's Book,* it would endure for a while longer, but it would never have the influence that Hale wielded in its glory days before the Civil War—an event she managed to avoid ever mentioning while the conflict was under way.

5. The Nineteenth-Century Finale

"THE SHADY SIDE OF FIFTY"

Elizabeth Cady Stanton spent 12 years on the lecture trail. Unsurprisingly, the strain began to take its toll. She injured her back when a wagon that was toting her between stops overturned. Then she contracted pneumonia. Eventually, at 65, she decided to devote herself to writing and limit travel to less challenging itineraries. She and Susan B. Anthony were camped out in Stanton's home in Tenafly, New Jersey, working on a history of the suffrage movement, when the 1880 election rolled around. The friends marched together to try to vote at the local polling place, an effort that ended when an inspector refused to let Stanton put her ballot in the box and she threw it at him. (Anthony was an old hand at attempting to vote, having been arrested in 1872 and put on trial for, in the words of the district attorney, voting when "at that time she was a woman.")

Stanton had promised Anthony their 50s would be terrific, but—irritation with the voting system notwithstanding—she was finding her 60s to be even better. She and her frequently estranged husband had reconciled, in a relationship that seemed to involve a good deal of affection but a minimal number of demands. She traveled through Europe. She was celebrated by the members of the National American Woman Suffrage Association (NAWSA), though she was never really as beloved as the more hands-on Anthony. She was supporting herself by her writing, which was as feisty as ever.

Her good humor and unthreatening appearance still allowed her to get away with a never-dwindling radicalism, especially on matters like sex, which had brought down so many other female lecturers. "Stately Mrs. Stanton has secured much immunity by a comfortable look of motherliness and a sly benignity in her smiling eyes, even though her

74

arguments have been bayonet thrusts and her words gun shots," noted the novelist Grace Greenwood. Stanton herself began to feel that the motherly look could go too far. "I have one melancholy fact to state which I do with sorrow and humiliation," she wrote a friend in 1888. "I was weighed yesterday and brought the scales down at 240." She vowed to begin dieting almost immediately and added: "Yet, I am well; danced the Virginia reel with Bob. But alas! I am 240!"

On the occasion of her 70th birthday, Stanton was invited to deliver an essay on "The Pleasures of Age." She said it took about a week "to think them up," but by the time she had finished composing, "I was almost converted to the idea that 'we old folks' had the best of it." Her research had not begun on a promising note. She told her audience that she had gathered a group of 70-plus friends for breakfast and challenged them to come up with examples of the brighter side of aging. One of her guests proposed that "perhaps one may find some pleasure in being deaf, as then you do not hear the nonsense of ordinary talk." Another said blindness, too, might be a blessing, "as then your eyes are shut to many things you fain would never see." It's hard to believe such a conversation actually ever took place—but this was before the age when public figures' remarks were vetted for accuracy.

Then Stanton quickly veered toward the positive: the ideal elderly woman spent most of her time in her library, where she would reread a favorite book or simply sit quietly in contemplation, reciting "inspiring sentiments in prose and verse" or playing "on some instrument." In the evenings, although her own dancing days might be over, she could still enjoy watching the young ones on the floor. Stanton followed with an admonition about the importance of a sound health regimen. All in all, it seemed a particularly strange prescription for happiness coming from an unstoppable lecturer who would soon be bemoaning 240 pounds while reporting that she had recently danced the Virginia reel.

With that perfunctory bow to traditional visions of old age out of the way, Stanton moved on to her favorite theme: chiding women who believed that once their children had grown they had nothing to live for—when there was so much work to be done! All the energy that had been directed to courtship, marriage, and motherhood was just waiting to find new expression. If women were lucky enough to have no serious money problems, she concluded, "surely each of us may take up some absorbing congenial work to dignify the sunset of our lives." It was a theme she would return to again and again in her seventies—that "on the shady side of fifty" middle-class women had the opportunity to start a whole new life, when they could turn their attentions away from family duties to fight for the family of man.

"NO LIMIT IF DEAD"

The controversial figures of the early women's reform movement were beloved celebrities by the end of the century. The obituaries for the Grimké sisters, who died in the 1870s, skipped over the angry mobs who had tried to burn down the halls where Angelina was speaking and focused on their gentle charity. The *Cincinnati Enquirer* eulogized Angelina as "a pioneer in the anti-slavery movement and a friend to the poor and needy" when she passed away in 1879. A Leavenworth, Kansas, paper pointed out, under the headline "Sensible to the Last," that Angelina had asked to be buried in an old dress so that all the good ones could be given to the poor.

Susan B. Anthony was a star—the woman who knew everyone, from presidents to African American heroes like Frederick Douglass to popular celebrities like Lillian Russell. The media, which had snarked about her spartan figure and wardrobe, now couldn't get enough of her. When Anthony collapsed on a trip in 1895, reporters rushed to her home. One Chicago paper telegraphed its representative: "50,000 words if still living, no limit if dead." No one seemed to have aged better than Anthony, whose real character the nation had finally learned to appreciate. "From being the most ridiculed and mercilessly persecuted woman, Miss Anthony has become the most honored and respected in the nation," Stanton wrote in her memoirs. It was not that Anthony had changed; it was the country that had come around.

No one in Anthony's generation of reformers seemed to be planning on retirement. Antoinette Brown Blackwell, the first woman to be ordained a minister in a mainstream Protestant faith, celebrated her 70th birthday with her first visit to Europe. When she returned, she wrote to Anthony, "I plunge again into work," with hopes that she could last at least another two decades: "Life is too short for all we would like to do but we will keep busy till the end." She had her wish. A friend described Blackwell at 90, still stalking off every morning for two or three hours of vigorous hoeing in the garden. The *Boston Globe* called her "in many respects the most remarkable woman in the country."

When Catharine Beecher was in her 70s she decided she wanted to go to college—specifically, to take a course at the elite Cornell University. The horrified president told her the classes were all male. "In fact, I prefer to take it with men," she replied serenely. Everything seemed to have worked out for Beecher, who preached the glories of domestic life without ever having one of her own. "I have been for many years a wanderer without a home, in delicate health, and often baffled in favorite plans for usefulness," she wrote. "And yet my life has been a very happy one, with more enjoyments and fewer trials than most of my friends experience who are surrounded by the largest share of earthly gratifications."

Catharine and Harriet, still plumbing the profitable domestic arts market, wrote *The American Woman's Home,* which tackled the aging issue, noting that for housewives "and still more to those who in public life have been honored and admired, the decay of mental powers is peculiarly trying." The remedy, the sisters wrote, was for their near and dear to pay "courteous attention to their opinions" and avoid any temptation to argue "or make evident any weakness or fallacy in their conversation." Perhaps it was a warning to their relatives.

Basically, the sisters argued that the most important job of the old was inspiring others with their patience and acceptance. It was an echo of the lectures by colonial ministers: when you don't feel you have any role to play in the world, you can still set a good example by not complaining. When the book was published in 1869, neither of the authors was preparing to follow that advice anytime soon. Harriet, about to enter her 60s, was on a manic series of speaking tours, and Catharine would soon be on her way to Cornell.

"BLACK AND NEUTRAL TINTS ARE DECLARED APPROPRIATE"

Lydia Maria Child had started a serious trend when it came to books on aging. They were very big sellers in the latter part of the nineteenth century. Most of them tried to be upbeat in the extreme. A prominent minister's wife produced a version in 1888 that included an elegy to gray hair: "beautiful in itself and so softening to the complexion and so picturesque in its effect that many a woman who has been plain in her youth is, by its beneficent influence, transformed into a handsome woman." That was a heck of a lot more encouraging than Lydia Child's promise back in the 1860s that as long as people maintained good temper and sincerity, they were unlikely to be "repulsively ugly in person after middle life."

Learning to love your gray made sense since hair color was still frowned upon — at minimum, it was regarded as an example of trying too hard. Also, women were expected to act their age when it came to dress. That basically meant really boring clothes. "We put bright colors upon our little children," explained an 1877 etiquette book. "We dress our young girls in light and delicate shades, the blooming matron is justified in adopting the warm, rich hues which we see in the autumn leaf, while black and neutral tints are declared appropriate to the old." The distaste for women trying to look young wasn't restricted to social arbiters. Sojourner Truth — who seemed to have a particular loathing for the fashion of big, feathery hats — complained about her fellow reformers: "... mothers and gray-haired grandmothers wear high-heeled shoes and humps on their heads.... When I saw them women on the stage at the Woman's Suffrage Convention, the other day, I thought, What kind of reformers be you, with goose-wings on your head, as if you were going to fly, and dressed in such ridiculous fashion, talking about reform and women's rights? [']Pears to me, you had better reform yourselves first."

Older women had left caps behind, but they did wear wigs, mainly to disguise a loss of hair. There's never been an age when women were eager to let the world know they were balding, but in the nineteenth century it was also seen as a sign that a parent or grandparent had suffered from syphilis. Hairdressers who fitted clients for wigs tended to do so in deepest secrecy, shooing even their assistants from the room. The nation also still frowned on the idea of older women using cosmetics to disguise their years, although that sort of thing did happen. In the cities, the well-to-do and daring could go to an "enameling studio" where their wrinkles were erased under a mask of wax and paste. "The hygienically furnished, well-kept beauty parlors have come to stay, and there are few women who will not feel better for visiting them occasionally as a supplement to their home treatments," decreed *The Woman Beautiful*.

At home, women would use ground starch or rice to whiten their skin. A pale complexion was the most sought-after beauty goal, and there were plenty of new products on the market that promised to help. Beauty experts were new favorites on the lecture trail. "Madame Yale" traveled the country talking on "The Religion of Beauty, the Sin of Ugliness" and selling her catalogue of antiaging products. Flouncing her thick mass of blond hair, she demonstrated exercises in a pink satin gym suit. "It would be hard to describe her form as anything but just 'perfect,'" hyperventilated a paper in Pittsburgh. But even the smitten writer seemed to have a little difficulty accepting Madame Yale's biggest selling point—she claimed to be 50 years old.

The end of the nineteenth century brought older Americans something more important than any skin whitener—teeth! "Perfectly fitting false teeth have done more to postpone age than any one physical cause," declared *Harper's Bazar* (the publication's original spelling) in 1885. A new kind of moldable rubber base made dentures much more comfortable—it had been around for a long time, but since the inventor was extremely litigious, it wasn't used widely until his patent expired in 1881. And even the strictest critic of artificial beauty enhancements had absolutely no problem with artificial incisors. *Harper's* celebrated false teeth and "the more uniform heating of houses" as improvements that "might almost have made age young again."

"DISEASE, PREMATURE DECAY . . . WILL BE SURE TO RESULT"

As America left the Civil War era behind and started flinging itself full tilt into economic expansion, conspicuous consumption, technological progress, and scientific inquiry, the medical profession began paying more attention to the effects of aging on female anatomy. Not all of their inquiry was helpful. The more scientists investigated the way women's bodies worked, the more they concluded that ovulation was pretty much the only game in town. ("Women's reproductive organs are preeminent.") Physicians regarded menopause as a shutting down of female energy that required rest and an extremely quiet lifestyle. One activity that was rigorously ruled out was sex — doctors thought it could be fatal for older women. The influential English physician Edward Tilt warned that any sexual desire in menopausal women was due to "a morbid impulse" and urged single middle-aged women to avoid taking a husband "without having obtained the sanction of a medical man." Psychiatrist Forbes Winslow worried that menopause might turn a woman who had never borne a child into an "ovarian manic" with "immodest sexual appetites." Possible remedies included "injections of ice water into the rectum or vagina, or leeching of the labia and cervix."

The vision of menopause as a truly unpleasant dead end started out in England, but it quickly spanned the Atlantic. John Harvey Kellogg, the cornflakes inventor who had tried corseting his wife's collie, produced a popular advice book in 1881 that decreed, "Sexual life begins with puberty, and, in the female, ends at about the age of forty-five years." If a woman insisted on retaining her erotic side, he added, "disease, premature decay, possibly local degenerations, will be sure to result. Nature cannot be abused with impunity." Kellogg had a lot of theories about menstruation, one of which involved the danger of having it begin too soon: "Females in whom puberty occurs at the age of ten or twelve, by the time their age is doubled, are shriveled and wrinkled with age. At the time when they should be in their prime of health and beauty, they are prematurely old and broken."

Middle-aged women in the later nineteenth century who complained about feeling ill were less likely to brew a home remedy and more likely to consult doctors, who were in turn very likely to tell them that their problems were all related to menopause. Sex was not the only thing menopausal women were being told to avoid. Tilt and other physicians warned them against risky behavior like reading novels, dancing, or going to parties. And you couldn't start preparing too soon. "We insist that every woman who hopes for a healthy old age ought to commence her prudent cares as early as the fortieth year or sooner," said an 1871 medical advice book. "She should cease to endeavor to appear young when she is no longer so and withdraw from the excitements and fatigues of the gay world even in the midst of her legitimate successes, to enter upon that more tranquil era of her existence now at hand."

Obviously not everyone agreed. Plenty of postmenopausal women had embraced the theory that the best days were still ahead and getting to them might require a good deal of moving around.

"THIS NEW IMPLEMENT OF POWER"

In 1895, Frances Willard published *A Wheel Within a Wheel*, a book about how at "the ripe age of fifty-three" she learned to ride a two-wheeled bicycle.

Willard was one of the great female leaders of the nineteenth century. Her political vehicle was the temperance movement, a cause we don't tend to think of as particularly liberating. But feminists of her era saw drinking as something that separated husbands from their families. Wealthy men went off to their private clubs, and the working class flocked to saloons — in Chicago in 1897, the saloons outnumbered the total of grocery stores, meat markets, and dry goods stores combined. While they were a source of friendship and support for many men, saloons existed mainly to encourage their clientele to drink as much as possible, as fast as possible. Left behind in the wreckage were the wives and children, and many middle-class reformers saw banning alcohol as the best way to solve the problem.

Willard was definitely a true believer in the cause. But she also wanted to build temperance into a huge political movement, with women at its head, working on "everything" — from suffrage to prisons to health reform. And health reform included lots of exercise. There were still holdouts in the general population — in Baltimore, a doctor claimed that putting female students in schools where they had to climb stairs "would affect future childbearing." But the tide was turning. Reformers were championing physical education classes for girls, and women's magazines extolled brisk walks or toe touching for their readers. Willard's doctor recommended bike riding as therapy for her severe case of anemia. She embraced the idea even though she needed friends to help support her — literally — during a long training period. In her 40s, Willard confided to her readers, she had tried her niece's three-wheeled bike, fell off, and broke her elbow.

But she got back on the saddle and bonded with her bicycle, which she named Gladys—"the most remarkable, ingenious and inspiring motor ever yet devised upon this planet." It had been a struggle, but Gladys was worth it, Willard told her readers. Then she explained why she had persisted:

- She was hoping husbands and wives might go biking together: "the more interests women and men can have in common, in thought, word, and deed, the happier will it be for the home."
- She liked the idea of "acquiring this new implement of power and literally putting it underfoot."
- "Last but not least, because a good many people thought I could not do it at my age."

The book was a bestseller.

6. Turn of the Century

The turn of the century was an exciting time for a select few older women. Most were still living quietly with their families, but there were some notable exceptions: Frances Willard had that bestseller about learning how to ride a bicycle at 53. Lillie Langtry, a spectacular British beauty, was filling theaters on both sides of the ocean when she was in her 60s. And everybody wanted to see Sarah Bernhardt, the French actress who played in America regularly—including four "farewell" tours, the last of which was extremely successful even though Bernhardt, then in her 70s, had undergone a leg amputation. In 1898, with the approach of the Spanish-American War, Annie Oakley, the Wild West show star, wrote to President McKinley, offering to place "fifty lady sharpshooters at your disposal" should hostilities break out. Oakley, who was one of the most famous people in the nation, was only 37 at the time. She would make a similar offer to Woodrow Wilson when she was 57 and then settle for touring World War I military camps to give shooting demonstrations to the recruits.

"One of the most remarkable changes in the lives of women in this country has been the postponement of old age," wrote Jane Addams, the settlement house reformer, peace crusader, and future Nobel Prize winner. Her essay was one of many victory laps by older women who wanted to point out how far things had come. (*Harper's Bazar* had noted triumphantly in 1885 that the modern grandmother "never has time to be 'looking toward sunset.'") The *Cosmopolitan* writer Nancy Woodrow told her readers that "[t]he woman who to-day is celebrated for distinctive charm and beauty, ripe views, disciplined intellect, cultivated and manifold gifts, would, two score years ago, have been relegated to the heavy ranks of the dowagers and grandmothers—forced by the stern conventions of prevailing opinion to confront the bitter knowledge that, just as she had gained a mastery of the rules, she was expected to retire from the game."

Women of all ages were doing more of everything. They were becoming much more economically important, both as consumers and as workers. Wives were making almost all the family purchases — many of them, store owners began to notice, were buying their husbands' clothes as well as their own. They were going out to restaurants with their friends, without male supervision. While the laws giving husbands control over their wives' property still needed a great deal of improvement, widows were no longer inevitably stuck living at the whim of a male heir. By 1890, more than 90 percent of the elderly women who lived alone or with their children on a farm owned the property in question. Many of the properties were small and poor, but still, they were theirs.

In the expanding American office place, women were everywhere — well, everywhere but the boardrooms. They were certainly in the classrooms. By 1905, virtually all the elementary schoolteachers were women, and they were getting better salaries. Although still far from lucrative, teaching was beginning to pay a living wage, thanks to union movements and the law of supply and demand — more young people were going to school and staying longer, increasing the competition for qualified instructors. Older women were seeing expanded job opportunities even in periods when economic contraction left men with fewer options. Marion Harland, an advice writer, reported that a doctor had told her: "When I want *good* work done, I look about me for a woman over forty-five years of age."

"MENTALLY MAKING AN ADDRESS"

As she moved into her 80s, Elizabeth Cady Stanton did begin to slow down. But she was still a much-in-demand writer, of everything from magazine articles to resolutions for the National American Woman Suffrage Association. And while she admitted she could no longer "clamber up and down platforms," she was still giving lectures — sometimes speaking for more than 90 minutes. On Stanton's 80th birthday, in 1895, Susan B. Anthony had organized a lavish celebration at the Metropolitan Opera House in New York, where dignitaries gave both gifts and speeches to the guest of honor, who was seated on a gold-and-velvet chair in the middle of the stage.

Then Stanton made a new splash, challenging popular beliefs about both religion and sex. She published a shocking bestseller—a feminist version of the scriptures called *The Woman's Bible,* in which she denounced the concept of virgin birth as "a slur on all natural motherhood." The NAWSA felt compelled to pass a resolution attesting that it had no official connection with "the so-called Woman's Bible." But Stanton was unruffled, and felt vindicated not long afterward when the *American Journal of the Medical Sciences* published a paper announcing that it was "now generally recognized" that menopause could be a boon to women, "an important aid to the preservation and increase of the vital forces." It was hardly going to be the end of medical diagnoses blaming "change of life" for every kind of complaint under the sun, but it was definitely a step forward.

Stanton lost most of her sight in her mid-80s, but she kept giving interviews and writing with the help of a reader and a typist. Her last article, on divorce reform, was published two weeks before her death at 86. It's possible that Stanton committed a kind of assisted suicide, getting a prescription for a drug overdose. She had said she wanted to be "speeded on to heaven" whenever she became a true invalid, and her family suspected she had, as usual, taken things into her own hands. Stanton quietly asked her daughter and maid to help her dress—black silk—and fix her hair. Then she stood up for a few minutes before she sat down at a table, fell asleep, and died. No one knew what she was thinking when she got to her feet for the last time. But her daughter Harriot, who became her successor as a leader of the suffrage movement, said she believed her mother "was mentally making an address."

"BEST WOMAN IN CHICAGO"

In 1906, four years after Stanton's death, the grand old women of the voting rights movement traveled to Baltimore for the NAWSA convention. "It is seldom that such a number of notable women gather in one city," gushed the *Baltimore Sun,* comparing Susan B. Anthony to Queen

Victoria. It was yet another example of the way the media had fallen in love with all the women it had reviled when they were in their 40s and 50s, just setting out to reform America. Anthony knew she would not live to see women get the vote. But she was still fighting. At a dinner given during the convention in honor of her 86th birthday, someone read a commemorative telegram from President Theodore Roosevelt and Anthony bristled. "I wish the men would do something besides extend congratulations," she sniped, noting that she'd have preferred if Roosevelt had said "a word to Congress" about suffrage. At the end of the evening, Anthony recalled some of the great women she had known — Stanton, Lucretia Mott, the Grimkés. And then, looking out over the assemblage, she announced: "Failure is impossible." Those would be her last public words.

Anthony's appearance was the emotional high point of the suffrage convention, but she was far from the only speaker people had come to hear. Jane Addams took part in a panel about health conditions in the cities and so impressed Dr. William Welch, the dean of Johns Hopkins School of Medicine, that Welch was moved to announce suffragists "are not such a queer lot of people as many suppose." Addams, then 45, was the daughter of a wealthy Illinois businessman. She had been depressed and at loose ends when she graduated from college and had dropped in on a London settlement house during a European tour. It was run by male college students, and Addams liked the work they were doing with the poor. She decided to do the same thing herself in Chicago — except with young people of her own gender. Her Hull House settlement provided a center for the immigrant community, a home for college-educated women who wanted to work with the poor, and a political staging ground to fight for issues from cleaner government to cleaner streets. Soon there would be projects like it in big cities around the country. One of the new breed of young social workers in Boston's Denison House was Amelia Earhart, who generated publicity for a settlement fund-raiser by flying over the city dropping leaflets about it.

Shortly after that suffrage convention, the *Chicago Tribune* named Addams "Best Woman in Chicago," after a balloting in which it suggested that only unmarried women could qualify for the honor. The paper said most of the voters it had surveyed felt "that the unmarried woman has a far better chance of being good than the woman who is burdened by the task of looking after a husband." In a way, it was an echo of all those early nineteenth-century stereotypes about old-maid aunts devoting their lives to selfless good deeds. But those aging spinsters were supposed to be working unnoticed in the background, living just to be useful to others. Nobody had imagined that one of them could wind up being extolled to the world as the *best woman* while wives and mothers were essentially declared ineligible.

Being single had never been more fashionable. "The modern 'old maid' is round and jolly, and has her full complement of hair and teeth, and two dimples in her cheek, and has a laugh as musical as a bobolink's song," wrote the novelist Fanny Fern happily. "[A]nd she goes to concerts and parties and suppers and lectures and matinees, and she don't go alone either; and she lives in a nice house, earned by herself, and gives jolly little teas in it." It was far better, Fern added, than the bad old days of living on a relative's charity and having to take care of "her sister's nine children." In popular magazines, writers urged that the term "old maid" be replaced by "bachelor girl" or "bachelor woman."

It was all about having an economic role in the world. Female college graduates, seeing a raft of career options, started plotting a single life — the proportion of women with degrees who married dropped as low as 50 percent. An essay in *The Woman Beautiful* looked back triumphantly on the days when a twenty-five-year-old was considered over the hill, since she had no real options outside of marriage. But these days, the writer added, "a woman of thirty-five is now considered most interesting and companionable, and many men find her more attractive than the inexperienced girl in her teens." Some forty-five-year-old readers might have preferred a more expanded vision, but that was covered in other articles — many, many other articles — extolling the New Woman. The New Woman was independent and energetic, and she could be any age at all as long as she went out and *did things.* "I fear you think the New Woman is going to wipe you off the planet but be not afraid," Stanton wryly told the men at her eightieth birthday tribute. "All who have mothers, sisters, wives or sweethearts will be very well looked after." While you could be a New Woman and married, it did seem — as the *Tribune* proposed — that it might be a lot easier if you were single.

"TO WRITE PAPERS, TO ADDRESS AUDIENCES, TO PRESIDE OVER MEETINGS"

In 1914, when Addams, then 54, wrote a piece for *Ladies' Home Journal* titled "Need a Woman over Fifty Feel Old?," her answer, unsurprisingly, was an emphatic no. More and more women, she told her readers, had been turning their later years into a golden period of achievement and communal action. And if anyone was wondering exactly how to get on that age-defying activist track, Addams had an answer: women's clubs. It was the clubs, she wrote, that allowed housewives with dwindling family responsibilities "to write papers, to address audiences, to preside over meetings." And to try to change the world. "These same elderly women who, in their youth, had been sheltered from any knowledge of crime and the ways of criminals...were often responsible for securing matrons in the police stations, teachers in the jail, the establishment of juvenile courts and the abolishment of vice districts," Addams wrote, going on to credit club women with fighting for proper sanitation, school nurses, and vocational schools.

Women's clubs were booming by the end of the century. It all may have started with a snub. In 1868, when Charles Dickens visited New York, he was feted at a dinner hosted by the New York Press Club. Among the members who had been looking forward to the event was Jane Cunningham Croly, a writer who had successfully broken into the new world of women's-page journalism under the pen name Jennie June. When the male members of the Press Club decided that women weren't invited to the Dickens dinner, Croly founded a group of her own that barred men. She named it Sorosis, and by the end of its first year it had 83 members, including artists, editors, poets, teachers, and writers, along with philanthropists, a historian, and two physicians.

The idea spread across the country, but most of the new clubwomen weren't professionals, like Jane Cunningham Croly. It was just the opposite — the clubs were a path to the outside world for women who had spent their early years as homemakers. Americans were still strongly opposed to the idea of working wives. Of course, some women did have to work in order to help support their families, but that was seen as a terrible reflection on their husbands. W. E. B. Du Bois wrote that in the "better class" of urban African American homes, "the wife engaged in no occupation save that of house-wife." Those voters for Best Woman in Chicago did have a point. While there were children at home, society expected their mothers to devote just about every waking moment to domestic responsibilities. And in return, they'd receive love from their family, respect from their community, and the joy of knowing they'd done their duty. But there was that catch: what did all those mothers do with their time once the children moved on? Elizabeth Cady Stanton had figured out an answer, but most women didn't have Stanton's drive—or her lifelong contacts with every important reform leader on the Eastern Seaboard. They were stuck. For most of American history, they had been told to sit down, rock, and contemplate their eternal reward. Then people like Lydia Maria Child started urging them to do something for other people. That might be interesting—particularly if it didn't involve all of Child's nostrums about sitting in the park and telling nursery rhymes to passing children. But what could they do and how could they do it?

The clubs provided that path. They usually started with self-education projects. The members would discuss books or read papers they'd prepared. Generally the topic was literary or historic—the role of the mother in Charles Dickens novels or Great Women of Roman Civilization. The audience was other housewives. But since most members were a few decades away from whatever schooling they'd enjoyed, the opportunity to present their ideas before a group of serious listeners could be daunting.

From a history of these early groups, an application for membership:

The undersigned feeling the need of something to stimulate her mental and moral culture, and believing the means may be the concentration in a literary society or body associated expressly to impart and receive instruction, hereby offers herself for a candidate for the honor of membership in the Edgeworthalean Society. She has long meditated this step, and has hitherto been withheld by a sense of her deficiencies and shame at exposing them to that honorable literary body; but knowing that shame often proceeds from pride, that great bar to the acquisition of knowledge, she intends laying it aside and coming forward as a simple learner to the feet of those whose years, if measured by their attainments, would far exceed those of

Your humble petitioner

"Dante is dead"

Even at that early, essay-reading level, the first clubs were controversial. "Homes will be ruined, children neglected, woman is straying from her sphere," warned the *Boston Evening Transcript* when the New England Woman's Club was founded in 1868. But as time went on, they became more of an honored community institution — one that members might see as a way to make new friends and find new interests, or even move up socially. Some never went beyond that: in 1914, Carrie Chapman Catt noted wryly that the association of women's clubs in Iowa barred groups that were interested in suffrage because "[n]o club with a purpose could be admitted."

But over time, as women's education improved, some clubs grew less excited about listening to their members deliver research papers and more interested in community activism. In 1904, when Sarah Chase Platt-Decker took over her post as president of the General Federation of Women's Clubs, she announced: "Ladies, you have chosen me as your new leader. Well, I have an important piece of news to give you. Dante is dead. He has been dead for several centuries, and I think it is time that we dropped the study of his *Inferno* and turned our attention to our own."

For an example of how the clubs evolved, let's look for a minute at the Women's Literary Club in Buffalo. It was founded in 1884 by Harriet Townsend, the 45-year-old wife of a wealthy merchant, for the purpose of "mental development." But Townsend pretty clearly had her eye on a wider target, and soon the club invited a speaker from the Boston Women's Educational and Industrial Union to give a talk on the group's work for social justice. Soon Buffalo had a Women's Educational and Industrial Union of its own, also headed by Harriet Townsend. The group raised money to purchase a large building for a headquarters, where members could meet and working women could come for exercise, education, and a nourishing lunch. It was not, Townsend stressed, going to be "an association of benevolent, well-to-do women, joined for the purpose of reaching down to help the poor and persecuted women, but a Union of all classes and conditions of women." Her success in getting her friends to regard themselves as the peers of factory workers may have been mixed, but the union did lobby successfully in the state capitol for divorce reform and in city hall for a police matron to protect female prisoners from being handled and searched by men. They also went to court on behalf of servants who were shortchanged by their employers. That project became so successful that eventually domestic workers found they could get their rightful wages by merely dropping the union's name.

In 1893, an 18-year-old homeless woman fainted from hunger in another upstate New York city, Rochester. Male police officers, seeing no other immediate option, carried her to their station, where she woke up in a jail cell. The story reached the ear of Rochester's most famous citizen, and Susan B. Anthony got angry. She contacted the local women's club, which had the presumably ironic name of Fortnightly Ignorance Club. Ignorance invited Harriet Townsend to come and talk about her work in Buffalo, and the Rochester Women's Educational and Industrial Union was founded. Soon it, too, was providing free legal aid and a comfortable place for working women to come to eat and relax, and pushing for prison reform. The beat went on.

Those were the women Addams praised for everything from establishing kindergartens to lobbying for laws ensuring a clean milk supply. And—no small point—creating a fuller life for themselves in their middle and later years. "One woman of sixty whom I know is most widely useful in many church activities," Addams told her readers, conjuring up the vision of a widow whose children were married and living far away but whose house had become "the center of beneficent activity, a place where a woman dwelt not alone but surrounded by the affection of countless friends." It seemed like a perfect second act—helping the world and defeating loneliness at the same time.

"THE MOSES OF HER RACE"

Very few of the women's clubs were integrated. At a convention of the General Federation of Women's Clubs in 1900, Mary Church Terrell—the president of the National Association of Colored Women—was

refused permission to convey greetings from her group after the Southern clubs in attendance threatened to resign. But there was a rich world
of black women's clubs, whose long tradition dated back to eighteenth-
century societies African American women had organized for mutual
protection and aid. Many of the nineteenth-century clubs began with
the same goals as the white groups: mental stimulation and general good
fellowship. "Clubs make women read and think in order that they might
not sit like idiots when some bright paper is being read," said a speaker
at the opening meeting of the Woman's Era Club in Boston. The Female
Literary Association in Philadelphia had a tradition going back to
the 1830s of hosting what they called "Mental Feasts."

The Booklovers Club in Washington, DC, began as a meeting place
for the capital's black female elite. It was founded by Josephine Bruce,
the wife of one of the black senators elected during the Reconstruction
era. Josephine, the daughter of an Ohio dentist, was a star of the integrated social life of post–Civil War Washington. (A reporter covering a
White House reception in 1880 decreed that "Mrs. Bruce's toilette was
considered one of the most tasteful and magnificent of the evening.")
But for all her glamour, Bruce was still pretty much stuck in her role as a
wife and mother until the club movement gave her a road forward.
When her son went off to boarding school, she began giving lectures for
the National Association of Colored Women, including one at Tuskegee
Institute, which led to a job there as a principal after her husband's death.

Most of the African American clubs needed very little time to morph
into centers of social action. The Woman's Era Club of Boston quickly
moved from delivering papers on African civilizations to protesting a
lynching in South Carolina. In 1896, Ida Bell Wells-Barnett, a Chicago
journalist who made the lynching of black men in the South into an
international cause, was honored at the founding meeting of the National
Association of Colored Women's Clubs. One of the gathering's high-
lights came when Harriet Tubman, the oldest member, introduced
Wells-Barnett's infant son as the Baby of the Association. Tubman was
still working and traveling, still suffering the indignities of segregation
when she was on the move. In 1905, she shared a ride to Rochester with
a white friend, both planning to attend a suffrage meeting the next day.
But after they parted at the train station, Tubman quietly went back to

the station lobby and sat there all night, aware that there were "no lodgings which would take in a woman of color."

In 1908, Tubman achieved her longtime goal of opening a proper residence for black needy elderly in her hometown of Auburn, New York. The *Auburn Citizen* wrote glowingly that now "the Moses of her race" could see that her "95 years have at last been crowned with success." Tubman was actually closer to 85, but she was nearing the point when she could no longer travel or live on her own. In 1911, she herself entered the Harriet Tubman Home for the Aged, where she died in 1913. "I go to prepare a place for you," she told the people gathered around her bed. At her burial she got — finally — full military honors.

"MORE AWED AND FRIGHTENED THAN IF THEY HAD APPROACHED ROYALTY"

It may seem like quite a leap to go from Harriet Tubman, Underground Railroad heroine, to Caroline Astor, doyenne of New York society. But they both reached their highest public celebrity later in life. Astor's role was mainly to preside over grand parties. While there had always been something resembling high society in the nation's largest cities, the whole scene had been pretty remote to the rest of the country. Then the Industrial Revolution created a bigger, more colorful population of rich people, and newspapers, with their new ability to print pictures of fabulously dressed partygoers, were eager to introduce the elite to the masses. Before long, weekend crowds were streaming up Fifth Avenue toward the homes of the socialites they'd been reading about, hoping to catch a glimpse of one of these new celebrities.

Astor made headlines virtually every year with her Opera Ball, where she would welcome guests wearing her famous diamond tiara, necklaces, and brooches — the general effect, one guest said, was like "a walking chandelier." "The people who came into her presence were more awed and frightened than if they had approached royalty," said Isadora Duncan, who once danced for Mrs. Astor's guests at a lawn party. The nation — or at least its biggest city — had apparently moved past the era when older women had to stand at the back of the ballroom and watch the young folks having fun. You could be elderly and still be the center of attention as long as it was your ballroom, and you were dripping with diamonds.

The woman known as "*the* Mrs. Astor" attempted to impose her standards on her city's social elite, shutting out people like Cornelius Vanderbilt, who had become fabulously wealthy rather recently — and, the old families thought, rather crassly. But Vanderbilt's daughter-in-law, Alva, gave a costume ball in 1883 that was so spectacular even Astor was forced to acknowledge her. Alva invited more than a thousand guests and, using the new Gilded Age tool of press relations, brought in reporters to admire her preparations. The event cost an estimated $250,000 — more than $6 million in today's money. "Amid the rush and excitement of business, men have found their minds haunted by uncontrollable thoughts as to whether they should appear as Robert Le Diable, Cardinal Richelieu, Otho the Barbarian, or the Count of Monte Cristo, while the ladies have been driven to the verge of distraction in the effort to settle the comparative advantages of ancient, medieval, and modern costumes," reported the enthralled *New York Times*. On the evening of the event, police had to be dispatched to hold back the crowds of spectators milling in front of the Vanderbilt house, hoping to see the wildly garbed attendees — who included Mrs. Astor.

Alva Vanderbilt was only 30 at the time of her big triumph, but she was just getting started. When she was in her 40s, she divorced Vanderbilt for adultery, shattering the tradition that a well-bred woman never got a divorce, let alone publicly pointed out that wealthy American males had a predilection for bedding people other than their spouses. She then married another rich man, Oliver Belmont. After his death, Alva, then in her 50s, became a generous supporter of the women's rights movement. She underwrote Alice Paul's National Woman's Party, which headquartered for a time in the Belmont summer home in Newport, where Alva draped the walls with purple-and-gold banners announcing: "Failure Is Impossible!" She also commissioned a thousand-piece tea service with cups inscribed "Votes for Women!" In 1912, Alva, 65, led a suffrage parade down Fifth Avenue, dodging tomatoes thrown from the crowd and comforting a terrified young marcher: "Brace up, dear. Pray to God. She will help you."

Around the country, wealthy women were finding ways to have an impact beyond overdressed balls. Chicago's Bertha Palmer, "the Mrs.

Astor of the Middle West," was 44 when she became nationally known for her role in the Chicago World's Fair. The Woman's Building, which she organized, was a spectacular display from 47 nations. Over in Baltimore, Mary Garrett, an heir to a fortune from her railroad-magnate father, seldom did anything more dramatic than give away money and hold parties for visiting suffragists. But the media still ran headlines about her every twitch: "Ants Ruin Part of House. Floor in Baltimore Residence of Miss Mary Garrett Gives Way"; "Miss Mary Garrett, the famous daughter of the late John Work Garrett, to spend winter at Bryn Mawr." And newspapers across the country printed a story that revealed the bathtub in her dressing room was lined with Mexican onyx.

Garrett did become a major philanthropist, particularly to Bryn Mawr, which became the first American women's college to offer a doctoral degree. In 1896, the *Washington Post* put her at the top of a story headlined "Old Maids of Wealth," which announced that the "number of unmarried women beyond the allotted age of girlhood who have a fortune of at least $1,000,000 is not small." The *Post* declared that the millionaire spinsters "have charming personalities, have wide circles of friends and probably would not exchange places with any married woman the world over." It was perhaps an unnecessary reiteration of the lesson we learned from Aaron Burr's widow, Madame Jumel: being rich makes a lot of things work out.

"IN LIFE'S MIDSUMMER"

By the early twentieth century, both the media and the celebrity class had broadened — a lot. New women's magazines celebrated entertainers like theater sensation Lillian Russell, whose fans speculated about her age and came up with everything from 40 to 65. The newspapers also took a keen interest in a new class of female scandal stars, who often took to the stage after their moment in the headlines. Today, we have reality shows, but at the turn of the century, people had vaudeville and popular theater, where they could go to see Lillie Langtry, who was not much of an actress but who had once been mistress to the Prince of Wales. Or Belle Boyd, a Civil War Confederate spy who acted out her adventures onstage while touring in the company of her third husband, 16 years her junior. Or even Madeline Pollard, a mistress of a prominent

Kentucky congressman who sued him for breach of promise when he married another woman.

Newspapers were full of stories and pictures about the female celebrities of the day: actresses and reformers and society queens. There were a great many ways to have adventures and become famous, from serving the poor to bedding a wealthy cad. And once women began showing up in contexts that had nothing to do with marriage and motherhood, they were no longer necessarily seen as over the hill when they passed 30. In fact, some public women's age progression was viewed like men's. When one newspaper finally resolved the mystery of Lillian Russell, it reported she was 46 — "in life's midsummer. May it be endlessly prolonged."

If one woman symbolized the turn-of-the-century era, it could well be Russell, the product of a Chicago finishing school, brought to New York at 18 by her suffragist mother, who dreamed of working with Susan B. Anthony. Lillian became a singer at a time when the theater was the most popular form of mass entertainment. Women's magazines celebrated her as the perfect beauty. The press happily chronicled her four marriages, her gold-plated bicycle, and the shorter skirts she popularized for wheeling. Everyone admired her "hourglass" figure—a 38-inch bust, a waist that with the help of considerable corseting could be squeezed into 24 inches, and 40-inch hips. Anna Held, a voluptuous Ziegfeld Follies star, was rumored to have had her lower ribs removed in order to better achieve the look. Russell, who had famous eating contests at Delmonico's restaurant with her longtime friend "Diamond" Jim Brady, once took the precaution of checking her corset in the cloakroom before she tucked in.

"Corpulency is the most perfect beauty"

The idea of connecting largeness with female allure was common throughout the Western world in the nineteenth century. "Corpulency is the most perfect beauty," Lola Montez, an Irish dancer who became a celebrity as mistress of King Ludwig of Bavaria, told her audience during an American lecture tour. Immigrant communities tended to regard weight as a desirable sign of prosperity, and they patronized theaters that gave them what they wanted. The ideal chorus girl was big breasted and fleshy. People who couldn't get to the theater themselves liked to admire the voluptuous stars on cigarette cards. The actress Eileen Karl, whose picture was a favorite, claimed that each of her thighs measured three feet around. "Big Legs and Chests Now the Rage," announced the *New York World,* in an article that proclaimed "the mass of theatre-goers regard a pair of ponderous legs as the acme of femininity."

Celebrating large figures didn't always work for older women—remember Susan B. Anthony—but the standards of beauty were changing in ways that made it easier for the non-young to feel included. The fashion look of the moment called for loose, flowing gowns with a curve that began at the chin and ended at the waist—a look that one historian suggested resembled "sagging breasts." Cosmetics had stopped being taboo. "It is no longer considered vulgar to aid nature when the good old lady withholds some of her gifts, though good form does not permit that such tiny artifices shall be noticeable," ruled a turn-of-the-century etiquette book. "The woman who feels the crying need of a bit of color in her lips or cheeks must apply it with infinite care." The authors helpfully included a recipe for rouge: "lavender vinegar 100 grams, spermaceti ten grams, rouge six grams, powdered talcum fifteen grams. Mix and filter."

Women were using switches of false hair to produce the effect of mass—long, thick, luxuriant tresses, preferably arranged in effortful piles on top of the head. "No woman under 95 was free from hair vanity," wrote Julia Foraker, the wife of a prominent Ohio politician, who recalled in her memoirs that when she was a student, her prim, middle-aged teacher asked to borrow her switch. Hair coloring was, in theory, still off the table. But Mrs. Astor, who ruled New York society well into her 70s, was unwilling to accept the fact that her hair had become both white and thin, and she began wearing brown or black pompadour wigs. The effect must have been startling, but the advantage of being Mrs. Astor was that no one pointed it out.

"HOW TO LIVE A HUNDRED YEARS"

In 1913, when Lillian Russell was in her 50s, she announced she was embarking on a new pursuit as a lecturer. Her first topic was "How to Live a Hundred Years."

"I began my career in Chicago as an entertainer. Now I am to begin a new career in Chicago—that of a missionary of happiness," she told the public. The lectures were extremely popular, the *New York Times* reported, "owing to the fact that for more than twenty years she had been known as one of the most beautiful women on the American stage, and it was remarked that despite the fact that she was well over 50 years old, she was still remarkable for her beauty." Russell died when she was 61—from complications after a minor injury. So her mission to help everybody live for a century was not entirely successful. But it was a good marker for another big change in American attitudes as the nation left the nineteenth century behind. The idea that aging was a problem to be solved through personal effort had moved beyond the world of health reformers. Average Americans were more and more inclined to think that if they followed the proper routine they could hold off wrinkles and lameness and ill health, and live longer than their parents and grandparents had imagined was possible.

The idea of conquering the effects of aging through beautiful thoughts endured, although readers were beginning to demand more practical suggestions. Russell herself had a beauty column that emphasized the lovely soul until the editor ordered her to refocus on lovely skin. And Lillie Langtry credited her complexion to the study of Buddhism until she ran into financial difficulties and hit the celebrity-endorsement route, announcing that she owed it all to Pears' Soap. But the nation's can-do spirit began to lean more toward the idea that people could make themselves healthy, young looking, and long-lived by diet and exercise. Russell—who eventually went from eating contests with Jim Brady to advice columns chronicling her war against weight—announced she was getting in shape through a regimen of rolling over 250 times every morning. The health reformers had been preaching the diet-and-exercise message for more than half a century, but it got much more attention when it came from Lillian Russell.

7. The Twentieth Century Arrives

"THE WHITEHEADS OF THE MODERN AGE"

America left the nineteenth century behind, but the publishing industry kept churning out those books of essays and poems targeted at the senior market—many variations on the theme of *Looking Toward Sunset* for the new generation. In 1915, the novelist Amelia Huddleston Barr came out with her entry: *Three Score and Ten: A Book for the Aged*. It was mainly a collection of conversations between Barr and her friends, all of whom seemed to have a convenient tendency to ask her opinion about everything under the sun. ("There is another question, Amelia. What keeps the soul in the body?") Between discourses on topics from bread making to the history of playing cards, Barr told her readers that in order to have "a vigorous old age" it was important to keep busy. She did not think that women should meddle in politics, but she very much approved of a 62-year-old friend who decided to fill up her spare time by investing in a hat store.

It's not clear how many 70-year-olds would have loved to receive *A Book for the Aged*, but Barr was definitely popular. And productive as hell. When she celebrated her 87th birthday in 1918, the local paper in her New York neighborhood noted that she was the "author of nearly 80 books" and had published three novels in just the last year. Parts of her *Remember the Alamo* would resurface much later in a John Wayne movie. Barr was feeling very upbeat, even though the United States had recently entered the hostilities that would come to be known as World War I. She told the reporter that the war would be "a good thing for America." The men who fought in it, she predicted "are coming back from battle better men than when they went in, and the women are going to rise to meet them."

Barr was right about ushering in a new era—though whether the men on the battlefield would have agreed that they were going through an improving experience is a different question. The war marked the real beginning of the twentieth century. Outside Amelia Barr's world, the options for older women went way beyond hat shops. Readers had been following the exploits of Nellie Bly, one of the first foreign reporters to make it to the Russian and Serbian conflict zone. Bly had been a barrier-jumping newspaperwoman since the 1880s, and thanks to her, Americans had gotten used to the idea that certain female reporters were going to do daring things in order to get a story. Inspired by the famous novel about an adventurer who goes around the world in 80 days, Bly circled the globe by herself in 72. She had herself committed to an insane asylum in order to expose its dreadful conditions. When the war broke out, she was 50, but the question of whether she was too old to be leaping into the trenches under fire never seemed to come up. "I was not afraid. I would not run," she assured her readers. "I thought another shot would follow. It will doubtless be better aimed. If it does, we shall die. And, if so, what then?"

Bly didn't have to find out. Soon she was out of the trenches and reporting from Hungary, where she was stopped by local soldiers who wondered if she was some sort of spy. A translator was brought in, and when she introduced herself, he cried, "My God! Nellie Bly!" Next, she proudly reported, he began speaking rapidly to her captors, explaining, "I have told them every child seven years old in America knows Nellie Bly."

So age was not an issue in Bly's World War I adventures. Except possibly to Bly herself: in 1918, she was trying to get permission from the Austrian ministry to tour Budapest, armed with a letter that described her as "born May 4, 1877" — 13 years later than her actual birth date. No one seemed to think it was unusual when other middle-aged women sailed off to France to do volunteer work. One of them was 50-year-old Molly Brown, who was famous as the "unsinkable" survivor of the *Titanic* disaster. "I am a daughter of adventure," Brown told the *Denver Post*. "This means I never experience a dull moment and must be prepared for any eventuality.... That's my arc, as the astrologers would say. It's a good one, too, for a person who had rather make a snap-out than a fade-out of life."

There did still seem to be some benchmarks — Jane Addams assured the world that there were plenty of energetic community activists "between the ages of fifty and seventy," but she didn't quite make it clear what would happen when the chairwoman of the town's anticorruption campaign turned seventy-one. Yet the media—in the grand tradition of the media—was ready to move on to the next big, or in this case older, thing. In 1911, the magazine *World Today* profiled "Some Grand Old Women" in the energetic army of "the whiteheads of the modern age." They ranged from a sixty-seven-year-old lighthouse keeper who was still rowing out to rescue distressed sailors to a centenarian who enjoyed taking rides in a race car to Rev. Antoinette Brown Blackwell, who was still preaching at eighty-three, "and her discourses are not back numbers, either."

"TO SEE ONE OLD WOMAN WHO IS NOT AFRAID"

Not everybody shared *World Today*'s enthusiasm. The *Atlantic Monthly* moaned that the "old lady" of 1907 lacked "the quiet serenity of life's afternoon." The problem, according to the magazine, was not so much the hard-rowing 67-year-old lighthouse keeper as the fashionable golfers who competed with their granddaughters "in their activities social, philanthropic, educational, and worldly." *Ladies' Home Journal* seemed to be yearning for that good old rocking chair. The magazine warned that no woman was going to be able to count on respect in old age if she is "on a dozen visiting committees to hospitals and asylums." All this, plus those club papers for the literary society—the magazine worried the new old woman would lose "that magnetism with which age and gentleness always appeal to men."

When it came to a rejection of quiet serenity, the champion might have been Mary Harris, a labor organizer universally known as Mother Jones. The list makers at *World Today* seemed to feel compelled to include her in their survey of overachieving seniors despite Harris's distinct lack of the apolitical middle-classness that popular magazines treasured.

Mother Jones wore black throughout her career, in memory of her husband and four young children, who had died in a yellow fever epidemic. She found a new family in the union movement, and from the time she was 50 she lived without a home, moving from one site of labor turmoil to another. "My address is like my shoes," she declared. "It travels with me wherever I go." She was most identified with the United Mine Workers, men who worked underground in caverns where women were prohibited. "She came into the mine one day and talked to us in our workplace in the vernacular of the mines," said one man who met Jones when he was young and she was in her 60s. "How she got in, I don't know; probably just walked in and defied anyone to stop her." The tiny gray-haired figure had a special genius for attracting publicity. In 1900, to drive off strikebreakers in Pennsylvania, she marched 15 miles with a parade of women wearing aprons, brandishing brooms, and beating on pans. The sheriff allowed them to pass, not foreseeing trouble. But as Mother Jones put it, "an army of strong mining women makes a wonderfully spectacular picture," and they successfully shamed the scabs out of the mines. In 1903, she led strikers' children on a three-week march from the textile mills in Pennsylvania to New York City.

In some ways, Mother Jones approached her career like Elizabeth Cady Stanton. That little-old-lady image was useful in softening views that could have been otherwise seen as threatening. (Urging strikers to bring their guns to one confrontation, she said, "If you should kill a rat, you are doing something everybody approves of.") When she arrived in Colorado in 1903, the *Denver Republican* reported: "You are surprised, astonished, incredulous to be informed that this eminently respectable and strictly conventional appearing old lady...should know aught of anything save the economy of a well ordered household." Like Stanton, Jones also prided herself on being a good traveler, no matter how unladylike the challenge. In one letter she described how she walked down a goat path in the mountains after midnight to get to her next rally: "I had to slide down most of it.... My bones are all sore today."

Mother Jones found her age so handy that she exaggerated it—she celebrated her 100th birthday when she was 92. "If you are too cowardly to fight, I will fight," she told one group of insufficiently militant laborers. "You ought to be ashamed of yourselves, actually to the Lord you ought, just to see one old woman who is not afraid." In her 80s—or what she said were her 80s—Mother Jones was working with striking miners in West Virginia. She was arrested and tried by a state military court for conspiracy to commit murder, which carried a possible death penalty. "Whatever I have done in West Virginia I have done it all over the United States and when I get out I will do it again," she said, refusing to offer a plea. The decision of the tribunal was secret, and while it appeared that Jones had been convicted, nobody was enthusiastic about executing, or permanently imprisoning, someone who looked like a great-grandmother. She was eventually freed to raise hell again.

Mother Jones was, obviously, one of a kind. And for all the new open-mindedness about age and women, the traditional patterns were still in effect all around the country. In 1906, *Harper's Bazar* published a series of essays by "An Elderly Woman," who said she was leading the life of an average middle-class grandmother—living with her daughter, trying to be useful, but aggrieved when there was a community problem to be solved and the younger people ignored her offers of help. "My fault was the irreparable one of belonging to the generation of those whose business it is to sit comfortable in the shade and wait—who can say for what?" she wrote. Elderly Woman found some joy in being able to support her grown children in times of trial and being a companion to her grandchildren when they had nobody else to play with, but she reported the same sense of ostracism older women had wrestled with a century before. Although to be fair, she did have a national magazine interested in publishing her complaints.

"I'M NOT WAITING"

All the talk about how age shouldn't be a barrier came at the same time when physicians and social scientists were thinking a lot about the elderly and erecting new roadblocks of their own. A cynical person might conclude that when the experts first took the trouble to really think about the older people in their midst, their immediate conclusion was that they should be nudged out of the picture. Businesses began to impose mandatory retirement; welfare advocates pressed for pensions and old-age homes for the needy. Their plans were well intentioned and frequently welcomed. But the coin had two sides. One was to create the first threads of a national safety net for the people who were about to become known as senior citizens; the other was to increase the barriers between elderly Americans and the world of the young.

That was hardest on men. Most women still didn't work for wages, and those who did usually labored in jobs they'd have been happy to trade for a pension if one was offered. Men, whose lives were tied to their image as breadwinner, were going to have a painful transition into the world of mandatory retirements if they worked at jobs they liked. Amelia Huddleston Barr, whose range of acquaintances was somewhat limited, class-wise, felt the whole idea of retirement for men was terrible: "If they only sat in their office and read the returns, their business would gain in every good way by their presence." In 1919, the Pennsylvania Commission on Old Age Pensions studied what happened to people who could no longer live in their own homes and concluded that children were much more willing to invite an elderly mother to stay with them. "Aside from the sentimental reasons involved, the presence of an old woman around the house—unless she is absolutely invalided—entails little burden, as she can be made useful in numerous ways," the commission reported. "This, however, is not the case with an aged man."

None of this is to say that women who had an active professional life were any more eager to give it up than men were. In 1912, when Antoinette Blackwell was 87, she and another octogenarian minister, Robert Collyer, were honored at a Unitarian gathering. Finishing his address, Collyer turned to Blackwell and said, "Here we are, two old pilgrims, sitting in the sunshine waiting for the angel to come," and bent over to kiss her forehead. Blackwell, who was nearly deaf, just smiled. The next day, when she learned exactly what he had said, she jerked her head up and announced that Collyer "may *sit* if he wants to, waiting for the angels. But I'm not waiting. I have too much to do."

"THE MOST POPULAR WOMAN IN AMERICA"

We call the time between the late 1800s and 1920 the Progressive Era, and there certainly was a lot of progress. Airplanes! Zippers! Hearing aids! The hamburger bun! Henry Ford's moving assembly line! Henry Ford's millionth car! Cities were exploding in size, immigrants arriving in multitudes, factories popping up everywhere. And politically, a reform movement tried to tackle the downside of all this change through better education, public health programs, anticorruption campaigns, and government initiatives to help the downtrodden.

It was the age of "trustbusting"—Theodore Roosevelt's crusade against the corporate monopolies that were ruthlessly crushing competition, which he began after reading a series in *McClure's* written by Ida Tarbell. In "The History of the Standard Oil Company," Tarbell documented how John D. Rockefeller, the richest man in America, colluded with the railroads to crush his struggling competition. It was probably one of the most influential pieces of journalism in American history, and it's pleasing to report that the author was a descendant of Rebecca Nurse, the elderly woman who was dragged out of her sickbed and tried as a witch in Salem.

Tarbell was in her 40s when she published the Standard Oil stories, and one magazine declared that they made her "the most popular woman in America." Or at least, the author amended, it would be a close race between her and Jane Addams.

In 1912, Roosevelt—then out of office and alienated from his successor, William Howard Taft—created the Progressive Party to mount a new presidential campaign. Addams seconded his nomination at the party convention. Her speech was another first-time-a-woman event, and not everybody was thrilled. Charles Eliot, the distinguished former president of Harvard, told a *New York Times* reporter that Addams's starring role at the convention was in "very bad taste." By putting an unmarried woman on the podium in such a prominent place, Eliot felt, the Progressives were setting a bad example for the rest of her gender, who ought to be marrying and repopulating the world. Addams was 51 by then and had a long-running romantic relationship with Mary Rozet Smith, a philanthropist and settlement worker. It's unlikely Eliot had any inkling of that—he was just an example of the sentiment in some quarters that the only women who should be participating in politics, or other public activities, were married women whose children had grown up.

"SILLY, VAIN, IMPERTINENT OLD MAID"

Addams was about to lose her most-popular status as America drew closer to war and she became increasingly identified with the anti-war movement. "Jane Addams is a silly, vain, impertinent old maid," fumed a paper called *New York Topics*, "who is now meddling with matters far beyond her capacity." A woman who could create the settlement house movement, speak to huge crowds at enthusiastic rallies, and lead battles against corrupt politicians without having anyone mention her age finally entered Old Maid territory by speaking out against a war.

One of the few House members who voted against entering World War I was Jeannette Rankin of Montana, serving her first term as the first woman ever elected to Congress. Montana was one of 12 states that had given women the right to vote by 1916. It was certainly a step forward — unless you chose to dwell on the fact that there were still 36 to go. Carrie Chapman Catt, the 57-year-old head of the National American Woman Suffrage Association, had despaired of getting Congress to approve a constitutional amendment and pursued a strategy of trying to gain the franchise one state at a time. It was a noble but extremely dreary effort. When it was all over, Catt would estimate that during 52 years of struggle women had conducted "56 campaigns of referenda to male voters; 480 campaigns to get legislatures to submit suffrage amendments to voters; 47 campaigns to get state constitutional conventions to write woman suffrage into state constitutions; 277 campaigns to get State party conventions to include woman suffrage planks; 30 campaigns to get presidential party conventions to adopt woman suffrage planks in party platforms, and 19 campaigns with 19 successive Congresses." It was no wonder people got tired of the strategy.

By 1913, the NAWSA was facing a rebellion from younger, more radical members, led by Alice Paul, who had spent time in London, where women routinely chained themselves to fences, defied the law, got thrown in jail, and went on hunger strikes for the right to vote. The women of England, Paul said impatiently, "are now talking of the time when they will vote, instead of the time their children would vote."

It wasn't the first generational gap the movement had experienced. Back when Catt was new to the cause, Susan B. Anthony was complaining that every young suffragist believed that if only she had been put in charge, the vote would be long since won. But by the 1913 convention, Catt was part of the old guard. She had been working for the vote before Alice Paul was born, and as the arguments continued throughout the

NAWSA meetings, she correctly predicted that the militants would eventually bolt. The only ones left behind, she said bitterly, would be "those of us who really want suffrage and not advertising."

Paul's radical faction had support from women of all ages. Harriot Blatch, Elizabeth Cady Stanton's daughter, was older than Catt, but like Paul she had spent a long time in London and was far more interested in drawing national attention with parades and demonstrations than in petitioning for more state referenda. Alva Belmont, who was in her 60s, was opening her pocketbook and her summerhouse to Paul's National Woman's Party. So was the "unsinkable" and wealthy Molly Brown. In the end, Paul's demonstrations and Catt's more moderate behind-the-scenes negotiating worked pretty well together. In 1920, for the first time, women got the right to vote across the nation in a presidential election. The winner was Warren Harding, who is generally regarded as one of the worst presidents in American history. It turned out that just having women in the mix was not a ticket to utopia. Lots of work lay ahead.

"IT IS NOT A DYE"

In 1915, a Kansas lawmaker proposed making it illegal for a woman to wear cosmetics "for the purpose of creating a false impression." The bill didn't go anywhere, but it's worth mentioning that the legislation would have exempted women over 44. The danger, apparently, was only in potential husbands being sold a misleading bill of goods. Beyond the traditional mating period, it was all right to go ahead and use some artifice.

The industry of beauty had come of age. Younger women were being urged to make themselves look desirable. Older women were being exhorted to make themselves look younger. Advertisers insisted both goals could be accomplished with the purchase of as many beauty products as possible. And the mass media came down strongly on the side of the folks who bought those ads—in 1908, the magazine *The Woman Beautiful* announced that longer life spans were due "to the physical care in beauty shops." There was still a strong prejudice against the idea of coloring graying hair, although a lot more women were beginning to try it. In 1919, *Milady Beautiful* ran an ad for "Dr. Olga Schiller's Gray Hair Restorer" that assured readers "IT IS NOT A DYE." Instead, Dr. Olga claimed to have come up with a magic wash that "brings back the original color of teh [*sic*] hair and keeps it so."

Beauty was one industry that had at least a bit of equal opportunity. Helena Rubinstein, the daughter of Polish Jews, opened cosmetics salons first in Australia and then, in 1915, in Manhattan—the beginning of an empire. Madam C. J. Walker built a successful business around hair treatments for black women. In 1916, when Madam Walker was 48, she returned to visit her birthplace on a Louisiana plantation, and the local white paper reported: "World's Richest Negress in Delta." By then she owned an elegant Harlem townhouse and was renovating a 34-room place in the country. In 1917, the *New York Times* ran a feature entitled "Wealthiest Negro Woman's Suburban Mansion" and described the home, in Irvington-on-Hudson, as having "a degree of elegance and extravagance that a princess might envy."

Walker, who was born Sarah Breedlove, had had an unhappy childhood. She lost her parents at seven, got almost no education, and was sent to work as a laundress when she was very small. She married at 14, had a baby, lost her husband at 20, and moved north. Her second marriage was terrible, and possibly as a result of the stress, her hair began to fall out. Later, she would say she was on the verge of becoming bald when she had a dream in which "a big black man appeared to me and told me what to mix for my hair. Some of the remedy was from Africa, but I sent for it, mixed it, put it on my scalp and in a few weeks my hair was coming in faster than it had ever fallen out."

Walker's treatment was marketed to women of all ages, and it may not have been anything more unusual than regular washings with a good shampoo, combined with scalp massages. But once she began offering to set women up in their own home salons with "Walker's Scientific Scalp Treatment," an associate reported that in Chicago and New York, black neighborhoods had "a Walker parlor on every corner."

"AN ILL-ADVISED EXPERIMENT FOR ONE OF HER YEARS"

In 1910, Robert Dickinson, a gynecologist at Brooklyn Hospital in New York, published a paper detailing his exhaustive study of more than 100 corset-wearing patients. Nobody, he contended, could "scrub floors or pick up baby or tennis ball without squeezing the bowels and shoving things out of place." There was no period in American history, it would seem, that didn't have a corset controversy. But it was a sign of the times that Dickinson included the tennis ball question. More and more women of every age were riding bicycles, playing tennis, and exercising in other ways that did not permit the restriction of a super-girdle. Yet an essay on "How to Remain Young" in *Harper's Bazar* warned every older woman that doing away with corsets was "an ill-advised experiment for one of her years if she wishes to look neat and trim and well-groomed."

The corset would survive, in one form or another. But the mature, curvy figure it celebrated was about to go into eclipse. Fashions were becoming looser, skimpier—for the body "as straight and yielding as a very young girl's," decreed one commentator.

The nation was approaching the 1920s, when there would be way, way more of the same.

8. The 1920s

"Our Wages Highest in World's History"

As decades go, the 1920s look pretty darned good. "Our Wages Highest in World's History, Hoover Declares," headlined the *New York Times* on December 2, 1927. A subhead reported that Herbert Hoover, the secretary of commerce, was expecting the country to enjoy perpetual prosperity. That part, um, turned out to be wrong.

While the big boom in incomes was enjoyed mostly by the people who were already pretty wealthy, it was hard for average citizens not to feel that things were skyrocketing for them, too. When the decade started, about a third of American families had cars — 10 years later, it was more than three-quarters. The impossible models of the early years, with the dreaded start-up cranks, had been replaced by versions that were easy for women to use, and women drivers were everywhere. You could buy a car or a house or a new home appliance with credit, and omnipresent advertisers were urging people to do just that. Americans were moving to the cities in droves — for the first time more than half the population lived in urban areas. The world of homemaking was transformed by the arrival of refrigerators, toasters, electric vacuum cleaners, and, gradually, washing machines. Along with a growing expectation that housework not be so much work. "If we get married, I'll keep house better than mother does hers," a girl promised her boyfriend in an ad for S.O.S, the new steel wool soap pads. "But I'm not going to turn into a slave. You men! You think drudgery is a sign of good housekeeping."

"this new girl"

It was, in many ways, a terrific time for women. They were going to college more frequently, getting better jobs, and losing some of their terror about the possibility of staying single. In London, the *Daily Telegraph* published a grim report on "Marriage in America" that theorized that since women in the United States could get good jobs, they did not want "a great, hulking, cranky man to wait on all the time." The paper claimed that 30 percent of New York's unmarried women fell into that category, while another 20 percent "will not marry an average man because they think there is a chance of trapping an American millionaire."

It was great to be a woman, but it wasn't so great to be older. The New Woman, who could be any age, gave way to the flapper, who most definitely could not. The flapper was the era's icon — daring and flashy and, to be honest, a bit of a brat. She was thin, with a boyish figure — the only foundation garment that was popular with the young was a bra that could flatten, rather than enhance, the bust. Curves were so out of style that a child who noticed a picture of Lillian Russell was heard asking her mother who the "fat lady" was. The flapper wore light, short skirts that showed off her legs, only partially covered with flesh-colored hose that she rolled down to the knee. A lawmaker in Ohio, in keeping with the grand and glorious tradition of state legislatures, introduced a bill to ban skirts that did not "reach to that part of the foot known as the instep." Someone in Utah proposed "fine and imprisonment" for anyone whose skirt rose "higher than three inches above the ankle," while a Virginia legislator, turning his attention upward, wanted to outlaw anything that displayed more than "three inches of her throat."

The flapper stayed out late, danced with abandon, smoked and drank, and made it clear she had little regard for the rules about sex and decorum that her parents had obeyed. "Repressions have been released . . . exhibitionism has changed from a vice into a virtue," complained V. F. Calverton, a leftist writer who was appalled by "this new girl, with all her emptiness of ideas and effusiveness of emotions." While a great many women didn't get any closer to the flapper model than a new hairstyle, the whole nation got the idea: the younger generation intended to live life full force and, of course, never get old.

"My candle burns at both ends," wrote Edna St. Vincent Millay, who was 28 when she published what was probably the poem of the decade.

It will not last the night.
But ah, my foes, and oh, my friends —
It gives a lovely light.

The new prototype was Zelda Fitzgerald, who arrived in New York in 1920 at the age of 19 with the novelist F. Scott Fitzgerald and married him three days later. The flapper, Zelda once wrote, "awoke from her lethargy...bobbed her hair, put on her choicest pair of earrings and a great deal of audacity and rouge and went into the battle. She flirted because it was fun to flirt and wore a one-piece bathing suit because she had a good figure, she covered her face with powder and paint because she didn't need it and she refused to be bored chiefly because she wasn't boring. She was conscious that the things she did were the things she had always wanted to do." It was a life plan that clearly wasn't going to last much past 25.

Zelda was, Scott Fitzgerald said, "the heroine of my stories," and the couple tore through America and Europe dancing on tables, getting into fights, and drinking nonstop, both conscious they were a bestselling brand. It all ended badly, with alcoholism, mental illness, and divorce. But while she lasted, Zelda was the perfect example of the fact that young, attractive women were no longer excluded from public platforms. While she was a talented writer, Zelda had a national profile in the '20s simply for being beautiful and outrageous and the muse of a famous novelist. Other women, far less dependent on a male partner, were also finding that if you wanted the world to pay attention to your message, there was nothing better than being young and comely. The time when women found it easier to get the nation's attention if they were unthreateningly matronly had vanished.

"More power to the Gloria Swansons"

The theater, which had long celebrated actresses with large voices, large gestures, and large figures, was no longer the most popular form of mass entertainment. Movies had taken hold — American producers were cranking out an average of 800 feature films a year for an eager national audience. In the all-American city of Muncie, Indiana, a survey found movie attendance was higher than church attendance. Casting directors wanted their heroines to have delicate figures and no facial lines that would be magnified on the big screen. When the plots didn't involve historic romance — sword fights and kissing — they celebrated saucy flappers or spunky little girls. The first great movie star, Mary Pickford, was cast as a child into her 30s. (A hardheaded businesswoman, Pickford co-founded United Artists at about the time she was playing Pollyanna and Little Annie Rooney before the cameras.) The rather creepy obsession with childlike women went beyond the films — when the first Miss America Pageant was held in 1921, the winner, Margaret Gorman, was a tiny 16-year-old who passed the time between events on a nearby playground, shooting marbles.

One exception to the trend was the popular world of blues singers. Two of the biggest names were Gertrude "Ma" Rainey and Mamie Smith, who achieved their peak popularity when they were long past their 20s. "To say that Ma holds her own with those of lesser years would be putting it in a small way," wrote an African American critic in 1928, when Rainey was 42. But Hollywood movies suggested there wasn't a whole lot of hope for anyone who wasn't flapper-sized. A female fan, taking the most positive attitude conceivable, wrote a letter to a movie magazine praising films' obsession with youth. It was, she argued, "keeping the modern woman slim and healthy and keen, as young at forty as her mother was at thirty and her grandmother at twenty." It was a deeply American sentiment — if the public suddenly became obsessed with youth, it was your job to start looking more youthful. "More power to the Gloria Swansons, the Elsie Fergusons, the Irene Castles and the Viola Danas!" concluded the fan, naming some stars who were still flying high in their late 20s and 30s. Alas, the women on her list would all be retired or pretty much washed up by the end of the decade. Gloria Swanson survived best, and we remember her now mainly for her 1950 role as the aged, demented former star trying to rekindle her long-dead career in *Sunset Boulevard*.

"MOTHER, YOU'RE LOOKING YOUNGER EVERY DAY!"

To get another slant on the way the world was turning, consider an ad from Gossard Corsets, which appeared in *Ladies' Home Journal* in 1922. The pitch began by mentioning the importance of foundation garments for "the young girl who isn't built like a willow wand" but then shifted quickly to the main target: "that other woman who hasn't been nineteen for dear knows how many years." The "other woman" couldn't expect a teenage figure to arrive on its own. "You've got to make up in cleverness what you've lost in youth. Your corsets are all that stands between you and that vague, shapeless bourne from whence no traveler returns—age."

Corset makers had always seemed to specialize in ads aimed at making older women feel suicidal, and this was hardly the first time in American history that an advertiser assured readers its product would make them look younger. But the interesting thing about the Gossard pitch is the target age. Middle-aged women were no longer being given tips on how to look as if they were closer to 30. Now the presumption was that 19 was everyone's ideal. A skin cream company ad in 1923 featured a girl announcing, "Mother, you're looking younger every day!"— which was pretty obvious since the mother and daughter had the same face in the picture.

Scanning through the media of the 1920s, you might be excused for assuming women consisted of three types: 19-year-olds, women trying to look as if they were still 19, and those for whom the ship of youth had sailed entirely. After a stretch of progress in which older women found social acceptance, the tide had shifted. The new consumer economy and its young target audience were the stars of the show. Their mothers might not have been consigned to a rocking chair with a hideous cap and shawl, but they might as well have been, given the dwindling attention the world paid to them. Sometimes in the 1920s their fate sounded even more horrible than that rocker. In an essay entitled "Human Junk," the editor of *Ladies' Home Journal* referred to the aged as a burden made up of people who "have been broken on the wheel."

The medical profession was on the same page about aging, but some researchers were coming up with what they regarded as . . . cures. "The alleged joys of old age have been imagined to console us in our downfall, which is considered inevitable and irremediable," wrote Dr. Serge Voronoff, a French surgeon. Voronoff made an international splash in the 1920s when he claimed he had "transformed" an elderly woman with the graft of an ovary from a female chimpanzee. "Her figure had again become erect, her movements alert; her face no longer wore the expression of pain that made it look so old." Best of all, the physician claimed, his patient "was again able to climb lightly her six flights of steps" and work 12 hours a day. He insisted his operation should be performed immediately "on a large scale" in all old-age homes. Voronoff was also enthusiastic about grafting slices of monkey testicles onto men's scrota, and eventually the medical world did figure out that he was off his rocker. But he was hardly the only physician expressing faith in science's power to eliminate aging. "Immortal life will be achieved by the aid of applied science; it is what the whole scheme of evolution moves forward to," predicted Dr. Charles A. Stephens, a popular writer. Good thing, since Stephens also wrote that getting old meant entering a period of "grossness, coarseness and ugliness."

"SOME OF US OLD MAIDS DO GO MAD"

"I'm hipped on Freud and all that," says one of the trendy young women in Fitzgerald's first novel, *This Side of Paradise*, referring to the idea that everything is about sex. Freud and sex were extremely popular topics in the 1920s, and anyone who was keeping up with the conversation knew that things didn't look good for postmenopausal women. "It is a well-known fact...that after women have lost their genital function their character often undergoes a peculiar alteration," Sigmund himself wrote. "They become quarrelsome, vexatious and overbearing, petty and stingy; that is to say, they exhibit typically sadistic and anal-erotic traits which they did not possess earlier, during their period of womanliness."

Freud was hardly alone. The psychological community in general tended to regard both spinsters and menopausal women as either (a) pathetically stripped of all sexuality or (b) overcome by sexual drives that could lead them to do anything, including seduce innocent boys. "It's been in the background of my mind every minute like a terrible obsession. I wonder I haven't gone mad," says a middle-aged teacher in *Black Oxen*, a bestselling novel. "Some of us old maids do go mad." One of her colleagues, the desperate woman continued, had lost her mind a few years earlier, and the doctors reported her ravings were "the most libidinous he had ever listened to." The theory that menopausal women were oversexed wasn't new. But the more freewheeling public conversation of the '20s made the discussion both more open and more inventive.

Black Oxen told the transformation story of a 58-year-old Austrian countess whose friends felt age had made her "withered, changed, skinny...God! Mary Ogden!" Mary returns in triumph with a new name and a stunning new look achieved through a miraculous breakthrough in glandular therapy. Not only is she a beauty who appears to be in her 20s; she is back to being *interesting*. "People growing old are condemned for prejudice, smugness, hostility to progress...but this attitude is due to aging glands alone," she explains to her eager friends.

It was, of course, fiction. But at the time, scientists really were experimenting with perpetual-youth therapies, transplanting ovaries from young women into their older patients. "The senile female becomes more vigorous, shows renewed sexual desire, exerts a renewed attraction of the male, and after a longer period of sterility is once more capable of becoming pregnant and producing offspring," claimed the Australian sexologist Norman Haire, who lectured in the United States. It was the newest version of the chimpanzee story, and it would be far from the last.

"SHRIVELED OR WADDLING OLD AND ALL THAT"

In the real world, medicine was making some progress in improving the quality of life for older people, without the aid of chimpanzees' private parts. Conditions like fistulas and a prolapsed uterus could be cured by surgery. Americans' diet, on the whole, was better. And there was a new option coming 'round the bend: plastic surgery. In 1922, *Ladies' Home Journal* sent writer Ethel Lloyd Patterson on a tour of cosmetic surgeons, to report back on whether a face-lift was a good option for the nearly 40 crowd. Patterson's conclusion was—not yet. But she was optimistic about the future. The way science was progressing, she predicted, "it soon will not be necessary for women to grow old at all—I mean shriveled or waddling old and all that."

The movies were full of makeovers for the middle-aged—dowdy matrons who miraculously reclaimed their youth by cutting their hair and putting on different clothes. New diet products flooded the market, some of them deeply suspect. Marmola, advertised as dried animal thyroid glands, promised women they could lose weight without "table restraint." Wearing a harness called the I-On-A-Co was supposed to send a mysterious force through the body that would cut fat.

Older women were following the younger generation's fashion lead: cropped hair and skirts that were dramatically shorter than in the previous era. The *Journal of Commerce* determined that the amount of fabric required to make a complete outfit had dropped, in 15 years, from 19¼ yards to 7. By 1927, there were 7,000 different cosmetic products for sale in the country, most of them lotions, creams, tinted foundations, and rouge. At the end of the decade, when Congress imposed tariffs on imported consumer goods, Congresswoman Mary Teresa Norton of New Jersey protested that while "lipsticks, perfumes and the like once were luxuries...Today they are necessities." Helena Rubinstein built a cosmetics empire that she presciently sold in 1928, netting $7.3 million — about $106 million today — just before the stock market crash. After the Depression hit and the value of the company plummeted, Rubinstein bought it back again, launching her own outreach campaign to convince investors — especially women investors — that they should sell her back their shares. She managed all this from her bed, where she was recovering from a hysterectomy.

The culture of the '20s allowed advertisers to be increasingly vocal about the evil effects of gray hair. ("She retires, a reigning beauty whose triumphs were the envy and despair of a hundred rivals. She awakes to tragedy! In the night relentless age had laid a silvering finger on her hair. Youth betrayed by Time!") But hair dyeing was still controversial: ads often referred to their product as a remedy for "prematurely graying hair," which suggested that customers just needed to rectify an error rather than purposely conceal the effects of aging. The real barrier was not so much mortality as practicality. Despite all the technological progress the nation was making, hair coloring hadn't really improved to the point where the hair in question didn't wind up looking rather peculiar after an application.

"THEY SHOULD HAVE BEEN BURIED IN IT"

The generation gap was most painful in the ranks of the middle-class women who had run the clubs, spurred the reform movements, fought for the right to vote, and written all those essays on how the key to combatting age was getting involved in things outside yourself. Now all that was out of style. "Causes sweep by them unheeded," wrote Margaret Culkin Banning, a 36-year-old novelist and women's rights advocate, in an essay denouncing her contemporaries as "The Lazy Thirties." The housewives who 10 or 15 years earlier had sent their children off to school and then marched into the world of charitable endeavors and reform politics were now just—sitting at home. "They are younger than women of that age have ever been before, more confident of retaining their beauty, less burdened by housewifery, and better educated," Banning said. But she added, "Their point in common is inertia, their utter lack of response to the battle cries that used to get women into action." The mantle of reform leadership, she concluded, "may flap emptily in the wind until it blows to rags."

The people being criticized tended to agree. Dorothy Dunbar Bromley, a New York essayist, wrote a famous article for *Harper's* in 1927 in which she dismissed feminism as irrelevant and irritating. The modern young woman, Bromley said, hated the very word because it suggested "either the old school of fighting feminists who wore flat heels and had very little feminine charm, or the current species who antagonize men with their constant clamor about maiden names, equal rights, woman's place in the world, and many another cause...ad infinitum." While her generation certainly appreciated everything the old reformers had accomplished, Bromley said breezily, the modern woman had no intention of picking up their leadership mantle—"indeed, she thinks they should have been buried in it."

If those older activist women of the Progressive Era had lost their sway, one of the reasons was because they had gotten what they wished for. In 1919 and 1920, voters approved amendments to the Constitution giving women the right to vote and prohibiting the manufacture or sale of liquor. The two signal goals of the reform movement had been achieved. But neither victory delivered quite what their backers had hoped.

People quickly became used to the idea that women were voting, and there was little or no talk of ever going back. The Nineteenth Amendment was a complete success on that count. But it was a flop in terms of effect. The women's vote—which was supposed to deliver clean politics, better education, health care for the poor, and a long list of other social goals—never really materialized. Women didn't turn out as often as men, and when they did, they voted pretty much the same as their husbands, brothers, and fathers. The best example of the failure of suffrage to live up to expectations was the sad case of the Sheppard-Towner Maternity and Infancy Protection Act. It wasn't a large program—just a modest effort to provide clinics in poor, mainly rural areas and to educate poor women about infant care. But it was exactly the kind of legislation female reformers had talked about. Congress passed it in 1921 with the expectation that the politicians who had voted for it would be rewarded by their new constituents. When one of the opponents argued that the bill would promulgate maternity clinics run by "ladies who have not had babies," a supporter noted pointedly that "old maids are voting now."

Then in 1929, the act was repealed. Partly it was due to lobbying by the American Medical Association, which felt Congress was encroaching on doctors' turf. Partly it was due to the increasingly conservative temper of the times—the public, with its eye on all that perpetual prosperity, worried about Bolsheviks and immigrants and militant labor unions. But none of that would have mattered if politicians hadn't discovered they didn't really need to worry very much about the women's vote.

"COMPETE ALL OVER AGAIN FOR HER OWN PRIVATE HUSBAND"

The second great victory of the early-twentieth-century women's movement was Prohibition, which reformers won with disastrous consequences. The idea of banning the sale of liquor was popular for a while—that was obvious, since the Eighteenth Amendment to the Constitution managed to get passed. But the moment faded. By the end of the decade, bootleg liquor was one of the biggest businesses in the country, and more than a third of all federal convictions were for violation of liquor laws. The link between the women's reform movements and Prohibition helped solidify the younger generation's conviction that older feminists were a bunch of irritating prudes.

Alcohol had always divided women from men in urban America. Middle-class husbands went off to their clubs to smoke and drink in a female-free atmosphere. In polite society, men retired together after dinner to share some port while their teetotaler wives went into another room to sip tea. Working-class husbands went off to the local saloon while their families worried whether Dad would blow his salary on whiskey. The impetus for Prohibition was the very real problem saloon life posed for poor women and children, but middle-class women's hostility to alcohol also had a lot to do with that dividing line. Most of them had no experience with drinking, and they could not comprehend that wine or beer or whiskey could be anything but a terrible social evil.

As it turned out, Prohibition made everything worse. Older women still stayed home with their tea, but men of all ages flocked to speakeasies, and the younger women went with them. Nightclubs were very much a part of the '20s culture — in fact, for icons like Zelda Fitzgerald, drinking seemed to be the entire point. There were, of course, millions of families in which everybody — male and female, young and old — abstained. But even they were reading the papers and going to movies, where the heroes spent a disproportionate amount of time wearing tuxedoes and flirting with flappers over martinis. The only people who had no part in this new scenario were older women. When they showed up in movie plots at all, they were generally sweet but passive mother figures. Or worse. In *Ankles Preferred,* a comedy about a struggling dressmaking business, the owners' non-youthful and unappealing spouses are introduced with close-ups of their fleshy ankles, complete with drooping stockings.

Older women's reactions to their new and extremely unattractive image ranged from unease to panic — much of it ginned up by the media — over the possibility of losing one's husband to a flapper hussy. Nearly 300 movies in the 1920s featured themes of infidelity, and the betrayal often involved an older husband and a younger woman. In *Dancing Mothers,* when flapper Clara Bow's respectable boyfriend gets angry with her for flirting with another man in a nightclub and threatens to tell her father, Bow shrugs and says, "Go ahead, he's right over there." And Dad was indeed right over there in a corner, romancing a young woman who was most definitely not Mom.

"Which wins, mature companionship or that baby stare?" writer Helen Bullitt Lowry asked in a *Harper's Bazar* essay called "The Evolution of a New Social Technique: Or How to Keep a Husband." (It appeared in May 1922 — the bridal issue.) Lowry was something of a flapper expert, having written about them extensively for every publication from the *New York Times* to *Southern Cultures*. "For the first time in the history of our modern civilization," she warned, " 'married men' are no longer taboo to the young philanderers.... As a consequence the older woman must go out into the social market-place and compete all over again for her own private husband."

The media speculated that while the flappers were out dancing with their beaus, male "lounge lizards" were partying with older women, or "flapper dames." It's not clear how many flapper dames there really were, but the idea that an older woman could get her revenge for all the disadvantages the era piled on her was another popular movie plot. In *Dancing Mothers,* Clara Bow's mother, played by 36-year-old Alice Joyce, tries to save her spoiled daughter Kittens from an affair, and winds up running off to Europe with Kittens's boyfriend herself, leaving her unfaithful husband and selfish child behind.

"THE PROMISCUOUS PAWING AND PETTING"

If the flappers were winning the war for the nation's attention, it was in part because they were such great consumers — eager purchasers of cosmetics, clothing, fashion magazines, hair products, cigarettes, and costume jewelry. They were the top targets of an advertising industry that was exploding — in 1920 people were exposed to six times the commercial ads they saw in 1900, and the numbers kept rising. "Today's woman gets what she wants," said an ad in the *Chicago Tribune,* notable for its attempt to cover all possible bases. "The vote. Slim sheaths of silk to replace voluminous petticoats. Glassware in sapphire blue or glowing amber. The right to a career. Soap to match her bathroom's color scheme."

Older women were well aware that they'd been pushed out of the public eye by daughters and nieces and granddaughters who didn't share the values they'd expected to hand down. To make things worse, not only were younger women bored by politics and good works; they also seemed to behave... really badly. Lillian Symes, another one of those alienated 30-somethings, noted that she and her friends had thrown jazz parties and believed in the right to smoke and drink. But, she added, they "considered overindulgence...'rather sloppy'" and were "thoroughly revolted by the promiscuous pawing and petting permitted by so many technically virtuous young women to-day."

It was all a terrible disappointment for Jane Addams. Never a fan of Prohibition, she was nonetheless dismayed by the nation's sudden obsession with drinking and sex. Addams was hardly alone. Vida Scudder, a prominent reformer and essayist who was teaching young women at Wellesley College, described the 1920s as the worst part of her career. Complaints about female college students had been building up for some time. In 1906, Wellesley professor Margaret Sherwood begged young women who were going to college for fun to consider another path: "If she longs for dramatic activity, is there not a stage? If she yearns for the trapeze, is there not a circus? Will she not leave our beloved college what it was intended to be, a place for training the mind?" Trying to bridge the gap, 69-year-old Addams gave a speech in 1929 in which she assured young women that her generation had no desire to boss them around "for we are ambitious to be remembered as comrades and not as mentors." She did the best she could, but by the 1920s, Addams had lost some of her influence. If there was a most-popular woman, it was probably someone like Clara Bow, who starred in dozens of hugely profitable movies built around the idea that girls just want to have fun.

"OBSERVE A WOMAN STEEPLEJACK"

Women continued to be the nation's most avid readers, but a lot of what they read was truly terrible. *The Sheik,* by Edith Hull, a sensational hit, was your basic falling-in-love-with-your-rapist trash. ("Why have I brought you here? You ask me why? *Bon Dieu!* Are you not woman enough to know?") During some years in the '20s, half the bestsellers belonged to female authors. That meant both a great deal and not very much at all, since we're sloshing between novels by the likes of Edith Wharton and Ellen Glasgow, on the one hand, and those celebrating rapist sheiks, on the other. Not surprisingly, female heroines in the classics tended to be more complicated, older, and less likely to wind up with a happy ending. In Wharton's *The Age of Innocence* the hero is stuck with his pretty young fiancée when he falls in love with her 30-year-old cousin, Ellen. Ellen loses the man. But at the end the reader knows — and this was a rather common theme in novels with older heroines — that she is a noble character and the youthful fiancée is a weak little thing who will never, ever make him happy. Glasgow's *Barren Ground* follows Dorinda from a poor farm girl of 20 to a successful businesswoman of 50. In between she's betrayed by her fiancé, suffers a miscarriage, and marries a man she doesn't love. But she outlives and outachieves all the major male characters and takes pleasure in her thriving dairy business: "Repose, dignity, independence, these were the attributes with which she faced middle age, for the lines in her face were marks of character, not emotion.... Though she clung to youth, it was the youth of the spirit."

Work was a new frontier for women in the '20s. One reason advertisers were so obsessed with flappers was that a lot of them were wage earners. People living in the decade — or at least the ones writing in the popular press — seemed convinced that the sky was the limit when it came to jobs. "Within the space of a single day, one can ride in a taxi driven by a woman, directed by traffic signals designed by a woman, to the office of a woman engineer, there to look out of the window and observe a woman steeplejack at her trade or contemplate the task of the woman blacksmith whose forge was passed on the way," announced one writer in 1929, going a little over the top. The chances of encountering a woman steeplejack were really pretty remote. And while the number of women professionals was soaring, most of them were in the traditional occupations, like teacher, librarian, social worker, and nurse. Nevertheless, the very fact that opinion makers thought female engineers and taxi drivers were a good idea was quite a leap.

While most women still expected to get married, they were less likely to view it as the single achievement that would determine their future happiness. For older women, that was a big step forward. They might have been urged to look as if they'd just graduated from high school, but popular culture was moving away from the familiar obsession about finding a husband or falling into the waste bin. "What has become of the useful maiden aunt?" asked an ad in a women's magazine, which showed a picture, dated "1900," of a woman who seemed to be teetering on the verge of middle age, dressed in black, and presumably waiting to be asked to do someone's chores. "She isn't darning anybody's stockings, not even her own," the ad continued triumphantly. "She is a draftsman or an author, a photographer or a real estate agent.... She is the new phenomenon in everyday life."

Once again, it's important to point out that the actual number of female drafters was pretty low. During World War I, women did take over some traditionally male jobs, but when the soldiers returned to reclaim their old places, that was generally the end of the story. Teachers continued to be underpaid — so much so that some rural areas were still recruiting their faculty from high schools. But there was no question that a woman who decided not to get married had options. The 80-year-old novelist Rhoda Broughton compared her youth in the middle of the nineteenth century to the dashing girls of 1920 and noted approvingly that the new generation would not have to endure the "intense dreariness of the afternoon of life" the way "single women of small means" had existed in earlier times.

The attitude toward the unmarried is one of the critical markers that determine how well women of any age will fare in society. If girls can't envision a full, happy life without a husband, then we're back in the early nineteenth century, with 18-year-olds betting their entire future on their ability to land an acceptable mate, fast. Another marker is whether women who do get married can also have careers. Only about 10 percent of married women worked in the 1920s, and the idea of working mothers was still extremely controversial. Sometimes it was celebrated. A bestselling novel, *The Home-Maker,* introduced the perfectly miserable Knapp family, which is transformed for the better when Lester, the father, falls off the roof and is paralyzed. Wife Evangeline, an obsessive house cleaner whose perfectionism was driving the kids mad, goes to work in the same department store where poetic Lester was a terrible failure. Lester loves being at home with the kids. Evangeline thrives and gets enormous raises. The children blossom under their father's tender care. The crisis comes when Lester seems to recover the use of his legs, threatening everyone's happiness. But Dorothy Canfield, the 46-year-old author, saved the day by introducing a sympathetic doctor who grasps the whole picture and announces that Lester should never try to walk again.

Canfield was not, however, the majority view, even in fiction. Another popular novel, *This Freedom,* featured Rosalie, a beautiful girl who becomes a successful banker while raising three children. Things seem to be going well, despite a certain amount of quiet carping from her husband. But when she hits middle age, her eldest son winds up in prison, her daughter dies at the hands of an abortionist, and her youngest son commits suicide. There's a hint of a happy ending when Rosalie quits her job to help care for her orphaned granddaughter, but it's fair to presume that the moral is not about the advantages of having a working mother.

That kind of dire attitude was common. Women's magazines regularly featured stories about children who died while their mothers were at work. *This Freedom* was such a smash that the *Literary Digest* sent out queries to all the married women listed in *Who's Who in America,* asking whether they thought a woman could "run a home and have a job, too." Even though such super-achievers would seem likely to come down on the side of working mothers, the response was distinctly mixed. "She can if she has brains," said one respondent, who then added unhelpfully: "Few women have brains." Alla Nazimova, an actress, announced that she had "not given my husband half the happiness he deserves." An editor theorized that two of her children, who died of cerebral meningitis, "might have been over-nervous because of my mental labors previous to their birth."

A survey of white-collar men in 1924 showed nearly two-thirds felt married women shouldn't work, and almost all the rest felt it was all right only as long as they hadn't yet had children. "Generally speaking, we have learned to expect that the children of gainfully employed mothers will be neglected, ill-disciplined, poorly nourished, and educationally irregular," wrote David Snedden, a leading educational theorist of the era. "Death-rates among the babies, truancy rates among the boys, and sexual immorality rates among the girls will be severely high." If women were going to both work and be mothers, the popular consensus seemed to be that the job should be as trivial as possible. One female social scientist recommended a sideline like "typing, sewing, preparation of gift cards, painted lamp shades and the like."

"What is a Woman 35 Years of Age to Do?"

Older women who wanted or needed to get a real job ran into a wall of age discrimination, which was perfectly legal. "What is a woman 35 years of age to do?" asked a letter to the *New York Sun* in 1928. "I am a capable stenographer, well dressed (but not flashily), look thirty but have been turned down time and again because employers have drawn the dead line at twenty-five." She wondered if all working women over 30 were supposed to "take chloroform." A doctor, being interviewed about hair coloring, decried all the available preparations as "either unsuitable or dangerous." But he added that he had come around a bit when an older patient simply told him: "It is impossible for a woman with gray hair to get a job."

A 1929 study found that many factories, stores, and offices were indeed reluctant to hire older women — and "older," in some cases, could cover almost everybody who had failed to keep that fabled 19-year-old complexion. The explanations ranged from pay scales to adaptability and the theory that younger people were "less moody and irritable." The discrimination was greatest in offices, less severe in department stores and factories. But there was one type of employment agency that seemed to have no trouble placing older women, the report added. "That is the group specializing in the supplying of domestic help."

Domestic help was the one area of the economy where black women predominated. They made up more than half the population of maids, cooks, and other types of household servants by 1930. The jobs tended to be low paying, physically demanding, and generally involved working for a housewife who had high standards about the way everything should operate. It was crazy to imagine that African American women labored as maids and cooks in other people's homes out of preference. But a stereotype of the happy mammy endured. She was like Aunt Jemima, the icon on the pancake-mix box. Aunt Jemima seemed to be modeled after a minstrel show figure, but as the product grew more and more popular, publicists offered more and more details about The Legend. One promotion told the story of a Confederate general and his aide, trying to avoid Union soldiers and starvation in a lonely struggle through Mississippi, who came across an isolated house and a friendly voice calling, "Lawzee! You chilluns pestah th' life out o' yo' po' ol' mammy with yo' evahlastin' appetite fo' pancakes!" Aunt Jemima was thrilled to see the white Southern soldiers, and her pancakes revived the weary men. Then, the story continued, after the war the general brought her and her recipe to the eagerly awaiting North. The copywriters had to make it clear that Jemima wasn't leaving the South because she was dissatisfied with her lot in life. So another ad recounted her departure from the old homestead: "How happy she had been on that old Louisiana plantation! How kind, how noble, had been her 'massa,' Colonel Higbee!"

In 1923, Nancy Green, who had spent many years portraying Aunt Jemima in promotion tours around the country, was struck by a car and killed. She was 89 and her life had encompassed much more than pancakes—Green had settled in Chicago and helped organize the large and prominent Olivet Baptist Church while speaking out against poverty and racism in her adopted city. But when she died, a number of papers mixed the actual facts of her life with the Jemima fiction. She was sometimes reported to be a former happy plantation cook. In the black press, columnist A. L. Jackson seemed to admire the canny way the ad men did their exploiting: "There is no good reason why some wide-awake young business man from our own crowd should not seize upon that skill and capitalize it for himself and for the Race as these white men did with Aunt Jemima."

"THE PRIVILEGE OF PRESIDING OVER A BODY OF MEN"

Once women had the right to vote, it seemed obvious that the next step should be elective office. That was one job that didn't come with age limits. The handful of women who made it into Congress in the 1920s were all middle-aged or older. The first female senator, Rebecca Latimer Felton, was the 87-year-old widow of a prominent Georgia politician, and a Progressive movement activist in her own right. (Like many

Southern women's rights advocates, Felton had racial attitudes that were not only unprogressive but downright chilling.) When Georgia's incumbent senator died in 1922, Gov. Thomas Hardwick needed a placeholder who would warm the seat — very briefly — until a special election could be held. He named Felton on October 3. She was sworn in when Congress reconvened on November 21. The next morning, she made a speech looking forward to the day when many women would serve in the chamber. Then her male successor was sworn in and she was gone.

Felton's stay was shorter than normal, but the fact that she was the widow of a former congressman was very typical. Ten women served in the House in the 1920s, and four were congressional widows. Another, Winnifred Huck, won an election to serve out the term of her deceased father. "I have come into the political world like a clap of thunder out of a clear sky," she announced rather grandly. During her brief tenure she took a strong anti-war stance that was broken briefly when she nominated her son to the U.S. Naval Academy — a move that forced the academy to waive its normal height requirement for Huck's diminutive offspring. Another early congresswoman, Katherine Langley, was elected to the seat that belonged to her husband, John "Pork Barrel" Langley, who was convicted of violating the Prohibition Act by trying to sell 1,400 bottles of whiskey. Ruth Hanna McCormick of Illinois was the daughter of Ohio senator Mark Hanna and the widow of a U.S. senator. Florida's Ruth Bryan Owen, the daughter of three-time Democratic presidential nominee William Jennings Bryan, was also elected in 1928 and joked that she was "the first Bryan who ever ran for anything and got it."

Everyone realized it was a less than stellar beginning.

The first generation of congresswomen tended toward short stays — most lasted just one or two terms. But there were exceptions. Edith Nourse Rogers took over her husband's seat when he died in 1925, but she was reelected on her own, again and again. When she died in office in 1960, Rogers had served an extraordinarily productive thirty-five years. "The first thirty years are the hardest," she said. Mary Teresa Norton, who was elected from New Jersey in 1924, remained in office until 1951. She was a protégé of Frank Hague, a boss of county politics who promoted her career in an attempt to co-opt the new women's vote before it became clear there wasn't going to be one. Norton was 49 when she was first elected to Congress. "I was starting a ... career more strenuous, exciting, and rewarding than I had ever dreamed of having—at an age when women of my mother's generation wrapped themselves in shawls and sat down by the fireside to await the end," she said later. Like Elizabeth Cady Stanton and the other pioneers of a much earlier era, Norton used her age to skate around the barrier against women and public life. When a man in the audience at one of her speeches shouted that women should be at home "looking after their children," Norton, who had lost her only child, replied, "How very, very fortunate they are to have children! That privilege has been denied me. If I had children, I'd certainly be at home with them now if they needed me. But since I haven't, I'm here talking to you about a new responsibility that has been given to women."

Norton became the first woman to run a House committee, when the Democrats took over in 1931 and she became chair of the Committee on the District of Columbia. "This is the first time in my life I have been controlled by a woman," one member complained. "It's the first time I've had the privilege of presiding over a body of men, and I rather like the prospect," Norton returned. She began the fight to give the District of Columbia self-government, a battle that continues to this day.

"PARTICULARLY INTERESTED IN WOMAN'S SPECIAL PROBLEM"

One less inspiring arena for women was the ever-expanding beauty-aid industry. Actresses had been extolling the glories of soaps and face creams for several generations, but the idea of using non-entertainers' endorsements was new. (Although, you'll remember, Henry Ward Beecher followed up his sex trial with a paid tribute to Pears' Soap.) After the suffrage battle was won, Alva Belmont appeared in an unusual ad for Pond's cold cream in return for a $1,000 donation to the National Woman's Party. The ad praised her work for women and added that Belmont—who would have been over 70 at the time—"also is particularly interested in woman's special problem of how to keep her force and her charm throughout her whole life." While Belmont was a rebel, it turned out she was not prepared to go as far as to allow her picture to be used in an advertisement, so the soap maker substituted one of her library. It's not every day you see a beauty product promoting itself with a picture of a room. Belmont's actual testimonial was pretty direct, even stern: "A woman who neglects her personal appearance loses half her influence. The wise care of one's body constructs the frame encircling our mentality, the ability of which insures the success of one's life. I advise a daily use of Pond's Two Creams."

Among the prominent women putting in plugs for commercial products was Eleanor Roosevelt, whose husband, Franklin, a former vice-presidential candidate, was preparing to run for governor of New York. In 1927, she announced in *Ladies' Home Journal* that she had a Simmons Beautyrest mattress in her home and found it "the most marvelous mattress in the world."

We'll be hearing more from her.

9. The 1930s

"I SAVED A LOT OF PEOPLE FROM A TRAIN WRECK"

Radio was king in the 1930s. Experts in the brand-new field of ratings reported that Americans were collectively spending "nearly one billion hours before the loud-speaker." Those speakers were still pretty bulky and confined to the house, so during the day, the target audience was mainly homemakers. It was a breakthrough in modern communications — mass entertainment that was directed at women who weren't particularly young. By 1936, half of all the daytime programming consisted of 15-minute, long-running melodramas whose sponsors gave them the generic name of "soap operas." The shows' heroines were people like Ma Perkins, the wise and kindly owner of a small-town lumberyard, the mother of several grown children, and a woman spunky enough to break up a black-market baby ring or foil a team of Soviet secret agents. And there was *The Romance of Helen Trent*, "the real-life drama of Helen Trent, who, when life mocks her, breaks her hopes, dashes her against the rocks of despair, fights back bravely, successfully, to prove what so many women long to prove in their own lives: That because a woman is 35 or more, romance in life need not be over, that romance of youth can extend into middle life, and even beyond." Helen, whose travails ran through 7,222 performances from 1933 to 1960, never married any of her 28 suitors and never turned 36.

Helen Trent had a rather glamorous life as a Hollywood designer, but many of the soaps' leading ladies were simple housewives or widows running a family business — Ma had to take over that lumberyard when Pa died. They had endless adventures, demonstrating that a woman over 35 could not only find romance; she could also solve murders, outwit gangsters, and survive plane crashes. The heroine of *The Story of Mary Marlin* was appointed to the U.S. Senate to replace her husband, who disappeared in Siberia. *Stella Dallas* told the saga of a humble farmhand's daughter who "saw her own beloved daughter, Laurel, marry into wealth and society and, realizing the differences in their tastes and worlds, went out of Laurel's life." But she came back, due to a stupendous run of emergencies that included one crisis in which Laurel was kidnapped by a sheik. "I had to go to the Sahara Desert and try to save her," the actress who played Stella recalled. "On the way I saved a lot of people from a train wreck."

"You Can Have My Job"

The 1930s were, metaphorically, one long train wreck. The decade began with the collapse of the stock market, and hard economic times continued until the Depression smashed into World War II in 1941. At the peak of the 1930s, a quarter of the working population was unemployed and the average family income dropped 40 percent. The flapper was useless when mortgages were defaulting and furniture was being repossessed. Blondie Boopadoop, the party-loving cutie who had a long-running fling with Dagwood, a dim-witted billionaire's son, in the popular comic strip *Blondie*, suddenly seemed wrong for the times. Her creator quickly married the pair off, disinherited Dagwood, and turned his heroine into a sensible, rather harried housewife whose husband was a low-watt office worker providing the comic relief. The time for frivolity was over and the ideal woman acted like a grown-up. Her shoulders got broader — even literally, thanks to the fashions of the day.

On the home front, women returned to old, inefficient, but inexpensive ways of housekeeping — the sale of glass jars soared as women stopped buying canned food and began putting up their own preserves. The media, which still had ads to sell, tried to depict spending as prudent and sometimes downright patriotic. *Harper's Bazaar* extolled Grandmother, who helped the economy by getting nice little extras for her carriage: "When Grandmother made the opportune purchase of a quality product she saw an economic law working out in her own little world, she received exceptional value for her money, and she enjoyed the gratifying sense of being a public benefactor."

You'll notice that Grandmother wasn't going to work. The nation definitely preferred to think she didn't need to. When the Depression hit, many housewives were compelled to look for a way to make money to help their suffering families. But they faced double prejudice—for being older and for taking employment away from men. The career girl had been eulogized in the '20s, but during the Depression, the media was trying to celebrate the women who kept the hell out of the job market. Magazines helpfully published articles with titles like "You Can Have My Job: A Feminist Discovers Her Home." The new villain was the woman who worked for "pin money"—extra cash she didn't really need. Even Frances Perkins, the future secretary of labor, denounced college graduates who thought it was fashionable to work at jobs that could have gone to their less educated, needy sisters. She complained that their "flimsy pay envelope acts as a sop to the fashion…even if it drains the pockets of their male relatives and forces out of a job another unskilled woman who needs to work in order to live."

The idea that women—especially married women—were only working to get money to buy "extras" was commonly held. George Gallup, the pioneer polling expert, said it drew a level of public prejudice usually reserved for "sin and hay fever." When the American Federation of Labor urged that "married women whose husbands have permanent positions…be discriminated against in the hiring of employees," a 1936 Gallup poll showed 82 percent of Americans agreed. Congress even passed a law making it illegal for the government to hire "married persons" whose spouses already had federal jobs.

But in the real world it was hard to find people who didn't need their paycheck. A woman who looked like a possible "pin money" pursuer to casual observers "may be supporting a family, she may be all alone in the world," argued Eleanor Roosevelt from the White House. Even if a woman was living with relatives who had jobs, Eleanor reasoned, "the day her earning power ceases she becomes an economic liability to her family and her country." The First Lady felt discrimination against older female workers was worse than discrimination against older men, reasoning that for a man "it may eventually be possible to find a place in farm work or in forestry work or in some other industry, but what is to happen to the woman who after working twenty to thirty years in one industry finds a slip in her pay envelope saying, 'Next week your services will no longer be required'? She knows no other skill or trade; she has been trained to the knowledge of only one machine."

The idea that laid-off middle-aged men could seamlessly slip into jobs in forestry belongs in the same pleasant-fantasy category as the female steeplejacks we saw in the 1920s. But Roosevelt was fighting against a major-league prejudice, and she was well aware that times were tough even for women who appeared to have lots of advantages. Those college graduates who were grabbing up the clerical openings were often trying to support themselves after their old professional jobs disappeared or were given to men. The women who did manage to keep working often got less pay. Strapped school boards kept cutting teachers' salaries. Their compensation averaged about $1,600 a year during the Depression—the equivalent of about $24,000 today. Even worse, some teachers discovered their paychecks never arrived, or that the envelope just contained the equivalent of an IOU. "As professionals, we're entitled to starve to death quietly and with refinement," Elsa Ponselle, a Chicago elementary school principal, dryly told the writer Studs Terkel. While the teachers protested, she said, there were no strikes or walkouts because "that would hurt the children. We determined on one thing: We were not going to hurt the children. We went on teaching whether we were being paid or not."

Businesses that employed older women as a matter of course—like department stores—began to mutter about younger workers being more flexible and, of course, cheaper. The only occupations where age was not a real drawback were "the needle trades, beauty culture and cafeteria work," said Ollie Randall, an official at an emergency work bureau in New York. "It is extremely difficult for a woman over 40 to get a job today, and many of the women now out of work were dismissed because of their age." Older black women were facing a triple threat when it came to discrimination, with race piled on top of age and gender. Over half of black female workers lost their jobs in the Depression, compared to about 30 percent of white women. The Philadelphia Public Employment Office reported 68 percent of the job availabilities it handled in 1932 and 1933 were for "Whites Only." Domestic service, where so many black women were employed, was in a free fall—the maid or nanny or cook was the first luxury to go when families faced economic problems.

"WE DIVIDED WHATEVER WE HAD"

Some of the few bright spots of the Depression were the accounts of beleaguered women supporting one another. "Back in the Thirties, when it was really tough, and nobody was working, we divided whatever we had with each other," Mrs. Willye Jeffries, a union official in Chicago, told Studs Terkel.

In Chicago, labor union members tried to wring money out of the local relief office to bury the indigent dead. On one occasion, Jeffries said, they mobilized under the leadership of "a white lady, weighed about two, three hundred. We called her Ma Kuntz," who waved a stick to keep the protest marchers in time while looking out for police who might attempt to break up the demonstration. The police finally arrived, Jeffries remembered, stared at Ma Kuntz and her stick, and then went away. "We stayed over two weeks on that first floor. We had blankets, we moved a piano in and we had a big time. We had plenty to eat 'cause those that weren't picketing saw that we had food every day."

The press was not all that enthusiastic about populist uprisings, preferring to promote the theory that things were getting better on their own. A *New York Times* story on a convention of the National Federation of Business and Professional Women reported that "much optimism was expressed by vocational experts" regarding job opportunities for the "beginner after 40." The report exhibited no skepticism whatsoever when a featured speaker — the personnel director of a department store — told the delegates, "The chorus line is almost the only line that should give pause to the mature woman job seeker."

Some women who couldn't find jobs tried to go into business for themselves, and the cheerleading media embraced the idea that those self-starters were likely to succeed. "I am now daily confronted, on Fifth and Madison Avenues, by thousands of prosperous lady milliners, lady dress designers, decorators and agents of various sorts, not to mention the ten thousand other ladies of breeding who are scattered among the city's fashion magazines, small shops, travel bureaus, picture galleries, publishing houses, tea shops and department stores," wrote a possibly overenthusiastic Frank Crowninshield, the editor of *Vanity Fair*. In truth, most of the female entrepreneurs were running beauty parlors in their kitchens or performing other one-woman services. And the chances of making any real money were minimal. A 1936 survey of single women on relief in Chicago found that the vast majority of the older recipients had been employed in the past, many of them running exactly the kinds of businesses other women were then being urged to start: dressmaking, hairstyling, or managing a rooming house.

"CEASE THEIR PERNICIOUS EFFORTS TO LENGTHEN THE SPAN OF HUMAN LIFE"

When all else failed, you moved in with your relatives. The number of three-generation families rose in both urban and rural areas. Older women generally fit more comfortably into their children's homes than men, but no extra mouths were all that welcome when people were having trouble feeding themselves. Chicago relief workers reported countless stories of elderly women whose children wouldn't take them in. Maude, a 51-year-old widow living with her daughter, lost her job and then cashed in her insurance policy to make ends meet. The daughter, who had been planning to inherit that insurance money, was so angry at its disappearance that she turned her mother out. Black families had traditionally welcomed needy relatives, but the strain was affecting them, too. The Chicago social workers told the story of Mary, a 53-year-old widow who had supported herself and her family for 40 years working as a domestic. When Mary lost her job in 1932, one of her sons refused to contribute to her support. Another was willing to take her into his home until it became clear Mary and his wife couldn't get along. The third had no home to offer and could give her only 25 to 50 cents each payday.

The Depression was bankrupting even people who had assumed they'd put away plenty of money for retirement. Carey McWilliams, a Los Angeles lawyer, watched its impact on "the kind of widows who are legion in southern California. Who had brought money out from the Middle West and had invested it in fly-by-night real estate promotions. They began to lose their property.... There was a feverish activity in foreclosures." Middle-class parents generally didn't have to worry about homelessness, but if they moved in with their children, the hostility did seem, at times, to be pretty intense. A writer in *The Nation* picked up on the venerable satire "A Modest Proposal" by Jonathan Swift and suggested, "Doctors will have to be warned to cease their pernicious efforts to lengthen the span of human life."

The media, looking for an upside, churned out stories on how to live happily in a multigenerational household. The unnamed but very cheerful author of "I Am the Mother-in-Law in the Home" reported in the *Saturday Evening Post* that while she had endured the death of her husband and two children, along with crushing financial reverses, the specter of living with her married daughter seemed like the most unendurable blow of all. However, after many struggles with her offspring and her high-strung businessman son-in-law, she won them over by learning to play piano and type, and reading her way through college courses at the library. The final triumph came when the author started listening to the radio to educate herself about sports and charmed the pants off a very important dinner guest by talking about racing "and then in progression mentioning the names of horses and riders with easy familiarity, which evoked veritable gasps from my astonished children."

LIVE ALONE AND LIKE IT

In 1936, Marjorie Hillis, an editor at *Vogue,* wrote a bestselling advice book, *Live Alone and Like It,* for women over 30 — divorced, widowed, or never married. As we've seen, a lot of people couldn't afford quarters of their own whether they wanted them or not. But economics aside, women who lived alone had always been regarded as either loony or pathetic. Now times were changing. A quarter-century later, Hillis's message would be echoed in *Sex and the Single Girl,* Helen Gurley Brown's 1962 smash hit that urged unmarried women to stop being "mouseburgers" and have a no-holds-barred social and romantic life. Hillis was not particularly enthusiastic about the sex angle, which she seemed to regard as something left over from the frivolous '20s. When it came to fornication, she warned, "the Woman Pays." But she was not at all opposed to the woman picking up the tab if she went out to dinner with a gentleman who was more strapped for cash than she was. "After all," she philosophized, "it's better to be brazen than neglected." Most of all, Hillis wanted each reader to be "a gay and independent person." So there were tips on how to throw parties in even the smallest apartments, how much to tip when traveling, how to mix cocktails, and how to cook for company. "A reputation for good cuisine," she counseled, "is an almost certain step towards popularity."

Like those optimistic female essayists of the nineteenth century, Hillis believed the answer to both aging and loneliness was to *do something*. But her list of suggestions was somewhat different. Instead of helping others, she wanted her readers to do things for themselves. Settlement houses didn't come into the conversation. Hillis urged her readers to focus on "friends, hobbies, parties, books and almost anything else that keeps you interesting." At one point, after offering a long list of options, Hillis added, "Be a Communist, a stamp collector or a Ladies' Aid worker if you must, but for heaven's sake be something." Aiding the poor was better than nothing, but she didn't seem to find it nearly as appealing as antiquing.

It was, in its way, a turning point. Hillis was hardly breaking new ground in urging readers to take care of their bodies and get exercise. (Mrs. deW, one of the book's many good examples, devoted so much time to physical improvement that "at home recently, she entertained the guests by standing on her head.") But the book's main secret for a happy later life was self-gratification: having the most elegant home possible, pampering oneself with breakfast in bed, lots of massages, and fun activities that make great cocktail party conversation. Her heroines took trips to the Andes or gave glamorous buffet lunches with the help of a low-cost "colored-maid-in-for-the-afternoon." They did not do community service. One of Hillis's cautionary tales was Mrs. O, a middle-aged divorcée who was "active in women's clubs and the movement to promote birth control" but lacked "any ability for graceful living at home." Some of O's friends, Hillis said crushingly, "have also thought that perhaps it was *not* so surprising that ten years or so ago, Mr. O ran off with his pretty stenographer."

"BUXOM BLONDE . . . AND I DON'T KNOW HOW NEAR 40"

While Americans were obsessed with radio in the '30s, they still got their visual models of glamour and the good life from movies. Given the times, audiences lost interest in the silly-teenager model of the flapper era. Most of the top stars were independent-looking women in their 20s or early 30s—Bette Davis, Katharine Hepburn, Greta Garbo, and a somewhat recycled Joan Crawford. People still loved a story about a little girl, but now the big child star was mercifully an actual child: Shirley Temple.

The '30s are widely regarded as a golden age of film, and as movies got bigger and their plots more complex, older women got a wide range of roles. Billie Burke played the blond and beautiful good witch in *The Wizard of Oz* when she was 54; Margaret Hamilton, the bad witch, was 38. It may have been payback in a way for Burke's being denied a leading role in *The Great Ziegfeld*, the Oscar-winning 1936 biography of her late husband, Flo Ziegfeld. The studio had decreed that she was too old to play—herself. On the other side of the coin, in the Marx Brothers movies Margaret Dumont personified all the things middle-aged women didn't want to be, a dignified dimwit who never got the joke. In reality, Dumont was an accomplished actress with an impeccable sense of timing who knew how to make her co-stars look good. When Groucho Marx got an honorary Oscar in 1974, he failed to mention his brothers in his brief speech, but he made sure to credit Dumont.

Jane Darwell, a late bloomer who made her first movie when she was almost 40, put in her time in five Shirley Temple films, usually as a helpful grandmother or housekeeper. But she also starred in the ultimate Depression drama *The Grapes of Wrath* and won an Academy Award for her portrayal of the stolid, brave, beleaguered migrant family matriarch who tells her husband, "We'll go on forever, Pa, 'cause we're the people." Spring Byington demonstrated if not range, at least the extensive opportunities available to an actress who specialized in playing wise and kindly mothers—she appeared in 47 movies throughout the '30s. Marie Dressler, a veteran theater trouper, had trouble finding work in what she called the "youth-mad" '20s. But when talking pictures arrived, she won a lucrative contract with MGM, and in her 60s she became Hollywood's top box-office attraction until her death in 1934. Dressler starred in one of the decade's smash hits, *Min and Bill*, a comedy-drama in which she got to have a romance—although hardly a glamorous one—with a hard-drinking fisherman played by Wallace Beery. She was not only a superstar honored on the cover of *Time* but an icon who could be brought into any American's home with Marie Dressler dolls or puppets or dresses. "She was the best-loved star of her time," wrote movie historian Earl Anderson. "She looked like your grandmother, or yourself. To hell with young love, to hell with getting rich. We had Marie." Dressler was wryly aware that her well-padded body had no relation to the normal ideals in women's magazines. "That's all me!" she told portrait photographer George Hurrell, patting her rear end when she posed for a series of film-star shots that were totally true to her sense of self. When she was nominated for a Best Actress Oscar for *Min and Bill* in 1931, Dressler laughed that she was pitted against Hollywood's most glamorous young women: "Imagine this old mud hen running competition with a star like Norma Shearer. Probably some pal tossed in my name to give me a plug and the crowd a good laugh." Dressler got the last laugh, however: she won.

In 1937, Walt Disney produced his first full-length animated movie, *Snow White*, which introduced generations of children to the idea that the evil witch was an old hag who spent her time trying to destroy youth and beauty. Not as cheering as the Marie Dressler story but in keeping with the theme: there were myriad movie roles for women who had passed 35, as long as they didn't involve sex appeal.

Then there was Mae West.

A stage star who specialized in comedy and—particularly—sex, West went to Hollywood in 1932 when her old pal the actor George Raft suggested she be cast in what was supposed to be his breakthrough movie. Gossip columnist Louella Parsons described the newcomer as "buxom blonde...fat, fair and I don't know how near 40." In fact, she was 39, and although her role was originally both minor and boring, West rewrote her part of the script, adding a bit in which another woman admires her jewelry and says, "Goodness, what beautiful diamonds!"

"Goodness had nothing to do with it," retorts West, in what remains one of the most quoted lines in Hollywood history.

Raft, who was totally overshadowed, said his friend "stole everything but the cameras." West also changed the tempo of the dialogue, speeding everything up until the veteran comic Alison Skipworth protested the way she was being pushed around. "You forget I've been an actress forty years," she told West indignantly. "Don't worry, dear. I'll keep your secret," said West, who was about to start breaking the age ceiling herself in the most public way possible.

Part of her genius was ambiguity — her ability to deliver the most salacious lines with an apparent tongue in cheek. That was somehow easier for middle-class audiences to accept from a woman who was, at least age-wise, not supposed to be doing that sort of stuff at all. It wasn't an act that lasted forever — by the 1940s West's career had collapsed. But in 1933, she was the biggest box office draw in Hollywood. She changed the ideal figure back to the Lillian Russell model, billed as "the gal with the hourglass figure that makes every second count." "I never worry about diets. The only carrots that interest me are the number you get in a diamond," she said airily. A Paramount publicity man posed her on a keg of beer, with the line "Mae West says drink beer and you'll get curves, gals."

It was quite a decade for films, and the grand finale came in 1939 with *Gone with the Wind*. It was based on the wildly popular novel, in which Scarlett O'Hara spends her 20s trying to survive the Civil War and the storms of love. Most of the older characters weren't all that much of a help, except, of course, for Mammy. We meet her at the beginning of the movie, disciplining the young Scarlett ("If you don't care what folks says about this family, I does"), and watch her stand by Scarlett and Rhett through their greatest crises. Mammy had no known personal life outside her devotion to the O'Hara family. She was even less independent than Aunt Jemima, whose rag-doll version at least had a husband and children. Hattie McDaniel, the veteran entertainer who played Mammy, was an old hand at that kind of role, having been Mae West's maid in *I'm No Angel* and Shirley Temple's maid in *The Little Colonel*. "Why should I complain about making $700 to play a maid?" she once demanded. "If I didn't, I'd be making $7 a week being one." McDaniel, 44, won an Academy Award for Best Supporting Actress for her Mammy portrayal — the first Oscar given to an African American. "I sincerely hope I shall always be a credit to my race and to the motion picture industry," she told the assembled diners at the awards gala. To accept the statuette, McDaniel had to make her way through a sea of tables—the first black guest ever invited to the dinner, she had been seated way in the back of the room.

While the movies treasured the memory of those pre–Civil War mammies, in the real South they were few and far between. Historian Catherine Clinton thinks the image of the asexual, middle-aged devoted slave who ran the whole household was conjured up as a counterpart to the young black women who were sexually exploited by the white men who controlled them. Being older—and generally unattractive—was important. So was the idea that Mammy loved her white charges more than herself. In 1934, the movie *Imitation of Life* presented an updated version of the same character in Aunt Delilah, a black maid who gives her boss, Bea, a pancake recipe that Bea turns into a successful company. When Bea offers Delilah a (minority) share in the business, the maid reacts in terror to the idea of being able to afford a house of her own. "Oh, honey chile, please don't send me away," she begged. "...I'se your cook. And I want to stay your cook." Delilah was played by Louise Beavers, who, like Hattie McDaniel, had also played a maid-confidante to Mae West. There was frequently a black maid in West's movies, and her job was mainly to admire whatever West's character was wearing or help the plot along by expressing approval of her next move. However, none of them gave the impression that they'd turn down a fortune in order to maintain the privilege of staying by West's side.

"I say: 'Try one. Try a skirt.'"

The Depression could be...depressing. The country decided rather quickly that one thing it needed was a good stiff drink, or three or four. In 1933, Utah provided the last necessary state ratification for repeal of Prohibition, and relatively few Americans were sorry to see it go. A study by *Fortune* in 1937 showed 30 percent of women regretted its demise, but only 15 percent of men. People were also eager for diverting gossip, and one of the most sensational stories of the era involved the newly crowned bachelor king of England, Edward VIII, who announced in 1936 that he was abdicating the throne to marry Wallis Simpson, a 40-year-old twice-divorced American. "I have found it impossible to carry on the heavy burden of responsibility and to discharge my duties of king, as I would wish to do, without the help and support of the woman I love," he said in what was regarded as—depending on your perspective—one of the most romantic or one of the most ridiculous moments in the history of the royal family.

Watching Simpson create an international sex crisis at 40 was something. The British public had many objections. One was her age, although her lover, who was referred to as "the young king," was actually a year her senior. There were persistent rumors that her hold over Edward was due to some sexual secret—perhaps erotic tricks she had learned during a sojourn in China. Whatever it was, most of the public decided they preferred Elizabeth, the plump, cheerful spouse of Edward's brother, who became queen. Wallis, who dieted on a single egg per day whenever she gained the slightest bit of weight, disparagingly referred to Elizabeth as "Cookie." After the abdication, Edward and his wife embarked on a new life as the Duke and Duchess of Windsor. Nothing in their later history suggested the British had lost much in the bargain—for one thing, they spent a lot of time hanging out with Nazi sympathizers—but the duchess gradually did become a fashion icon, with her simple, rather severe style of dress and her super-slender frame. She had her pillows embroidered with the motto "You can never be too rich or too thin."

The rich part was probably true, but given the fact that so many people were worrying about starving to death in the '30s, extreme thinness wasn't all that popular. Fashions tended toward fuller figures—skirts were longer, and shoulders were padded. The change in the ideal of the perfect figure was so dramatic, "one might almost have thought a new anatomical species had come into being," said one commentator. Corsets were back in a less rigid form, and bras came with cup sizes. Perhaps the biggest fashion discovery was pants. Sporty young women had begun playing golf or tennis in them, and the film star Katharine Hepburn wore trousers all over the place: "Any time I hear a man say he prefers a woman in a skirt, I say: 'Try one. Try a skirt.'" But it was hardly a trend that swept the nation. Studio executives tried to confiscate Hepburn's pants and were dissuaded only when she threatened to walk around the lot naked. During World War II, four female pilots who had been grounded by the weather in Georgia were arrested for violating a local law against women wearing slacks on the street at night. It was going to be a slow transition, but these were the first stirrings of a change that would eventually spread so far that even older, full-figured women would feel comfortable wearing pants everywhere from church to the campaign trail.

"THE PITILESS HAND OF TIME"

While the nation may have abandoned its obsession with 19-year-olds, it had most definitely not lost interest in urging older women to look "youthful." And when it came to the beauty industry, the battle was still frequently described in ways that made the first wrinkle sound as traumatic as, say, the first spot of leprosy. "Many women do not realize that day by day the pitiless hand of Time is writing a tragic story on their faces," said a 1930 ad for Dorothy Gray skin products. "First he traces fine little lines at the corners of eyes and mouth. These lines seem harmless enough, but they lead to a cruel sequel. They mark out an easy path for deep, unsightly wrinkles. The ugly wrinkles swiftly follow, to stay and destroy your loveliness." Actress Edna Wallace Hopper, who was in her 60s, urged the readers of women's magazines to purchase Edna Wallace Hopper's Special Restorative Cream. "I've been booked from one theatre to another as 'The One Woman in the World Who Never Grew Old,'" her ads announced. "At a grandmother's age I still enjoy the thrills of youth." Edna claimed she often got come-ons from "boys scarcely above college age." It was, perhaps, the new version of bragging that people mistook you for your daughter.

It's not surprising that women were seduced by the idea of battling time, since some of the arguments for growing old gracefully were depressing in the extreme. Thurman Rice, a physician who published innumerable pamphlets and books on the question, cautioned people who were approaching 40 not to panic, since the woman "who can relax a bit at this time and smile indulgently at the mad struggle for beauty and youth has before her many happy days of comparative quiet and serenity." Married couples, he promised, could have lives "of placid, uneventful domesticity," while unmarried women... well, the unmarried women would probably have to resign themselves "to the prospect of a lonesome and possibly bitter old age."

On the brighter side, the media seemed to be rediscovering the middle-aged market, and Americans of both sexes were reading books like *Life Begins at Forty* and *Who Says Old!* Walter Pitkin, the author of *Life Begins at Forty,* theorized that middle age would be particularly terrific for well-educated women, who spent their thirties getting over the effects of women's colleges, which he seemed to feel included both overcerebration and unattractive dress. Pushing the thought much further, women's magazines went back to running articles celebrating the glories of aging. "Here is a woman of seventy-five who is eagerly interested in life and about to undertake a new business of some scope," offered one. "Another woman of eighty drives herself alone across the continent from Minnesota to California and back every autumn and spring."

Among the women who had been living—and fighting—in the public eye for years, aging in action was a natural theme. "Instead of slowing down, as a woman who is older than she used to be is supposed to do, I seem to be taking on new responsibilities every day in every way," said Mary Church Terrell, the civil rights leader, when she was in her 70s. "I do not feel old. I intend never to grow old." Her friends, Terrell noted, kept telling her to take it easy, but "I am just not built that way. I can walk faster and farther than either one of my daughters without feeling it. And I have greater power of endurance than either one of them has. I can dance as long and as well as I ever did although I get very few chances to do so." The fact that there were few dancing opportunities was a definite source of irritation: "There seems to be sort of a tradition that after a woman reaches a certain age she should not want to trip the light fantastic, and that even if she is anachronistic enough to wish to do such an unseemly thing, she should not be allowed to indulge in this healthful and fascinating exercise." Frustrating as that was, Terrell, a tireless organizer and educator, was not left sitting bored in the cold. At 86 she was still out filing suits against segregated restaurants.

"WHEN I SHOULD UNDERSTAND THAT I AM AN OLD LADY"

During the Depression, Jane Addams experienced another surge of popularity—economic trauma reminded the country of what they had loved about her all along. She received a flood of honorary degrees.

Good Housekeeping gave her a sort of national equivalent of that Best Woman in Chicago award, and in 1931 she was awarded the Nobel Prize. Franklin Roosevelt, the eighth president she had advised, felt that Addams "understands more about the real people of the United States than anybody else does." Addams had supported Herbert Hoover in the 1932 election, remembering the work they had done together on international food relief during World War I. But she happily embraced both FDR and the New Deal, sending Roosevelt telegrams urging him to take various positions or congratulating him on the wisdom of doing what she had already recommended. "They made me feel as if I were still in the frontline trenches," she wrote to her nephew. "Probably one never gets over that feeling, though. I have always wondered when I should understand that I am an old lady."

Perhaps never, since Addams believed the secret to staying young was to be "continually filled with a holy discontent," and her targets only expanded as time went on. She fought against segregated housing and capital punishment, and led a drive to increase public sympathy for unwed mothers and their children. In 1930, Addams celebrated her 70th birthday along with Hull House's 40th anniversary. (They weren't actually the same date, but like Mother Jones, Addams was perfectly happy to adapt her age to the cause at hand.) She no longer ran the settlement house on a day-to-day basis, but she was still an active presence, holding office hours every day so residents and visitors could come and talk. The Depression had sent a new flood of people, seeking help finding jobs, food, clothing, or just a sense of community. Some of the women who had come to work as Hull House residents had been there almost as long as Addams herself—at the anniversary party there were nine veterans of more than 30 years.

Addams was at home, recovering from surgery, when she received word she had won the Nobel Prize. She gave most of the award money to the Women's International League for Peace and Freedom. And she was sadly unable to go to Norway to give her Nobel lecture. She suffered from perpetual bronchitis, and her weight—which was close to 200 pounds despite her small stature—made it difficult for her to get around. But when both political parties held their presidential conventions in Chicago in 1932, she rode at the front of the peace demonstrators who staged a mobile protest march.

She still traveled, with her longtime companion Mary Rozet Smith. Their relationship had begun back in an era when women frequently had intense, lifelong friendships, sometimes sharing the same bed and writing passionate letters when they were apart. By the 1930s, the nation had passed through its Freudian period, and many people presumed their relationship was physical. No one ever really knew, but in 1934 when Smith died of pneumonia, Addams's life pretty much ended as well. "Jane grieved every day after that," wrote her biographer, Louise Knight. Her doctor had banned her from living at Hull House, and she stayed with various friends while continuing to write and pursue her lifelong quests for peace and helping the poor. In 1935, she was hospitalized with a sharp stomach pain that turned out to be advanced cancer. Addams was 74. She told her friend Louise DeKoven Bowen that she was not afraid to die: "I know I'll go on living, and I want to know what it's going to be like." While they were waiting for that last ambulance, Bowen recalled, she went into Addams's room to tell her the driver would not arrive for another hour. "That's all right, for that will give me time to finish the book I'm reading," Addams replied.

Her body lay in state at Hull House, where thousands walked past the coffin and the neighbors stood at tenement windows that looked down on the funeral service. She was buried near her parents and siblings, under a stone that read "Jane Addams of Hull House and the Women's International League for Peace and Freedom."

The Depression gave the nation a new appreciation of the older reformers, who had been fighting for justice and equality for so long. As they died, there was a sense of a passing of the torch. In 1932, Alva Belmont, the battling suffragist socialite, died at 80. At her funeral the casket was draped, at her request, with a banner reading "Failure Is Impossible." Mother Jones, the union leader who had exaggerated her age to shame young men into following in her fierce footsteps, celebrated her 100th birthday on May 1, 1930, when she was really turning 92. It was, she knew, going to be the last hurrah. She was living, mainly bedridden, in the home of friends in Maryland, and with some effort, she walked down the stairs to greet a crowd of birthday visitors, including labor leaders, politicians, and a delegation of 100 unemployed men. "A wonderful power is in the hands of women...but they don't know how to use it," she told the whirring news cameras. "Capitalists sidetrack the women into clubs and make ladies of them. Nobody wants a lady. They want women." It was her last public appearance. She died six months later, and her body went by rail to a cemetery in Illinois, where she was buried near the graves of mine workers who had been killed during a strike. Thousands of mourners greeted the coffin.

There had been an earlier requiem Mass in Washington, where Mary Harris Jones was remembered before a church packed with both dignitaries and working men and women. "Her zeal and earnestness in behalf of the poor will be a pleasant memory long after her body is gone," said the priest. Elliott Gorn, Mother Jones's biographer, noted that those words "made her seem just another charitable old woman, not the fiery organizer who led angry workers in their quest for justice. But he was merely following a trend that reduced the militant warrior to an old saint that hid the angry matriarch of laboring families behind the sweet grandmother."

"THE OPPORTUNITY FOR DOING SOMETHING USEFUL"

Eleanor Roosevelt moved into the White House as a former settlement house worker. She had introduced her fiancé, Franklin, to the world of the immigrant poor, taking him on a visit to a tenement, where he "could not believe human beings lived that way." After they married and he was felled by polio, she enabled him to continue his political career by becoming his "legs"—a mission that was much more to her taste than traditional marital duties. She helped build the organization that allowed him to run for governor of New York, working with labor unions and women's groups, and eventually becoming an official in the Democratic Party herself. Her good friend the journalist Lorena Hickok claimed Eleanor "was better known to politicians around the state than her husband was." It was a role she would carry on through his presidential campaigns and more than a dozen years as First Lady.

There are some people who seem middle-aged even when they're young, and Eleanor was definitely one of them. (Her mother, to Eleanor's great dismay, nicknamed her "Granny.") The lucky ones also never seem to get old, chugging through a kind of energetic maturity forever. The 48-year-old First Lady who moved into 1600 Pennsylvania Avenue in 1933 did not seem much different—or much older—than she was at 30, and it would be the same way when she worked at the United Nations in her 60s. Her energy was prodigious. In the White House, she divided her day into 15-minute meetings, broken by stints of calisthenics, horseback riding, and laps in the White House pool. (She once visited the White House usher's office for a meeting wearing her yellow bathing suit, an encounter the man never quite got over.) Eleanor traveled all over the country as First Lady—she was on the road more than she was in the White House. She visited slums, miners' homes, impoverished farm families, correctional facilities. One day, when FDR asked where his wife was, his secretary replied, "In prison, Mr. President."

"I'm not surprised, but what for?" retorted FDR.

When the "bonus army" of unemployed workers marched on Washington, Eleanor led them in a round of old war songs. She was at the head of the first presidential fact-finding tour of Puerto Rico. She wrote a daily newspaper column and, with the help of two assistants, personally answered up to 400 letters a day. The pleas for help were unbearable. Many desperate women wrote to the First Lady begging for secondhand clothes. "I can sew and would only be too glad to take two old things and put them together and make a new one," wrote a woman in Philadelphia. "I don't care what it is, any thing from an old bunch of stockings to an old Sport Suit or an old afternoon dress, in fact. Anything a lady of 40 years of age can wear."

Eleanor Roosevelt was the ultimate embodiment of the Lydia Maria Child theory of successfully growing old: "If any one were to ask me what I want most out of life, I would say—the opportunity for doing something useful, for in no other way, I am convinced, can true happiness be obtained." Her home life never seemed to offer her real satisfaction; the Roosevelts' marriage had devolved into a working partnership after Eleanor discovered Franklin was having an affair with her social secretary. She raised five children she loved, but she was never totally comfortable in a maternal role—Franklin's overbearing mother kept telling her grandchildren that Eleanor will "only bore you. I am more your mother than your mother is." But on the road, the First Lady was in her element, speaking and organizing and constantly taking controversial stands. She criticized the spending-cut strategy of the early New Deal and was far ahead of her husband on racial equality, inviting black leaders to confer at the White House. She was denounced as a "Jezebel" by the Woman's Christian Temperance Union for condoning drinking in moderation. She was hardly a fashion trendsetter—it took her years in the public spotlight before she gave up wearing her black hairnet. Never having been a beauty, Eleanor learned to be comfortable with her looks. "My dear, if you haven't any chin and your front teeth stick out, it's going to show on the camera plate," she said with cheerful resignation. The administration's critics constantly made sport of her appearance, but she managed to ignore it. "Every woman in public life needs to develop skin as tough as rhinoceros hide," she said.

Eleanor loved being on the move, preferably by herself. She was disappointed when Franklin wanted her to ride from New York to his presidential inauguration on a private train full of friends and future cabinet members. She had planned to take the family dogs to Washington in her blue Buick convertible. As First Lady, she refused to allow a Secret Service agent to be with her every time she went for a drive. In a compromise with the White House security officials, she agreed to travel with a revolver, which she practiced shooting until she was fairly proficient. She was stunningly approachable. Once in 1933, while she was sitting in her car at a gas station, a young homeless man approached Eleanor begging for money. She gave him 10 dollars—and an invitation to call at her New York residence. The man followed through but was sent away by a guard. When the First Lady heard what had happened, she went out and found him lingering at the corner. She invited him for dinner, then later found him a job with the Civilian Conservation Corps, where he rose in the ranks, all the while corresponding with Eleanor, who eventually became godmother to his daughter. When the future civil rights leader Pauli Murray, then a student at Howard University law school, wrote criticizing the president for his failure to do more for minorities, Eleanor herself wrote back, triggering a correspondence, an invitation to come and "talk things over," and eventually a lifelong friendship.

"HOW FINE IT IS TO PLAY THE GAME TOGETHER"

The New Deal brought a flood of women to Washington, and for the first time they were working at key points throughout the government. Frances Perkins took over the Labor Department and became—this is ironic, but remember we're talking cabinet titles here—the first female secretary. Carrie Chapman Catt, then in her 80s, proudly wrote to Eleanor that she had always had a "collection of statesmen" hanging on her wall but that now "I have been obliged to start a new collection and that is one of stateswomen."

It was quite a group. Barbara Armstrong, the first woman law professor in America, was the architect of the administration's historic Social Security program. Nellie Tayloe Ross, the former governor of Wyoming, became director of the U.S. Mint—a job she kept until 1952. Mary McLeod Bethune, an inexhaustible educator and civil rights leader, was head of Negro Affairs at the National Youth Administration. Bethune was with Eleanor at a legendary gathering of New Dealers in Birmingham, where the infamous sheriff Bull Connor had announced that the audience would have to be segregated. When blacks and whites were seated on their opposite sides, the First Lady came in with a folding chair and sat in the middle of the aisle. After the enthusiastic crowd finally finished applauding, one of the white organizers called on Bethune, referring to her as just "Mary."

"My name is Mrs. Bethune," she replied.

It seemed, in retrospect, to be a small thing, said Virginia Foster Durr, a white civil rights leader who was at the meeting, "but that was a big dividing line. A Negro woman in Birmingham, Alabama, called Mrs. Bethune at a public meeting."

Virtually all the new Washington women were old enough to have grown up in the Progressive Era, fighting for voting rights. "The friendships that were formed among women who were in that suffrage movement have been the most lasting and enduring friendships—solid, substantial, loyal—that I have ever seen anywhere," wrote Frances Perkins, who joined the administration at 52. They had worked in settlement houses, led clubs that fought for urban sanitation, clean politics, and consumer rights. They had been mentored by people like Jane Addams and had supported each other through the unsympathetic 1920s. Now they were finally addressing many of the issues the suffragists had believed would be taken care of when women got the vote. In 1938, Rep. Mary Norton shepherded a bill through the House that abolished child labor and created the first minimum wage—25 cents an hour. It was, she said, the high point of her public life.

The New Deal women tended to hang out together, and there were times when they really needed that sense of having one another's backs. When Perkins arrived at her desk on the first day of work in the Labor Department, she discovered her resentful predecessor had filled it with roaches. (She was hardly a novice when it came to dealing with male resistance—she always wore black dresses, believing that men responded best to women who reminded them of their mothers.) Perkins was one of the central figures of the administration and one of the closest to the Roosevelts. She had graduated from Mount Holyoke, worked at Hull House and at the New York City Consumers' League. She was having tea with friends in 1911 when the Triangle Shirtwaist Factory, a sweatshop crowded with overworked, underpaid young immigrant girls, caught fire. Perkins was part of the horrified crowd who saw workers trapped in the upper floors of the building leap out of windows to escape the flames and fall to their deaths on the sidewalk. She became executive secretary of a citizens committee formed to investigate the disaster, and eventually one of the nation's experts on worker safety issues. Governor Roosevelt named her industrial commissioner and offered her the Labor post when he became president. Perkins, whose husband suffered from psychiatric problems, was the support of her family, and she was reluctant to move to Washington to take the cabinet job. Molly Dewson, the Democratic Party official who was serving as the pipeline bringing women into the administration, refused to listen to her reservations. "Don't be such a baby, Frances," she told her friend. "You do the right thing. I'll murder you if you don't."

Dewson, who had graduated from Wellesley, served in the Red

Cross in France during World War I and had been head of the New York City Consumers' League. Eleanor Roosevelt brought her into Democratic politics in 1928, and they worked hand in hand to move women into FDR's administration. "How fine it is to play the game together all these years, isn't it?" Perkins wrote after a particularly fruitful luncheon. Dewson recalled that whenever she wanted serious support on an important subject, "Mrs. Roosevelt gave me the opportunity to sit by the President at dinner and the matter was settled before we finished our soup."

"OH NO; TERRIBLE, THE DOLE!"

Besides the roaches, Frances Perkins found her new desk in the Labor Department was stuffed with more than 2,000 "'plans' for curing the Depression." Most of them were clearly impossible, but she was taken by several suggestions that involved giving the elderly flat payments every month. At the time, there was virtually no such thing as a private pension. Some states had old-age assistance programs, but the highest gave the equivalent of about $550 a month in today's money. In most states, they got little or nothing at all. When Perkins was commissioner of labor in New York State, her friends had told her about the British system for old-age and unemployment insurance. People who had been to England "thought it was such a nice idea that Lady Jones' maid had a little book, and when Lady Jones paid her, she wrote in the maid's little book and that was going to take care of the maid when she was old — when she was 70 years old or 65 years old, she could collect something. Now wasn't that a good idea? Thousands of people thought it was a fine idea." Perkins got Governor Roosevelt to send her to England to study the system, and although she was horrified by the amount of government paperwork it required, she became a convert to the concept we now know as Social Security.

It was quite a battle. Americans always had been adamantly attached to the idea that people were responsible for their old age; if they failed to save enough to prepare on their own, relatives should shoulder the burden. And giving money to the elderly was tied up in the public mind with aid to the unemployed, which was even less popular. When the subject of unemployment insurance came up, Perkins recalled, business-men would say, "Oh no; terrible, the dole!" Then she "would mention old-age insurance to them to make it easier, but they would say, 'No, that's the dole too. I don't believe in the dole.'"

The country was still politically conservative in 1932, so the Democratic platform on which Franklin Roosevelt ran for president simply called for a study on the causes of unemployment—"as though anybody hadn't studied them in years," Perkins sniped. Once elected, FDR created a Committee on Economic Security, with Perkins at its head. The committee was supposed to study the possibility of a national program for the unemployed, the aged, and health care, but—in a moment that would presage the rest of twentieth-century politics—it quickly dropped the health care part as too complicated. And work on the unemployed and the aged was hardly treated as an administration centerpiece. Just to prepare its proposal, the committee had to borrow actuaries from the Lions Club and a friendly life insurance company.

Long term, the committee decided, the answer to the problems of the elderly should be a program that people paid into while they were working. That way, their benefits would "come to the worker as a right" and not be restricted to the very needy. Thus was born the Social Security system, which was approved by Congress in 1935. It was desperately underfunded. Even though it wasn't established under the Department of Labor, Perkins said, her staff "had to carry it the way you carry a dependent child." She loaned workers to the Social Security Administration, including the critical statisticians, and put them up in her Labor offices, giving the top official a "large, handsome, red-upholstered, high-back chair...so that he could look like a king." While the chair came out of her own office, Perkins admitted it was also "somewhat uncomfortable."

"THE TASK MAY WELL PROVE INSUPERABLE"

At the time Social Security was first passed into law, somewhere between a third and half of Americans 65 and over were dependent on their family or friends for their support. The new program was slow to start, and when it did, monthly benefits began at a princely $22.60 — well under $400 in today's money.

The world into which Social Security was born presumed men were the family breadwinners and that benefits would normally be based on a husband's income. Married couples did get more than single people — the government acknowledged that the wife had to eat — but if the wife worked, chances were it wouldn't be reflected in their check. And if a nonworking wife lost her husband before age 60, she got nothing. Ditto for many who were divorced. The country would spend the next decades wrestling with the program's deficits. One of the biggest was everyone it left out, including domestics and agricultural workers. That was a lot of people, particularly minority women. Mary Anderson of the U.S. Women's Bureau found herself seated next to Mrs. Roosevelt at a lunch and was delighted to hear the First Lady nagging her to do something about the nation's retired cleaning women, nannies, cooks, and laundresses. But nothing happened. The argument was that it was too complicated to try to cover people outside the normal work-for-a-company system. "The task may well prove insuperable," said Secretary of the Treasury Henry Morgenthau Jr. It was ironic, given Perkins's initial introduction to the program through Lady Jones's maid. Many people thought Congress wanted to exclude domestics simply because they tended to be non-white. Years later, Perkins would say that the administration gave up on universal coverage and gradually "let them take out one group after another; no objections, just so we got the basis of the bill." The Social Security Act was a huge compromise, but it was still a start for what would become one of the largest and most popular parts of American government. And when it passed, Frances Perkins threw a party.

"IT WASN'T THAT I EXPECTED ANYTHING, MIND YOU"

Ida May Fuller, a retired secretary for a Vermont law firm, was just passing by a government office when she decided to drop in and ask about that new Social Security business. Fuller, who was known as "Aunt Ida" in her neighborhood, was a Republican, and she had never been all that enthusiastic about government programs. But she had noticed, while she was working, that a deduction had started coming out of her paycheck.

"It wasn't that I expected anything, mind you," she said later.

The people in the office urged her to fill out some forms. On January 31, 1940, she received a check for $22.54—the first Social Security benefit ever.

10. The War

"BUILDING A PLANE TO BOMB HITLER"

In 1943, World War II was under way, and *Life* magazine introduced the nation to Helen Dortch Longstreet, a worker at a bomber plant near Atlanta who was a riveter like Rosie in the celebrated song. ("She's making history, working for victory...") Longstreet had the additional distinction of being 80 years old. "I am going to assist in building a plane to bomb Hitler... to the Judgment Seat of God," she told the interviewer.

Longstreet was part of a very wide change in Americans' attitude toward older working women. As usual, it was the economy that dictated a new way of thinking. World War II swept nearly 16 million American men, not to mention 350,000 women, into the military. The home front—particularly the defense industry—was desperate for workers. People who had lost their jobs during the Depression were snapped up. School boards that had a policy of firing teachers who got married were suddenly writing to their former employees, asking them to return. Four million women entered the workforce during the early years of the war, but by 1943, there were virtually no more unmarried women to hire, and married women were turning out to be hard to recruit—even when government propaganda offices, going for the hard sell, warned them that a "soldier may die unless you man this idle machine." Eleanor Roosevelt urged the government to create an industrial draft for reluctant housewives, but her husband—who was no fan of the draft even for men—preferred cajolery.

"Women, women, women were needed," the *Christian Science Monitor* reported in a story about a massive recruitment drive for New Jersey's industrial plants, which boasted having corralled new hires up to the age of 79. "As to how old they were [and] what experience they had, the 1,000-odd employers behind the drive seemed not at all concerned. It was almost as if someone had promised 'no questions will be asked.'"

Of the 6 million women who went to work at a paying job during the war, more than 1.5 million were between 45 and 65. Another quarter of a million were over 65.

"how 'Grandma' received word of her promotion"

Do you remember Jeannette Rankin, the Montana Republican who was elected to Congress even before the nation had universal suffrage, and then promptly lost her seat when she refused to vote for America's entry into World War I? In 1941, Rankin, 60, had finally made her way back into the House of Representatives after spending more than two decades working for peace, consumer rights, and other causes that had been on the original suffragist agenda. She was less than a year into her term on December 7 when Japanese planes attacked the U.S. naval base at Pearl Harbor. Her life went into an awful rewind. On December 8, Congress voted to declare war on Japan. Rankin couldn't get a word in during the debate—the Speaker of the House, knowing her pacifist history, refused to recognize her. When they got to her name in the roll call, she finally had her chance. "As a woman I can't go to war, and I refuse to send anyone else," she said, casting the single "No" vote. As she left the House, an angry mob went after her, forcing Rankin to lock herself in a phone booth until the Capitol police could escort her to her office, where she again had to barricade herself in. Everybody disagreed with her. "Montana is 100 percent against you," her brother cabled helpfully. Papers issued angry editorials. In one, Kansas's *Emporia Gazette,* the famous editor William Allen White denounced Rankin's vote, then added, "But, Lord, it was a brave thing." It was also the end—again—of Rankin's congressional career.

There were eight other women in Congress. The 66-year-old Mary Norton of New Jersey came to the House accompanied by her doctor, having dragged herself out of a sickbed to vote for the war, despite a fever of 103 degrees. "There are so many things I'd like to do," she said during the mobilization. "How I wish I were about 20 years younger. But never mind—where there's a will there's a way and I'll find it." Edith Nourse Rogers, a Republican from Massachusetts, had been one of the first House members to denounce Nazism while most of her colleagues were still pushing neutrality. One of Rogers's top priorities was to improve the status of women who volunteered to serve overseas. She had worked in France during World War I, when women, except for nurses, were treated as contract employees who had to get their own housing, buy their own food, and work with no legal or medical protection from the government. She was determined that this time would be different, and she pressed for an official Women's Army Auxiliary Corps, later shortened to WAC.

Given the demands of the war, the military acknowledged it was going to need women in noncombatant roles to free up men for the front lines. But the official vision of their role was less than stirring. Assistant Chief of Staff John Hildring noted that "we have found difficulty in getting enlisted men to perform tedious duties anywhere nearly as well as women will do it." The generals did not envision women as part of the actual team, certainly not a team that had rights and benefits and possible military careers. In fact, a prime feature of the generals' view of female recruits was their disappearance as soon as the hostilities ended. "The WAC who shares your Army life will make a better postwar wife," the War Department advised.

Rogers had gotten a watered-down version of her WAC bill passed before the Pearl Harbor attack, despite virulent opposition from some of her colleagues, who hated the whole idea of women in the military. "Who will then do the cooking, the washing, the mending, the humble homey tasks to which every woman has devoted herself; who will rear and nurture the children?" demanded one congressman. But in the end, the bill passed easily, and in 1943, Congress finally voted to make the WACs part of the regular army. Applications poured in from women aged 21 to 45 who met the government's basic requirements. As in World War I, the older volunteers often said they were taking the place of family members who couldn't enlist or died in the early fighting. Esther McGowin Blake was a widow with two grown sons when the elder, Lt. Julius Blake, was reported missing in action. She joined the WACs and served in Alaska in an air force division. Later, in 1948, she signed up for the air force itself, on the "first minute of the first hour" when it became legal for women to enlist.

The military service, like the civilian world, was willing to drop all its age restrictions if the crisis was severe enough. Ruth Cheney Streeter, 47, was turned down by the Women Airforce Service Pilots as "too old." But the marine corps was won over by the fact that she had a commercial flying license. Lorena Hermance just made the 45-year-old limit when she officially became the first grandmother to join the WACs. With 20 years' experience in telephone communications, she expected to be assigned to work near her family in California. "Most of the officers are under thirty and have no home ties," she wrote in her diary, noting that she had promised her husband she would not volunteer to go overseas. "Mine may not be the most exciting corner of this war," she admitted philosophically, "but there is obviously a great deal to be done here so I shall stay at home and do it."

Hermance did apply for Officer Candidate School, although she seemed reluctant to admit she had ambition. "I'm not sure I want to be an officer but I'm darned if I want it on my record that I'm too stupid to be one," she wrote in the diary, which she was keeping for her grand-daughter. She did well in school, then discovered that as a newly minted officer, she was being transferred—overseas. "Out of the whole regi-mental group, in which I was the only one who did not request overseas duty—guess who is going overseas...I received my orders today," she wrote. "The old involuntary volunteer, Lorena. I simply don't know whether to laugh or cry." She was sent first to General Dwight Eisen-hower's headquarters in Algiers and later to the Italian campaign, where she worked to keep communications running—the only woman in a group of 50 British and American officers. One day she was startled when her superior officer called and asked, "How are you, Captain?" It was, she wrote, "how 'Grandma' received word of her promotion."

The idea of sending a grandmother into a combat zone—and the "Grandma" designation continued to obsess the nation—should have been inconceivable. But the public has always had a handy ability to blank out inconvenient realities. Red Cross volunteers, who drove their "clubmobiles" into the war in Europe and North Africa to make dough-nuts and serve coffee to the troops on the front lines, were almost always referred to as "girls" although a number were in their 30s when they entered the war. More than 50 died in service. Eleanor Stevenson, who was 41 when she arrived in Italy, recalled working under fire to deliver thousands of hot soups and coffees during a heavy storm. At one point, she wrote later, "things got so bad the boys insisted that we Red Cross girls get into the clubmobile and go six miles down the road out of shell range, where we sat until daylight.... When we set up housekeeping again, it was pouring, and there were three or four inches of soupy, watery mud in the tent housing the doughnut machine." During the Battle of Mignano, the clubmobile came under direct fire that took out both the women's latrine and their beloved doughnut machine.

The military didn't go out of its way to tell the folks at home that it had women in their 40s risking their lives to serve coffee to the soldiers. But some of the worst things that happened to American women overseas were stories everyone knew. They involved the nurses. When American bases in the Philippines were overrun by the Japanese early in the war, army and navy nurses set up field hospitals for the retreating forces, ministering to soldiers and civilians on the floor of the jungle itself, fighting off rats, snakes, and swarms of malaria-bearing mosquitos. Their work became legendary via popular, if somewhat overwrought, movies. (Veronica Lake saved her comrades by walking up to a Japanese patrol with a grenade tucked in her bra; Donna Reed served on Corregidor Island wearing military overalls and pearls.)

The real nurses were a bit less glamorous. Josie Nesbit, a 47-year-old lieutenant who boasted a size 13 shoe, provided maternal sympathy to the women who worked in a huge Japanese prisoner of war camp and became known as the Angels of Bataan. They remained prisoners until the end of the hostilities, tending their patients every day, despite lack of food and horrific surroundings. "Admittedly, I tired more quickly and much of the stamina I had in the past may have been somewhere lacking," Nesbit recalled, but "there was absolutely no time for self-pity."

Captain Maude Davison, 57 by the end of the Battle of Bataan, was in some ways Nesbit's opposite. A short, stocky woman who wore her white hair tied back in a bun, Davison was nicknamed "Ma" although she was not in the least bit motherly. She insisted on strict military discipline, and while the rigorous order she enforced might not always have won hearts, many believed it gave her nurses the sense of structure they needed to survive. By the end of the war, when the prisoners were subsisting on a 700-calorie daily ration, Davison's weight had dropped from 156 pounds to 80. But despite massive fatalities at the camp, all her nurses survived. "With meager equipment, extremely short of help, and under the most trying circumstances, every nurse without exception conducted herself in a manner which solicited the highest praise," reported an aide-de-camp to General Douglas MacArthur, who attributed their "sterling conduct" to Davison's leadership. After the war, Davison's admirers, including MacArthur, recommended that she be awarded the Distinguished Service Medal, but the officials in charge of making the decision decreed that "chief nurse of a field command is not considered a position of great responsibility in the Distinguished Service Medal sense" and gave Davison a lesser Legion of Merit award instead.

"Granny has gone to work in the war plant"

On the home front, almost half of all American women were employed, including a record number over 35. They tended to be more reliable than younger women, who sometimes racked up terrible absentee records trying to deal with the scarcity of childcare. "Granny has gone to work in the war plant," enthused the *Evansville Courier and Press*, in a story about an Indiana engineering company's chapter of—yes!—the War Working Grandmothers of America. *Fortune* printed a photo of Ah Yoke Gee, a middle-aged welder in a California shipyard, with the caption "Chinese Woman: She hasn't missed a day's work in two years." The story celebrating Gee's patriotism didn't mention that she was unable to vote since American law stripped native-born women of their citizenship if they married Chinese immigrants.

The War Department—whose enthusiasm over grandmothers wielding power tools knew no bounds—wanted to publicize older women workers to lure more of them into jobs. But it also wanted to prod the employers, whose need for help didn't always overcome their biases against older workers. For a while, as one historian noted wryly, employers seemed determined to find the "mythical thirty-year-old woman whose children were grown." A forty-two-year-old lawyer went to her local employment office and "was told that if I were still in my twenties and a good stenographer I could be used, but that no employer wanted 'old women past thirty.'"

With employers resisting while the government demanded that older women step up, the country was definitely having a problem with mixed signals. Readers of *Independent Woman,* a publication of the National Federation of Business and Professional Women's Clubs, shared stories about simultaneously being courted and snubbed. "I cannot quite understand the whole situation," wrote one correspondent who said she had been recruited by the WAVES (Women Accepted for Volunteer Emergency Service) for a navy procurement job because of her particular qualifications, then was told she had flunked the physical: "A health record of being absent less than two weeks in twenty-five years of continuous service could not compensate for corrected eyesight and corrective dentures." Not everyone was sympathetic. Another letter to *Independent Woman,* from "a woman in the forties who has been working in Washington since June, 1942," complained that her contemporaries were too picky and rigid. The middle-aged woman whose story had started the dialogue, she noted, resisted one job offer because the government agency refused to give her time to find a place to live before beginning work. A newly minted college graduate, the writer contended, would have bunked with friends while she enjoyed "the weird and wonderful experiences incident to getting located."

As workers got increasingly scarce, age discrimination grew less tolerable. A Connecticut woman, Louise Fillebrown, who had tried to sign up for defense work after Pearl Harbor, found "this wasn't so easy.... The specter of age reared its ugly head whenever I struck out in the direction of an employment office." But as time went on, she noticed the increasingly prominent WOMEN WANTED ads in the newspapers, tried again, and found a job easily. "The age limit rose from forty to forty-five, forty-five to fifty; and then, in the more congested factory districts it disappeared altogether." Fillebrown had a great time doing factory work. "Near me worked a gray-haired mother—riveting away to protect a sailor son. Further on was a mother-and-daughter team making planes by day and sleeping together in a single bed by night." The women had a nice home 40 miles away, but in a world of gas rationing, commuting was impossible.

The end of bias didn't apply to black women, no matter what their age. At the peak of the labor shortage, a United Auto Workers survey of several hundred factories found only 74 open to hiring African Americans. President Roosevelt found the situation appalling. "In some communities employers dislike to hire women. In others they are reluctant to hire Negroes. We can no longer afford to indulge in such prejudice," he said. But even if African American women were last in line, many eventually did get jobs that had a double payoff: patriotic pride plus a considerable salary jump. More and more domestic workers found they were able to leave behind the world of laundry and housecleaning. In Los Angeles before the war, over half of the non-white women who worked were in domestic service. But that figure dropped to 15 percent once other options opened up. The change was, of course, much to the dismay of the women's former employers, who found it impossible to "get help." In the South, there were rumors of "Eleanor Clubs," secret groups that encouraged servants to demand higher pay and even — heaven forbid — the right to sit down at the table and share the meals they prepared for their employers. Some white Southern housewives were convinced club members were hanging around the stores gloating while they watched their former employers go through the humiliation of shopping for their own groceries.

"THE IDEAL WOMAN CLERK"

The country was staring at a tremendous shortage of women working at the bottom — stores couldn't find clerks and restaurants had no waitresses. While the War Department was begging housewives to go to work in the defense industry, the director of the United States Employment Service urged those who didn't feel they could become riveters to "free hardier men and women for essential war jobs by taking full or part time work in their own neighborhoods, in bakeries, drug stores, laundries, restaurants and stores." Members of the National Association of Retail Grocers told a reporter at their annual meeting that they had decided "the ideal woman clerk...is a matron of 30 or more, who has had experience in planning meals for her own family and who takes a keen interest in nutritional values of various foods." The grocers claimed they had been dying to hire such women for ages but had been constrained until the war by public opinion.

Secretary of Labor Frances Perkins told a luncheon for trade unions in 1942 that employer prejudice against older women was "breaking down." But those open-minded bosses were not necessarily running an assembly line. "The woman over 50...will doubtless be surprised to find she is wanted, not to work in war plants, but to be dishwasher in a local restaurant or factory," reported the *New York Times*. That may not have been welcome news for any 50-year-olds who needed a healthy paycheck, but the media had its marching orders—the war effort needed those dishwashers and waitresses. It might be rather painful to see women of 60 or 70 toting heavy trays in restaurants, *Woman's Home Companion* noted cheerfully, "until you see the pride in their bright eyes."

Everybody was expected to do something. On radio, the soap opera heroines all joined in the war effort, running canteens at home and battling Nazis...everywhere. Helen Trent, still 35, fell off a cliff while trying to rescue a truck full of wartime supplies but lived to fight another day. Ma Perkins's son was killed in combat, a plot development that caused an outcry among listeners who felt the public didn't want to be reminded that their own children might face a similar fate overseas. A number of other characters were injured, and soap operas being what they were, their wounds frequently came with amnesia. The husband of the heroine of *Rosemary* returned from overseas a total mental blank. When he recovered, he recalled having married another woman and fathered a child with her.

Nonfictional women had plenty of opportunities to volunteer, as anything from nurse's aides to air-raid wardens to farmers. More than 1.5 million women joined the Women's Land Army, which helped keep American farms going when many of the regular agricultural workers were in the military. The *New York Times* reported on Mary Carpenter, a 47-year-old New York housewife, who reasoned, "My husband works at night and sleeps all day. My son's away. I might as well be working on a farm." It wasn't perhaps the most stirring endorsement in war propaganda, but the *Times* did manage to mention that the recruits—who worked for extremely modest salaries — had a uniform that was "not only practical but attractive."

Even when they were keeping house, women were reminded they had a war to win. The author of *Thrifty Cooking for Wartime* compared them to generals "united in one great army, for one noble purpose — VICTORY. Just as necessary as shouldering a rifle is the shouldering of our responsibilities at home." Everyday items from sugar to gasoline were rationed, and the government urged its kitchen generals to regard rationing as both a blow against the enemy and a dieting tool. "Mrs. America," the target of so many war-effort advertisements, was always married, middle-class, white, and 30 to 50 years old, with children who were in school or grown. She had a lot to do, from working in defense plants to looking for food with her ration card. But the ads never suggested that American men who were not serving in the military attempt to shoulder a little of the housework.

For a while, the government threatened to limit the consumption of rubber by banning the manufacture of girdles. Untiring pamphleteers suggested that women "grow their own muscle girdles by exercising," but eventually this turned out to be one rationing war the authorities couldn't win. "Uncle Sam certainly does not want American women to wear garments that would menace their health or impair their efficiency, especially during wartime when every ounce of energy and effort is needed," protested *Hygeia*, in an article titled "Fitting the Feminine Form." The controversy was a marker in the history of foundation garments, which had gone from instruments of torture to relatively comfortable elastic underwear. Eventually the government would promote wearing them as a way for defense workers to avoid fatigue.

"I MARVELED AT HER HARDIHOOD"

Eleanor Roosevelt experienced the war on every conceivable level short of grabbing a machine gun and heading for the front lines. She worried about her four sons, who were all in the military service. She unsuccessfully pressed her husband to accept more Jewish refugees. She spoke out on behalf of African Americans, who were being discriminated against in both the military and the war industries. When the overcrowding, housing shortages, and conflicts over hiring and promotion started race riots, a letter printed in a paper in Jackson, Mississippi, announced: "It is blood on your hands, Mrs. Roosevelt." Eleanor once asked the president, who was struggling to wring votes out of the Southern Democrats in Congress, if he minded her speaking out. "No, certainly not. You can say anything you want," Franklin replied. "I can always say: 'Well, that is my wife. I can't do anything with her.'" She visited the troops fighting in the Pacific, traveling alone to the front, but worried that if the soldiers were told a female celebrity was coming, they'd expect a movie star and be disappointed. But by all reports, the men were thrilled. Admiral Halsey, commander of the Pacific Fleet, had not loved the idea of a visit from the First Lady, but he was won over. "I marveled at her hardihood, both physical and mental," he reported. When Eleanor visited the wounded, some of them terribly injured, Halsey said the expressions on their faces as she leaned over them was "a sight I will never forget. She alone accomplished more good than any other person who passed through my area."

Republican critics claimed she was wasting taxpayer money on "junkets."

Half of the American public adored her, according to a Gallup poll, and about 40 percent felt fervently that she ought to stay home and behave like a proper wife. She was working inhuman hours, always on the move, always stopping to speak to whatever soldiers, farmers, housewives, or defense workers she thought would be buoyed by a brief conversation. She was possibly having the most extraordinary middle age of any woman in American history. "I'd never have believed it possible for a woman to develop after fifty as you had in the last six years," her friend Lorena Hickok wrote to her after FDR's 1940 reelection, which had begun with a rancorous nominating convention that was calmed and moved by the First Lady's address. "This is no ordinary time," she told the crowd, "no time for weighing anything except what we can best do for the country as a whole."

Eleanor had made thousands of friends. But she was always seeking that one, ever-elusive relationship with someone for whom she would be the most singular, beloved person in the world. At one point it seemed that she might have found it with a young leftist named Joseph Lash.

They met on a train to Washington in 1939. Lash, 29, had been summoned to testify before the House Un-American Activities Committee in his capacity as an officer in the Student League for International Democracy. (In the long tradition of the Left, even though Lash was nearly 30 he counted himself as a student for political purposes.) Eleanor took a shine to Lash and the friends he was traveling with. The next day, she joined the audience in the committee room to show her support.

"When I was testifying, Mrs. Roosevelt appeared and the hearings weren't finished and we were supposed to come back the next day," Lash recalled. "She said, 'I can take six of you.' So she scooped us into her limousine. And lo and behold we were having dinner with the President. And that night we spent at the White House and the next morning she came to the hearings again. The hearing room came alive. Everyone was on their toes." Taking young people under her wing and inviting them to dine at the White House was standard operating procedure for Eleanor, but her relationship with Lash was, by any measure, unusual. She invited him to spend time with her at Val-Kill, the cottage at Hyde Park Franklin had built to give his wife a little space when his mother was in residence at the main house. (Under Eleanor's ministrations, the "cottage" not only became warm and comfortable; it grew to twenty rooms.) The two of them swam, hiked, and talked into the night on the front porch. Lash was a melancholic, insecure young man, and later, looking back, he thought that his unhappiness "reminded her of her own when she was young." It was a particularly lonely point in her life. The president was otherwise engaged, her children were grown, and Lorena Hickok, the well-known reporter who became a dear personal friend, had begun to move on. "She had a compelling need to have people who were close, who in a sense were hers and upon whom she could lavish help, attention, tenderness. Without such friends she feared she would dry up and die," Lash wrote later.

Eleanor's relationships with both Lash and Hickok were so intense that people naturally speculated about whether there was a sexual side. Hickok, who was definitely a lesbian, was 39 when she first met Eleanor, in 1932, and they shared letters that certainly sounded romantic. ("Hick darling, I want to put my arms around you . . . to hold you close.") But they were of a generation of women who wrote love letters to their female friends as a matter of course and no one ever knew for sure. During the war, when Lash was still single and serving in the military, he and Eleanor met on occasion at hotels, where they spent most of the time talking in her room. "Separation between people who love each other makes the reunion always like a new discovery. You forget how much you love certain movements of the hands or the glance in the person's eyes or how nice it is to sit in the same room & look at their back!" she wrote him.

Later, Lash's wife, Trude, said she was sure the relationship had been platonic: "Joe had a room next to hers and came into her room. He was very tired. He had not slept all night. And she said, 'Why don't you lie down, Joe,' and sat on the bed next to him and talked with him. And I'm sure that was all." Unfortunately, Lash was under surveillance by the ever-eager Army Counter Intelligence Corps, which was suspicious of his leftist past, and agents bugged Eleanor's hotel room. A hotel worker told the First Lady what was up, and Eleanor—who apparently saw nothing improper about her behavior—complained to the president's staff. FDR was outraged, and the intelligence operations were overhauled. And although no one ever was sure whether it was a direct reaction to the incident or not, Lash was shipped overseas. After the war, Eleanor would continue her friendship with Lash and his new wife, for whom she actually helped play matchmaker. She wrote thanking them for letting her "share your evening after the wedding," adding "I am very grateful and love you both very much." But she never did seem to find that one elusive person for whom she would always be first. And as the war neared a close, she also lost her role as First Lady.

11. The 1950s

"WITHOUT MY HUSBAND'S ADVICE AND GUIDANCE I FEEL VERY INADEQUATE"

On April 12 of 1945, Eleanor Roosevelt was attending one of the many events that filled her life when she got a call summoning her back to the White House. She intuited the crisis that was coming. Nevertheless, before leaving she returned to the charity musicale in progress, waited until the next break in the entertainment, and apologized for "leaving before this delightful concert is finished." Then she sat in the car "with clenched hands all the way" until she arrived home and was informed that Franklin had died.

Widowhood is a common fate—at the time President Roosevelt died, most women were widows by the age of 70, as were more than a quarter of those 55 to 64. But that didn't make it any less traumatic—both because of the personal loss and because a wife's identity was generally wrapped up in her marriage. Even though she was one of the most famous people in the world, Eleanor was no exception. "I shall hope to do what I can to be useful, although without my husband's advice and guidance I feel very inadequate," she wrote to a diplomat who sent his condolences. Without Franklin she was no longer First Lady. She no longer had her role, or her White House staff, or even her White House home. She also, of course, no longer had her husband of 40 years, who, despite their sexual separation, had been a beloved partner. For a further heartbreak, Eleanor had to deal with the discovery that he had not been alone when he died. Lucy Mercer Rutherfurd, whose affair with Franklin had crushed Eleanor in 1918, had been there, too. And the visit, along with many others in recent years, had been arranged by their daughter, Anna, who believed that Lucy's companionship relaxed and soothed her ailing, exhausted father.

Eleanor returned to Hyde Park, which was filled with the Roosevelts' Washington possessions. Franklin's dog Fala was there waiting, and he became her constant companion. But the house was—at least by

Eleanor's standards — short on people. For a while, she felt at sea. Then in December the new president, Harry Truman, asked her to go to London as a delegate to the United Nations, the new world body Franklin had struggled so hard to establish. At first, she was mainly there as The Widow. Eleanor herself volunteered that she had no particular qualifications for the job. She had to prove herself, and as the only woman in the American delegation, she was determined to be better prepared than any of the men. She pored over State Department papers, reading everything that could possibly be of use, putting in 18 to 20 hours a day. If she failed, she felt, there would "never be another woman on the delegation."

Overachievement worked out wonderfully, and the delegates elected her to chair the committee drafting a Universal Declaration of Human Rights. It began, originally, with the idea that "all men are born free and equal," but the opening was amended to declare the equality of "all human beings." Despite foot dragging from the Soviet Union, the Declaration was adopted in 1948. Eleanor Roosevelt had embarked, at 64, on another incarnation.

The end of the war had brought changes for almost everyone. Soldiers came home; families were reunited. Prisoners of war were released. Maude Davison — the leader of the nurses known as the Angels of Bataan — was 59 when her internment camp was liberated in February of 1945, and her health was about what you would expect from a woman who had been working on a starvation diet. After receiving a medical discharge in 1946, she married an old friend, Charles Jackson, a widower. Their life together was quiet — and rather short. Davison passed away 10 years later, the first of the nurse-POWs to die. She had never gotten that Distinguished Service Medal.

Davison's fellow POW Josie Nesbit retired from the service in 1946 as a major. She married another internee, William Davis, and sent birthday and Christmas cards to the women she had served with for almost 50 years, until she died just 9 months short of her 100th birthday.

"YOU'RE NOT GOING TO LIKE IT, GEORGE. SHE'S AN OLD MAID."

Non-veterans were in transition, too. By January 1946, the number of working women was down four million from its peak in 1944. Some were laid off or fired to make room for returning soldiers. Many went happily home of their own volition. Among those who didn't, older women were particularly prominent—more than 80 percent of those 45 and over said they wanted to remain in the workforce. It made sense. Their children were mostly grown and the demands of homemaking continued to dwindle. Thanks to the New Deal, more than 90 percent of American homes had electricity, and the ever-improving home appliance market kept simplifying chores like washing and cooking. Besides canned goods, consumers were beginning to have access to a raft of frozen foods, including the legendary "TV dinners," which might not have been great cuisine but did offer the option of speedy meal preparation.

After some postwar churning, older women were once again encouraged to work outside their homes. The prejudice they'd faced in earlier times had abated—the country had gotten used to seeing them holding down jobs. But, as always, it was the economy that really dictated attitudes. Postwar America was booming, and while employers no longer needed women to run power drills, they desperately needed more clerks, office workers, teachers, and nurses. And a lot of them would have to be older, since young women were quitting work in droves to marry returning soldiers and start families.

By 1950, the average female worker was in her 40s. Younger women, keenly aware of the shortage of men due to war casualties, were beginning to obsess about early marriage. "A girl who hasn't a man in sight by the time she is 20 is not altogether wrong in fearing that she may never get married," wrote an essayist in the *New York Times*. "Not so long ago, girls were expelled from college for marrying; now girls feel hopeless if they haven't a marriage at least in sight by commencement time." In 1940, just a little more than half the young women between 20 and 24 were or had been married. By 1955, it was more than 70 percent, and the prospects for the other 30 percent were portrayed as bleak in the extreme. In the postwar classic *It's a Wonderful Life*, an angel shows George Bailey what the world would be like if he had never been in it, and George asks to see his wife, Mary. "You're not going to like it, George," the angel says somberly. "She's an old maid. She never married." Mary is a miserable, seemingly frigid librarian. The actress Donna Reed was in her mid-20s when she played the part.

"MY MOTHER LIVES WITH US"

One of the most significant social changes in postwar America was its spectacular building boom, fueled by GI loans, which helped young marrieds buy the homes of their dreams in developments that seemed to spring out of nowhere. Suddenly a quarter of all families were living in the suburbs, generally in brand-new neighborhoods composed almost entirely of younger couples. The physical distance between parents and their grown children expanded overnight. And the idea of multigenerational families, which already had been growing unpopular, fell even further out of favor.

"My recently widowed mother feels that I am obligated to take her into our home," complained a writer to Eleanor Roosevelt's question-and-answer column If You Ask Me. Roosevelt responded that older people were better off living alone: "We are usually not good for our children or for their children when we live with them.... Older people can help from experience, but sometimes they have had too many experiences to make it wise for them always to be around the young." Perhaps some of Eleanor's contemporaries who read her comments thought they might feel extremely independent, too, if they had a top job at the United Nations.

Those positive magazine stories about how mothers and their married daughters learned to share a home were replaced by articles that stressed the desirability of getting Mom to go somewhere else. An essay in *Harper's* quoted a middle-aged woman expressing her dismay that "My Mother Lives with Us," and it offered no happy ending — just an acknowledgment that "Susan's catalogue of grievances was, unhappily, all too familiar." The media didn't neglect the dark side of the trend. "Right now there are thousands of old people, men and women isolated in the loneliness of a rooming house, with only the camaraderie of a park bench to give them social solace ... in forgetting our elders, we have forgotten our own hearts," opined *Ladies' Home Journal*. But the suggestions for a solution usually involved setting the elders up in a ... separate place. Another *Ladies' Home Journal* article from the same period extolled clubs where "oldsters" could get together and learn to paint or play instruments.

That was exactly the kind of thing many in the target audience dreaded. "The social planners assume that we are lonely and offer us defenses, which will also keep us out from underfoot," mused Hannah Trimble, a 60-something retired Indiana teacher. But, Trimble wrote in the *New York Times,* "I shall never be able to sit happily in a neighborhood club and roll clay worms in the palm of my hand, and I refuse to end a busy life making potholders on weaving frames which have been brought up by civic bureaus."

If Trimble thought the tone of these discussions about the elderly was incredibly patronizing, she was incredibly right. A speaker at the American Home Economics Association in 1956 offered a list of suggestions for how to live the good life past 65, ranging from "Cultivate quiet interests" to "Limit your range of physical activities." A physician writing in the journal *California Medicine* theorized that aging men tried "over-compensation" to prove they were as strong or as clever as ever. But the typical older woman, he said, went for hypochondria — fearing her loss of beauty and fertility, "she finds an easy rationalization for this threat in the development of physical complaints, since society's attitude is much more indulgent to illness in the female."

There was always that question of exactly when "old" started. In *Ladies' Home Journal,* Eleanor Roosevelt wrote, "Age is a matter of the mind as well as of the body." But she went on to conclude, "Ordinarily, old age is supposed to begin at sixty. After that you are more or less living on borrowed time, and after seventy most people count each year as an unusual gift." It was true that the life expectancy for an American woman at the time was about seventy. But one like Eleanor, who had made it to sixty-five, could reasonably hope to see eighty.

Still, by the standards of the time, Roosevelt was being generous. In 1950, the *New York Times* ran a story titled "Business Now Holds Women 'Old' at 35."

"CONTROL BY AGING FEMALES"

Not everybody was happy that women were living longer. The Population Reference Bureau, a nonprofit research group, issued a warning in 1955 that the country could be taken over by elderly women since their numbers were increasing so much faster than those of men. "In terms of voting power, ownership of land, and corporate equities, the United States could be seen on the road toward a gerontomatriarchy — control by aging females," it announced ominously. The acclaimed biographer Catherine Drinker Bowen had noticed the sentiment. "In short," she wrote wryly, "we who used to be carried off decently in our forties and fifties by apoplexies, stomach ulcers, and general debility now remain on the scene until seventy or eighty-odd, presumably retired from work and cluttering up the continent from Biloxi to Alaska." People were reading *Generation of Vipers,* Philip Wylie's perennially bestselling harangue about domineering mothers who turned their sons into emasculated conformists. Women had gone through American history being told they weren't worth anything if they didn't bear children, and now Wylie had turned "Momism" into Public Enemy Number One. She was "a middle-aged puffin with an eye like a hawk that has just seen a rabbit twitch far below. She is about twenty-five pounds overweight, with no sprint, but sharp heels."

On the plus side, the growing numbers — and purchasing power — of older Americans encouraged scientists to tackle medical conditions that had hitherto been regarded as a natural and untreatable part of the aging process. In 1943, a writer in *Harper's* had called arthritis "medicine's neglected stepchild" because of the lack of research devoted to alleviating it. He quoted a venerable physician who said that whenever a patient with arthritis came into his office "I always want to jump out of the window" because he had so little to offer. But by the 1950s, people were beginning to demand more effort. "The dread disease arthritis is the most chronic malady in the United States," said the *New York Times,* as it begged readers to donate to research seeking a cure. The next year, in a similar plea, the paper announced: "Today there is hope in the struggle against arthritis, though scarcely a decade ago there was no hope at all." Much of that optimism was directed at cortisone, a new medication Americans were being told would be an "elixir of life" for people suffering from age-related diseases like arthritis and hardening of the arteries. Scientists were finally figuring out how to produce cortisone in quantities sufficient for mass use. "Today it is reassuring to know that *the great majority of arthritis cases can be greatly helped,*" said an ad from the Metropolitan Life Insurance Company. As usual, it was an oversell, featuring reports of crippled patients who could "walk, run and even dance" after a couple of days' worth of treatment. Cortisone never became a miracle cure, but it was a breakthrough—those unhappy doctors finally had something to offer when an arthritis case walked in.

On a less elevated level, Geritol was introduced in 1950, as a new cure for what sounded like a new ailment: iron-deficiency anemia, which TV viewers were informed was really just "tired blood." Ads for Geritol were omnipresent on early television. Directed at older people, particularly women, the promotions featured authoritative-sounding male announcers—or a young and concerned-looking Betty White, who told "you really busy gals" that if they dragged around the house or had a "weak, rundown condition," Geritol was a surefire way to "feel stronger fast."

Geritol was a postwar version of Lydia Pinkham's nostrums. It was 12 percent alcohol, plus iron and some B vitamins. Consumers were only supposed to take a small dose, but if they kept sipping, the effect would be approximately the same as tippling champagne. As time went on, the FTC would require the Geritol makers to point out that "the great majority of tired people don't feel that way because of iron-poor blood." But nevertheless, the ads kept showing frustrated hubbies dragging their exhausted wives around the dance floor until Geritol transformed the missus into a red-hot mama.

"They had fulfilled their destiny as seed-pods"

The medical world had a more ambitious answer to older women who consulted their doctors about feeling tired and run-down: the sex hormone estrogen. It wasn't a sudden development. You may remember the French scientist back in the 1920s who claimed he had an elderly patient racing up six flights of stairs and working 12 hours a day after she got an implant of chimpanzee glands. A quarter of a century later, scientists in Missouri were reporting that they'd injected female prison inmates, 64 to 89 years old, with a combination of testosterone and a female hormone to stupendous outcomes: "Women who formerly had shown no desire to help in making beds and serving meals now helped nurses, entertained themselves and found joy in life," Waldemar Kaempffert reported in the *New York Times*. A Los Angeles doctor, E. Kost Shelton, extolled hormone therapy at a meeting of the American Geriatrics Society the following year. "Formerly, most women who survived until the fifth or sixth decades expected to be and actually were senile in both appearance and perspective," he said cheerfully. "They had fulfilled their destiny as seed-pods and were willing to dry up and blow away."

Chimpanzees aside, scientists had been isolating estrogen in their labs since the 1920s with an eye toward helping postmenopausal women. By the 1940s, "estrogen replacement therapy" had become fairly common. When doctors figured out how to administer it as a pill instead of an injection, the treatment really took off. Estrogen was also showing up in beauty products—Helena Rubinstein promised that her Estrogenic Hormone Cream would help prevent "tragic signs of age—dryness, wrinkles, crepey throat, old-skin hands" in women "over 35." It wouldn't take terribly long for the medical community to get skeptical about those creams, and in 1961, the American Medical Association would denounce them as dangerous and ineffective. It was the beginning of what would become a half-century roller-coaster ride with estrogen therapies.

The theory that menopause was the end of real life for women was still going strong, thanks in particular to Freudians who claimed that menstruation was the female equivalent of a penis and menopause naturally brought on castration anxiety. Helene Deutsch published an influential two-volume work called *The Psychology of Women*, which theorized that menopause sent women into out-of-control sex and other irresponsible adolescent behavior. The theory posited that a minority—including, presumably, people like Deutsch—could escape the worst effects through careers or working on public welfare. It may have been the first time Lydia Maria Child's ideas about solving old age by working for others were expanded to include prevention of nymphomania.

"STARS ARE AGELESS!"

Hollywood reflected that postwar dried-seed-pod theory about older women. In 1950, Bette Davis starred in *All About Eve* as a Broadway legend who feels her career is ending because she is turning 40. It was quite a switch from the era of Sarah Bernhardt happily emoting in her 70s. That same year, the trauma of aging drove *Sunset Boulevard*'s former movie queen Norma Desmond so dotty that she shot her much younger lover when he dumped her. Desmond, played by Gloria Swanson, is introduced at the beginning of the movie holding a burial service for her beloved chimpanzee — which is, it seems, the best she can do in terms of having a child. She is living in her old Hollywood mansion, served by a former director turned devoted servant and surrounded by old Hollywood friends who are as divorced from reality as she is. "There's nothing tragic about being fifty — not unless you try to be twenty-five," the much younger Holden character tells Norma as he heads for the door, setting the stage for a finale that will leave him face-down in the swimming pool. Then, as Joe floats away, Norma looks up at the sky and says, defiantly, "Stars are ageless!"

(Both Davis and Swanson were nominated for the Best Actress Oscar for their performances. Historian Lois Banner theorizes they divided the vote for fans of mature performances, giving the actual prize to 29-year-old Judy Holliday for *Born Yesterday*. Later, Swanson would complain about "the ghastly American worship of youth.")

By the end of the 1950s, Hollywood was so enamored with the teenage audience it sometimes seemed producers were forgetting everybody else. The ultimate example was *Gidget*, a surfer flick in which the only female over the age of 18 is Gidget's mom, whose big moment comes when she tells her daughter that "to be a real woman is to bring out the best in a man." The older women who appeared in movies in the postwar era were pretty much like their immediate predecessors: recognizable faces who popped up regularly, usually playing worried mothers, wise grandmothers, and faithful maids. Marjorie Main, who specialized in sassy old dames, was in 34 movies in the 1940s and kept it up in the 1950s, eventually switching to television. In 1958, she made her final appearance in an episode of *Wagon Train*, a popular western. Main played her usual comic role as a crusty, outspoken old bat who nonetheless has a spark of sex appeal. The writers paired her off with an aging cowboy, but not before she conducted a flirtation with one of the co-stars, Ward Bond, a character actor who was more than a decade younger.

Getting a younger man in the 1950s—even for a minute—was a rare feat. Main was one of many examples of veteran actresses who found bigger and better roles on TV. The new medium was looking for brand names at a time when very few well-known performers wanted to be seen on what was frequently referred to as "the boob tube." Spring Byington, who had been popping up forever in supporting roles in motion pictures, got her own series, *December Bride*, in which she played a widow living with her daughter and son-in-law, who were constantly trying to marry her off—a comedy tailor-made for a decade in which keeping Mom from moving in was a long-running obsession. Ann Sothern was 49 when she began playing Katy O'Connor, a glamorous assistant hotel manager, in *The Ann Sothern Show*. "Katy, all the fellows fall for Katy," the theme song announced, " 'cause Katy makes them whistle for more." Lucille Ball was in her 40s when she starred in the smash TV hit *I Love Lucy*, which was succeeded by similar sitcoms that kept her onscreen for more than 20 years.

"EVERY WOMAN OVER FIFTY SHOULD STAY IN BED UNTIL NOON"

The postwar world was supposed to be all about young suburban couples, but the best-known fashion icon of the 1950s was First Lady Mamie Eisenhower, who was 56 when her husband, Dwight, was elected president. Mamie was eight years older than Eleanor Roosevelt had been when she arrived at the White House. But Eleanor was a reprise of those turn-of-the-century women who strode through life with their eye on social reform, not clothes or hairstyles. Mamie happily regarded herself as a fashionable dresser. Her style was far from haute, and it wouldn't be all that long before commentators would shudder at the memory of her tightly curled bangs. But there was something about Mamie that appealed to the moment. When one of her halter-top sundresses was described as making her "look more like a girl than a mature woman," she retorted, "I hate old-lady clothes. And I shall never wear them." Her designer, Mollie Parnis, decreed that her client was "proving that a grandmother needn't be an old lady. She's made maturity glamorous."

"Mrs. Dwight D. Eisenhower is expected to give a lift to the fashion industry," the *New York Times* noted approvingly after the 1952 election. "The millions who cheered Mrs. Eisenhower during the campaign tour noted that she always was well groomed, in simple little suits or dresses of good lines and flattering cut, that her hats were right and her gloves were spotless." Unlike Eleanor, Mamie did not work with her husband's party in an organizational way, but she apparently had no objections to being marketed in his political campaign. Supporters were encouraged to sing songs like "I Want Mamie," to wear "I Like Mamie" buttons, and even to use tape dispensers featuring Mamie's picture. When Eisenhower made appearances, the crowd would regularly yell, "Where's Mamie?" until she appeared from behind a curtain, crying, "Here I am!" In 1956, Eisenhower's reelection campaign ran an ad praising housewives as the custodians of American values. "They like Ike," the narrator continued. "And here's someone else they like—Ike's beloved Mamie." Women were urged to go to the polls and "keep our first lady in the White House for four more years."

As First Lady, Mamie did not hold press conferences, but she was happy to be photographed modeling her latest fashions. The nation became fascinated with "the Mamie look" and read obsessively about her inaugural ball gown, with massive petticoats that gossips said took three hours to properly arrange, covered by a gown festooned with 2,000 hand-sewn rhinestones. The dress would reappear on knickknack shelves across the country in the form of Mamie figurines. *Life* extolled the First Lady's "pretty neck and shoulders," and she repeatedly showed up on the lists of the world's best-dressed women. Her passion for pink spurred a national craze for the color, and when America learned that Mamie had pink bathrooms, millions of homes adopted the same scheme.

She also broke new ground with her public displays of affection with Ike, whom she frequently kissed and hugged in front of the cameras. In 1955, when the president suffered a heart attack, Mamie stayed in a hospital room next to his, demanding little in the way of special treatment—except for a pink toilet seat. Her public image was a mixture of traditional housewife and mink-wearing lady of luxury. She caused a political mini scandal in 1958 when she took a government plane home from Phoenix, where she had been staying at a spa that specialized in helping middle-aged women lose weight. She made no secret of how much she loved breakfast in bed. ("Every woman over fifty should stay in bed until noon.") During their evenings alone, she and Ike liked to eat dinner off trays in front of the TV — or two separate TVs since they preferred different programs, which they managed to hear while they dined in the same room. The cuisine, reportedly, was sometimes just one of those new frozen TV dinners. Everyone knew that Mamie liked to play canasta, loved charm bracelets, watched the soap opera *As the World Turns,* and wore a pink housecoat with a pink bow in her hair during her mornings at home.

Mamie was a genuine trendsetter, which spoke to the fact that older women had significant clout in matters like style in the postwar era. The fashion industry was constantly announcing a youth takeover, but the moment was slower to arrive on Main Street than the experts predicted. Meanwhile, it was an era of pearl chokers, mink coats, and shirtwaist dresses. The "New Look" unveiled by Christian Dior in 1947 featured a long, full skirt, but it required an extremely narrow waist, which once again would have to be achieved through serious corsetry. Foundation garments — happily with newer, more comfortable synthetic fabrics — were omnipresent. There were girdles for teenagers, girdles for stout women, girdles for thin women, girdles to be worn while washing the kitchen floor. Everybody was expected to suffer for their looks, one way or the other.

The Mamie bangs may look dreadful to a modern 56-year-old, but they were designed by Elizabeth Arden, the fashion titan who became one of the first women to appear on the cover of *Time.* Some financial experts of her era believed she had earned more money than any woman in American history. The looks she designed weren't so much for young women as for older women who wanted to appear younger — another client of Arden's was Wallis Simpson, the Duchess of Windsor. Arden stressed heavy makeup, firming facial exercises, and — pink. Pink was definitely the color. It was while returning from an Elizabeth Arden spa that Mamie got in trouble for taking that government plane.

"They've Messed with the Wrong One Now"

At 86, Mary Church Terrell was still picketing, protesting the segregation of restaurants and theaters, and filing civil rights suits. She lived long enough to see the Supreme Court's decision banning segregated public schools in *Brown v. Board of Education*; she died two months later, on July 24, 1954, at age 90. Mary McLeod Bethune, who had been the central African American figure in the Roosevelt administration, was still in action in Washington, where President Harry Truman appointed her to a committee on national defense. "I am now 78 years old and my activities are no longer so strenuous as they once were," she wrote. "I feel that I must conserve my strength to finish the work at hand." She was completing her autobiography and trying to organize a foundation to continue her fight for wider educational opportunities for African Americans. "Sometimes I ask myself if I have any other legacy to leave," she wrote. "Truly, my worldly possessions are few. Yet, my experiences have been rich. . . . So, as my life draws to a close, I will pass them on to Negroes everywhere in the hope that an old woman's philosophy may give them inspiration."

Faith in community work as a way to combat the effects of age was alive and well. The generation of black women carrying the banner in the 1950s were middle-aged, and they had been in the civil rights movement before most white Americans were even aware there was such a thing. When whites learned better, it was through Rosa Parks. She was 42 — long past her youth by the standards of 1955 — when she refused a Montgomery, Alabama, bus driver's demand that she give up her seat to a white passenger. She was equally unmoved when he threatened to have her arrested. "You may do that," she said calmly. He did, and the rest, as we say, is history. Parks had worked for 12 years with the Montgomery chapter of the National Association for the Advancement of Colored People (NAACP). To the world, she was a stupendously respectable, unthreatening-looking woman who appeared in court wearing a demure black dress with white cuffs and a small velvet hat. "They've messed with the wrong one now," cried a teenager in the crowd around the courthouse. While the nation watched, Montgomery blacks staged a yearlong bus boycott protesting segregation, organized largely by African American teachers and social workers.

We tend to look back at the civil rights movement and see young people sitting in at lunch counters, organizing Freedom Rides, and risking death to register black citizens to vote. But older women were at the center of the early movement, because they had always been leading behind the scenes. First and foremost was Ella Baker, who had gone to college in Raleigh in the 1920s and then shocked her family when she rejected the normal black-middle-class career of teaching to become a community organizer. She was a perpetual mover, in the tradition of Elizabeth Cady Stanton and Eleanor Roosevelt, happiest when she was on a train, working through her papers and traveling toward another mobilization.

The civil rights movement, when it came onto the national stage, was perceived as something led almost exclusively by men. In part, that was because the men preferred it that way. Andrew Young, who would later become mayor of Atlanta, remembered feeling that people like Ella Baker "were too much like my mother. Strong women were the backbone of the movement, but to young black men seeking their own freedom, dignity and leadership perspective, they were quite a challenge." Baker was one of the first organizers of the Southern Christian Leadership Conference, but she and its charismatic leader, Dr. Martin Luther King Jr., didn't get along. She was an SCLC acting director, but when the position was made permanent, the job went to a younger man. "After all, who was I?" she asked bitterly. "I was female, I was old."

"AN AMAZING WOMAN — DON'T KNOW HOW SHE STAYS SINGLE"

Meanwhile, in Washington, Rep. Mary Norton, who had passed the historic legislation outlawing child labor and winning workers a minimum wage, was bemoaning the fact that "women do not organize as they could to help elect women! They could, because of their numerical strength, control elections, but it is my opinion they never will." She had reason to be discouraged — when she announced her retirement in 1950, there were only 10 women in Congress, and over the next decade, the number never managed to inch up to 20. "Congresswoman Norton is perfectly remarkable," Eleanor Roosevelt would note in 1954. "She insists that she is 79 years old, but nobody would know it by watching her!... Old age which comes as gracefully as it has come to her is certainly nothing to be feared for she is more interesting and a more entertaining companion today than she was 40 years ago."

The women who were elected to Congress were still frequently widows but with vastly different ideas about what to do with their inherited political careers. On the one hand, there was Vera Bushfield, who served as her husband's successor as senator from South Dakota in 1948 but wasn't in office long enough to get sworn in. On the other, there was Margaret Chase Smith, who succeeded her husband in the House, then ran for the Senate, becoming the first woman to serve in both chambers. At the time she moved up, she was in her 50s—a veritable juvenile by Washington standards. It gave her the opportunity to craft a quarter-century career of breaking barriers and standing up to some of the most vicious forces in postwar America.

Margaret Chase had grown up in the Maine mill town of Skowhegan, the oldest of six children. Her father, a barber, was a mean drunk. Her mother worked in factories, stores, restaurants, and laundries to help support the family. By the time she was in high school, Margaret was working, too. She particularly liked being a telephone operator, and it was through that job that she met Clyde Smith, who called one day to ask the time. Smith, a successful businessman more than 20 years her senior, was interested in politics and women. He "had a reputation for liking the girls, especially younger girls," Margaret told her biographer. Divorced, he pursued her and enough other flames to keep her perpetually insecure about his intentions. She graduated from high school and eventually became circulation manager at a local paper—of which Smith was co-owner.

She also started joining women's clubs, the versions that stressed business and professional networking as well as culture and civic improvement. While she was still in her 20s, she became head of two of the biggest and most impressive clubs in Skowhegan, forging friendships with other hardworking, self-starting women—relationships that would come in handy when she moved into politics.

She was still attached to Clyde, who was in the state legislature and looking for the next step up. They finally got married in 1930, when Margaret was 32 years old. Her new husband was 55, in bad health, but eagerly promoting himself as the next Maine member of the U.S. House of Representatives. He also continued his outside love life—a few months before he married Margaret, Smith fathered a baby girl with a local factory worker. Near the end of her life, Margaret looked back and remembered her marriage: "[A]s great a man as Clyde was, he was not as devoted to me as you seem to think," she told an interviewer. "Let me limit my observations to saying that he gave me many heartaches." But whatever the failings of their union, Clyde and Margaret forged a very successful political partnership. She joined the staff of his Washington office, her duties expanding as her husband became more and more disabled from what was apparently advanced syphilis. She appeared as his surrogate in his reelection campaign in 1938, racing back and forth between Maine and Washington, and growing so confident in her role that she promoted her own foreign policy, which differed sharply from her husband's. (While Clyde was an isolationist, Margaret believed both in military preparedness and Maine's share of the defense industry.) Clyde won reelection, but he was failing physically. In early 1940, he issued a plea to his constituents to give Margaret his seat in the case of his death: "I know of no one who has the full knowledge of my ideas and plans or is as well qualified as she is to carry on these ideas and my unfinished work for the district." It was a serious underestimation of Margaret's capacities, but it held the day. After Clyde died, Margaret replaced him in a special election with only token opposition.

She had more trouble with the regular general election in the fall of 1940, when four other Republicans felt a man deserved the seat. Given the rhetoric from her opponents, a Portland newspaper columnist noted that the campaign was being waged less on ability than on a "question of sex." She whomped them all, along with her Democratic opponent in November. Much later she referred to 1940 as "a pretty heavy year." She had watched her husband die while managing his Washington office, and run in three elections in five months. She had also signed an agreement providing monthly payments to the illegitimate daughter Clyde had fathered.

In Congress, Margaret Chase Smith refused campaign contributions, set records for roll-call attendance, and personally responded to every constituent's letter on the day it arrived. But she also sought serious policy-making power—some of her major issues were civil rights, the Equal Rights Amendment, and a strong military. In 1948, she ran for senator. It was an unheard-of goal. Only a few women in American history had gotten to the Senate, and all of them had initially made it through appointment—except, carping historians might point out, Gladys Pyle of South Dakota, who won a peculiar contest for a two-month term when the Senate was out of session in 1938.

By then, Smith had developed a close relationship with the House Naval Affairs Committee's chief counsel, William Lewis Jr., 31. Smith was the only woman on the committee, and some of the male members had trouble dealing with her presence through lengthy meetings. Lewis was tasked with giving them a break by taking Smith for an after-dinner walk. He later became her executive assistant, and the two were both politically and personally inseparable. Speaking about the relationship in her old age, Smith said she could not marry—particularly marry a younger man—"and keep my job." She added: "I wish that I had made more time for love." Lewis urged her to run for the Senate, then organized her campaign, which was regarded as a long-shot gamble at first. The national party wasn't enthusiastic, given that in the House she was not a reliable Republican vote; her preference for bipartisanship had started early. And no woman had ever won an election to the Senate in her own right. Smith wanted the job so much she gave up her long-standing opposition to campaign contributions.

She needed all the help she could get. There were whispers about her morals and much louder claims from the Right that she was a Communist sympathizer who had supported suspect institutions like the United Nations. At this point, her detractors didn't focus on her age. Most of the talk was about her gender—sympathetic stories often stressed attributes like her cooking skills. It sometimes seemed as if every story about Smith's achievements included some reference to her muffin recipe.

She had more notable strong suits. For instance, in the run-up to the election, Smith was on a congressional trip to Iran when the plane's engines faltered. The lawmakers were put into life jackets in anticipation of a possible crash landing over the ocean. To calm her fellow passengers, Smith coolly pulled out several harmonicas she had purchased for her young relatives and led everyone in singing. When the plane landed safely, and the survivors were marveling over her performance, one admiral who had been on board offered: "An amazing woman — don't know how she stays single."

The plane story — plus another moment when she slipped on the ice while campaigning, broke her elbow, had the cast set, and still managed to make it to her next appearance — convinced the electorate that if she was not manly, she was definitely spunky. Smith won the election in a landslide.

Senator Margaret Chase Smith was a military hawk and a vigorous anti-Communist, qualities that would get her into trouble later in her career. But she was appalled by Joe McCarthy, a new Republican colleague who had just arrived from Wisconsin and was soon making headlines with his claims that the government was "infested with Communists" plotting to help the Russians win the Cold War. His accusations became national news, and other senators joined in the witch hunt. Most of the rest stayed quiet out of fear of being branded Communists themselves if they objected. Careers were being ruined, and government employees were terrified. Smith, who served on two committees with McCarthy, didn't like the situation.

In June of 1950, Smith rose in the Senate and offered her "Declaration of Conscience." The American people, she told her colleagues, "are sick and tired of being afraid to speak their minds lest they be politically smeared as 'communists' or 'fascists' by their opponents." As a loyal Republican, Smith said, she did "not want to see the Republican party ride to political victory on the Four Horsemen of Calumny — Fear, Ignorance, Bigotry and Smear."

Her speech did not stop McCarthy, who temporarily got revenge when he succeeded in getting Smith thrown off his Senate Permanent Subcommittee on Investigations. (He replaced her with newcomer

Richard Nixon.) He encouraged speculation that she herself was a Communist — or at least a "fellow traveler" — and promoted a primary challenge when she ran for reelection. But Smith won with no trouble, and in December 1954, she was also the winner when the Senate voted to censure McCarthy. She was even mentioned as a possible vice-presidential nominee in 1952 and 1956. (The job, like the committee slot, went to Nixon.) She entered the 1960s as a national figure. In Illinois, a teenager named Hillary Rodham opened up a copy of *Life* magazine that featured a story on Smith and was amazed. "I had no idea there was such a woman," she recalled.

"Is our guest famous for travel?"

While Smith's star was rising, Eleanor Roosevelt was ending her official relationship with Washington. In 1952, the new president, Dwight Eisenhower, had opted not to renew her appointment to the United Nations. She certainly didn't retire from the public stage — she continued writing her newspaper column and averaged 150 speeches a year. "Is our guest famous for travel?" one of the panelists on the popular game show *What's My Line?* asked when Roosevelt appeared as the mystery celebrity of the week. In 1959, she starred, improbably, in a television ad for Good Luck margarine. Butter substitutes were still regarded with some dismay, but Eleanor announced, in her unmistakable voice, that "[n]owadays you can get margarine like Good Luck, which really tastes delicious. That's what I've spread on my toast." While extremely generous to charities, Eleanor also managed to make a healthy annual income — the equivalent of about $800,000 in today's dollars. Once, when she was at a dinner at Brandeis University, the emcee suffered a sudden stroke, and Eleanor quickly stepped up and took over. "No, I have not slackened my pace," she wrote to a friend in 1954. "At least, not yet. I probably shall. Everybody does." Note the "probably."

Time, commenting on how "Mrs. Roosevelt had changed during her years alone," decided that "although she has aged visibly," she was looking better than ever — quoting "one fascinated Frenchman" as saying "Madame Roosevelt is becoming beautiful." The magazine credited the transformation to a car accident in which several people were injured and her "face was smashed against the steering wheel." Bizarrely, *Time* told its readers that "the aftermath was a happy one" since "Mrs. Roosevelt's protruding front teeth were broken in the accident; the porcelain caps which replace them subtly changed her whole face and gave her a sweet, warm and gentle smile." The magazine also appreciated a weight gain that, the anonymous authors said, had given her "a comfortable and matronly air."

She did seem to have come to a good place. "At 70, I would say the advantage is that you take life more calmly. You know that this, too, shall pass!" she wrote. Asked about her accomplishments on her birthday, she told reporters that she had gotten the most satisfaction from the United Nations work. But basically, she said, "I just did what I had to do as things came along." Whatever spare time she had was often devoted to answering letters—the ones that involved impossible requests for appearances often got an apology of "Ack—regret no time." There were signs of aging. She became deaf in her right ear, and her gift of falling asleep at will, anywhere, became less controlled. "It can be awkward if she's in company," said Nina, one of her grandchildren. "I keep a very close watch. If I catch her just as her head is nodding, one tap of the ankle is enough. But once her head reaches her chest, it takes a good old-fashioned shake."

She devoted endless hours to campaigning for Adlai Stevenson, the Democratic presidential nominee in 1952 and 1956. Her relationship with the former Illinois governor was personal as well as political. Joseph Lash felt that while "Adlai did not interest her as a man," she loved his keen mind. If Stevenson at times seemed to rely on her too much, Lash added, "that too was not unflattering. The worst thing was not to be needed." She continued to develop intense friendships similar to the one she had with Lash himself.

Eleanor met Dr. David Gurewitsch through Lash's wife, Trude. He treated her in 1946 after the car accident that broke her teeth and then became an intimate friend, traveling all over the world with the former First Lady, keeping in constant correspondence during their separations, and escorting her to dinners and other evening events. (The most modern person of her day on many matters, Eleanor did not believe a proper woman went out alone after dark.) She kept a picture of him on her night table and took another with her in a leather frame on her trips. His future wife, Edna, who later wrote a book on the relationship, called it "an intimate but platonic union."

"You know without my telling you that I love you as I love and have never loved anyone else, and I am grateful for the privilege of loving you and thankful for every chance to be of help," she wrote to him on his birthday in 1955.

Gurewitsch, who always referred to her as "Mrs. Roosevelt," carefully kept his independence. He dated women and eventually got married. If Eleanor suffered, she never did anything to alienate him. She and Edna Gurewitsch eventually became close friends. When Eleanor was 75, she and the Gurewitsches bought a house together in Manhattan. While Eleanor was never going to find the kind of passionate intimacy she had been searching for in her marriage and later life, she was spectacularly successful in surrounding herself with people who loved her.

She had also started a friendship with another young activist, Allard Lowenstein, who irritated her staff by showing up at her Hyde Park home with a pack of friends without any advance notice. Her social secretary pointed out to Eleanor that she would have been angry if her children behaved like that. "By now," she replied, "you ought to know me well enough to know that I like young men."

12. The 1960s

"I'LL WAIT"

In 1960, after 27 years and 7,222 episodes, *The Romance of Helen Trent* went off the air. After a multitude of unsuccessful relationships, Helen was left with her final flame, John, who asked her to marry him — in six months, after he finished a run for the Senate. "Oh yes, I'll wait six months, darling. I'll wait," said Helen.

She was, presumably, still 35.

If you were one of the women who actually had been getting older while listening to Helen all that time, the 1950s was a pretty decent decade to be not-young. You could work if you wanted — particularly if you craved a job as a teacher, nurse, clerk, or receptionist. You could shop in stores where Mamie fashions were on every rack, and watch people your own age occasionally play sexually attractive working women on TV.

But change was coming around the corner, looking about 20 and wearing a miniskirt. Everybody felt it in the air — some sooner than others. A convention on beauty and style for senior citizens, sponsored by New York City's Golden Age Clubs in the late 1950s, promised to show the audience how to "cast off the black guard of defeatism and despair into which a youth-geared civilization has cast them." Mamie Eisenhower was about to be replaced by 31-year-old Jacqueline Kennedy, the third-youngest First Lady in American history. (The other two, in case you're interested, were 24-year-old Julia Tyler, who married widower John Tyler near the end of his term in office, and 21-year-old Frances Cleveland, who caused so much excitement when she appeared in public that her husband, Grover, had to hide her on a farm outside Washington.) Like Mamie, Jackie Kennedy was extremely fashion conscious, but nobody ever referred to her look as matronly.

Styles had already begun evolving — skirts were getting shorter and narrower, and the fad for the chemise, or "sack," dress foreshadowed an era that would celebrate the small busted. "What would become of Gina if I showed myself thus?" demanded the buxom 1950s sex symbol Gina Lollobrigida.

Many less famous women were asking themselves the same question.

"LIFE EXPECTANCY BY THE YEAR 2000 WILL BE 120 YEARS"

We look back on the 1960s as a time of youthful rebellion, sexual liberation, and overall social turmoil. But all that took a while to get started. The first wave of the baby-boom generation that was going to dominate the culture—for what would seem to their seniors and juniors like eternity—was still in high school in 1960. The suburban-housewife ideal was still...the ideal. A *Ladies' Home Journal* poll in 1962 found almost all young women "expect to be married by 22. Most want 4 children." And while many wanted to work until those children came, "afterward, a resounding no!"

Employers hoped that when the young women said they didn't want to work "afterward" they were thinking short-term. The booming economy couldn't afford to have them all stay home forever. Because of the low birth rate in the 1930s, there were fewer workers available in the 25 to 44 age group, so at the dawn of the 1960s, business leaders like the National Association of Manufacturers were broadcasting the news that there were greater job opportunities for older people. The number of women 45 and older who worked in 1962 was double that of 1947. The jobs tended to be along the low-paying clerical line, and as had happened during the war, the fanfare about employment opportunity was accompanied by complaints about age discrimination. An advice column urged women returning to the workforce to avoid the entire subject of birth dates: "If your interviewer persists, try to be casual and tell him that one of the signs of aging successfully in a woman is to be able to lie successfully about her age. After all, we all know that the best 20 years of a woman's life are between the ages of 28 and 30!"

Hard to imagine that working out.

The ranks of older Americans continued to expand. The average life expectancy in 1964 was 70—up from 47 at the turn of the century.

"The American Medical Assn. has estimated that if medical progress continues at its present rate, the life expectancy by the year 2000 will be 120 years," the *Los Angeles Times* reported in 1961.

Okay, maybe not. But for the first time increases in life expectancy reflected medical victories over diseases that affected older people. In the earlier part of the century progress mainly had been in fighting ailments that tended to kill the young — which were often the result of poor sanitation, and other public health issues. Then antibiotics and other "miracle" drugs reduced fatalities from infectious diseases like influenza. For a while the medical community seemed to wonder if anything more could be done. But scientists have a hard-to-repress need to solve problems. Doctors got much better at handling heart attacks and performing surgeries that stopped them from happening in the first place. Researchers developed medicines to reduce blood pressure and cholesterol. Older Americans healed themselves, too. Smoking, which had been on the rise since the turn of the century, started to decline.

"OLD AGE ISN'T THAT BAD!"

Thanks to Social Security — which had been expanded to include domestic and farm workers — the people who lasted through their 60s and beyond were better fed and more likely to be living relatively comfortable lives. The suicide rate among the elderly began to fall in the 1930s, and kept going down — with the most dramatic decline in the late 1960s, when the rise in Social Security payments was particularly high and Congress had added on Medicare.

Because 65 tended to be the point at which people qualified for age-related benefits, it became a common demarcation line between "middle-aged" and "elderly." But that last category was getting pretty crowded, and society began seeing substrata. In the national imagination, at least, one's 60s were a pleasure-seeking life of retirement. Americans in their 70s were "senior citizens" the media mainly tried to portray as not that old at all. One *Chicago Tribune* columnist, under the sort-of-encouraging headline "Old Age Isn't That Bad!," quoted an expert who claimed, "A national survey showed half the respondents believe you're not old till 80!"

People in their 80s who made the news were usually treated as either miraculous exceptions or adorable, albeit wrinkled, babies. "A woman of 83 recently won first prize in the bridge tournament on a Pacific liner carrying 700 first-class passengers," marveled the *New York Times*. *Ebony* celebrated a 79-year-old great-grandmother who "dances a mean mambo" and in another feature reported on a trip to Canada by a Cleveland Golden Age Club, where a good time was allegedly had by all even though one of the members tripped, fell, and was rushed off to the hospital. "The oldsters had a very young time," the magazine decreed.

The habit of calling older people "oldsters," alas, continued.

So did the freedom with which older women were denigrated in the media. Dr. Joseph Peck, a bestselling author, contemplated "what makes old folks tick" and theorized that while retirement left both men and women at loose ends, "[s]he, however, can survive her boredom tho it may be killing for everyone around her. One bored old lady can create more disturbance in a household than a Communist in a new-born republic." Describing the way "an apparently healthy woman" ages, Dr. Paul Poinsard wrote in a medical journal that she "makes life miserable for all those around her by her irritability, criticism and anger, aroused at the slightest issue." While a woman whose children are grown might have the time to do things she always wanted to do, the doctor wrote, that wouldn't help because "she has not developed the capacity for enjoyment."

Advice on how to avoid this kind of fate continued unabated. And if there was one particular theme, it was self-improvement. "You must be interested in your life. If you're not, change it," recommended Anita Colby, billed as "America's foremost authority on beauty after 40." She advised her readers to "[d]ecide what you want to do and work toward doing it, even if it means perhaps going back to school." While it sounded as if Colby was less than enthusiastic, the idea of continuing education was getting popular. In a way, it was a successor to those women's groups decades before, in which members gathered to present reports on subjects like the fashions of ancient Rome. But the idea of spending your later years helping others was still somewhat in abeyance. At a symposium on "The Emotional Basis of Illness" in San Francisco in 1968, one of the expert speakers suggested that menopause was hardest on women who were "dominated by what psychiatrists know as 'narcissistic ego strivings.'" Those narcissists, he said, "are often club women, the PTA leaders, the volunteers for government reform, hospitals or war work. They are known as 'pillars of strength' in the community." Mark that as a kind of milestone—the very women who had long been celebrated for overcoming the effects of age by directing their attention toward serving the community were being pointed to as the "narcissists" who were going to take menopause worst.

"WE WANTED TO LOOK NICE"

Yet there were still people who insisted on trying to save the world—or at least keep it from exploding. In 1961, Dagmar Wilson, a 45-year-old mother of three, was visiting with some friends in her backyard outside Washington, DC, trying to figure out a way to organize housewives against nuclear testing. Concern about the arms race between the United States and the Soviet Union was already widespread, but in a still-conservative era, speaking out against it was controversial. Wilson felt the message might be delivered best by mothers—particularly middle-class, middle-aged mothers. "We wanted to look nice to emphasize the fact that this was who we were.... We felt this in itself expressed the urgency of our concern," she said. They started Women Strike for Peace and planned a demonstration, using a telephone tree in which friend called friend. The response went beyond their wildest dreams. Six weeks later, 50,000 women marched in demonstrations around the country, calling for an end to nuclear tests and pointing to the danger of radioactive fallout poisoning babies' milk. Both Jacqueline Kennedy and Nina Khrushchev, the wife of the Soviet prime minister, responded. "As mothers, we cannot help but be concerned about the health and welfare of our husbands and children," Mrs. Kennedy wrote supportively. Her husband added a deeply restrained compliment, calling the marchers "extremely earnest."

It was a new version of the Elizabeth Cady Stanton tactic: delivering an otherwise radical message through the filter of gray-haired maternity. Or, this time, particularly well-dressed maternity. Cora Weiss, one of the youngest members of the WSP leadership, remembers trying to live up to her colleagues' standards. "I arrived at one Fifth Avenue demonstration wearing a cherry-red suit," she recalled. "Right away one of my elder sisters said: 'Your lipstick clashes!' That was the end of me that day."

The women's timing was right—Americans were very worried about nuclear war. They had practiced "duck and cover" routines in school, and those new suburbanites were building fallout shelters in their basements, where the whole family was supposed to huddle if a bomb fell. Wilson was the daughter of suffrage supporters, and like the suffragists, she understood that the country paid attention when prominent matrons appeared willing to get arrested for a cause. The WSP demonstrators wore white gloves, nice hats, and shirtwaist dresses. Some of them picketed the White House in mink coats. When Wilson and her associates were summoned to appear before the House Un-American Activities Committee in 1962 to answer questions about possible Communist infiltration into their group, their supporters filled the hearing room with flowers and babies. It was pretty much the death knell of HUAC. "I had the opportunity not only to confront my accusers but also to make them look like idiots," Wilson said happily. One newspaper headline read: "Peace March Gals Make Red Hunters Look Silly."

"A MATTER OF AGE AND SEX"

Dagmar Wilson was not, of course, the first woman to take on congressional anti-Communist witch-hunters. Margaret Chase Smith had delivered that spectacular denunciation of Joe McCarthy in the 1950s, a speech so brave and powerful it became legendary. The political consultant Bernard Baruch declared that if it had been made by a man, he would have been the next president of the United States. And even though Smith was burdened with the wrong gender, she did get mentioned as a possible vice-presidential candidate. In 1964, when the very conservative Arizona senator Barry Goldwater was a front-runner for the Republican presidential nomination, Smith's fans pointed out that since she came from the moderate-to-liberal end of the party, she could provide a potential balance.

As soon as the idea came up, commentators started obsessing about

Smith's age. George Dixon, a columnist at the *Washington Post*, joked about "The Barry-Maggie Ticket." The pair had great experience in military matters, he wrote, and "not even their most scurrilous traducers could accuse them of being too youthful." At the time, Goldwater was 54 and Smith was 65, which Dixon seemed to consider extremely elderly. "Senator Smith is one of the few Senators to omit her age from the Congressional Directory," he jibed, "but I know how old she was previous to 1900!" (Smith was born in 1897.) He was writing at a time when the country was being led by the first president born in the twentieth century, and John Kennedy made Americans newly youth conscious when it came to their leaders in Washington. Never mind that Kennedy's predecessor, Dwight Eisenhower, served from age 62 to 70. There was nothing particularly remarkable about Smith's age. But you wouldn't have known it from the campaign to come.

Smith said she was not interested in second place. "I am only thinking of the Presidency," she told the *Boston Globe*. It was a long shot, but if there was going to be a serious woman candidate in the twentieth century, it seemed as if Smith might be the right one to make the move. Many Republicans found Goldwater too conservative and the other likely candidate, New York governor Nelson Rockefeller, too liberal. Some of Smith's allies hailed the idea of her running, but other Republicans who ought to have been enthusiastic were doubtful. Nellie Tayloe Ross, the woman who had once been governor of Wyoming, called Smith a "lovely person" but claimed she lacked the necessary "physical stamina."

The media seemed incapable of discussing Smith's campaign without describing her as "silver-haired." She complained that "almost every news story starts off with 'the 66-year-old Senator.' I haven't seen the age played up in the case of men candidates." The *Los Angeles Times* reported on the interview with a story that was headlined: "66-Year-Old Sen. Smith Hits Age Talk."

On January 27, 1964, at the Women's National Press Club, Smith announced she was running for president, in a speech written by her companion-aide Bill Lewis, who would become her campaign manager. It would be a long-odds candidacy under any circumstances: she had no real organization or paid staff, and her insistence on being present for every Senate vote left her only two weeks to campaign in the crucial New Hampshire primary. Rather than give speeches at high-profile rallies, she did what she had always done in Maine and went from coffee shop to workplace to women's club, shaking hands and chatting with the voters.

The focus on her age continued. Richard Wilson, a columnist for the *Los Angeles Times*, called it "a disqualifying factor." In other matters, he wrote, she was better suited for the presidency than many of the recent occupants of the White House. Her only problems were "a matter of age and sex." And for Wilson, the two were intertwined. The best age for a politician to run for president, he opined, was in the 40s or early 50s—but that was the time when "the female of the species undergoes physical changes and emotional distress of varying severity and duration." Ah, menopause.

The campaign didn't really go anywhere—besides everything else, Smith attempted to relate to the average voter by sharing her muffin recipe, which the press glommed on to so intensely it virtually became the entire campaign. But she did make history, becoming the first woman ever to have her name placed in nomination at a major party convention. Silver hair and all.

"Women Are People, Too"

Meanwhile, in the New York City suburbs, a housewife in her late 30s had been typing up a manuscript about all the ways middle-class, college-educated women were being walled off from the world, doing chores that were nothing more than busywork, slowly losing their identities—and maybe their minds. It was, of course, Betty Friedan's *The Feminine Mystique*, which would be previewed in a *Good Housekeeping* article in 1960 titled "Women Are People, Too." It wasn't exactly a fire-breathing headline, but considering the social revolution it introduced, maybe it made sense that the magazine decided to be so desperately cautious.

Title notwithstanding, "Women Are People, Too" drew floods of letters from women who felt they knew exactly what Friedan was talking about. They had gone to college with men—often getting better grades — acquired the requisite engagement ring by senior year, moved off to a model house in the suburbs, and raised a small crop of well-bred children. They were often still in their 40s when the youngest child married, and they were separated from the network of relatives and family friends who had occupied previous generations. The new appliances guaranteed that their critical housekeeping duties were minimal. There was plenty of entertainment on TV but a bewildering sense of "Is that all there is?"

Friedan was terrific at describing their frustration, and she proposed remedies that from our current worldview seem extremely modest. She told her readers to find work they cared about in "art or science...politics or profession" and then to keep the commitment going through classes or volunteer work while they waited for the opportunity to return to their careers. It was not necessarily the Lydia Maria Child plan of doing good for others — unless your ultimate career goal was in, say, social work. And Friedan did cannily note that the meaning of volunteer activities had changed — the passions for civic improvement of the early part of the twentieth century had given way to short-term, uncontroversial suburban-housewife projects that one interviewee called "committees I don't care about." Back in the day, Friedan wrote, women's community activities "almost always had the stamp of innovation and individuality, rather than the stamp of conformity, status-seeking, or escape." No more.

The book was written for and about an important, but rather narrow, audience. Future critics would note that Friedan showed no interest in the problems of working-class women. Domestics could not have been anything but offended when she noted that in the past "certain institutions concerned with the mentally retarded discovered that housework was peculiarly suited to the capacities of feeble-minded girls." *The Feminine Mystique* was also basically a book for middle-aged women. Friedan's view of younger housewives was strictly that of an observer. ("They seem to get younger all the time — in looks, and a childlike kind of dependence.") Very few people over 55 show up at all. Anybody who hadn't embarked on a committed, passionate career of some kind before then, Friedan seemed to feel, was pretty much beyond hope.

The book made Friedan a feminist star, and very soon she would help create a national movement. She began visiting Washington, where she hung out with what she called an "underground network of women"— middle-aged careerists who had taken it for granted they would have to work twice as hard as a man to achieve half as much, but couldn't resist trying anyway. They included people like Marguerite Rawalt, a tax attorney who had always yearned to be a judge, or to move up to a government post where she could make a real impact. But she always seemed to wind up assisting a man. In 1961, when she was 65, Rawalt saw her last chance. She desperately wanted a slot on the Foreign Claims Settlement Commission, which was charged with resolving claims made by Americans whose property had been seized by other countries. She was highly qualified, and for once, Rawalt had a crucial political connection—a longtime association with the new vice president, Lyndon Johnson. The official who did the screening was appropriately awed by all the agencies she'd served in, all the projects she'd shepherded through, all the people she had known and helped along the way. "And now for the $64,000 question. How old are you?" he asked. When she told the truth, Rawalt could see on his face that her chance was gone.

Another woman Friedan came to know was Pauli Murray, an African American lawyer who, after a life of immense struggle, had landed a job with a major law firm only to discover that as the sole woman, the sole minority, and a newcomer 20 years older than her peers, she was always going to be a triple outsider. She didn't stay long, moving on to a pioneering career in the civil rights movement. She also armed herself with a pile of credentials, acquiring a doctorate from Yale, teaching in Ghana and then at Brandeis University, and finally becoming an Episcopalian minister.

And there was Esther Peterson, the highest-ranking woman in the Kennedy administration, with the inevitable title of director of the Women's Bureau, an agency of the Department of Labor. In her mid-50s, she wore her graying hair the old-fashioned way, with a braid on top of her head. One adversary dubbed her "the woman with the tight hairdo." Peterson helped convince the president to create the Presidential Commission on the Status of Women, headed by Eleanor Roosevelt. The former First Lady's relationship with Kennedy had begun rather badly. She disapproved of the money his father had lavished on his campaign and his failure to appoint any women to his cabinet. "Men have to be reminded that women exist," she snorted. They eventually made a sort of peace, and Kennedy reappointed her to the United Nations and to the National Advisory Committee of his new creation, the Peace Corps. But his most important peace offering was that Commission on the Status of Women. While the administration higher-ups certainly never expected it to do anything important, it had the critical effect of bringing together hard-charging women from around the country, along with politically savvy Washingtonians like Marguerite Rawalt.

The commission members—a whole generation full of experience, talent, and frequently thwarted ambition—were gathered in Washington for a meeting when the women began to complain about the way the Lyndon Johnson administration was failing to enforce the part of the new Civil Rights Act that prohibited employment discrimination on the basis of sex. One thing led to another, and by evening a crowd had gathered in Friedan's hotel room to figure out what to do. There was a lot of talk about forming a women's version of the NAACP, to organize protests and pursue court cases on behalf of equal rights. Sometime that night, the National Organization for Women (NOW) was born.

"Do you mean, dear, that you think you would not be bored?"

Eleanor Roosevelt was never able to take a very active role in the Commission on the Status of Women, although member Pauli Murray said her own work was a "memorial" to the First Lady, who had personally answered Murray's 1938 letter criticizing FDR's racial policies and become a lifelong friend. Eleanor spent her last years in New York, living with David and Edna Gurewitsch. At the beginning, the trio would go out for evening entertainments, all organized by Eleanor. "Typically we three would hurriedly gulp our dinner in Mrs. Roosevelt's apartment downstairs, then dash out, David in the lead, to hail a taxi," Edna wrote. "Anxiety was high and breath was short as we reached the theater or concert hall in the nick of time." Finally, Edna suggested it might be easier if the three of them stayed home on occasion. Eleanor, she said, reacted with surprise: "Do you mean, dear, that you think you would not be bored?"

Apparently the most admired woman in America was shocked to discover that her housemates were willing to spend time together without some special diversions to keep their spirits up. But once convinced, Eleanor happily shared evenings with the Gurewitsches in their home unless there was a really interesting invitation to something in the outside world. It was undoubtedly helpful for her to have David, who was also her physician, close at hand. At 77 she was still appearing on television, writing her columns, and regularly entertaining her grandchildren and great-grandchildren. But she wasn't well. In 1960, her doctors discovered she had anemia, which they treated with steroids, which then activated a dormant case of bone-marrow tuberculosis, a rare condition that would eventually kill her.

She continued her life as close to normal as possible and pressed on with her work, writing another book, working with the Commission on the Status of Women, and chairing a committee to investigate the lack of government protection for the Freedom Riders who were fighting to integrate mass transportation in the South. She prided herself, Edna Gurewitsch recalled, on her self-sufficiency—even in the still-foreign world of domesticity. Once, on a plane returning to New York, she told Edna she would make breakfast for herself when she returned home. "Marie has left bread in the toaster and put water in the teakettle and taken the teacup out. I will do the rest," she said proudly. It was, by the standards of her life, a high mark in culinary achievement.

But her niece remembered that her aunt "didn't seem her old self." Eleanor began retracing the stops of her life—visiting Campobello Island, where she and Franklin had summered with their children, and receiving guests at her old cottage in Hyde Park. Finally, she began planning her funeral (plain wooden coffin). She died on November 7, 1962. President Kennedy ordered all United States flags around the world lowered to half-staff in tribute.

"AN AIRLINE OR A WHOREHOUSE?"

The focus of NOW's new "NAACP for women" was equal employment opportunity. Marguerite Rawalt organized a little band of volunteer lawyers to take the cases to court. She was retired and newly widowed.

The death of her husband, Harry, weighed heavily on her, and she welcomed the ungodly schedule of travel and meetings: "I seem to lose myself that way, and make up for the lack of Harry at home to care."

One of the landmark cases involved flight attendants, who were at the time all women—and women who were required to retire if they got married or when they reached 35. It was, airline executives insisted, a crucial perk for business travelers to be greeted by a young, attractive, single woman when they got on a plane. "What are you running, an airline or a whorehouse?" demanded Rep. Martha Griffiths of Michigan, when the House held a hearing on the matter.

It was because of Griffiths that the flight attendants got their hearing in the first place. In 1964, when the Civil Rights Act was wending its way through Congress, a few Southern conservatives proposed adding an amendment that would protect women as well as minorities from discrimination in hiring and promotion. Most members took it as a joke, or an attempt at distraction, but Griffiths grabbed on to the amendment and—with the help of Margaret Chase Smith in the Senate—pushed it into law.

After it passed, flight attendants were the first people in line to press their complaint. They had double ammunition, since the Civil Rights Act had been followed by the Age Discrimination in Employment Act of 1967. But passing a law and changing the world are always two different things. Even the government could be oblivious. Two years after that law against age discrimination had passed, the Department of Health, Education, and Welfare contacted the American Association of University Women, looking for the names of women "between 25 and 35" who might be good fits for federal job openings. After howls of protest, the department revised the request to women under 50.

Critics complained that the legal system still didn't know what to do with companies that only discriminated against older women. When age came up, employers could point to all the gray-haired men who were on the payroll, and when sex came up, they might be able to trot out a raft of female 27-year-olds. Decades later, women would still be going to court claiming they'd been tossed out of work after being referred to as a "prune" or an "old hag."

On the plus side, in 1973, flight attendants won the right to turn 36.

"DON'T TRUST ANYONE OVER 30"

While Friedan and her contemporaries were organizing NOW and taking age discrimination cases to court, on the nation's college campuses all hell was breaking loose. Those postwar baby boomers had finally arrived, and they were determined not to be silent like their parents' generation. The nation first noticed something was going on in September of 1964 when Katherine Towle, the dean of students at the University of California at Berkeley, announced that student groups could no longer use a popular plaza to solicit support for "off campus political and social action." Towle, who was then 66, was the first woman ever to be named dean of students at Berkeley. Earlier she had been the first director of the women's marines and was one of the first officers in the Marine Corps Women's Reserve to serve in World War II. She would say later that she sympathized with the students' position but had no authority to do anything except enforce the administration's policies.

Anyway, the deed was done and the free speech movement was born, along with the slogan "Don't trust anyone over 30." (Jack Weinberg, an environmental activist at Berkeley who originated the line, said many years later that he hated being attached to it for life but added wryly, "I've become more accepting of my fate as I get older.")

While the student movement was definitely anti-authority, the young protesters actually trusted quite a few people over 30. Bettina Aptheker, who was one of the Berkeley leaders, remembers one critical moment when the students tried to stop a police car from hauling away one of their group. (It was, yes, Jack Weinberg.) The standoff lasted for two days—the car surrounded by hundreds of students surrounded by hundreds of police officers, and everyone very nervous. Aptheker has a vivid memory of Ann Fagan Ginger, a 39-year-old local lawyer, "getting up on top of the police car and giving us instructions on what was legally required if we got arrested. She was great—very calming."

Aptheker also has fond memories of Dean of Students Towle, who was hauled in to testify for the prosecution at a trial for the arrested protesters. Student sit-ins had blocked her office for days, but Towle praised the young people for creating paths so visitors could make their way through. "She might as well have been a defense witness. She was that great. She was very sympathetic to us." Twenty years later, when Towle was in her 80s and in a nursing home, Aptheker visited and brought her a bouquet of roses.

As campuses erupted, there were almost always supportive over-30 figures in the background—Emily Taylor, the 49-year-old dean of women at the University of Kansas, stood up for a group of feminists protesting in the administration building, warning the chancellor that if he arrested them, he'd have to arrest her, too. And outside school, there were plenty of young women who wanted to hang out with people like Pauli Murray—who mentored, among others, future congresswoman Eleanor Holmes Norton. Dorothy Day, the founder of the Catholic Worker Movement, spent her 60s and 70s counseling an entire generation of draft resisters, runaways, and other assorted rebels, and was a hero to young radicals. Still, getting older did not appear to be something the youth were planning to do themselves. "Hippie women over thirty have that lean and desperate look," reported Vivian Estellachild, a chronicler of the counterculture movement.

As the decade went on, young Americans declared their moral superiority from sea to shining sea. "A world like this deserves contempt," said Deborah Smullyan in her commencement speech at a high school in suburban New York. "Only goodness in our generation can counter the decadence of the society we are inheriting. And our generation is good." It was one of many, many graduations of the era in which a spokesperson for the students announced that the adults had built a world that was, in the words of Hillary Rodham of Wellesley, "not the way of life for us. We're searching for more immediate, ecstatic, and penetrating modes of living."

"A CLASSIC EXAMPLE OF LIBERAL MOTHER-DAUGHTER CONFLICT"

In 1963, Women Strike for Peace won their goal: the United States signed a limited nuclear weapons test ban treaty. But they were hardly through. They were among the first Americans to oppose the Vietnam War—still wearing dresses, nice hats, and frequently picketing in high heels. And the members were out in full force in 1968 when Jeannette

Rankin—the former congresswoman who had voted against both world wars—led a big women's anti-war rally in Washington. Rankin, 87, was at the head of 5,000 demonstrators, the largest gathering of women for a political protest since the suffrage era. It took place on the opening day of Congress, and the police barred access to the Capitol grounds. All the protesters could do was deliver a petition to House and Senate leaders, and then gather for the rest of their program at a nearby hotel.

They were, as we've seen, careful to be decorous. They had been picketing the government for what felt like forever, and they had always tried to make it clear that while their aims were radical, their deportment was...not. But as the gathering convened in the hotel auditorium, a much younger group took the stage, carrying a papier-mâché coffin decorated with hair-spray cans and garters, and a blond-haired dummy that was supposed to represent Traditional Womanhood. They were from New York Radical Women, heralding a new generation gap within the women's movement. When they finished their performance, they stalked away to another part of the hotel. Amy Swerdlow, one of the organizers of the march, followed along with many of her friends—all in their 40s—expecting to hear the younger generation argue for more aggressive tactics to press for an end to the war. "What we found, however, were young women rushing to the mike to speak passionately, but often incoherently, about the way in which the traditional women's peace movement condoned and even enforced the gender hierarchy in which men made war and women wept," Swerdlow recalled later.

Swerdlow felt the young people regarded her and her comrades as part of the problem—the older generation who had graduated from Radcliffe or Smith, then retired into domesticity. She had tried to negotiate with New York Radical Women before the march, when they demanded that Women Strike for Peace pay for an extra hotel room for them to hold their counter-gathering. In the end, the organizers had agreed—even though they realized they were putting up money so the younger women could have a venue to produce an attack on them. It was, Swerdlow observed, "a classic example of liberal mother-daughter conflict."

There were no set age lines between the feminist old guard and the new radicals. But in general, the women who had been working for equal rights for a long time were fighting for a place at the table when it came to everything from jobs to national defense policy. The most radical wing of the new guard wanted to burn down the table entirely, wiping out patriarchy, marriage, and maybe even traditional parenthood. Some of the most vocal—and most publicized—new arrivals also wanted to get rid of cosmetics, sexy dresses, and anything else women wore with an eye toward pleasing men. The old guard was at a loss. "I don't want people to think Women's Lib girls don't care about how they look," Betty Friedan told the *New York Times* as she had a quick hair curl that made her 20 minutes late for a huge march for equality that she organized in the summer of 1970. When Friedan wound up appearing on TV with Roxanne Dunbar, one of the followers of the new dress creed, she accused Dunbar of being "scruffy." The wounded younger woman noted that she had appeared in "my very best army surplus white cotton sailor trousers."

By then, Friedan had become a kind of metaphor for the gap. "She misrepresents the case for feminism by making people believe that reform is the answer," said Sally Kempton, a member of the new wave. "The problem is more fundamental. The entire society has to be upended. And on top of that, she projects the star image, the elitist, which is totally out of whack with what we believe. And there she goes, in sexually suggestive clothing, saying she is the spokesman for the movement. She is not the movement mother; that is Simone de Beauvoir." Beauvoir, the French philosopher and feminist, was certainly less attached to the economic and cultural status quo than Friedan was, but she also had the great advantage of being an ocean away, writing in a different language and staying out of the young American feminists' faces.

Friedan, on the other hand, was everywhere, and sticking to her guns. At a college speech in 1970, she urged the students not to be seduced by "the bra-burning, anti-man, politics-of-orgasm" school of thought. She was suspicious of lesbians in the movement—in 1969, she warned feminists against the "lavender menace." (Later she would recant, saying that at the time, her attitude toward homosexuality had been "very square.") And she was proud of her clothes and figure.

"Feminists all over the country have admitted to me that they enjoy looking pretty and dressing up," Friedan told a meeting of the Colorado NOW in the 1970s. By then, she argued, American women had become "more secure as people and this enables them to enjoy the traditional things about being women—like nail polish and eye shadow."

Some of the most outspoken young women disagreed totally. And since NOW was still the center of feminist action, many of them joined up and tried to transform it. Their numbers weren't really all that large, but they attracted massive media attention. NOW co-founder Muriel Fox remembers picking up a Sunday *Times Magazine* and reading a story about the "Second Feminist Wave" that quoted the 29-year-old president of NOW's New York chapter, Ti-Grace Atkinson, comparing marriage to slavery and looking forward to the day when those "legal contraptions" were gone and children were raised communally. "We felt she was going to disgrace the entire feminist movement," Fox recalled. And the next NOW meeting, Fox said, "produced an unfamiliar outpouring of hippies.... We old-time NOW members asked each other, 'Who are those people?'"

One of the reasons for the vast difference in perception was the attitude toward men. While the original NOW founders confronted male politicians and sued male employers on a daily basis, many of them lived with liberal-to-left male partners who were sympathetic and sometimes extremely supportive—Fox's husband, Dr. Shepard Aronson, was chairman of the New York chapter of the NOW board. Many of the younger women had come up through the anti-war movement and the student left, where the male radicals could sometimes be thuggishly macho and where women's issues were generally regarded as an unwelcome distraction.

"And so she stood among the weeds"

The generational battle seemed to be everywhere, although some communities hoped they were at least somewhat exempt. *Ebony* contended that "elder people of the Negro race have higher status among their people than elderly whites enjoy." But the age gap was there, and growing. The *Chicago Daily Defender*, one of the nation's most prestigious black newspapers, ran a short piece in 1960 called "This Is Life: Old Woman," which used the metaphor of a decrepit house: "The basement door gaped open, its door, wide, loose, sagging, as though many children had gone through it. No one came to see her anymore. No one wanted to go inside her and take her warmth, or look through her eyes, or smell her or touch her.... And so she stood among the weeds of her isolation, and not even a rat would go inside her."

One major generational point of contention centered on hair. Younger women had begun to wear Afros—the natural style that violated the beauty standards of some older women, who had been raised to believe that straight, well-controlled tresses were the ideal. "Lord have mercy!" laughed Elizabeth Hayes Patterson, recalling the reaction. Patterson, a former associate dean at Georgetown University Law School, was particularly afraid that her new Afro would offend her grandmother, who was a hairdresser: "I did worry about her feeling a kind of rejection of what she had done all her life." But while her grandmother would definitely have preferred to see Elizabeth keep straightening her hair, there was no drama. Other families didn't necessarily adapt as smoothly. Septuagenarian Florence Price told interviewers about a friend who went to pick up her daughter at the airport and discovered the girl had grown an Afro: "My friend just stood there in that airport, looking at her daughter, and screamed." Price, whose daughter had an Afro, too, sympathized: she called the style "just a disgrace."

"WITH A SMOKE MASK OVER HER NOSE, LISTENING PATIENTLY"

In the civil rights movement, the middle-aged female organizers who spent their lives fighting racism had too much to think about to worry about ageism. If they had a second "ism" to battle, it would have been sexism. "Around 1965 there began to develop a great deal of questioning about what is the role of women in the struggle," Ella Baker said later. "Out of it came a concept that black women had to bolster the ego of the male.... I personally have never thought of this as being valid."

Baker had already turned her attention to the younger generation, becoming the guiding hand in organizing the Student Nonviolent

Coordinating Committee (SNCC). It was, in the beginning, a reflection of Baker's own vision of blacks and whites, men and women, young and old, working together to empower the grass-roots communities. The students called Baker "our Gandhi" or "*fundi*," a Swahili word for a person who teaches the next generation necessary skills and wisdom. She worked with no salary or even official title, moving from town to town, listening all night to the students' smoke-filled debates, demanding no concessions to either her age or her asthma. One former SNCC member recalled her "sitting in on these SNCC meetings that ran for days — you didn't measure them in hours, they ran days — with a smoke mask over her nose, listening patiently to words and discussions she must have heard a thousand times." Diane Nash, who became one of the leaders of the black college students who staged sit-ins at segregated lunch counters, met Baker when she was 18. Baker was, Nash recalled, "the first older person I had known who was so progressive. And I needed that reinforcement. It was important that someone like her thought we were right. It was really important when things got hot and heavy."

Baker's vision of community organizing left little room for ego. Even if white resistance to the idea of black people voting in the South had not been so vicious, it's likely that younger civil rights workers would have gotten restless with her patient, low-profile approach. But the violence was terrible, and the national media was paying attention to new voices like Stokely Carmichael of the black power movement. (Word went around the movement that Carmichael had once joked the proper place of women in the movement was "prone." Much later, he denied the quote, saying, "A woman like Ella Baker would not have tolerated it.") Eventually all white members were expelled from SNCC. It was no longer an Ella Baker organization, and while Baker refused to separate herself from the young people she had nurtured for so long, she did gradually drift away, focusing most of her attention on international issues.

Young people, white and black, were tired of compromise and of taking cues from their elders. When NOW was a young and pioneering organization, members predicted it could someday become an "NAACP for women." But both NOW and the NAACP were suddenly being dismissed as old-fashioned and way too timid. To make the chasm clear, some of the radical feminists referred to the older NOW membership as "Aunt Thomasinas."

"JUST WORLDLY ENOUGH, RELAXED ENOUGH"

Of all the social revolutions that broke out in the 1960s, none was more popular than the sexual revolution. In 1962, Helen Gurley Brown, then 40, published *Sex and the Single Girl,* her clarion call on behalf of unmarried women—"the newest glamour girl of our times." It was not really an assault on matrimony. Brown's argument was that if women had fun—including a lot of sex—and worked on their careers when they were in their 20s and 30s, they'd make a much better match later on. Marriage, she decreed, "is insurance for the *worst* years of your life. During your best years you don't need a husband." Brown herself had married a wealthy, successful, and extremely supportive movie producer, David Brown, when she was 37 and "just worldly enough, relaxed enough, financially secure enough... and adorned with enough glitter to attract him."

Her book was, in many ways, a successor to *Live Alone and Like It,* the 1936 bestseller by Marjorie Hillis that instructed single women on how to live a fabulous life, give great parties in tiny apartments, and turn their itty-bitty bedrooms into glamorous retreats. Hillis, however, had not really encouraged extramarital sex; Brown couldn't get enough of it. She told one associate that during her single days she'd made love to 178 men. A lot of women were interested in following her example, although perhaps at a less ambitious level.

If Brown had a liberated vision of how old a woman should be when she got married, she still couldn't escape the age obsession. In her early 40s, she was looking for work and had an interview with the brilliant Mary Wells Lawrence, who was about to become one of the most successful advertising executives in the country. Lawrence offered her a job, Brown accepted, and they were chatting away when suddenly Brown stopped and abruptly said she didn't want the job after all. "She looked at me very strangely," Lawrence recounted years later, "and said, 'You know, I take that back. I'm not going to work for you. I won't work for you. You are younger than me.'"

In 1965, Brown got to be in charge herself. She became the editor of

Cosmopolitan, a famous literary magazine that had fallen on very hard times and was in grave need of a makeover. And make over she did. The newly nicknamed *Cosmo* brought into the mainstream the idea of sex as a normal and extremely important part of every woman's life. It was revolutionary, even if its content was a far cry from the intellectual fare the magazine had originally been known for. Brown referred to her readers as "my girls" and warned her film critic that his strong reviews were upsetting to young women who "only want to know about a movie they can go to on a Saturday night date at the drive in." Then she added abruptly: "They write to me about their menstrual problems."

FEMININE FOREVER

Brown's "girls" weren't the only ones worrying about menstruation. Menopause — which was frequently referred to as "the menopause" — was a big topic. And the discussion was moving in two entirely opposite directions. Many experts maintained that it was a natural part of life, and it was time to stop making it a big deal. "In the higher educational level, the enlightened woman doesn't fear or complain about the menopause," Professor Bernice Neugarten, of the University of Chicago, told an audience. Neugarten, one of the nation's foremost experts on the psychology of aging, had a PhD, but the *Chicago Tribune,* in reporting her speech, followed tradition and referred to her as "Mrs. Neugarten."

Other experts were making "change of life" sound less like a change than a deep plunge downward. After *Sex and the Single Girl,* one of the books that helped define the sexual revolution was Dr. David Reuben's wildly popular bestseller *Everything You Always Wanted to Know About Sex* (*But Were Afraid to Ask).* Reuben's readers got the equivalent of a course in sex education, including, critics pointed out, some information that was bigoted (homosexuals were trying to "solve the problem with only half the pieces"), weird, or just plain wrong — *Playboy* helpfully ran a list of 100 errors. Toward the end, Reuben turned to menopause: "Once the ovaries stop, the very essence of being a woman stops," he decreed. He went on at some length about how the absence of estrogen leaves the unhappy woman "as close as she can to being a man.... Not really a man but no longer a functional woman, these individuals live in the world of inter-sex." If women saw menopause as the beginning of the end, Reuben concluded, they "may be right. Having outlived their ovaries, they may have outlived their usefulness as human beings."

You are not going to be surprised to hear that Reuben was a cheerleader for hormone replacement. The idea that there was a perpetual fountain of youth tucked away in hormones had been around for decades, but in the 1960s, it boomed. Robert Wilson, a New York gynecologist, made a huge splash with his book *Feminine Forever,* which told female readers how to avoid becoming a "prematurely aging castrate" by using hormones to avoid menopause completely.

"It shows how women who already have gone through the anguish of menopause can experience the phenomenon of Menopausal Reversal," promised an ad for the book, "and grow *visibly younger* day by day until they are transformed into the exciting, vibrant females they were before the 'change'!" It's not hard to see how that grabbed attention. "One gynecologist on the staff of George Washington University in Washington, DC, says she has been besieged by women patients who bring Dr. Wilson's book into her office with paper clips attached to various pages," reported *Science News.*

The pharmaceutical industry was thrilled at the idea of a new market made up of virtually all the older women in the country, and it enthusiastically pressed the case for hormone replacement with ads that made menopausal women sound pathetic in the extreme. "There we were—my husband at the peak of his career—busy, successful...but no time for me," said a woman in one ad for Premarin, an estrogen tablet. "I'd lie awake night after night, more depressed every day. This wasn't a 'change,' it was a catastrophe." Ayerst Laboratories produced a film that showed a woman in a nightgown, sitting before a fireplace, talking about how her children were grown and her husband was "away a great deal," leaving her alone in the evening to wonder whether he was stepping out with a younger woman. The idea that estrogen could keep a husband from straying was central to Wilson's theories. While postmenopausal women would still be "castrates," he wrote, with estrogen her "breasts and genital organs will not shrivel. She will be much more pleasant to live with and will not become dull and unattractive." He compared menopause to diabetes and estrogen replacement to insulin.

Wilson, who had been a gynecologist in Brooklyn before his fame sent him rocketing to a Park Avenue office in Manhattan, was a great spinner of tales. He claimed he had once been visited by a mobster who displayed his pistol and announced that unless his menopausal wife's behavior could be improved, he was planning to kill her. His theories about estrogen were based mainly on one rather sloppy study of about 300 middle-aged women. "Since recent medical progress made menopause and its consequences fully preventable, I believe it becomes the obligation of doctors to tell every woman that she can now remain feminine for life," Wilson wrote in 1966, when he was taking his victory lap after the book's publication. He provided charts to illustrate when women would need hormone therapy, which began with 5 percent of those from 17 to 29, ratcheted up to "about 40%" of women in their 30s, and then covered pretty much everybody on up to 85.

Feminine Forever had hardly hit the shelves before there were reports the FDA was investigating Wilson's relationship with G. D. Searle and Co., the manufacturer of Enovid, which happened to be just the kind of drug Wilson was extolling. Later, the *New Republic* would obtain the tax-exempt filings of the Wilson Research Foundation—a nonprofit headed by Wilson's son—and determine that manufacturers of estrogen made up a huge portion of the contributors. Wilson's son eventually said that estrogen manufacturers had also paid the expenses of writing *Feminine Forever*.

"THE LOVELY CATACLYSMIC RESULTS"

By the beginning of the 1960s, Helena Rubinstein was fading—perhaps it was just as well, considering the direction the styles of the times were headed. Her long-suffering personal secretary wrote to a friend in 1964 that his boss "has had double pneumonia, a heart attack, inflamed arteries.... She was ninety-two on Christmas day and yet she has now completely recovered and dictates, on average, sixty-four letters a day. Two secretaries have already had nervous breakdowns and a third has developed a strange rash!" She had also weathered a break-in—three men posing as florists forced themselves into her bedroom at gunpoint. The nonagenarian saw them and was said to have declared, "I'm an old woman. Death doesn't frighten me. You can kill me, but you can't rob me...now get out." She slipped the keys to her safe down her nightgown and began shrieking—sending the robbers fleeing with only about $100 from her purse.

When Rubinstein died, in 1965, Elizabeth Arden was unmoved by her longtime competitor's demise, but she was deeply disturbed that the newspapers mentioned Rubinstein's age in her obituaries. Arden, who was eight years younger, was definitely not preparing for her own passing. "Death...was a subject Miss Arden refused to contemplate and any reference to it met with icy silence," said a friend. Just four years before she died, at 85, Arden went real estate shopping in Ireland and bought herself a castle.

The passing of the two fashion icons coincided with the end of an era of sophisticated, rather mature glamour. "There's no middle age anymore," a *Chicago Tribune* essayist mourned in 1967. "There are the young young, the middle young, and the old young." It was a new version of the 1920s many-variations-on-19. The *Tribune* writer quoted a psychiatrist who announced that Americans no longer saw any positives in aging: "We used to look forward to being grandparents. Now grandma isn't home baking cookies; she's frugging at the hot spots." Grandma might have replied that it's possible to both cook and dance, but there was no denying that the 1960s were in many ways an echo of the 1920s—if you weren't young, you at least had the responsibility to try to disguise the fact. Otherwise there was...wrinkling. According to an ad in *Vogue* for something called Youth Cosmetics cream, the arrival of the first wrinkle was a warning about "careers and happiness ruined by the ravages that time can cause the unprotected face."

For decades women had been turning to plastic surgery to remove the signs of age, but it had always been a rather hush-hush matter. Now people were reading about it everywhere. "Plastic surgery is admittedly expensive, not covered by Blue Cross, horribly uncomfortable for a few days—but oh my foes and oh my friends—the results!" wrote Helen Gurley Brown in 1964. "The lovely cataclysmic results are the kind you can't get any other way." She began her long romance with facial reconstruction with a nose job, and then went on to endure many, many more procedures over the course of her long life. Her husband declared himself shocked by "the self-inflicted pain," but it was pretty clear she wasn't doing this for a man.

They had seen the future, and it was lifted. "[S]omeday women and men will enter the hospital for the removal of wrinkles and jowls in much the same way as they keep their weekly appointment at the beauty salon or barber shop," promised the *Chicago Tribune*. And it couldn't start soon enough. "Twenty years ago women started having their faces lifted at age 60 and they probably had 'time' for only one lift. Today, most start in their late 40s," plastic surgeon Dr. Wilmer Hansen told the *Los Angeles Times*. He was, at the time, one of only eight physicians who specialized in plastic surgery in Los Angeles — obviously there was still a long way to go. Hansen also enjoyed the old-school tendency of male experts to make fun of their female patients. ("If exercise did much good, a woman's face — particularly around the mouth — should be wrinkle-free, because there is no place on a woman's body that gets more exercise.") Helen Gurley Brown, not surprisingly and not secretly, was an ardent fan and often bragged that she had never taken a day off work in her life "except for cosmetic surgery."

For all the emphasis on youth, there was also a celebration of gray hair — or at least beautiful, lush, charming gray hair. "My hair's gray — Now, I love it that way!" announced a happy woman on what appeared to be a romantic cruise with her husband in an ad for Come Alive Gray rinse. The ads tended to feature women who looked rather young to have gone gray on their own. And there were still some doubts about whether letting nature take its course was a good idea. "The crucial question," a *New York Times* article announced, was "whether men will whistle at (or otherwise pursue) a gray-haired woman." To find out, the writer took a survey — it was a sign of the times that being whistled at on the street was regarded as desirable, and that mature men were pleased to discuss their preferences. The *Times* quoted a vice president of American Airlines generously announcing, "A woman's hair is the last thing I look at when deciding whether to whistle."

It was becoming a lot easier to conceal gray with home hair coloring sets, but it was not necessarily more socially accepted. Certainly nobody broadcasted the news. "A feeling of smugness, like that of a World War II suburban volunteer who recognized a Messerschmitt, always accom-

Being a seventeenth-century colonist didn't mean you were doomed to an early demise. Tavern keeper Anne Pollard of Boston lived to be 104. *(Massachusetts Historical Society)*

Dolley Madison had an answer to the challenge of gray hair—she favored wearing turbans decorated with artificial dark curls. And she apparently didn't share the prevailing social prejudice against rouge. *(Bettmann / Getty Images)*

Mum Bett, a Massachusetts slave, won a lawsuit in 1781 arguing that her enslavement was unconstitutional. She took a new name—Elizabeth Freeman. *(Massachusetts Historical Society)*

A nineteenth-century lithograph that depicts "Stages of Woman's Life" consigned each 70-year-old "always to church and in her place." Then it was time for a "second childhood," and finally women became "useless cumberer[s] on the Earth." *(Bettmann / Getty Images)*

Lydia Maria Child captured public attention with her housekeeping hints and rather sappy poetry about the joys of old age. Many of her fans had no idea she was also an ardent abolitionist. *(Library of Congress)*

Sojourner Truth, escaped slave turned abolition crusader, returned to the lecture circuit after the Civil War. She mournfully noted that rather than report on her message, the newspapers "seem to be content simply in saying how old I am." *(Library of Congress)*

Protected by their aura of gray-haired respectability, Elizabeth Cady Stanton, left, and Susan B. Anthony managed to have plenty of adventures on their lecture tours. Anthony once spoke while standing on a pool table, and Stanton got to play cards with soldiers on a train. *(Library of Congress)*

Dress reformers who bemoaned tight corsets and heavy floor-length skirts thought bloomers— loose-fitting trousers— were the solution. But they drove the establishment crazy and weren't very flattering. *(Division of Rare Books and Manuscript Collections, Cornell University Library)*

Frances Willard was famous as a reformer and temperance movement leader. Then she made a big splash in 1895 with her book on how she learned to ride a bicycle at "the ripe age of fifty-three." *(Courtesy of the WCTU Archives, Evanston, Illinois)*

Caroline Astor would wear so many diamonds at her famous Opera Ball that one guest said she looked like "a walking chandelier." *(Courtesy of the Metropolitan Museum of Art, gift of R. Thornton Wilson and Orme Wilson, 1949)*

"Stagecoach" Mary Fields was a legendary driver in the Wild West. She was still so popular in retirement that when her Montana hometown barred women from saloons, the mayor granted her a special exemption. *(Ursuline Convent of the Sacred Heart)*

The press speculated endlessly about how old the glamorous Lillian Russell was at the height of her show-business career. The answer turned out to be 46— "life's midsummer." *(Library of Congress)*

Turn-of-the-century theater fans loved voluptuous stars. Actress Eileen Karl claimed that each of her famous thighs measured three feet around. *(Ohio State University, Jerome Lawrence and Robert E. Lee Theatre Research Institute, photograph courtesy of Knowledge Bank)*

Marie Dressler reached her peak fame in a well-padded middle age, when her comic roles made her what one historian called "the best-loved star of her time." *(Donaldson Collection / Getty Images)*

Mother Jones with miners' children. The tough union activist found her little-old-lady aura so useful that she constantly exaggerated her age. She celebrated her 100th birthday at 92. *(Newberry Library)*

Rebecca Latimer Felton of Georgia became the first woman to serve in the U.S. Senate, in 1922. Her term lasted one day. *(Library of Congress)*

Settlement house founder Jane Addams, once described as the most popular woman in America, became a leader of the anti-war movement before World War I. Suddenly she was being denounced as "a silly, vain, impertinent old maid." *(Hull-House digital image collection, Special Collections and University Archives, University of Illinois at Chicago)*

Margaret Dumont was an accomplished actress who specialized in dignified-dimwit roles that made comic costars like Groucho Marx look good. (*Duck Soup, 1933, Paramount Pictures*)

When Eleanor Roosevelt went to visit troops in the Pacific during World War II, she worried the men would be disappointed that they weren't getting a dazzling movie star. They were, by all reports, thrilled. (*FDR Library / NARA*)

Captain Maude Davison, center, along with fellow nurses Josie Nesbit, left, and Helen Hennessey, before their capture by the Japanese during World War II. Davison led the women, who would become known as the Angels of Bataan, through a captivity during which her weight dropped from 156 to 80 pounds. (*International News Photos / Getty Images*)

The disappearance of young men from the civilian workforce during World War II opened up opportunities—not just for older women but for younger minority women as well. Here, welder-trainee Josie Lucille Owens works on ship construction. *(Library of Congress)*

Ida May Fuller, a retired secretary, applied for a new Depression-era program with no expectation there would be any reward. She was surprised in January 1940 when she received $22.54—the first Social Security check. *(Associated Press)*

A World War II rationing card. Wives were urged to help the war effort by working in defense plants. But almost nobody suggested that the men who were still at home should lend a hand with the housework. *(Pocumtuck Valley Memorial Association Library)*

Mamie Eisenhower with her 1953 inaugural gown. It was pink—naturally—with more than 2,000 hand-sewn rhinestones. *(Nina Leen / Getty Images)*

In the 1950s, television offered a whole new world of opportunities for older actresses. Ann Sothern was 49 when she began playing a glamorous hotel executive in *The Ann Sothern Show*. *(NBC/Photofest © NBC)*

Margaret Chase Smith didn't get a whole lot of votes when she ran for president in the Republican primaries in 1964, but she did become the first woman to have her name placed in nomination at a major party convention. *(Margaret Chase Smith Library)*

Rep. Martha Griffiths and her election van. Listening to airline executives explain why they needed their stewardesses to be young and attractive, she demanded, "What are you running, an airline or a whorehouse?" *(Courtesy of Archives of Michigan)*

Middle-aged, middle-class women who were worried about the arms race in the 1960s started Women Strike for Peace. They believed their message would be most effective if delivered by well-dressed matrons. *(Bettmann / Getty Images)*

Ella Baker left the traditional teaching path for middle-class black women and became one of the most effective organizers of the civil rights movement. *(© 1976 George Ballis / Take Stock / The Image Works)*

When Gloria Steinem turned 40, a guest told her she didn't look it. Her reply—"This is what 40 looks like"—became what she called "my most quoted line." *(Associated Press)*

"I do not feel old. I intend never to grow old," decreed educator and civil rights leader Mary Church Terrell. She proved her point: at 86 she was still filing suits against segregated restaurants. *(Courtesy of the Moorland-Spingarn Research Center, Manuscript Division, Howard University, Washington, DC)*

Mae West attempted to rejuvenate her career as a Hollywood sex goddess by costarring with Tony Curtis in *Sextette* at age 84. It was generally regarded as a bad plan. *(© Crown International Pictures / Photofest)*

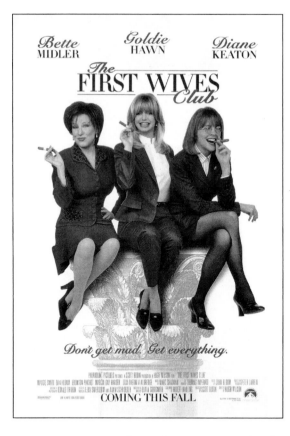

One of the surprise hits of the 1990s was *The First Wives Club*. Women moviegoers seemed to love watching Goldie Hawn, Diane Keaton, and Bette Midler get revenge on husbands who dumped them for younger women. *(© Paramount Pictures / Photofest, photographer: Andrew D. Schwartz)*

Helen Gurley Brown wrote her famous *Sex and the Single Girl* to assure women that they could have careers and plenty of sex in their 20s and 30s and then still catch a highly desirable mate. *(Elizabeth Lippman / Contour by Getty Images)*

Barbara Mikulski had many triumphs in a career that would make her the longest-serving woman in the history of Congress. One of them was breaking the unwritten slacks-ban rule in the Senate. *(Tom Williams / CQ Roll Call / Getty Images)*

Michelle Obama hosted "bootcamp weekends" with her friends while she was in the White House. It was, she said, a reminder that if they wanted to take care of others, "we need to take care of ourselves first." *(Barack Obama Presidential Library / NARA)*

While many people in Washington were obsessed with physical fitness, no one had a more famous workout routine than Supreme Court justice Ruth Bader Ginsburg. *(Courtesy of Magnolia Pictures)*

Hillary Clinton accepted the Democratic presidential nomination in a pantsuit—white, in hono the suffragists. *(Joe Raedle / Getty Images)*

panies the spotting of a dye job," the *Times* reported. Clairol ran a mammoth ad campaign promising customers that they could keep it a secret: "Does she or doesn't she? Hair color so natural only her hairdresser knows for sure." The ads, which quickly became classics, often featured a woman with a child—to make it clear Clairol was for moms, not "fast" women. Shirley Polykoff, an ad copywriter who became an industry legend with the Clairol campaign, would not allow her employers to raise her salary above $25,000 because she did not believe her pay should be higher than her husband's.

When the '60s began, only about 7 percent of American women dyed their hair. Within a decade, the practice was so common the government stopped putting hair color on passports.

"TEARING APART HUMAN ORDER"

As the '60s went on, and those twenty-something baby boomers became the center of everything from fashion to civil disobedience, older women began dressing more and more like their juniors. "This historian observed a Boston matron on the far side of fifty, who might have worn a graceful palla [mantle] in ancient Rome, dressed in a miniskirt and leather boots," complained Brandeis professor David Hackett Fischer. To be fair, Fischer also noted that he'd seen a man in his sixties "who might have draped himself in the dignity of a toga" wearing hip-hugger jeans and a tie-dyed T-shirt.

Twiggy, the famous 91-pound British model, epitomized an era when the Duchess of Windsor's slogan about never being too thin became a national mantra. Twiggy, whose real name was Lesley Hornby, measured 31-22-32. "It's not really what you'd call a figure, is it?" she asked. But it was the look of the moment, and mature women like Helen Gurley Brown tortured themselves to keep their bodies as reedy as possible. "Skinny is sacred," Brown decreed.

In a win for everyone of every shape, underwear was getting more comfortable—tights and pantyhose replaced girdles and nylons. And slacks, which would transform the way older women dressed in the near future, were beginning to make an appearance. In 1961, *The Dick Van Dyke Show* made history of sorts when it introduced a happy homemaker, in the form of Mary Tyler Moore, who wore pants while she did the housework. Many women were already doing that in the comfort of their homes, but it would be a while before the idea of wearing slacks in public would become popular for women of all ages. "Back then...women got dressed up to go to the store," a beauty care executive recalled.

We live in an era when it's perfectly okay for a woman to wear pants to church or to work, or to be nominated for president. It's sometimes hard to remember how daring that seemed back in the wild 1960s. "To sum up, wherever women wear men's dress, it is to be considered a factor in the long run tearing apart human order," a prominent Vatican cardinal declaimed in 1960. Slacks wearers who weren't afraid of tearing human order apart still had to worry about where they could get pants when they wanted them—they often had to buy men's versions and adapt them. Levi's discovered that about 15 percent of its jeans were being purchased by women.

The tide was turning, with the help of women like Mary Tyler Moore and Rep. Charlotte Reid, a 56-year-old Illinois Republican. In 1969, she became the first woman ever to wear pants on the floor of the House of Representatives. "I was told there was a lady here in trousers, so I had to come over and see for myself," one of Reid's male colleagues told the *Washington Post*.

"Mobile still and more affable than rumor would have it"

Walt Disney spent the 1960s sticking to the values he'd long espoused, producing big, animated features that taught children the villain was almost always an ugly old woman—this was the decade of Cruella de Vil. His *Mary Poppins* began with a line of very old and very cranky-looking applicants for the nanny job, being blown away by a miraculous gust of wind that brings a youthful Julie Andrews floating down under her umbrella to save the day.

Nevertheless, older women did appear in top-grossing films of the '60s, occasionally in lead roles. Rosalind Russell, 54, starred in *A Majority of One* as a widow who moves to Japan to be with her daughter and son-in-law, and falls for a Japanese businessman. (Love triumphs over familiar objections to an interracial romance.) Accepting Russell as the romantic heroine was probably much easier for audiences than accepting Alec Guinness as the Japanese suitor. Russell was a leading woman throughout the early part of the decade, starring in *Gypsy* as the fabulous Mama Rose in 1962 and returning a few years later as a nun in *The Trouble with Angels,* a comedy in which a Who's Who of older actresses played teachers attempting to educate schoolgirls, played by women in their early to mid-20s.

Bette Davis, in her 50s, ran into a rough patch in her career but made it perfectly clear she intended to keep on keeping on. In 1962, she placed an ad in the help-wanted section of the *Hollywood Reporter,* reading: "Mother of three—10, 11 & 15—divorcée. American. Thirty years' experience as an actress in motion pictures. Mobile still and more affable than rumor would have it. Wants steady employment in Hollywood. (Has had Broadway)." It was, she claimed later, a joke. She'd had a string of hits, although the biggest were roles as a washed-up actress who serves her sister the pet parakeet for lunch in *What Ever Happened to Baby Jane?* and as a dotty plantation owner whom everyone believes decapitated her youthful lover in *Hush...Hush, Sweet Charlotte.*

One of the defining movies of the '60s was *The Graduate,* a coming-of-age comedy about an alienated 21-year-old who's seduced by one of his parents' friends, the nefarious Mrs. Robinson. By now it's hardly necessary to mention that Dustin Hoffman, who played the hero, was only six years younger than Anne Bancroft, who played Mrs. R. The role made Bancroft a star, and it's interesting to think of what might have happened if Doris Day had accepted an offer to play the part. Day, who turned down the role because it involved nudity, had become famous in the '50s, playing what some critics called "a perpetual virgin" who held off male suitors wanting to Go All the Way. In the '60s, she went from chaste date to virtuous housewife, whose fidelity was tested in a row of films with silly plots and huge box office returns. She was the most popular star of the era, but she wasn't immune to the forces that had sent a previous generation of older female movie stars to TV. By the time Day hit 46 she was playing a widow on *The Doris Day Show.*

Middle-aged actresses continued to emigrate to TV, but there weren't many roles along the lines of the sexy working girl Ann Sothern had portrayed earlier. Bette Davis, during her low-employment period, showed up on episodes of *Wagon Train* and *Perry Mason*. Agnes Moorehead, who had starred in films like Orson Welles's *Citizen Kane*, enjoyed a whole new career at 64 in the TV comedy *Bewitched*, playing every man's nightmare of a cranky mother-in-law who could also cast spells. Barbara Stanwyck, whose movie career during the 1940s made her the highest-paid woman in America, switched to TV and scored a hit with *The Big Valley*, starring as the matriarch of a powerful California ranching family in the Old West.

Among the film stars who wound up playing someone's mother on television, Stanwyck may have gotten the most active parts—her character was taken prisoner, trapped underground after a cave-in, and locked in a mental asylum by her enemies. It was a sterling accomplishment for an era when TV had entered into a love affair with Men Who Rode Alone. Viewers could watch cowboys on the move in shows like *Have Gun—Will Travel*, and modern all-male variations like *My Three Sons* (a widower and his boys), *Route 66* (two young men on the highway), and above all *Bonanza* (the saga of an Old West patriarch who had been married and widowed three times, producing three sons who shared their father's talent for falling in love with women with short life spans).

13. The 1970s

"I THINK I'LL KEEP HER"

Geritol, which had faded a bit from the national consciousness in the 1960s, bounded back in 1972, with a famous commercial in which a husband spoke to the camera while his wife draped herself over his shoulder, smiling like something between a model and the brainwashed resident of a creepy commune.

"My wife's incredible," the man boasted while violins played. "She took care of the baby all day, cooked a great dinner, and even went to a school meeting—and look at her." The woman kept snuggling and smiling. "She looks better than any of her friends," bragged her spouse. "She takes care of herself—gets her rest, does her sit-ups, watches her diet. And to make sure she gets enough iron and vitamins, she takes Geritol every morning. Makes me take it, too." The violins continued as the announcer explained that Geritol has "more than twice the iron of ordinary supplements," and then it went back to the happy couple.

"My wife," the master of the house concluded as his grateful, silent helpmate beamed. "I think I'll keep her."

The 1970s were great for memorable-in-an-awful-way ad lines. It was, after all, the decade of "You're not getting older, you're getting better." That was Clairol, assuring women that they never needed to let "any guy put you down because of your age." It may have been a comfort, although, as a *New York Times* essayist noted, the woman in the ads tossing her shining mass of hair did not really look old enough to worry about the problem: "[I]f she's over 25, I'll eat my bottle of bleach."

But "My wife...I think I'll keep her" had a special resonance. In Garry Trudeau's popular *Doonesbury* comic strip, runaway housewife Joanie Caucus, married to Clinton, told the gang that her turning point came when one of his bowling buddies complimented her French fries: "Clinton leaned back in his chair, and said with a big, stupid grin, 'My wife, I think I'll keep her.' I broke his nose."

"GERIATRIC TRIUMPH"

Doonesbury, which debuted in 1970, featured a large cast of characters who started at Yale, moved on to form a commune, and then marched through the rest of the twentieth century marrying, reproducing, and pursuing careers. Joanie Caucus — slightly battered by life but determined to move along — was the female star. She was 38, older than her pals, and eager for a new start. She wanted a career as a lawyer, and although she worried that no law school would take "a middle-aged woman," she was accepted at the University of California, Berkeley, where Doonesbury fans followed her fictional progress avidly. She got so many letters from enthusiastic supporters that Trudeau's mailman assumed he and Joanie Caucus were living together. Three years later, when it would have been time for her to graduate as part of the class of 1974, Trudeau was invited to give the law school's commencement address. "And they put a mortarboard on her chair in the front row," he remembered later. Joanie began her career in her 40s, eventually becoming an aide to Rep. Lacey Davenport, the eccentric Republican who became a beloved part of the cast of *Doonesbury* characters.

The nation couldn't help noticing how much Lacey resembled Rep. Millicent Fenwick of New Jersey. Both had been in their 60s when they were elected to the House. Both were fiscal conservatives who had a passion for truth, justice, and the underdog. And there was something about their age, honesty, and outspokenness that made them both compelling. The real-life Fenwick had spent the Depression trying to raise her two children on a limited income while swimming under the debts of the fashionable husband she'd divorced. She had worked as a feature writer for *Vogue* and, in 1948, had authored *Vogue's Book of Etiquette.* Her grandson Joseph Reckford remembers that Fenwick would describe her *Vogue* days as "a waste of time" when she would have much rather been working on civil rights. But deep in her heart, he added, "I think she really loved that stuff." While researching the etiquette book, his grandmother went to the Pentagon to find out whether civilians should wear military decorations they'd received during past service. "The chief of protocol didn't have an answer. So the two of them sat down and wrote the rules."

"It was not dull to be around her," Reckford said. "Not warm and fuzzy, but really interesting." Fenwick was nearly six feet tall, thin, with perfect posture and a speaking voice that reminded many people of Katharine Hepburn's. A reformed cigarette chain-smoker, she decided to substitute a pipe after her seventh grandchild was born: "I thought I reached the age when my conduct would not scandalize society."

Fenwick became involved in the civil rights movement well before it was a popular cause for white Northerners. "When she was with *Vogue*, she made sure black models were in the pictures," said Reckford. She worked with the NAACP and, later, a fair housing group and the Legal Aid Society. It was an era when liberal Republicans could do that sort of thing, and Fenwick was also active in party politics. When she ran for the New Jersey state assembly in 1969, she became one of only two women in the 80-person body. And since she was the pipe-smoking grandmother of eight with the Katharine Hepburn voice, she was... noticeable.

In 1974, Fenwick decided to try for a newly available seat in the House of Representatives. Another Republican, Tom Kean, wanted it, too. Both were moderate-to-liberal members of their party, and there was a general assumption that Fenwick, who was 64, would defer to Kean, who was 39 and had been a leader in the state legislature. Fenwick said later that she might have complied but "there was something about that expectation that got under my skin." She stuck it out and won the primary by 76 votes. During the race, her driver-assistant, a recent college graduate, was floored by Fenwick's "enormous bundle of energy.... She worked me to death, I'll tell you that.... It was fifteen- to eighteen-hour days normally, particularly as fall rolled around." In the final election, voters couldn't help noticing that during debates, she easily outlasted her much-younger opponent. "I'd be glad to stay and talk as late as you like," she wickedly told the audience as the Democrat appeared ready to topple. She won and became a freshman in Congress at 64. Her election was described as a "geriatric triumph."

We'll refrain from revisiting the fact that a 64-year-old man elected to the House of Representatives would have been regarded as unremarkable. Fenwick became a famous figure in the 1970s—mainly because of her accomplishments but also in part because so many people believed she was *Doonesbury*'s Lacey Davenport. When both Lacey and Millicent were appointed to the House Committee on Ethics, Reckford said, "Grandma had to acknowledge there was a connection." And she did proudly display one of the original cartoon panels in her bathroom. It featured a campaign ad for Lacey with the slogan "Davenport. As indispensable as sensible shoes."

In the real world, Fenwick carried around a red bag full of constituent letters to which she'd respond — with her own handwritten missives — while sitting at her desk in the House during debates and speeches that almost no one else ever stayed around for. "She said she could learn a lot from just listening. She thought that was her job," her grandson recalled. Early on, Fenwick found the idea of staff so intrusive that when constituents would call, she'd pick up the phone herself and say, "They are too busy. Talk to me." She had an impressive attendance record — at one point in her House career it was estimated she was present for 99 percent of the votes. In 1975, she was on the cover of *Parade,* which called her "the Republican version of Eleanor Roosevelt," though "the taut elegance of her looks and assertiveness of her manner are more reminiscent of Katharine Hepburn."

While her language was elegant ("I think that's something you will come to regret saying"), Fenwick was fearless when standing up to even the most powerful members of Congress. She had a long-running feud with Wayne Hays, the irascible chairman of the House Administration committee. Hays had power over all the day-to-day operations of Congress — like elevators. When one elevator operator offended him, he had the operators' seats removed so they had to work standing all day. "That was the sort of petty thinking she hated," Reckford said. "She'd confront him and get threatened. He said he'd take away all her staff."

On her 65th birthday, Fenwick went on a fact-finding tour of Vietnam and Cambodia with a congressional delegation that included another nationally famous woman from the House: Bella Abzug, the outspoken New York Democrat who was 10 years her junior. "I always like style, and she has style," Abzug once said of Fenwick. "We both have a sense of ourselves. We're both women of the world." At one point the two went on a long side trip to investigate allegations about wrong-ful imprisonment in Vietnam. Fenwick thought the claims were unfounded. Abzug disagreed. They got into an intense fight during which Fenwick said, "Listen here, Bella Abzug, I can scream just as loudly as you and I've got just as bad a temper." When the encounter ended, Abzug nudged Fenwick and said, "That was fun, wasn't it?"

"AND THEY SAID I DIDN'T DO ANYTHING"

Fenwick was one of just 19 women in the House when she came to Congress. It was a small but formidable crew. There was, for instance, Rep. Shirley Chisholm, of Brooklyn, who in 1972 had become the first black politician to run for president on a major party ticket. Her campaign was hopelessly underfunded, and resented by some of her male colleagues, who seemed to feel a black man deserved to be first. (Chisholm later said she felt "far more discrimination being a woman than being black.") Despite it all, she did receive 152 first-ballot votes at the Democratic National Convention.

There was also, of course, Bella Abzug. And Barbara Jordan and Elizabeth Holtzman, both of Watergate investigation fame, and Margaret Heckler, of Massachusetts, who'd be a leader in organizing a congresswomen's caucus to fight for equal rights legislation. Arriving two congresses after Fenwick was Geraldine Ferraro, who would go on to become the first woman nominated for vice president by a major U.S. party. Most of the women were in their 40s or early 50s, which was pretty youthful by congressional standards. "Old" was a relative adjective when it came to Congress. In 1975, reformist "Young Turks" overturned the seniority system and tossed out 81-year-old Wright Patman as a committee chair in favor of 62-year-old Henry Reuss, who was regarded as a veritable boy wonder.

Fenwick never got a chance to work with Margaret Chase Smith, who had been among the most influential Republicans in a Senate dominated by Democrats and had continued to irritate Republican leaders with her independence. Smith opposed President Richard Nixon's attempt to nominate Clement Haynsworth and then G. Harrold

Carswell to the Supreme Court—both men had abysmal records when it came to civil rights. But she was, and always had been, a fiscal conservative and a hawk on foreign affairs and the military. As the Vietnam War became less and less popular, Smith's pro-war stance enamored fewer and fewer of her constituents. She was also suffering from very public ailments—arthritis forced her to use a cane and ride through the Capitol in an electric cart. Hip replacement surgery put her out of commission for four months, causing her to miss roll-call votes for the first time in thirteen years. Then Bill Lewis, her companion, suffered a heart attack. Smith's concern overwhelmed any of the old demands for public discretion. "Bill needs me and I need him," she told a reporter when she chose to miss more votes in order to stay with Lewis at the hospital. When the reporter asked her if she was speaking on the record, Smith said, "I don't care. Nothing matters if Bill doesn't live." Lewis did recover, and her remark triggered a front-page story in the Sunday *Maine Times* on the senator and her aide's "special relationship," which the paper called "one of the greatest love stories on Capitol Hill."

When Smith, 74, ran for reelection in 1972 against a 48-year-old Democrat, Rep. William Hathaway, she had to battle rumors about her health, questions about her reliance on Lewis, voters' exhaustion with the war she still supported, and charges that she had, after all these years in Washington, lost touch with her constituents. "In polite society one does not publicly discuss a lady's age," wrote a congressional observer in the *New York Times*. "When the lady happens to be United States Senator, however, and her age is 74 . . . the subject becomes a common topic of political discourse." As so often happens in these sagas, the new guy won. While Smith remained in a sort of seclusion, Lewis read her brief concession speech, congratulating Hathaway and thanking her supporters. Then Smith sadly returned to finish her term in Washington. Even the women, she felt, had deserted her. The president of the Maine chapter of NOW decried Smith's support of the war and said the senator "represents everything women in the liberation movement want to eliminate." Smith, wounded, never forgot the attack. "Here I was," she said in an interview nearly 20 years later, "a woman with this background and this record—I cosponsored ERA throughout my Senate tenure, stopped [Senate Republican leader] Everett Dirksen from knocking the word 'sex' out of the Civil Rights bill, got women full regular status in the Armed Services, and championed many women causes in Congress—and they said I didn't do anything."

"A FEW PEOPLE CAME OVER AND WE HAD TEA"

In 1972, the Equal Rights Amendment finally got its day in Congress. Alice Paul, lifelong soldier for the cause, was 87 and on the other side of the generation gap she'd help create in the suffrage era. During the Vietnam anti-war protests, a group of female college students decided that, since they lacked draft cards to burn, they'd burn their voter registration cards. They called Paul and asked her to join in. Paul, who had undergone arrest, hunger strikes, and force-feedings to get the right to vote, wasn't enthusiastic. But the ERA—a simple constitutional assertion that both genders had the same rights—was something almost everyone could rally around. After last-minute obstacles thrown up by a few very determined leaders, it sailed through the House, 354–24. When it passed the Senate, 84–8, some of the male senators gave their seats to House colleagues who had been heroines in the struggle, so people like Martha Griffiths and Bella Abzug could be there on the floor for the big moment.

A moment like that seemed to call for a celebration. At least sort of. One of Paul's colleagues recalled that "a few people came over and we had tea." Then everyone went right back to the phones, calling to lobby the state legislatures. Thirty-eight states had to ratify the ERA to make it part of the Constitution, and eight legislatures instantly approved it by unanimous votes. Two dozen more followed quickly, and it seemed as if victory was just around the corner. But then ratification started slowing down. In 1978, as the deadline approached, the ERA was three states short of victory. Congress extended the deadline but to no avail.

There were all sorts of reasons for the backlash—most notably the newly muscular politics of the social right. But there was also a genuine fear and anger on the part of traditional housewives, whose role had been dismissed by many of the younger activists. For generations full-time homemakers had been celebrated — sometimes in the smarmiest terms possible — as the heart of the family and the molders of the future. Now they were the object of pity, women who had missed out on the chance to have careers. Nobody wanted to be thought of as "tired, pre-occupied domestic servants beset by incomprehensible troubles." But that was the sort of language young feminists used frequently — when they weren't comparing housewives to slaves or prostitutes.

And there was something worse than the lack of respect. People were losing confidence in the idea of marriage for life. The 1970s was the decade when divorce started booming. More than a million couples split up every year, and the whole country became aware that statistically speaking, every new union had a one-in-two chance of not making it to the finish line. In 1983, the federal government would note that the number of divorces had set a record for the eighteenth straight year and was three times as high as it had been in 1962.

Getting divorced was becoming much easier, to the relief of many people of both sexes. But men were still the major breadwinners in most families, and many older women were haunted by the image of the devoted wife being abandoned by a husband looking for a younger model. Phyllis Schlafly, the leading force behind the anti-ERA movement, frequently pointed out that the famous baby-care expert Dr. Benjamin Spock — who made headlines when he announced he was eliminating all sexist language from his child-rearing books — "walked out on his faithful wife, Jane, to whom he had been married for forty-eight years, and took up with a younger woman: Dr. Spock was truly 'liberated' from traditional restraints." On the other side of the political divide, Millicent Fenwick's archenemy Rep. Wayne Hays divorced his wife of twenty-five years to marry a secretary who worked in his Ohio home office. The Hays story became even more of a cautionary tale about unreliable men when Elizabeth Ray, a twenty-seven-year-old clerk on his House committee, got jealous and told reporters she was being paid a healthy salary simply to be Hays's Washington mistress. ("I can't type, I can't file, I can't even answer the phone.") The great power broker was finished. And on the day Hays fell, as her grandson recalled, Fenwick "acted immediately to get the seats back in for those elevator operators."

"HOW ABOUT 'DISPLACED HOMEMAKER'?"

The fear of losing a husband to a younger woman certainly wasn't new—remember all those middle-aged wives in the 1920s fretting about predatory flappers. But the idea of the isolated, older woman left on her own after a lifetime of keeping house had a particular resonance now that a younger generation was being trained to expect that women would have careers and the ability to bring home some money of their own. The women who had gotten married under the old rules were facing divorce when the idea of alimony was becoming increasingly unpopular. It had never really existed for most people—only about 14 percent of wives whose marriages broke up were awarded any kind of spousal support, and less than half of those actually got the payments their husbands were supposed to provide. But at least society believed, in theory, that they deserved compensation for their years of family service. Now judges felt even freer to demand that ex-wives—especially ex-wives whose children were grown—be able to take care of themselves.

For most of the older generation, the idea of life without a husband and his financial support was terrifying. "We're a minority you may not have thought much about," 55-year-old Laurie Shields told the *Chicago Tribune*. "But our plight is very real, especially those of us recently divorced or widowed. People our age were raised to believe marriage meant security.... The assumption, unfortunately, is unwarranted." Divorce, of course, wasn't the only cause of displacement in the 1970s. More than half of women 65 and over were widows. Combined with the older women who were divorced or had always been single, that left two-thirds more or less on their own. And there weren't many services available if they needed help. "If a town had a lunch program for the elderly, that was considered a big deal," recalled Ron Wyden, who was then a young Oregon lawyer.

It was a problem waiting to be noticed—and in order for that to happen in America, it was necessary for someone to give the problem a media-friendly name. That happened in the early 1970s, when Tish Sommers, an organizer for NOW, was carrying a chicken casserole out to the porch where her housemates—a commune of older women activists—were ready for dinner. "How about 'displaced homemaker'?" she asked her friends. And from there, a movement was born.

Sommers was a displaced homemaker herself, although with a more adventurous history than the norm. She'd been a dancer and community organizer, and during World War II, when she failed a test to become a defense factory worker due to poor hand-eye coordination, she started a day-care center for the mothers who had made the grade and joined the assembly line. She'd once had an affair with a married man 20 years older—it was, she'd later tell a biographer ruefully, "a typical example of an older man picking up a younger woman, going off trying to rejuvenate." She married, divorced, and then married a man 10 years her junior. By the time she hit middle age, she was living a relatively traditional life—wife of a professor at the University of Washington, Cub Scout den mother. Then the 1960s kicked in, and Sommers's husband began attending encounter groups and seeking the ever-elusive "inner self." He eventually told Tish that while he "thought I was a very good person, he didn't love me." She was crushed. They divorced.

Sommers was in her 50s. She had money, thanks to a family inheritance, but she was experiencing all the disorienting feelings that come with being suddenly single at a later age. Always a NOW activist, Sommers started a special task force that eventually grew into the Older Women's League. Besides being one of the great acronyms of the era, OWL had the advantage of Sommers's financial support, which funded training-counseling centers for the first wave of newly single women who now knew they were displaced housewives.

Meanwhile, the issue caught on with the media. In 1976, *Ladies' Home Journal* published "The Discarding of Mrs. Hill," the story of a 53-year-old lifetime homemaker who lost her husband to stomach cancer. Since he had died before retirement, his wife got no pension, and she was stunned to discover that she was too young to be eligible for Social Security. The family savings had been depleted by Mr. Hill's illness, and when his wife tried to find a job, employers were unenthusiastic about a middle-aged applicant with no prior experience. Her grown daughters sent her money—not enough to help much, yet enough to make her feel guilty. It was a story guaranteed to unnerve any reader who was counting on living out her life with a husband's support. When the magazine left Mrs. Hill, she had a part-time job at a nursing home and was about to lose her house.

Ideas about what to do were springing up everywhere. The Gray Panthers, like OWL, was sparked by the frustration of a political activist facing old age. Maggie Kuhn had worked for the Presbyterian Church, overseeing social welfare programs. But even the church had mandatory retirement, and when Kuhn turned 65, she was out of a job, and starting a new movement of her own. The fact that her new group's name was a play on the Black Panthers was a pretty good hint that it was not going to be middle-of-the-road. The Panthers were intergenerational and all-purpose, fighting for nuclear disarmament as well as displaced-homemaker legislation; they opposed both federal cuts in student loans and compulsory retirement. They also pushed for smaller, more immediate issues—in New York, the Panthers successfully pressured the city's Transit Authority to acquire buses that could "kneel" for the elderly and other riders who had trouble negotiating the first 16-inch step. Age, Kuhn argued, was "a great universalizing force"— everybody, whatever race or gender, was growing older every day.

"Right out of the box, she began to push this message of age and youth in action together," said Ron Wyden, who had started a senior-citizen legal-aid program in Portland. "Listening to her, you'd get intoxicated with the sense of citizen power. I couldn't stop smiling. I thought—this is really what community organizing is all about." It was through the Panthers, Wyden said, that he decided health care was "far and away the most important issue" to tackle. And Wyden was a very useful person to influence since he'd eventually go into politics, be elected to the U.S. Senate, and become the top-ranking Democrat on the committee that handled issues like taxes, Medicare, and Medicaid. "I adored Maggie," he recalled.

While older women were worrying about a lonely, impoverished old age, younger women were getting a pretty clear message that, for them, times had changed. The American economy, so strong since World War II, suddenly faltered. Good-paying union jobs in manufacturing began to disappear. American families were going to find it harder and harder to maintain a middle-class standard of living on one salary. Girls in high school and college understood that when they went out into the world and married, they'd probably still be expected to help bring in income. For the first time more than half of adult American women were working outside the home for pay. It was a new middle-class model. Girls went to college to find a career, and then maybe a husband. Boys dreamed of a future wife who would be attractive, sympathetic — and a good earner. Inevitably, the country lost all interest in groups that tried to make nonworking wives feel more connected to the outside world. In 1974, the *Los Angeles Times* reported a "poignant indication of the state of things: Norwalk Women's Clubhouse was purchased by Weight Watchers Inc., that group apparently being larger, stronger, richer and with a more secure future than the once-dominant women's clubs."

"BUT WE WERE GOOD DINOSAURS"

In 1969, New York City police raided the Stonewall Inn, a gay bar in Greenwich Village. The patrons and their supporters protested, and the confrontation became known as the Stonewall riots — America's introduction to the gay rights movement. Organization quickly followed. At an early meeting of the Gay Liberation Front, among the attendees were Kay Lahusen and her partner, Barbara Gittings. They were both in their late 30s, and they had been activists for more than a decade — Gittings had been one of the founders of the New York chapter of the Daughters of Bilitis, a national organization for lesbians, in the 1950s. But they were made to feel decidedly unwelcome by the younger people, who called them "dinosaurs."

It shouldn't have been surprising that an idealistic movement for social change was ridden by ageism. After all, the student left had been born only a few years earlier, vowing to never trust anyone over 30. "I came out in 1976, at the age of forty-five, in Venice, California," recalled Tita Caldwell. "It was a wonderful, exciting time to be a lesbian feminist. But for me there was a problem. Almost every woman was at least

10 years younger than I was." Caldwell wound up feeling "discouraged and invisible." But she turned things around, joining Old Lesbians Organizing for Change (OLOC), a support and social activism group that is still going strong in the twenty-first century. Lahusen, equally undeterred, bought two stuffed dinosaurs, which she carried around to gay rights meetings. "We were dinosaurs in a way," she said, "but we were good dinosaurs."

Older gay women hit a trifecta on the discrimination front. They had to battle all the normal problems of trying to find good-paying jobs because they were women, but they had been frozen out of the early women's liberation movement by people like Betty Friedan because they were gay. Then their time seemed to have come — the gay community was coming out and standing proud. But most of the early rebels were young and irritated at having to deal with anyone who reminded them of their parents.

A great many older lesbians had spent their lives concealing their sexual identity, and the new gay movement was too youth-centric to offer them much support. Some found a home in groups like OLOC or SAGE, which was started to provide services to gays and lesbians who had been isolated by age. Chris Almvig, one of the co-founders, recalled her first client, Audrey, who was homebound and alone. She had been getting a lot of help from her neighbors, who had no idea she was gay. And Audrey was afraid to tell them. Almvig discovered that when Audrey's neighbors came over to bring her groceries, "she turned the portrait of her lifelong partner who had passed away face down on the piano so that they couldn't see it. When we came to visit she was able to talk with us about her. This was of monumental importance to the heart of the work that we were learning how to do — to cater to the needs of our LGBT elders that we were only just recognizing."

"Older Women, Younger Men — Why Not?"

In March of 1974, *Ms.* magazine threw Gloria Steinem what she recalled as "an omelet party at some restaurant in the neighborhood" for her 40th birthday. It produced what the endlessly quoted Steinem later called "my most quoted line." Another guest, a reporter, politely told her that she didn't look 40. "And I said, just off the top of my head, 'This is what 40 looks like—we've been lying for so long, who would know?'"

While almost nobody else really looked like Gloria Steinem did at 40, she was making some serious points. Women's lives had changed in so many ways. They certainly didn't think their chances of marriage and a family had evaporated at 30, and many expected to be hard at work on careers that lasted into their 50s or 60s. But hitting your 40s was still frequently a disquieting marker. "We've been ignored so long that I got the impression that many women stopped being women at 45," said Faire Edwards, a participant in the White House Mini-Conference on Older Women. (If older women were going to get a government conference, it was still going to be a mini.) "What do we do, turn into pumpkins maybe?" Gail Sheehy, who in 1976 published her mega bestseller *Passages*, about the stages of adult life, described 35 to 45 as the passage to—well, middle age. Sheehy told her readers it could be a great period for a woman, when the kids were grown and "she is released to soar into realms undared on wings untested." Yet Sheehy, who was still in her 30s at the time, wasn't ready to imagine what the entire trip would look like. The book stopped exploring the stages of life at 50.

Less cheery essayists were more explicit about the downside of moving past 40. Susan Sontag wrote a diatribe against "The Double Standard of Aging" that echoed—in a more political and intellectual way—all the complaints the previous generation had made about the different way society regarded older men and older women. "Women become sexually ineligible much earlier than men do," she declared. "A man, even an ugly man, can remain eligible well into old age. He is an acceptable mate for a young, attractive woman. Women, even good-looking women, become ineligible (except as partners of very old men) at a much younger age." She blamed capitalism for the Western world's youth worship. People with less elevated outlooks made the same complaint. Participants in the mini-conference opined that while gray hair on a man seemed to connote sexiness and power, "a woman with gray hair is perceived as sitting by the fireplace rocking, with a white cap on her head." Things weren't quite that bad. If gray hair made women look like candidates for a rocking chair, the obvious solution was not to have any. There was certainly no longer shame in washing it away—about 33 million women were using hair color in the 1970s.

Despite the long-held biases against such unions, more women were beginning to take younger husbands. Conventional wisdom still held that the man was supposed to be the senior partner, but 16 percent of the marriages in 1970 involved older women with younger men, and the proportion went up to 22 percent by the end of the decade. "They're finding, like men, that they can be more attractive in maturity than they were in the awkwardness of youth, more adept at romance, more skillful sexually, more stimulating socially," announced an article in the *Saturday Evening Post* titled "Older Women, Younger Men—Why Not?" The article also pointed out that there were 2,000 American women over 55 married to men under 25 and theorized that there were probably more "if women admitted their real age to the census taker." If the *Saturday Evening Post*—the magazine that made Norman Rockwell a household name—felt the idea was sensible, that did suggest a rather expansive consensus. "The only time the mature woman is 'over the hill' is when she's heading for the next tee on the golf course," the *Post* essayist announced stoutly. Singer Dinah Shore, who was in her mid-50s, embarked on a long-running relationship with actor Burt Reynolds, who was 20 years younger. The affair gave a huge boost to Shore's career, and didn't seem to hurt Reynolds's, either.

If the world was taking a somewhat more welcoming view of older women, there were good reasons. The nation had been obsessed with youth in the 1960s, in part because the first wave of the humongous baby-boom generation was hitting its 20s. By the mid-1970s, the first boomers were pushing 30 and perhaps beginning to take a whole new look at what it meant to be . . . non-young.

"NEW MIDDLE-AGE CRISIS"

The world's vision of aging women had always been based, in large part, on maternity. You reproduced until menopause; then when the last child was grown you were probably in your 60s and elderly. Middle age became a semiofficial stage of life when families got smaller, and mothers discovered that their child-rearing was over when they were in their early 40s. But by the 1970s, the timetable was more or less retired: women were delaying pregnancy to work on their careers, then beginning motherhood at a point when earlier they might have been deemed to be on the cusp of old age. Everything was shifting in the direction of more choices and fewer restrictions based on your date of birth.

That was good news. So was the fact that women whose children were grown frequently had careers of their own to keep them busy. So was the fact that older Americans were living longer. You know there's a catch coming, right? The media discovered a "sandwich generation" of women who had to care for both their own youngsters and elderly parents. And while almost nobody specifically blamed either the babies or the older people for creating the problem, the results could seem pretty grim. "Never before has any group had to carry the burden of both their parents and their children at the same time for so long a time," wrote an essayist in a 1977 *Los Angeles Times* piece called "New Middle-Age Crisis: Being a Mother to Your Parents." A couple with the pseudonyms of Carolyn and Walter Johnson had finished raising two children and Walter was at the peak of his law career when Carolyn's 87-year-old mother got sick and moved in with them. A few months later, their elder daughter got divorced and came home with her 3-year-old. "Soon Carolyn's mother and daughter were arguing about how to discipline the 3-year-old," the paper reported. "Walter Johnson worked longer and longer hours to avoid the nasty scenes at home. Carolyn found herself caught in the middle—a phrase repeated often by those in similar situations." It was, University of California professor James Peterson commented, a new phenomenon—at least in terms of size and scope. And "the middle generation is carrying the load."

The children who preferred to avoid the load were looking more and more to nursing and retirement homes when their parents needed new living accommodations. There were many types, from housing developments with extra services for health care and entertainment to what were basically hospitals for old people. Even the more approachable models gave many women nightmares. "If we don't do something now, when we are older they will have us playing bingo," warned an OWL member at a 1977 meeting in West Los Angeles. "They are patronizing with seniors. They treat them like children. They sit them down and give them coffee and cake." Another member nodded. "What's worse are the arts and crafts."

One of the early OWL solutions was communes — the idea of older single women getting together, pooling their money, and establishing group housing just the way the 20-somethings did. Maggie Kuhn, founder of the Gray Panthers, didn't like the idea of segregating seniors, and she was living at 75 with a "family of choice" in Philadelphia that included seven younger men and women, ages 21 to 39, along with six cats, a poodle mix, and a tank of tropical fish. One of the younger residents admitted, "At first I was a little bit hesitant about moving in with an older woman. I have gentlemen friends, and I worried what Maggie might think about my having them over. When I mentioned it to her, she said, 'It's all right with me. Do you mind if I have them over, too?'"

In her autobiography, Kuhn wrote that denying sexuality in old age "is to deny life itself," and described some of her own affairs, including one with a university student 50 years younger. Ron Wyden had friends who lived in Panther communes — which Kuhn liked to refer to as "shared housing" — and remembers their enthusiastic descriptions of life with housemates ranging from 70 years to 15 months. And the fact that Kuhn was sleeping with some of the younger residents, Wyden said, "was certainly a topic of discussion."

But in most of America, the idea of communes never took off. Nursing homes started booming. Almost nobody went to them enthusiastically, but older women, schooled in the dark feature stories about grandmother-in-the-bedroom, had stopped expecting they would wind up living with their offspring. In middle age, they were already telling each other they didn't want to be "a burden." And there was more money to pay for their keep — along with Medicare in 1965, Congress had authorized Medicaid to pay for the health care of low-income Americans, and a large chunk of that spending went to nursing homes. The vast majority of nursing home residents were elderly women, almost all widows.

By the 1970s there were 23,000 nursing homes in the country, and there was also, for the first time, a sense of alarm about what happened to the people who wound up living in them. It spawned at least 50 major newspaper investigations and multiple probes by congressional committees. They discovered horror stories, like a Senate report of "a woman suffering from a fever of 106...found by a member of her family lashed to a chair." A *Chicago Tribune* investigation uncovered "[a] woman left so little tended that maggots, apparently anticipating another death, already had infested her body."

Far more common than those spectacular stories of neglect and abuse were patterns in which nursing home residents were drugged into compliance. One Senate subcommittee was particularly disturbed about the way patients were given tranquilizers "to keep them quiet and to make them easier to take care of." Another subcommittee reported that tranquilizers represented nearly 40 percent of medication administered in nursing homes.

"Mother's Little Helper"

Drugs were not just an issue for nursing homes. While national attention was directed at drug use by rebellious youth, older, better-off, play-by-the-rules Americans were engaged in a serious romance with psychotropic drugs — particularly tranquilizers. An extensive four-year national study conducted in the 1960s found that tranquilizer use had gone from about 7 percent of the population in the mid-1950s to 26 percent a decade later. Except for among very young adults, tranquilizers were much more popular than stimulants. ("The younger respondents apparently want to wake up rather than go to sleep," mused the study's author.) And women were far more likely to use them than men. By the '70s, one in five American women were taking tranquilizers, and an estimated one to two million women were addicted to them.

America had been enamored of tranquilizers since the 1950s, when a scientist named Frank Berger was testing a new muscle relaxant on monkeys and noticed that the animals — which had been so vicious lab workers had to wear face guards and thick gloves when dealing with them — suddenly became downright mellow. ("Where they wouldn't previously eat in the presence of human beings, they now gently took grapes from your bare hand.") The drug was repurposed as a sedative for humans. Its popularity was partly thanks to a rebranding: a colleague told Berger that the world didn't really need new sedatives — "What the world really needs is a tranquilizer. The world needs tranquility. Why don't you call it a tranquilizer? You will sell ten times more." The newly named tranquilizer, called Miltown, came on the market the day after Mother's Day in 1955 and quickly became a favorite in Hollywood, where entertainers spread the word to the public. The popular television comedian Milton Berle told his fans he was "thinking of changing my name to Miltown Berle." By the end of the decade, Miltown was popular across the country, and although the presumption had been that hard-working men would be the natural market, women picked up on the idea fast. A 1957 time capsule buried in Tulsa, Oklahoma, that was supposed to show the future what life was like for typical Americans included a woman's purse, containing bobby pins, gum, cigarettes, a compact — and a bottle of tranquilizers.

By the end of the '60s roughly two-thirds of tranquilizer users were women. Betty Friedan thought they were a symptom of the "problem that has no name" and the horrors of full-time homemaking: "You wake up in the morning, and you feel as if there's no point in going on another day like this. So you take a tranquilizer because it makes you not care so much that it's pointless." Feminists weren't the only people focusing on the problem. The Rolling Stones had sung snidely about "Mother's Little Helper." ("What a drag it is getting old.") The nation was certainly being urged to worry — newspapers and magazines in the early 1970s were full of headlines like "Housewife Is a Junkie." Physicians complained at a Senate hearing that drug marketers were recycling the rhetoric of the women's liberation movement — one such ad recommended Ritalin "for environmental depression...engendered by such problems as the constant assault of noise...ecologic pollution and social unrest." An ad for a tranquilizer-antidepressant showed a housewife in an apron, staring unhappily at a huge male foot. "FAILURE...She had a hypercritical father in her formative years. Her husband follows in the same pattern," said the copy. "[T]hey have whittled away at her self-confidence considerably—which causes anxiety and depression."

"Some people didn't even tell their own children"

By the 1970s, the Miltown generation of wives and mothers was moving on past child-rearing and perhaps wondering whether middle age would involve more or less need for tranquilizing. One of them was Betty Ford, a congressman's wife the country would come to know very well.

Before we get to Ford's troubles with drugs and alcohol, let's start this story at the beginning. Richard Nixon had barely cruised to reelection in 1972 before his administration was engulfed in what we would come to call the Watergate crisis. It was an action-packed couple of years. First, Vice President Spiro Agnew had to step down after he was implicated in a tax-evasion, money-laundering scandal. Congress picked Gerald Ford, the Republican minority leader of the House, to succeed Agnew. Then Nixon was forced to resign and Ford became the only American president to reach office without ever having run in a national election.

Ford had been president just a few weeks when his wife, Betty, underwent a mastectomy. It had started out as a fairly simple case—she'd been having a routine exam when the doctor discovered a lump. "When they told me I had to be operated on," Betty recalled later, "I protested and said I had a schedule to keep and couldn't possibly take time out." She went back to her schedule, hosted a tea for Lady Bird Johnson, and then entered the hospital the next day. Surgeons removed the nodule, discovered it was malignant, and then brought her back into the operating room for removal of her breast. Tests showed the malignancy didn't seem to have spread, and the First Lady returned to her social obligations. There was no recurrence.

Her openness about what had happened was, by the standards of the day, stunning. The public knew about the mastectomy before she went home. And this was a time when almost nobody talked about having cancer, and certainly not breast cancer. The general presumption was that cancer was a death sentence, and one so grisly it should not be shared, period. "Some people didn't even tell their own children," said Betty Rollin, the author of a breakthrough memoir, *First, You Cry*, about her experience with breast cancer. Ford's story, with its good-news ending, changed the conversation entirely. Women flooded into clinics for mammograms and began self-examining. One of them was Happy Rockefeller, the wife of Vice President Nelson Rockefeller— Ford, having moved up from vice president, appointed Rockefeller to take his old job. Happy found a small lump, and a biopsy showed the Second Lady, too, had a malignant growth. What followed was a story similar to Betty's—mastectomy and a determination that the cancer had not begun to spread. "We're very grateful to Betty Ford for her example to all of us," the vice president told reporters.

The double White House saga stunned the nation. Breast cancer was a major cause of fatality in middle-aged women—deadliest for women in their early 40s. Mammograms were just being introduced, and very few women performed self-examinations—the feeling was that if cancer was fatal, there was no point in trying to find out if you had it. Ford became the national model for a new way of thinking, and she was happy to be a symbol for early detection and treatment. At one point she made her rationale political: "There had been so much cover-up during Watergate that we wanted to be sure there would be no cover-up in the Ford administration." But in general, she simply expressed gratitude that she could be useful: "I'm sure I've saved at least one person—maybe more." She was definitely a help. In part because detections were coming earlier, breast cancer survival rates improved, particularly for older women.

Ford was not the first famous woman to tell her breast cancer story. In 1972, Shirley Temple Black, the former child superstar who had served as a United Nations representative during the Nixon administration, discovered a lump that also turned out to be cancerous. Like Ford, Black was extremely open with her story—she held two press conferences to discuss it. Unlike Ford, she did not give her surgeons the go-ahead to remove her breast if a malignancy was discovered. "The doctor will make the incision, I'll make the decision," Black said. She wound up having a modified procedure.

In the 1970s, the idea of a patient making such a judgment herself was unheard of. As Ford's daughter Susan observed, when the doctors took you in to check a lump for malignancy, you woke up and "either had a Band-Aid or no breast." But some rebellion was blooming. In 1972, the *New York Times* profiled Rosamond Campion, who had refused to sign the papers that would allow surgeons to remove her breast if they found evidence of malignancy. Her surgeon, Campion said, warned her she'd be "dead in three weeks." But when cancer was indeed discovered, Campion flew to Cleveland, where the Cleveland Clinic doctors performed what the *Times* called "a highly controversial operation" that left her breast intact. "There is a small underground of hospitals and surgeons who are willing to do a local excision," reported Campion, who wrote a book about her experience. At the time, she seemed able to tick them all off on one hand ("one in Manhattan — and one in Litchfield, Minn.").

Meanwhile, Betty Ford was trying hard to make people think of breast cancer surgery as a normal part of health care. She told the press that she'd heard women say they'd rather lose an arm than a breast — "and I can't imagine such talk. It's so stupid." It's hard to appreciate now what a breakthrough it was that this was becoming part of the national conversation. Nancy Brinker, who founded the Susan G. Komen Breast Cancer Foundation, said the media was originally so unnerved by any mention of the word "breast" that her staff had to describe the disease to the press as "female cancer."

"If Betty Ford can do it so can I"

Ford had an unusual background for a presidential wife — she was a former dancer who had been married before. When she and Jerry Ford fell in love, the ambitious young politician kept the news of their engagement secret from his conservative constituents until he won a difficult congressional primary. After the wedding finally occurred, they had four children in quick succession. Jerry was moving steadily up the Republican ranks, often on the road, appearing at campaign rallies or fund-raisers. Betty, who was left taking care of the children, was tortured by a pinched nerve in her neck — it was the beginning of a long list of ailments that would afflict her for the rest of her life. Eventually — but quietly — she suffered a nervous breakdown and began seeing a psychiatrist.

When Jerry Ford became president, the media, sensing the public's desperate need for some normalcy in Washington, portrayed the new First Family as extremely midwestern, homey, and uncomplicated. But Betty was quietly in treatment for the pinched nerve and a growing arthritis problem, becoming increasingly addicted to painkillers and suffering from the alcoholism she had developed over those long years of solitude while her husband pursued his career. The public, who had no idea, loved her. Her breast cancer emergency came just after Ford had pardoned the much-loathed Richard Nixon, and the nation's attitude toward the First Family swung from outrage back to sympathy.

She was not a woman to be overly discreet about serious subjects, and cancer was hardly the end of her story. In 1975, she told a TV interviewer that she would not necessarily be surprised if her daughter, then 18, told her she was having an affair. "You just cost me 10 million votes — no, you just cost me 20 million votes," her husband joked as the White House was deluged with 28,000 letters, mainly critical. It was emblematic both of Betty's distance from social conservatives in the Republican Party and of America's move to the second stage of the sexual revolution — when older, average people who had no plans for a torrid affair themselves became inured to the idea that a lot of extramarital intercourse was going on. In 1969, 68 percent of Americans said they were opposed to sex before marriage. By 1973, the majority felt it was okay. "No woman can be her glowing best without being in love," decreed a writer for *Harper's Bazaar,* counseling older women on how to turn their lives around. "An affair? If you have a going marriage... well....Despite recent writings, I'm not a bit sure that extra-marital carryings-on are right for everyone." The idea that a writer in a mainstream fashion magazine would suggest that even some married women might find their lives improved by extramarital sex was still — pretty new.

Betty Ford never endorsed affairs — beyond that one fabled remark about her daughter, she just made it clear she enjoyed sex with Jerry.

When she told a Washington columnist that nearly the only question she had not been asked was how often she slept with her husband, the columnist asked, "Well, how often do you?"

"As often as possible!" she replied.

She was a fun First Lady. On a trip to China in 1975 Betty took off her shoes and danced with the children at a school she was visiting. She pushed her unsuspecting and fully clothed husband into a swimming pool while a photographer was recording a day in his life. When Susan and a friend were having a sleepover in the Lincoln Bedroom, she put on a sheet, walked in, and terrified the girls by reciting the Gettysburg Address.

Betty was hugely popular when her husband ran for a full term in 1976. But Jerry was less so, and Jimmy Carter won the election. The president had lost his voice during the final hours of campaigning, so it was his wife who read the concession announcement. Post-election Jerry Ford was once again on the road, giving speeches, fund-raising for his party, and playing in golf tournaments. The children were off on their own, and Betty was alone — not a widow or divorcée but a kind of displaced house-wife all the same. She was supposed to be writing her memoirs, but her long-term alcohol and prescription-drug use, mixed with loneliness and a loss of her sense of mission, turned her into what Betty herself called a "dopey pill-pusher, sitting around nodding." Susan organized a family intervention. Just after her 60th birthday, Betty checked into an alcohol and drug treatment program at Long Beach Naval Hospital.

She was less enthusiastic about making her drug and alcohol use public than she had been about breast cancer, but she nonetheless was frank about her situation. And once again, Ford's candor was transfor-mative. Women who would never before have discussed such a problem picked up the phone. "The reverberations from her latest bombshell already are being felt in alcoholism treatment centers," reported the *Chicago Tribune*. "A spot check of such centers in the Chicago area shows a noticeable increase in the number of women seeking help for drinking problems as well as an increase in the number of husbands and children referring their wives and mothers for treatment." A representative of the South Suburban Council on Alcoholism told the paper, "Some of the women have told us that 'If Betty Ford can do it so can I.'"

Experts said the number of women alcoholics was about equal to the number of men. But their problem was less well known and carried a greater stigma. Ford's candor was immeasurably helpful. She was also very conscious of the fact that women alcoholics were less likely to get treatment than their male counterparts, and she began a fund-raising crusade to create a facility with space divided equally between the sexes. In 1982, the Betty Ford Center was opened, and a few years later she was honored for her work by the National Association of Alcoholism Treatment Programs. "Awards are often given to people who are old and decrepit because you don't think they'll be around much longer," the 67-year-old Ford told the audience. "Well, if that's your idea, it's premature because I don't plan to retire—and I plan to be around for quite a while." She was right—she lived to be 93.

"I GAVE UP BEING SICK AND STARTED PLAYING A LOT OF GOLF"

Part of Ford's problem had stemmed from the pain of her arthritis. It was the bane of so many otherwise healthy older women and so seemingly intractable that women's magazines, in desperate search of some good news, sometimes just fell back on positive thinking. One writer described a friend so crippled by arthritis she "walked with difficulty, could barely wiggle her gnarled fingers." Then one day she seemed... transformed. Even her fingers looked straight. The author claimed that when she inquired about what had happened, her friend simply said: "I gave up being sick and started playing a lot of golf." It was Beautiful Thoughts all over again. Lydia Maria Child would have approved— although she'd have wanted a few good deeds thrown into the mix.

For those who preferred medical intervention, there was hip replacement therapy, but it had always been a terrible ordeal with mixed results. Margaret Chase Smith tried that method in 1968, and the operation— followed by months of hospital rehabilitation sessions—left her exhausted and contemplating retirement. But things were about to change. In 1970, Smith's other hip was giving her pain, and she had a second replacement surgery. The technique had changed so much in two years that Smith was back in full swing in only a matter of weeks.

In the 1970s, hip replacement became one of the fastest-growing fields in surgery. There would be between 20,000 and 25,000 performed in 1972 — up from fewer than 5,000 in 1970. Of course, it was far from an overall arthritis cure, but for some victims, it seemed almost magic. In fact, the media reported on it with the same sense of wonder it had used in days of yore to describe those imaginary estrogen therapies that made elderly retired housekeepers suddenly race up and down the stairs and become pregnant. "Four weeks ago an elderly woman arrived at a New York City hospital in a wheelchair," reported the *New York Times* in 1972. "Crippled by arthritis, she was unable to walk or even stand erect. Last week she left for home on her own two legs, aided only by a cane." This time, the results were frequently as good as advertised. The keys to the breakthrough included joints made from new alloys and the use of a cement, known as methyl methacrylate, to keep the replacement together.

"CASH IN ON THAT INVESTMENT OF YEARS"

As American women fought for rights and respect and power in the last decades of the twentieth century, older women were visibly part of the team. They were everywhere — marching for liberation and helping to support their families and working out at the gym. But it was not as if the nation had embraced the idea that a woman should actually look her age. The specter of wrinkles still showed up in ads for beauty products, and wrinkles had the same air of doom as they did in the decades before. "It is a gradual process, this facial aging," warned an ad in *Harper's Bazaar*. "Then one day you attend a class reunion...or chance to run headlong into an old beau...or renew your lipstick in the unrelenting brightness of the sun. Then you see what has really happened, and it hits you: *this* is what those around you see and live with, every single day."

The clarion call of cosmetic surgery became ever louder. It was depicted, more and more, as a business decision. "The brilliance of intellect, the advantage of experience and competence can be hindered by exterior aging for both men and women," counseled *Harper's Bazaar*.

"To look as young and vital as your mind is, is not only desirable, but often necessary if you are to cash in on that investment of years." Betty Ford, after her release from the alcohol and drug treatment center, made her next headline when she announced she was having a face-lift. "Isn't it wonderful? I'm 60 years old and I need a new face," she told a reporter. The public seemed to prefer the idea of former First Ladies growing old gracefully — and without surgical intervention. But Ford was cheerfully determined. A lot of male politicians had privately had hair transplants, she told the press. "I prefer to grow old looking as well as I possibly can."

Still, there was always the Beautiful Thoughts route. "Hypnotize yourself into thinking 'I am unshakably, unquenchably, deliciously myself and thus I am *young*,'" commanded a writer in *Harper's Bazaar*. But the much more common message was that women who wanted to keep their looks could only do so with lots and lots of intervention. In another very different article, *Harper's Bazaar* suggested women could look 30 for 20 years — as long as they had the help of "invaluable aides-de-camp," which included "hairstylists, colorists, visagists, plastic and reconstructive surgeons, masseuses, manicurists, pedicurists..."

"WHO CAN TURN THE WORLD ON WITH HER SMILE?"

In 1978, Mae West tried a comeback with the release of *Sextette*, in which at 84 she played an ageless sex goddess who had six husbands. When asked why she was starring in another film, West said, "Public demand. They'll see me as they always like to — as myself. You know, sort of sexy." The rest of the world didn't agree. "One eye sometimes sags," wrote Vincent Canby in the *New York Times*, "and the voice, despite Hollywood's electronic skills, cracks like the voice of the old lady she really is. Under these circumstances, the sexual innuendoes are embarrassing. Granny should have her mouth washed out with soap, along with her teeth." Critics of the future, watching replays, weren't much less horrified, although one Chicago reviewer, after calling *Sextette* one of "the world's all-time worst movies" added supportively, "[T]hat doesn't detract at all from its immense charm and lewd fascination." It was West's last encore. When she died, in 1980, the *Los Angeles Times* obituary noted that she had starred in only 12 films. "No one else had ever established so secure a place in film history on the basis of so few roles, but then no other woman had become a sex symbol after making her screen debut at 40, either."

The movies of the 1970s weren't all that friendly to women in general—it was the decade of frat boys (*Animal House*), three men on a boat (*Jaws* and *Jaws 2*), two guys and a gimmick (*The Sting*), mob guys with Diane Keaton looking worried (*The Godfather*), *Superman, Rocky, Smokey and the Bandit,* and *Blazing Saddles.* When actresses did get major parts, it was generally in stories about young love (*Love Story, Grease, American Graffiti*). Older women were pretty much cut out of the picture. In her early 50s, Shelley Winters did have a leading role in the action-disaster movie *Poseidon Adventure,* in which she played an aging former competitive swimmer who saves hero Gene Hackman. Of course, the effort caused her character to collapse with a fatal heart attack.

On the plus side, Ellen Burstyn won an Academy Award for her work as a 30-something widow in *Alice Doesn't Live Here Anymore* and mesmerized the country as a terrified mom in *The Exorcist*—although all the attention in that one, of course, went to the kid with the spinning head. At 46, Audrey Hepburn played Maid Marian in *Robin and Marian,* opposite Sean Connery—for once, the male star was about the same age as the actress playing his romantic interest. Ruth Gordon made a huge splash in 1971 with her starring role in *Harold and Maude,* a movie about a young man obsessed with death who falls in love with a 79-year-old woman who's obsessed with—well, "with life." Maude does commit suicide with sleeping pills when she turns 80, but she makes it clear this is a positive move. ("Go and love some more.") Many viewers found the movie wonderful; many found it...strange. But Gordon was on a late-life roll. She'd received an Academy Award for Best Supporting Actress (*Rosemary's Baby*) when she was 72 and told the audience, "I can't tell you how encouraging a thing like this is."

Television still offered a broader vista for older actresses, even though TV had moved beyond the early years when any former movie star, whatever her age, was a real catch. Mary Tyler Moore was in her mid-30s when she debuted her comedy about a Minneapolis TV producer who was — big breakthrough — unmarried and 30. "Who can turn the world on with her smile?" the show asked, and there was Mary, by herself, dancing under an umbrella. The show ran from 1970 to 1977, and during that time Mary remained single and unconcerned about her age. It was one of the most popular shows of the era — even Betty Ford made a guest appearance. But when *The Mary Tyler Moore Show* first arrived onscreen the initial reviews were tepid at best. The *St. Petersburg Times,* while celebrating "the return of a delightful and talented actress," found it hard to get excited about "the life of a 30-year-old spinster."

In 1973, the show's creators added Betty White, who was then at the ripe old age of 51, to the cast. White, whom we first met in those early Geritol commercials, was hired to appear as Sue Ann Nivens, a cooking show host with a sickly sweet on-air personality who was, behind the scenes, a man-hungry, sharp-tongued cynic. The producers had presumed the single, middle-aged, and extremely sexually active Sue Ann was so off-putting no one would stand her for more than an episode or two, but the writers — and the audience — loved her, and White won two Emmys for the role.

The 1970s were a breakthrough era in television. *All in the Family,* the benchmark comedy about the racist misogynist Archie Bunker, made history of a sort when it featured an episode about Archie's wife, Edith, going through menopause. But that was nothing compared to the moment in 1972 when Bea Arthur, 50, arrived as Maude, the title character in an *All in the Family* spin-off about an outspoken and sexually active middle-aged liberal. Maude took Miltown and drank until she woke up one morning in bed with a neighbor. She had an abortion at 47 — two months before the *Roe v. Wade* Supreme Court decision. Eventually she wound up in Congress. Bea Arthur called Maude "the Joan of Arc of the middle-age woman."

So older women were certainly visible. But those who showed up on TV were almost always in comedies. In a *New York Times* essay, Caryl Rivers complained that they were never "the lawyer who fights for justice, the doctor who makes the vital decision, the candidate for

Congress, the reporter on the trail of the story." Well, there was Maude
going to the House of Representatives, but that happened at the very
end of the series' last gasp. And Mary Tyler Moore, Rivers complained,
might have been on TV through her 30s, but she always looked "like a
gorgeous 25-year-old." Why, Rivers asked, was the entertainment
world still a place where the double-chinned John Wayne or the silver-
haired James Stewart could be a romantic hero while women of the same
age were only stars of the Bette Davis model, settling for "bit parts or
chopping-people-to-bits parts." Maybe, she theorized, it was because
"the media are still male-dominated, with the male ego as the retina."
The discussion would continue for decades to come.

"I see the awful pants"

In 1972, a reader wrote to the *Hartford Courant*: "Could you advise an
older woman, say one beyond age 60, what to do about the pantsuits
women are wearing? I don't like them. In fact they are contrary to my
training since girlhood on what a woman should wear. Yet everywhere I
go—to the grocery store, to meetings, even to church, for heaven's
sake—I see the awful pants." Nobody could know then, of course, that
in the twenty-first century a 68-year-old woman would run for president in pantsuits. But the *Courant* advice columnist warned that it was "a
fashion that may not pass. Women like them, what with no girdle and no
nylons and freedom from eternally pulling down a skirt."

Some older women resisted. "I'm 45, and I've been working too long
in a skirt to go to pants now," said Alicia Munnell, a senior vice president at the Federal Reserve Bank of Boston. "The miniskirt is the first
fashion trend that I've not adopted. I waited it out. I will wait out pants."
But it turned out, there was no real retreat. Women began wearing pants
to the office, to restaurants, and to formal social events. After a while,
nobody was surprised to see a 70-year-old woman in jeans. School
boards that had busied themselves preventing married women from
teaching earlier in the century were now voting to allow their faculty to
wear pants to school. Older women were showing up in slacks or pantsuits so often that in 1975 a *New York Times* style commentator suggested

that "the more adventurous woman" might want to "look for a new kind of fashion excitement."

Getting comfortable with the new look took time — and the helping hand of marketers. In 1971, Jack Winter, a Milwaukee-based pants manufacturer, organized an advertising campaign to promote slacks in the workplace. He also distributed pro-slacks petitions for women to sign and hand in to their employers, which promised, "We will not wear freaky far-out things that have no place in the office." Slacks became a union issue, too. "The beginning of the new spirit in the offices came a few years ago when employers imposed dress codes that decreed we couldn't wear pants to work," wrote Margie Albert, a steward for the Distributive Workers of America. "Women rebelled. They petitioned, sent delegations to management, or simply agreed that on a particular day they'd all wear pants. We relearned the old truism: 'In unity there is strength.'"

In 1973, at a bill signing, President Richard Nixon turned to Helen Thomas, the 53-year-old veteran reporter for United Press International, and asked, "Helen, are you still wearing slacks? Do you prefer them actually? Every time I see girls in slacks, it reminds me of China." Then it got worse. "This is not said in an uncomplimentary way, but slacks can do something for some people and some it can't," the president continued. "But I think you'll do very well. Turn around." As the president, the attorney general, the FBI director, and other dignitaries stood smiling, Thomas, who was wearing white pants and a navy-blue jersey shirt, dutifully did a pirouette. "Do they cost less than gowns?" Nixon asked the reporter. When she replied in the negative, the president concluded, "Then change." To more male laughter. But a few weeks later, the White House lifted its prohibition on female employees wearing pants. The deputy press secretary claimed it was because temperatures had been decreased to conserve energy.

"In the past, women after 25 started to dress like matrons," wrote Lance Morrow in *Time* in 1978. "But the vivid costume party of the [19]60s taught women of all ages to wear almost any damn thing they pleased. Fashions are more subdued now, but many women, of all generations, have escaped the typecasting of dress."

"Hello, girls"

In 1974, Maggie Kuhn was invited to the Ford White House for the signing of the Employment Retirement Income Security Act, which established minimum standards for pension programs in private industry. It was a good day, and Gerald Ford jovially asked her, "Young lady, do you have something to say?"

"Mr. President," Kuhn replied, "I'm not a young lady. I'm an old woman."

It was a salvo in the ongoing battle to get a little dignity. Helen Gurley Brown was attempting to make peace with women's liberationists but ran into trouble with the nouns. "Twelve of us — I almost said girls, but they say I must stop that and refer to us as women — sat about and related our hang-ups," Brown wrote in an editor's note about her first consciousness-raising session, admitting she had been on her eighth hang-up when she was told to relinquish the floor. The session was a success, but it was going to be rather difficult to get the author of *Sex and the Single Girl* and the editor of a magazine that defined its readership as "that *Cosmo* girl" to drop the g-word.

The problem of being addressed in an irritating-to-insulting way wasn't limited to older women — the male veterans of the 1960s New Left were still around and still referring to their female companions as "chicks." During the student occupation of a building at Columbia University, two protesters got married by a clergyman who asked whether the bride, Andrea, would "take Richard for your man" and whether the groom would "take Andrea for your girl." To a cheering crowd, he then pronounced them "children of the new age." Who had been joined as man and girl. Madeleine Kunin, a state legislator climbing the very difficult ladder of politics in Vermont, went to a Democratic convention in Kansas with another female lawmaker, one of the state's top political leaders. They were greeted on arrival by the governor, who called out, "Hello, girls." Kunin, who later became governor herself, recounted the story more than 30 years later. She had never forgotten the moment. The difference between "women" and "girls," she decided, had become "the Maginot line of feminism."

The only road out of "girls" territory seemed to dead-end at "gals."

After a certain age, you could not be strong without being an "old gal." The *Chicago Tribune*'s positive report on the health of the mother of former president John Kennedy ran with the headline "'Tough Old Gal' Rose Kennedy OK After Surgery." A *Los Angeles Times* celebration of a 92-year-old fashion designer who finally got her college degree reported that Irene Horvath had been a "spry 72-year-old gal" when she went back to school. And then there was the media's fondness for describing any older woman, whatever her achievements, as a "grandmother" whenever possible. *Washington Post* editor Ben Bradlee tried to call a halt, ruling that "words like 'divorcée,' 'grandmother,' 'blonde' (or 'brunette') or 'housewife' should be avoided in all stories where, if a man were involved, the words 'divorcé,' 'grandfather,' 'blond' or 'householder' would be inapplicable. In other words, they should be avoided." But a few months later the paper announced that Lenore Romney had been nominated for the U.S. Senate, "a 60-year-old grandmother making her first bid for elected public office."

14. The 1980s

"[I]T'S NOT TRUE. BUT IT FEELS TRUE."

In 1984, Gloria Steinem celebrated her 50th birthday in a much bigger way than the decade before, when her offhand comment about "this is what 40 looks like" had become part of the national consciousness. While Steinem had meant it as a jibe against women's tendency to lie about their age, it had evolved into a thought about what 40 could look like if you put your mind to it. Or if you were Gloria. It was pretty much the same story when she turned 50, although the backdrop had certainly changed. She arrived at the Waldorf-Astoria "not in blue jeans but in blue silk, her arm circled in a serpent-shaped rhinestone bracelet, her bare shoulders dusted with glitter," reported the *New York Times,* quoting another attendee as saying Steinem looked "younger, thinner and blonder than ever."

Steinem did color her hair, and she had always watched her weight. But she hadn't had plastic surgery, and she often told people who asked about her exercise regimen that she worked out by running through airports during her endless travels. If she had changed, she told a reporter, she was "more radical" than when she was younger. She was certainly more focused on fund-raising for feminist causes. The $250-a-plate 50th birthday celebration was going to the Ms. Foundation, to support its publications and education projects. Included in the crowd of about 750 was Diane Sawyer, the 38-year-old former Nixon aide who was beginning a new career as a TV journalist. Garry Trudeau, the creator of Lacey Davenport and Joanie Caucus, was there with his wife, Jane Pauley. So was Helen Gurley Brown, still going strong as the *"Cosmo* Girl" editor at 62. Carol Burnett, 51, told a journalist: "I remember when my grandmother turned 47—I wept. Now it's a whole new world for women."

People were trying to think about their passing years not as getting old so much as evolving into new spheres of life. But the message from

254

the media wasn't universally encouraging. In 1986, *Newsweek* ran an infamous cover story announcing that an educated white 40-year-old woman was "more likely to be killed by a terrorist" than to marry. As the story told it, there was "an arid demographic study" that "confirmed what everybody suspected all along: that many women who seem to have it all—good looks and good jobs, advanced degrees and high salaries—will never have mates." The numbers were even less promising, the magazine said helpfully, if you were black.

The story was deeply inaccurate—the numbers were garbled, and *Newsweek* eventually retracted it, although it took 20 years to do so. Meanwhile, it haunted an entire generation. In Nora Ephron's *Sleepless in Seattle,* a friend tosses the factoid at Meg Ryan, and when Ryan protests, "That statistic is not true!" her friend replies, "That's right—it's not true. But it feels true."

"NOT SO DIFFERENT FROM COMMUNES"

Women who had gotten married before the new imaginary deadline still had a very good chance of eventually winding up without a partner. Tish Sommers frequently pointed out that 52 percent of women over 65 were widowed, compared to 14 percent of men. "Older men often remarry, while women rarely do," she said in 1981, adding that nine times as many men over 65 tied the knot "despite the larger number of women in this age bracket." The chances of a woman avoiding this sense of displacement by moving in with an extended family of children and grandchildren were minimal. Multigenerational families—home to a quarter of Americans before World War II—had bottomed out at about 12 percent. And communes never did seem to work out.

Still, there were newer options. In the 1980s, researchers attempted, for the first time, to count the number of people living in retirement communities. They estimated there were nearly a million—not much in a population of 27 million Americans 65 and older, but still a sizable chunk of people. Opinions on the benefit of these communities were varied. Betty Friedan couldn't understand "why people would voluntarily put themselves into an age ghetto." On the other hand, Charles Longino, a director of social research at the University of Miami, felt retirement community residents had "significantly fewer problems of loneliness and social isolation" as well as "more positive self-regard." Longino believed the communities were "not so different from communes. First they came together in retirement, then followed a strong community commitment, then an effort to share their resources with others they cared about."

That communal spirit didn't necessarily span the generations. In 1989, retirement community residents were worried about a new federal law that could keep them from discriminating against families with children. "Older people who live in communities of their own age with no children live longer and live happier without all the stress, noise and turmoil," said the head of the Seniors Civil Liberties Association, which filed suit to try to overturn the law. They were pretty successful. Residential developments that could prove they were only for "senior citizens" generally managed to ban anyone under 18 from moving in with their older relatives. To make it clear they meant business, some retirement communities instituted anti-children patrols.

"A WOMAN IN THEIR HOME TO DO THE HOUSEHOLD CHORES"

Almost anywhere older people were gathered — with the possible exception of golf courses — women dominated the population. In 1980, the Census Bureau counted three women for every two men over 65, with the gap getting larger as the age progressed. There were two women for every man over 85. While that meant women enjoyed the prospect of a longer life, the men knew that while they were around, they had the advantage. In Leisure World, a residential community near San Francisco, the *New York Times* reported, "women outnumber men 5,224 to 2,842. Residents say that no one is in more demand than a man who is handy with tools and is willing to do minor chores, such as repairing a sticking door or hanging a picture.

"Elsewhere," the *Times* continued, "residents of retirement communities said that it was common for a man to be besieged with offers of meals from women within a few days of his wife's death." The writer quoted a male resident of a retirement community near Tucson as complaining, "If another women [*sic*] brings me one more casserole at dinner time I'll scream." An 81-year-old man at a community in Long Island reported there were 70 widows and only four widowers, so "the minute they find out you're single, the pressure is incredible." But experts said the women's goal tended to be companionship and an escort to social events, while men who had lost their wives wanted a replacement. "They were looking for a woman in their home to do the household chores and take care of them," said a professor at the University of South Florida who'd been studying life in retirement communities.

It was a familiar story — men had almost all the advantages, except for longevity and self-sufficiency.

"ONE NEGATIVE... YOUR AGE"

"Twenty years ago, 'midlife crisis' was an affliction that struck only men," *Ladies' Home Journal* essayist Roberta Grant declared in 1987. But now that women had more career opportunities, she continued, they also had more opportunities for emotional crises when their career options began to narrow or fade. More choices, Grant warned, meant more "chances to make wrong choices — and, hence, to be discontent."

In the 1980s, everybody talked about women "having it all" — husband, children, career. But, of course, that meant having more to lose. Your job was supposed to fill the vacuum that came with an empty nest, but as Grant pointed out, jobs didn't last forever, either. Still, the *Ladies' Home Journal* editors did not traffic in unhappy endings, so their story about midlife crises was really about midlife opportunities. Erica, who had devoted herself to a Wall Street job that turned out to be unsatisfying, started a new career as a journalist and moved in with a great guy 10 years her junior. A 43-year-old cosmetics executive discovered she was "trapped in middle management," then found a new set of life options via a video dating service. The magazine's psychology columnist assured readers that midlife brought an "incredible feeling of security and freedom.... It's a time for women to go after what they really want out of life."

The determined optimism of the "having it all" era did presume that women could look upon midlife as a chance for a big turnaround. You could emulate Elizabeth Cady Stanton and that first generation of change-of-life suffragists—devote yourself to home and family until the kids were launched, then fling yourself into a career. A newer option was to focus your 20s and 30s on work and then hope for a late-breaking pregnancy or a happy adoption after you hit 40. Or you could follow Erica's lead and hook up with a younger man. That was happening more and more, although relatively speaking, the marry-your-junior option was still mainly reserved for men. When Jane Fonda, who was one of the decade's wonder women, embarked on an affair with media mogul Ted Turner, Turner told her a relationship between two overachievers who were passionate about politics and social issues was perfect except for "one negative... your age." At the time, Fonda was 51 and Turner 50. Shortly after that romantic interlude, Fonda had an eye lift and breast augmentation and began dating an Italian hockey player turned actor, 16 years younger than herself. "He makes me feel like a girl again," she told reporters. Fonda flew to Milan to meet her boyfriend's mother, who looked her over and said she was "too old to give Lorenzo babies."

That was that. Fonda married Turner in December 1991. After the ceremony, the bride served her guests fresh quail she had shot herself.

"I am looking forward to my first hot flash"

If we're contemplating overachievement, we have to spend some more time with Jane Fonda. In the 1970s, she had won an Oscar for Best Actress, opposed the war in Vietnam with such vehemence that her career appeared to be destroyed, and then quickly won another Oscar. In the 1980s, she published *Women Coming of Age,* a super-positive look at life in the late 40s. "I'm getting lines and gray hairs, but I want to think of menopause as an adventure. I am looking forward to my first hot flash," she wrote. Fonda made a notable third career out of being middle-aged. She published a famous workout book, which sold 2 million copies and was translated into 50 languages. That was followed by the release of the bestselling workout video in history and the creation of a workout empire that earned $20 million by the end of its first year of operation. She also starred in *9 to 5,* a huge hit in which she played a displaced housewife who teamed up with Lily Tomlin and Dolly Parton to triumph over a sexist boss. Then she purchased the rights to *On Golden Pond,* a drama about an elderly couple and their slightly estranged daughter, making it into a movie in which she played opposite her father, Henry.

The Fondas were themselves semi-estranged, and Jane had suffered all the traumas of a daughter with a very successful and somewhat remote father. Suddenly she was giving him a big career opportunity — the role won Henry an Academy Award for Best Actor, an honor that had hitherto eluded him. The relationship between Jane and Katharine Hepburn, her film mother, was apparently less rewarding. Fonda theorized in her autobiography that Hepburn felt "vulnerable" about her age when they were together. "She was a legend, yes, but I was the younger actress who because of youth was currently more of a box office draw — and I was only one Oscar behind her." The movie would go on to win Hepburn her fourth, a record that still hasn't been broken.

"BUT I FOUND THAT I REALLY COULDN'T KEEP UP WITH THEM"

On Golden Pond was a winner for Fonda personally, professionally, and financially. But it was the workout videos that made her an icon for contemporaries struggling with weight and muscle tone. She was the latest — and most successful — incarnation of female celebrity fitness gurus like Lillian Russell, who had urged her followers to roll over 250 times every morning if they wanted to live to be 100. Fonda's success inspired other middle-aged actresses to produce their own, generally less demanding exercise programs. "I went out and I bought all these other tapes, which are excellent but I found that I really couldn't keep up with them," said Debbie Reynolds, 51, as she led a room full of older actresses and entertainers, including Shelley Winters, who served as sort of groaning comic relief. Angela Lansbury, 62, released a video called *Angela Lansbury's Positive Moves: A Personal Plan for Fitness and Well-Being at Any Age.* Besides the exercises, it included a scene of Lansbury getting into a bubble bath and talking about sexuality. Neither Reynolds nor Lansbury achieved Fonda's level of super-success, but they both seemed to do better than singer Pat Boone, then in his 50s, who made an exercise video aimed at "mature adults" with Connie Letney, the owner of a chain of exercise centers marketed to people 50 and above. The *Chicago Tribune* described Letney as "a svelte older lady who does a fine job. Too bad that Pat is too busy preening and cracking jokes to follow what she's doing."

"I've had my day"

In 1987, Jane Fonda enthusiastically signed up to play the lead in *Music Box,* the story of a lawyer who defends her Hungarian immigrant father against accusations that he ran a death squad during World War II. The project somehow morphed into a hot ticket despite its dark plot, and the high-profile filmmaker Costa-Gavras agreed to direct. Suddenly word came down that the 47-year-old Fonda was too old for the part. The scriptwriter, Joe Eszterhas, convinced her to do an audition—something established stars never did—and he felt she did a "terrific" job. But the director was not swayed and the studio paid Fonda $1.25 million to disappear quietly. Jessica Lange, 12 years younger, got the part instead.

It hardly seemed fair, especially since Hollywood appeared to be on a roll when it came to scripts written for actresses in their 40s, 50s, and beyond. Shirley MacLaine won an Oscar for *Terms of Endearment,* in which she played a grandmother who hated being called a grandmother. At 41, Cher won the Best Actress award as a widow who found new romance in *Moonstruck.* Olympia Dukakis won the Best Supporting Actress Oscar for her role as Cher's mother. At the time, Dukakis was only 56, but she had no complaints. "After that, we were able to send our children to college with no problems," she said, calling up another aspect of the sandwich generation—women not only went directly from caring for their kids to caring for their parents; they leaped immediately from paying college bills to fretting about retirement.

So you could play a romantic lead in your 40s, but not necessarily... a lawyer.

When she reached her 70s, Katharine Hepburn announced she was retiring: "I've had my day—let the kids scramble and sweat it out." That lasted approximately six seconds. Then Hepburn agreed to star in a Broadway play, which won her a Tony nomination, and she went on working until she was 87. Mainly she made TV films. For all the expansion of opportunities in film, television continued to be the place that offered older actresses the most chance to stretch. The old TV classic plot about Guys in a Group, from *M*A*S*H* to *A-Team*, had expanded during the Mary Tyler Moore era to the Gang at Work, of mixed sex and age. Then suddenly there were all-female starring casts, from *Cagney & Lacey* (cops) to *One Day at a Time* (divorced mom and daughters). In *The Golden Girls*, another sharing-a-house comedy, the cast was much older, and the audience loved it. *The Golden Girls* was one of the most popular shows of the era, featuring two widows, a divorcée, and the divorcée's 80-year-old mother, all living together in Miami. Bea Arthur, the star, was 63 when the show started off. Estelle Getty, who played her mother, was 62 — yet another example of the malleability of actresses portraying elderly mothers. Rue McClanahan played Blanche Devereaux, who was active on the dating circuit, entertaining a steady stream of suitors. Blanche, who went through her 50s and into her early 60s during the run, had a silky wardrobe and an eager sexuality that was one of the show's breakthroughs. Although perhaps it wasn't necessary that the creators gave her initials that spelled BED.

The Golden Girls — which also gave Betty White yet another new career at 63 — ran for seven seasons and drew more than 27 million viewers to its finale. You couldn't exactly say it was a celebration of age, given all the puffy-thigh jokes. But it had good humor and a story arc that was very much built on the displaced women phenomenon — the 80-year-old mom became homeless when her retirement home burned down. When they weren't jibing each other about going to the bathroom in the middle of the night, they were luxuriating in their semi-communal living arrangement. ("We were all so lonely and then by a miracle we found each other.")

"THEY DON'T BUY ANYTHING. THEY EAT CEREAL. THEY DRINK COKE."

The biggest star turn for an older woman came with *Murder, She Wrote*, a detective series in which Angela Lansbury played a bestselling mystery writer who solved real-life killings in her spare time. Lansbury began the series in 1984, two weeks before her 59th birthday, and ended it at 70, when she switched back to her theater career. *Murder, She Wrote* was on CBS, which had decided that gearing their programs toward older women made business sense, given their relatively high purchasing power. It was not a philosophy shared by its competitors. "The networks seem to be chasing people 20 and under," Lansbury complained. "Why? I don't know. They don't buy anything. They eat cereal. They drink Coke."

The pro-youth programmers argued that younger people would never watch shows starring people their grandparents' age, but older viewers would eventually tune into popular programs about kids. It was a theory very similar to the one about targeting your movies toward men because women would always watch guy shows, but not vice versa. "Shows that can generate heat with younger audiences tend to be shows that have a greater potential of turning into major hits," said Perry Simon of NBC. "Shows that start off with an older audience rarely bring younger audiences in."

If women wanted to be really paranoid about the way TV regarded them as they aged, there was always the famous elevator moment on *LA Law*, a TV drama of the gang-at-work genre. There were several female characters on the show, and Rosalind Shays, the Older Woman, was the unpopular one. Played by Diana Muldaur, Shays was a difficult personality, and she slept with the boss. But she was also a pretty good lawyer, and perhaps the creators were afraid if she hung around too long they'd wind up making her sympathetic. So in one fabled episode, Rosalind was rejected by her lover as they stood at an elevator door, calmly told him "I don't want to talk about it" as the door opened, and then walked into — an empty elevator shaft.

Muldaur had no idea what was going to happen to her character until she opened the script. "I was as shocked as everybody else," she said. "I thought maybe I had asked for too much money!" The episode was titled "Good to the Last Drop."

"TOO OLD, TOO UNATTRACTIVE AND NOT DEFERENTIAL ENOUGH TO MEN"

In 1981, Christine Craft, the 36-year-old co-anchor at KMBC-TV in Kansas City, vanished from the screen. It probably wasn't a great trauma for viewers since she'd only been on the job for about eight months. But it was a moment that reverberated. Craft claimed she was demoted because she was "too old, too unattractive and not deferential enough to men." She filed a lawsuit, and the trial brought out details that made it very, very hard to believe the station's claim that her dismissal was just a matter of falling show ratings. The ratings were actually up, and the market research firm that recommended her demotion had conducted focus groups in which viewers were asked questions like "Is she a mutt?" It was a story awash with implications about age and gender. A *New York Times* editorial noted Craft said she was told that Kansas City viewers "liked warm, pretty things" delivering their news. TV news management, the editorial complained, was way behind the times: "There are few female film stars under 40; one of the biggest, Katharine Hepburn, is 73; and nobody ever called Bette Davis 'a warm pretty thing.'"

Women news anchors—an unheard-of phenomenon a few decades before—had become commonplace, thanks to the Federal Communications Commission's order for affirmative action plans. Claims that good-looking women were being given preference were complicated by the fact that on TV everybody was supposed to be attractive. But the age issue was clearer. There were approximately 1,200 local news anchors in the early 1980s. About half of the men were over 40. Only 3 percent of the women were. And while 16 percent of the men had managed to stay on the job after they passed 50, there was no such thing as a 50-year-old news anchorwoman.

Media executives pestered by claims of age discrimination liked to point out that TV reporter Dorothy Fuldheim had signed a three-year contract with her Cleveland station, WEWS, just before her 90th birthday. Fuldheim would, in fact, eventually sign a contract that was supposed to last until she was 115. But she was unique and very much in the tradition of beloved local institutions. She was also a good example of the rule that when a profession is new, disorganized, and low paying, women thrive. When she was first hired, at age 54, in 1947, WEWS was the only television station operating between New York and Chicago.

Barbara Walters became the first woman to co-anchor a national news broadcast in 1976, when she was 47. Her brief stint in the job was something of a disaster, thanks to her partner, Harry Reasoner, who made it abundantly clear he didn't like having her sitting next to him every night. "I remember reaching toward him at the end of one broadcast, in a friendly manner, just to touch him on the arm. He recoiled, physically recoiled, in front of millions of people," Walters wrote in a memoir. There was a happier story under way on the local level—in Seattle, Jean Enersen, a young reporter at KING-TV, had been named co-anchor in 1972. The outside world didn't necessarily notice she was making history, perhaps because there was no drama to her story. "Other than being turned down numerous times, my experience was pretty positive," she recalled. "I was lucky—I worked for a station that was founded by a woman." She was also lucky in having a male co-anchor who was "totally supportive." Enersen stayed at her job for a record-breaking 42 years.

Christine Craft, by the way, was awarded $500,000 by a jury who agreed she had been discriminated against by the news station that demoted her. But the Kansas City judge tossed the award out and ordered a new trial, pointing to what he claimed was Craft's "below-average aptitude" in matters of clothing and makeup. The next jury came back with exactly the same pro-Craft verdict, but it was overturned on appeal. The Supreme Court declined to get involved. And that was that. Craft worked for a while in California TV news, then went back to school and became an attorney specializing in employment law.

"I'm Outraged by the Whole Idea"

The 1980s were the heyday of the "power suit"—pantsuits with broad shoulder pads, thick lapels, and tailoring that didn't emphasize the figure. Their arrival was, at least in part, a reflection of the fact that women's presence in management positions had nearly doubled between 1972 and 1985. The suits looked so very, very powerful—some critics said "aggressive"—that they didn't last all that long. On the other side of the fashion spectrum, the miniskirt returned, forcing women who had worn them in the '60s to decide whether they were still a good idea. "A miniskirt doesn't suit you if you're over age 40," decreed Jean Shrimpton, the 44-year-old ex-model who had helped popularize the trend the first time around. "I'm outraged by the whole idea," Betty Friedan told the Los Angeles Times. "It's like trying to put women into girdles again."

While Friedan was anti-mini, she did assure the reporter, "I still have good legs." That was the appeal of the skirts: many older women who bemoaned the toll age had taken on their bodies still felt their legs were holding up just fine. (Two decades later, actress Diahann Carroll would publish a memoir titled *The Legs Are the Last to Go*.) Helen Gurley Brown, who didn't necessarily accept the idea that anything was going to go, loved the new trend. "Betty Friedan takes it all too seriously," Brown, 65, told a reporter in an interview she gave while wearing a skirt three inches above the knee.

"I GUESS I JUST *EXPECTED* IT"

While slacks were just about everywhere, women hoping to be elected to public office stuck to dresses. "I didn't ever wear pants, and the reason I didn't was that I didn't want people to think I was trying to be a man. I had to be very careful about things like that," recalled Geraldine Ferraro, who made history when she became Walter Mondale's running mate in 1984. Having a woman on the national ticket was a moment that thrilled women who had come of age in the '50s and '60s. And some of them were shocked when their own daughters . . . yawned. "I guess I can understand how some older women, like my mom, would get all sentimental over it [Ferraro's nomination]," Erin Murphy, a 24-year-old graphic designer, told the *Los Angeles Times*. "But, I don't know — it just seemed *reasonable* to me. I thought it was nice. But it wasn't any big drama. I mean, I certainly wasn't surprised . . . I guess I just *expected* it."

We'll see some more of that particular generation gap a few decades down the line.

Ferraro had a lot of problems during the campaign, from scandals about her husband's finances to the overall difficulty Mondale was having with Ronald Reagan. But her age was never a factor. At 48, she was a spring chicken by the standards of presidential/vice-presidential candidates. But if you wanted to see a battle over age issues, you could have checked out Michigan. Martha Griffiths, who had retired from the House of Representatives, returned to politics at age 70, when James Blanchard, the Democratic candidate for governor, made her his running mate. They won and remained a successful team until 1990, when Griffiths was 78 and Blanchard dropped her from his ticket, claiming she was getting increasingly frail. Griffiths rejoined that it was a bad idea to offend an elderly woman when it was women and the elderly who had made him governor in the first place. Blanchard stuck to his guns but lost reelection. "I don't know if I feel vindicated, but I think it clearly shows that I won it for him the first two times," Griffiths said.

In 1980, Millicent Fenwick ran for reelection to another term against a 26-year-old Democrat who promised not to bring up the age issue "unless she does." She won with nearly 80 percent of the vote. Fenwick kept getting more famous. TV's *60 Minutes* did a profile: "This old-fashioned lady is also a thoroughly modern woman... she is an elegant, literate, dead-honest legislator whose somewhat patrician manner gets on some people's nerves and amuses others." The *Wall Street Journal* claimed that Fenwick was "unique" in American politics: "a 72-year-old pipe-smoking patrician who wears a heart pacemaker and rarely works less than 12 hours a day."

Like Fenwick, that pipe story never seemed to get old. But then her congressional district was eliminated during the every-10-year redrawing of the boundaries. There was no place for her in the House — it was either move up or go home. On Thanksgiving of 1981, in bed with a cold, she wasn't sure. "I lie here now, 71 years old, wondering endlessly whether or not to run for the Senate next year," she wrote in her journal. "I've never thought I was ambitious, but is it pushing me now?" She ran and won the Republican primary — at a steep cost. She had never liked taking campaign donations, so she spent $776,000 of her own money on the effort. Then she ran up against Frank Lautenberg, the Democratic nominee, who had more cash than Fenwick and a far greater willingness to spend it. "She had never raised money until the Senate race and then she was unprepared for it," her grandson Joseph Reckford said. "She had a professional consultant, but she let him go."

One of her eccentricities was a refusal to leave Washington while Congress was in session — a practice other House members regarded as near insanity. Fenwick was not in New Jersey for much of the campaign, and her organization was a mess. Lautenberg had no compunctions about pointing out that he was 14 years younger. "The last thing I wanted to do was assault her," he said, "but I thought it was important to remind the voters of age, because to develop standing, starting out in your seventies, it would be harder to garner seniority and ranking positions." He also referred to her as "eccentric," a term he claimed was not the least bit age related. One way or the other, Lautenberg won. Whatever issues he had about age in the Senate seemed to dim as time passed. He ran his own final campaign in 2008, when he was 84, and died in office in 2013.

"I think it hurt her a lot," Fenwick's grandson said of the loss. "But she didn't show it. She had no patience with self-pity." Rebounding, Fenwick accepted an appointment by Ronald Reagan to be permanent representative to the UN Food and Agriculture Organization in Rome. She went happily to Italy, where she promptly replaced the Cadillac that was assigned to her with a Ford. "I am accredited to an organization that is trying to feed the hungry. There's something very inappropriate about that," she said of the expensive car.

"She loved that work," recalled Reckford. "Absolutely adored it." Since Fenwick's job covered much of the impoverished world, he added, "She would talk about nothing but Africa. She wanted me to leave law school and go to Rwanda." He decided to stay put, much to his grandmother's disappointment. "She thought I was wasting my life. She was never big on higher education."

"IN HER LONG GOODBYE"

The age requirement for First Lady, once Jackie Kennedy left the job, seemed to have crept upward. Except for Rosalynn Carter, who started at 49, and Barbara Bush, who was 63, all the presidents' wives from Lady Bird Johnson through Laura Bush were in their 50s. Nancy Reagan entered the White House at 59, and she went for a look of mature-Hollywood glamour. She was not a particularly age-conscious woman— perhaps that was due to a sense that everything related to birth dates was subjective. When filling out Nancy's birth certificate, her mother made herself four years younger; eventually Nancy dropped two years from her own age and eliminated her father from the document entirely, since he had abandoned the family. By the end, one biographer jibed, the only two accurate pieces of information on her birth certificate were "her sex and her color."

She was, however, very conscious of fashion and of her weight. A slightly catty *Chicago Tribune* writer compared her to the Duchess of Windsor and announced the First Lady was "much prettier" although "they shared the same bony dress size and apparent fear of food." Her husband was her obsession, and while everybody liked happy marriages, feminists were somewhat appalled by how far she went in her devotion. ("My life began with Ronnie.") While he was in office, she wasn't particularly popular. Critics sniped about her $200,000 presidential china, and a Washington postcard showed "Queen Nancy" in a fur cape and crown. When doctors discovered cancer in her left breast, Nancy was open about the mastectomy that followed and urged other women to have annual mammograms, but she did not spark the same national applause that Betty Ford had. Even when her husband was shot, the nation's appreciation of her devotion was mixed with reserve. While polls showed natural public sympathy, there were also lots of eyebrow-raising stories about Nancy's use of an astrologer to warn her if Ron was ever going to be in danger again.

Nancy Reagan became a real national heroine late in life, after her husband developed Alzheimer's disease. "Later, in her long goodbye with President Reagan, she became a voice on behalf of millions of families going through the depleting, aching reality of Alzheimer's, and took on a new role, as advocate, on behalf of treatments that hold the potential and the promise to improve and save lives," said President Obama after her death. She spent more than a decade standing by her husband's side as he declined, and her vigor in supporting Alzheimer's research caused her to break with President George W. Bush, who opposed embryonic stem cell research due to its connection to abortion.

THE BAG LADY PAPERS

Even before Ronald Reagan became a victim of Alzheimer's, he was a supporter of medical research—in 1983, as president, he signed a resolution declaring National Alzheimer's Disease month, which sent federal funding for the then little-known ailment up from $1 million to $11 million. The government's contributions soared in 1994 when he announced his own diagnosis and hit about $700 million in the year after his death. It was not, until then, regarded as a problem that generally afflicted men.

During the first congressional hearing on Alzheimer's in 1980, one of the psychiatrist-experts lamented: "We have a classic notion of what the disease is, and unfortunately, we have a stereotype. It is—and I hate to be sexist, but because there are more older women than men, it is usually sort of a little old woman who is doddering around, sitting in a geriatric chair, not knowing time, place or person. This is not the way we see the disease." In fact, some of the other stereotypes made the one about doddering old women look peachy. "They steal. They shoplift. They're violent. They 'expose' themselves in public," warned a sensational paperback on Alzheimer's titled *The Living Death*.

At about the same time, American women—particularly the ones living in large cities—were becoming obsessed with the image of the shopping bag lady. The bag lady was a mainly urban phenomenon—dragging her earthly possessions around in a suitcase or a shopping cart, talking to herself, and sleeping, homeless, on the streets. Even for people who were in no real danger of ever becoming homeless, she represented things they knew did happen to women on every rung of the economic ladder: ending up alone, perhaps demented, avoided by the rest of society.

The bag lady legend might have begun in 1979, when Irmgard Meyer, described as "a 'shopping-bag lady' who wandered the streets of midtown Manhattan homeless and alone," was found raped and suffocated near Grand Central Station with 90 cents in her pocket. Further inquiry revealed Meyer was a former employee of a New York ad agency who had thousands of dollars in assets, including some land in the Southwest. Nobody knew what had happened to her, but women around the country read the story and shivered at the idea that everything could fall apart—your marriage, your job, your sanity. The image scared even the impossibly wealthy. Oprah Winfrey said she once rejected her financial advisers' suggestion about stocks and hoarded $50 million in cash as a "bag-lady fund." Sherry Lansing, the former chair of Paramount Pictures, told the *New York Times* that her recurrent nightmare was being a homeless woman sitting on the street when her ex-husband drives past in a Rolls-Royce and tells his blond partner she was "just someone I used to know."

While homelessness would continue to be a major problem in American cities, new social service programs were reasonably successful in getting the shopping bag ladies off the streets. But there was still something about the image that nagged at women who had absolutely no reason to worry they'd become one. In 2011, Adrienne Arsht, the chairwoman of TotalBank, told an interviewer while discussing her philanthropy that she was constantly fighting to "get over the fear that I'll give it all away and be a bag lady." Alexandra Penney, a former bestselling author and magazine executive, lost all her investments in the Bernie Madoff scandal of 2008. She did still have all the jewelry she had bought in her prime, telling herself that "if you're ever a bag lady, you can sell it." She went on to become a successful photographer and blogger — and the author of a book called *The Bag Lady Papers*.

15. The 1990s

"WHEN THE CURTAIN WAS SUPPOSED TO FALL"

Perhaps it was a coincidence, but when Meryl Streep turned forty, she got three scripts in quick succession in which her character was a witch.

Streep ignored the offers but wasn't surprised. "It's over," she told her husband. She had been starring in films rapid-fire—classics like *Sophie's Choice, Silkwood,* and *Out of Africa.* But she was traveling all over the world to shoot them, and her children were getting tired of always being the new kids in class. The family settled down in California, where her job options were narrower. She had just finished making *Ironweed* with Jack Nicholson, a film she did not really see as a career boost—she played "an old drunk of indeterminate age. Maybe she was fifty, maybe she was—who knows? Sixty?"

Well, it obviously wasn't over after all. Streep was nominated for an Academy Award for her *Ironweed* starring role. She went on to make a dozen movies in the 1990s, including *The River Wild,* an action drama in which she played a whitewater rafting expert who foils a pair of armed killers, and *The Bridges of Madison County,* a romance about a traveling photographer and a lonely housewife, for which she received another Academy Award nomination. *Bridges,* which was based on a bestselling novel, was a huge hit. Streep co-starred with Clint Eastwood, then sixty-five. "I was forty-five and the studio felt I was too old," she recalled. But Eastwood, who also produced and directed the film, went to bat for her. "His mother liked me and he loved his mother," Streep theorized.

Looking back, Streep thinks she worried most about aging when she was approaching forty. "That was the time when the curtain was supposed to fall. For my immediate predecessors, that's when it did fall." But, she discovered, she could "surf the wave" that had washed away previous generations of actresses. It was more than just continuing to work and finding a wise-mom or sassy-old-dame niche. She was getting all kinds of roles—in romances, action movies, musicals. It was, she felt, partly because older women were becoming a larger part of movie audiences. And the people making decisions in Hollywood began to include a number of female executives. Dawn Steel became president of Columbia Pictures in 1987. And if she was not the first woman to become powerful in Hollywood, Nora Ephron said later, "she was the first woman to understand that part of her responsibility was to make sure that eventually there were lots of other powerful women." Ephron herself produced and directed the very successful *Julie & Julia* when she was in her late 60s. And Nancy Meyers was in her 50s when she made *Something's Gotta Give*.

Being a Hollywood pioneer wasn't always rosy. Steel had been head of production at Paramount when she was in her early 40s and was overthrown while she was in the hospital, giving birth to her daughter. "I don't know how to tell you this, babe, but you got fired while you were in labor," her husband told her. But within six months, she got the job at Columbia.

So things were looking up. But in life as in Academy Award nominations, Meryl Streep proved to be an outlier. There were still plenty of examples that illustrated Hollywood's general allergy to aging. In 1997, Riley Weston, a writer and actress who felt she was being aged out of Hollywood, celebrated being 30 by shaving over a dozen years off her age. (It helped that she was tiny and wrinkle-free.) She began submitting screenplays in her new identity as a precocious teenager and was quickly hired to write for *Felicity*, a TV series about a first-year college student. She made *Entertainment Weekly*'s list of the "100 Most Creative People in Entertainment." And Disney offered her a juicy screenwriting deal. Then someone blew the whistle and the deals were dead. "In a business fraught with age bias, I did what I felt I had to do to succeed," she explained. You could appreciate her dilemma, but it's pretty clear that when it comes to figuring out how to overcome age discrimination, pretending to be a teenager is not a long-term viable option.

"THEY'RE GOING TO HAVE TO CARRY ME OUT FEET FIRST"

Show business was a particular challenge, age-wise. Career advancement opportunities for older women were growing in many other professions, and the country was noticing—really noticing—how many older women were staying in the workforce, or reentering it after a period of full-time homemaking. In 1950, less than a quarter of the workers 55 and over were women. By 1993, it was 44 percent.

There were some obvious explanations for the change. The proportion of young working women had jumped in the 1970s, so it was logical that the proportion of women working in late middle age would show a similar increase a couple of decades later. Also, women dominated fields like retail that tolerated older workers best. And they needed the money. One survey of women 55 and older who were divorced, separated, or widowed found that only 5.5 percent got income from pension investments. And less than 2 percent of those who were divorced got alimony. Nonmarried women over 65 got, on average, 72 percent of their living from Social Security. A quarter had Social Security and absolutely nothing else. And, of course, gay women who had been living together in committed relationships for decades got no additional benefit whatsoever when their partners died.

By 2000, the average monthly Social Security check for a woman would be $696, compared to $928 for men. That $696 would translate to about $1,021 now. And the story of how far Social Security would take you depended a whole lot on where you lived. A 76-year-old woman at a 1998 White House panel told President Bill Clinton that her $915 a month allowed her to "live very well, independently and . . . without assistance from my sons" in Bristol, Tennessee. Another woman, a home care aide who was still working, seemed to be getting a similar income, but it left her living "paycheck to paycheck" in Seattle. There were no panelists reporting from New York City, where, in the 1990s, the average one-bedroom apartment cost about $1,500 a month.

So extra cash was definitely an incentive to avoid retirement. But a lot of women who didn't have serious financial problems still wanted to keep working because they found the prospect of a life of leisure boring. Ruth Cambron told the *New York Times* it was a vacation cruise that did it. "That convinced me not to retire. I did not want to feel useless," she recalled. (There does seem to be something about cruise ships that sends certain people over the edge.) Some happily married women found that staying home all day with a retired husband was just too much togetherness. Pauline Phillips, who wrote a popular advice column under the name Abigail Van Buren, said that was one of the more common problems she heard about from her readers. "Dear Abby" herself announced in 1993, when she was 75, that she planned to keep working forever: "What would I do? Boy, they're going to have to carry me out feet first." She turned the column over to her daughter full-time in 2002, when she began suffering from Alzheimer's disease.

"Forever Young"

Time followed up its covers on unwanted old people (1970), old people in revolt (1977), and old people enjoying their "fun years" without necessarily paying the bill (1988) with a 1996 cover titled "Forever Young." Researchers, the magazine told its readers, "are starting to talk about the likelihood of people living well into their second centuries with the smooth skin, firm muscles, clear vision, high energy and vigorous sexual capabilities they once could enjoy only in youth." Further reading revealed that while scientists were learning a great deal about the way the aging process worked, there hadn't actually been any big leaps in changing it. Still, *Time* reported, there were lots of "new therapies" that might provide a breakthrough, "from melatonin to antioxidants to hormone-replacement therapy to the intriguing hormonal precursor DHEA."

It was the same old story, but there were always new "miracles." In 1995, the book *The Melatonin Miracle* inspired *Newsweek* to produce a cover piece that featured the owner of a natural-foods store in Rockledge, Pennsylvania, simply answering her phone with "Yes, we have melatonin!" Melatonin, a hormone secreted by the pineal gland, was being touted as the newest way "to reset your aging clock." But eventually expectations narrowed. It would march into the twenty-first century known mainly as an over-the-counter sleep medication.

DHEA, that "intriguing hormonal precursor," was, like melatonin, the beneficiary of a new federal law that allowed dietary supplement manufacturers to avoid FDA scrutiny by simply noting in their ads that the products "have not been evaluated by the Food and Drug Administration." Besides slowing aging, DHEA was, at one point or another, supposed to do everything from prevent cancer to burn fat. "Some enthusiasts say that a daily dose of the substance has taken 20 years off their chronological ages," reported a health writer in the *New York Times*. Like most of the miracles, DHEA ran into that old devil: research. The Mayo Clinic conducted a two-year study on its effects on elderly men and women. "Our data provide no evidence that either DHEA or low-dose testosterone is an effective antiaging hormone supplement and argue strongly against the use of these agents for this purpose," the scientists concluded.

It's not that there wasn't medical progress in addressing problems that accompanied aging—like diabetes or arthritis or emphysema. But that was about improving the quality of your life as you got older, not averting aging altogether. And the public still was obsessed with that fountain of youth, egged on by the frequent publication of well-marketed books touting some new magic potion. In 1998, it was *Grow Young with HGH: The Amazing Medically Proven Plan to Reverse Aging,* by Dr. Ronald Klatz, which touted human growth hormone. "In a few decades, the traditional, enfeebled, ailing elderly person will be but a grotesque memory of a barbaric past," promised Klatz, who had a medical degree from the Central America Health Sciences University in Belize. The "consequences of *not acting,*" he insisted, "are far worse than the consequences of acting."

Women were also being barraged by stories about hormone replacement therapy (HRT). Anyone watching the news in the late 1990s might reasonably believe that HRT would help prevent everything from colon cancer to tooth loss to Alzheimer's disease. Premarin, the most popular version, was the bestselling prescription drug in the country in 1992. The manufacturers did not overpublicize the fact that the name was a reference to its source, *pregnant mares' urine.* Six million women were using it regularly.

There had already been questions about its long-term effects. In 1991, a Senate subcommittee on aging held a hearing on menopause and estrogen, in which expert witnesses basically agreed that...more research needed to be done. There was, chairman Brock Adams noted, "no public health policy" on whether HRT was good, bad, or indifferent. Representative Pat Schroeder, who had been complaining long and loud about the tendency of medical researchers to use men as the basis for their studies, suggested that one of the reasons there hadn't been more effort to study menopause was that "ageism against women is much heavier than ageism against men.

"I am delighted to be here today and finally see menopause come out of the closet, see it come out and become a legitimate health care issue rather than a joke," she said, adding that "there are days when I think if I hear one more 'raging hormone' joke I will have a little trouble retaining my self-control."

It would have been hard not to feel that if men had menopause, a lot more well-researched answers would have been available. But things were changing—thanks to champions like Schroeder and Bernadine Healy, who in 1991 became the first woman to head the National Institutes of Health. Under Healy, the NIH would launch a massive study of postmenopausal women, known as the Women's Health Initiative.

"My wife is 61 years old. How old is she going to be when this study is completed?" Brock Adams asked. The senator, a big supporter of government spending on women's health, wouldn't be around to pursue the issue. In 1993, he was forced to retire after a number of women accused him of sexually molesting them after giving them drinks laced with drugs.

Sigh.

"WHAT SIXTY LOOKS LIKE"

In what had clearly become a ritual, friends threw Gloria Steinem a "This is what sixty looks like" party to celebrate her birthday milestone and raise money for her charities. (Steinem's funeral, they told one another, was inevitably going to be a fund-raiser.) "She's Elizabeth Cady Stanton and Susan B. Anthony and Emma Goldman all rolled up into one—and she still doesn't gain any weight," announced Bella Abzug. Steinem, who had always talked about living to be 100, said she hoped to be alive in 2030 to "see what this country will be like when one in four women is 65 or over."

Not all feminists were as serene as Steinem. "When my friends threw a surprise party on my sixtieth birthday I could have kicked them all," recalled Betty Friedan. She felt as if her loved ones were "distancing me from their fifty-, forty-, thirty-year-old selves." She was depressed for weeks. But that was back in 1981. Friedan was pretty good at reinventing herself, and five years later, she'd be researching a new book on women and aging. Her sixty-fifth birthday, in 1986, was a bash, featuring more than 200 people who came from around the world to put on "a musical comedy about my life, a celebration of life that transcended age." This all happened at the Palladium, "the new 'in' disco in New York...and later we all went downstairs and danced."

Friedan's book took a little longer to write than she had anticipated. By the time *The Fountain of Age* came out, in 1993, she was past 70 and irate that anyone might regard that as over the hill. Retirement, she felt, was outdated—everyone should routinely expect to keep working into their 80s. Friedan specialized in angry tours of the sins of the mass media, and in her new book she had plenty of targets for her outrage. While people—especially women—were living longer and accumulating more assets for their later years, she wrote, "there was a curious *absence*—in effect, a blackout—*of images of people over sixty-five*, especially older women, doing, or even selling, anything at all."

Well, there was Angela Lansbury solving all those crimes on TV. But Friedan was never a fan of on-the-one-hand-this-on-the-other-that analyses. She was looking for the enemy, and she was especially offended by the advertising industry's attempts to portray older people as geriatric children. She found a Massachusetts restaurant chain offering a "kiddieburger" to "all kids under 10 and over 65" and a poster inviting the "young at heart" to have a "Senior Birthday Party at McDonald's" with cake and paper hats. There was also a book, called *Teaching and Loving the Elderly,* that proposed enriching "the poor childlike senior citizen" with intellectual challenges like identifying which states were in the 13 colonies.

"DON'T TALK ABOUT GOLDEN YEARS TO SOMEBODY WHO IS OLD"

Friedan also hated being introduced as "the mother of the women's movement"—a term she felt was used to separate women her age from younger feminists. (She quoted a 70-year-old theologian who had been invited to speak at a conference of female ministers and discovered that she had been sectioned off into a tiny group labeled "Our Foremothers.") She'd hit upon an important distinction: even in places where discrimination was taboo, there seemed to be a big difference between including older (i.e., middle-aged) women and accepting those who were seen as just plain old. When the National Women's Political Caucus held its first big meeting in 1971, the founders formed a policy council that had only one member under 35 and none whatsoever over 65. The younger women immediately protested being ignored, but no one said anything about the other end of the equation.

"[T]he message has gone out to those of us over sixty that your 'Sisterhood' does not include us," wrote Barbara Macdonald, a feminist in her seventies. Macdonald told her younger colleagues in the movement they were just like men, treating her generation "as women who used to be women but aren't any more. You do not see us in our present lives, you do not identify with our issues, you exploit us, you patronize us, you stereotype us. Mainly you ignore us."

The idea that women could keep working into their 70s and 80s was new — sort of. There had always been paragons like Antoinette Brown Blackwell, who was preaching sermons at 83 and getting paeans in the early twentieth-century press. But they were celebrated for being remarkable rarities. As the twenty-first century loomed around the corner, things did begin to shift, and soon the sight of a 70-year-old college professor or an 80-year-old museum tour guide would hardly raise an eyebrow. Younger women, planning long-term, were much less likely to expect that their lives in the public world would end with the arrival of their first Social Security check. But the failure of that fountain of youth to materialize meant that even icons who planned to go on forever discovered that aging often brought physical restrictions no amount of healthy living could stave off. "You have to be a good sport, you have to take things in good spirit, you have to accept what has to be accepted and try to put up with whatever happens to come," said Millicent Fenwick. She had retired from a United Nations job at 77 — her daughter was suffering from leukemia and her own health was slipping. So she returned to her home in New Jersey, anticipating something less than a rebirth. "Don't talk about golden years to somebody who is old," she said.

She tried to keep busy—fund-raising for her favorite causes and cheerleading her favorite issues. When she was 80, a woman with a similar name died and word spread that the former congresswoman had succumbed. Fenwick lounged happily on her patio, startling people who called with condolences by answering the phone with "Fenwick here." When local reporters came to check on the rumors, she'd give them the necessary clever retort, then try to engage them in a discussion of current events. She died—really—in 1992, at 82. "We all admired her and looked up to her so much," her grandson said. "Even though sometimes it seemed like she gave her best energy to other people."

A few years later, the *Doonesbury* heroine and Fenwick alter ego Lacey Davenport passed away in her early 90s after a struggle with Alzheimer's. In her final appearance, she saw her late husband, Dick, returning to take her to their next home. First, Lacey told him, she needed to primp a little: "I have to put on my face!"

"I think He's seen you without it, Dearest," said Dick.

In his comic strip, Garry Trudeau has written about aging as well as anyone in America. And he was unique in combining a celebration of older people with an acknowledgment that there was always going to be an end. That's a topic most elderly celebrities have preferred to steer clear of. In her mid-80s, Katharine Hepburn did volunteer to an interviewer that she was looking forward to dying: "Must be wonderful, like a long sleep." But it wasn't anything she was scheduling immediately. She made another movie appearance, playing Warren Beatty's aunt, and was in the TV movie *One Christmas,* for which she received a Screen Actors Guild nomination at 87. Hepburn died in 2003 at age 96.

"I WAS GETTING WAY TOO FAR OUT ON THE LEDGE"

The public wasn't exactly yearning for stories about famous people's decline and death. They preferred news about late-life comebacks, and there seemed to be plenty. Margaret Chase Smith's career certainly looked finished when she lost that Senate reelection battle at 74, to a Democrat who tried to depict her as a cranky behind-the-times relic.

But she slowly rebuilt her life, traveling with Bill Lewis on a Woodrow Wilson National Fellowship Foundation visiting professorship that sent her around the country to talk with students about everything from the evils of Richard Nixon to the battle for women's rights. Then Lewis died suddenly, of a heart attack. Smith was overwhelmed that the love of her life, who was 15 years younger than she was, had gone ahead of her. But she recovered again, throwing herself into her work, traveling, speaking. As time passed, her biographer Janann Sherman wrote, "Smith was gradually transformed from a querulous old woman and washed-up politician into a living legend and a symbol of all that was good about a Maine that was rapidly fading away."

She died at 97 in 1995, an excellent answer to complaints that all the opportunities for older women belonged to the middle-aged. She was, of course, Margaret Chase Smith, but she still was a symbol for women of all ages—that it was possible to find new purpose late in life, even after failure or personal loss.

Helen Gurley Brown, like Smith, hit a period when her former admirers began to feel she had definitely stayed too long at the fair. Brown was still editing *Cosmo* at 70, but her message of sexual liberation had failed to evolve with the times. She still claimed, for instance, that chasing secretaries around the office and stripping off their underpants was great fun for the secretaries as well as the bosses. "I have this possibly benighted idea that when a man finds you sexually attractive, he is paying you a compliment," she wrote, in a 1991 opinion piece for the *Wall Street Journal*.

In 1996, *Cosmo* announced that Brown, 73, was going to leave—slowly. The new editor, Bonnie Fuller, would be moved in very gradually, and at the end Brown would still be editor of the magazine's international editions, with an office and travel expenses. Brown acknowledged it was something she would never have done on her own—"They had to tell *me* it was over." But she did admit that "at seventy-four, I was getting way too far out on the ledge (to put it mildly) to continue to be guru of an eighteen-to-thirty-four-year-old reader."

Brown had long resented the indignities, large and small, inflicted upon her by age; she was outraged when a young woman offered her a seat on the bus. But like many other media celebrities, she worked things out by writing a book. *The Late Show* was about everything from shopping to estate planning to—naturally—sex. (She warned her readers there was a chasm "as wide as Sunset Boulevard" between older women who have sex and those who don't.) She also traveled the globe, opening new versions of *Cosmo* in countries where her message about enjoying life when you're young and postponing marriage didn't seem old hat.

Brown seemed to have figured out how to move on, but she had not figured out how to get past her lifelong obsession with her looks. When she was eighty, the author Eve Ensler came to visit and discovered Brown doing sit-ups. "Don't mind me," Ensler recalled her saying. "Eighty years old, [o]ne hundred sit-ups twice a day, I'm down to ninety pounds. Another ten years, I'll be down to nothing. But even then I won't feel beautiful." It wasn't one of your more uplifting visions of aging, but there did seem to be plusses to her obsession with the physical. She mentioned that she and her husband, David, had just had sex two days in a row: "He's feisty, always has been."

"MOM HAS THE HOTS"

The feistiness bar seemed to be tilting toward women. In 1992, two academic researchers released a much-discussed report on the sexual attitudes of middle-aged Americans. Men, the study found, became more and more interested in emotional satisfaction, while women focused on physical desire. Or, as the *Washington Post* put it, "Now that dear old dad is finally looking for a tender moment, mom has the hots." The researchers—biological scientist David Quadagno at Florida State University and sociologist Joey Sprague at the University of Kansas—found that half the men over 45 they sampled wanted sex mainly to satisfy romantic urges, while 60 percent of the women were primarily interested in the sex.

"It may be that it takes people half their sex lives to see the other half of themselves," said Sprague. "Men finally find out that it's okay to feel good about loving somebody, and women feel it's all right to feel pleasure. The stereotypes are broken. Men have hearts, women have bodies."

Everything in the story of American women does tend to converge. Education, equal rights, careers, economic power—it all came together, bringing a constantly expanding vision of what you could do, and how long you could do it. Sex included. Publishers were helpfully producing books like *What to Do When He Has a Headache: Creating Renewed Desire in Your Man*, and pharmacies were stocking lubricating gels. The *Washington Post* reminded its readers that back in the day, Benjamin Franklin had counseled men to pick older women for lovers "because they have more knowledge of the world." The story generously skipped over Franklin's observation that "in the dark all Cats are grey."

"Babe, District Attorney, and Driving Miss Daisy"

One of the surprise hits of the 1990s was *The First Wives Club*, in which Goldie Hawn, Diane Keaton, and Bette Midler played old college friends who meet up many years later to get revenge on husbands who had dumped them for younger women. "There are only three ages for women in Hollywood," Hawn's character complains at one point. "Babe, District Attorney, and Driving Miss Daisy." It was not, if you listened to the reviewers, a particularly great film. But it definitely hit a nerve with its target audience.

"They're showing up at movie theaters en masse—some, like the fifteen members of a women's group in Minneapolis, Minnesota, in stretch limos and evening gowns," reported *Time*. "They're calling in to drive-time radio stations, like Raleigh, North Carolina's WRAL-FM, which solicited listeners' divorce horror stories and revenge fantasies—and found its switchboards lighted up like Times Square." It was possible *Time* was overestimating the number of women who went to the movie in evening gowns, but the reporter did come up with a 52nd birthday party for a New Yorker named Patti Kenner "in which 60 of her female friends gathered for cocktails, then adjourned to a Manhattan theater to hoot and laugh their way through all 105 minutes of *The First Wives Club*." The movie also drew lots of praise from a support group in Hollywood called LADIES (Life After Divorce Is Eventually Sane), which included the ex-wives of actors Gene Hackman, Michael Landon, and Jerry Lewis. "The public thinks that money makes it different for us, but I've seen firsthand first wives of Oscar winners who moved from mansions to little apartments" — or even, for a while, to their cars, said Lynn Landon.

Two lessons from this story: the specter of the displaced homemaker still loomed large; and older women were a potential movie audience of serious proportion. That second point didn't seem to hit home very quickly in Hollywood, where the stars of *The First Wives Club* complained that they had to take substantial pay cuts to get the film made yet weren't offered much in the way of raises when the studio was mulling a sequel. It was, Goldie Hawn claimed, "because they were afraid of women of a certain age."

"MRS. CLINTON BELIEVES THAT PANTS CAN BE ELEGANT AND PRACTICAL"

The pants warriors were making their way toward a triumphal victory march in the 1990s. Senators Carol Moseley Braun and Barbara Mikulski broke the unwritten slacks-ban rule in the Senate in 1993. Braun, 45, was an accidental rebel, simply donning a suit she'd worn frequently at her previous job in the Illinois legislature. She was the first African American woman to win entrance to the Senate, but when she walked onto the floor, the gasps she heard were not about racial breakthrough. Mikulski, 56, knew she was ignoring the Senate dress code. It was a snowy day, and the meteorologists were promising more bad weather. "I just really wanted to be comfortable," she said. "I'm most comfortable wearing slacks. Well, for a woman to come on the floor of the Senate in trousers was viewed as a seismographic event."

Mikulski, like Braun, was a pioneer — at the time, she was on her way to becoming the longest-serving woman in Congress and a powerful, perpetually outspoken committee chair. "I might be short," the four-foot-eleven Mikulski said, "but I won't be overlooked." In 1995, Mikulski, then 59, was slightly injured in a mugging outside her home in Baltimore. The robber, her spokeswoman said, "pushed her to take the purse. She pushed him back." But rebellious as she could be, Mikulski didn't try to break the pants barrier without alerting the Senate president pro tempore, Senator Robert Byrd. She got at least a tacit approval and made her breakthrough. "You would have thought that I was walking on the moon," she said.

Pants weren't new to Congress—Rep. Charlotte Reid had worn black bell-bottoms onto the House floor in 1969. But the Senate had continued to be a no-go zone, and it drove some of the female staff members nuts. "We've heard from women staff that in the 1980s, if they came in to work—if they were called in on an emergency basis—they needed to keep a dress to put on quickly or they had to borrow one if they had to appear on the Senate floor," Senate historian Richard A. Baker told the *Washington Post*. Once Braun and Mikulski made the break, the grateful staff followed their lead and the dress code war was won forever.

But the big breakthrough was happening in the White House, where Hillary Clinton was a huge fan. "Mrs. Clinton believes that pants can be elegant and practical," said a spokesman for the First Lady, who confirmed that Hillary "wears pants about once a week." She was the first, and so far the only, First Lady to pose for a presidential portrait in trousers. "Why must she dress that way?" demanded fashion consultant Tim Gunn. "I think she's confused about her gender."

When Clinton became the first First Lady to run for the U.S. Senate, the Hillary campaign uniform was a black pantsuit with a pastel blouse. Celebrating her election, she recalled the morning she had announced her candidacy, the summer before: "And sixty-two counties, sixteen months, three debates, two opponents and six black pantsuits later, because of you, here we are." It seemed like a smart response to the ability of male candidates to wear the same basic suit every day without inducing any comment. But Clinton said she got tired of it, and when she ran for president, the pantsuits evolved into multiple bright colors.

"MIDLIFE IS THE BEST PLACE TO BE"

In 1999, the *New York Times* announced that a new study had determined that "Middle Age Is Prime of Life." The news came from an ambitious 10-year research project on Midlife Development in the United States (MIDUS) that kept track of nearly 8,000 Americans 25 to

74. And the winning life stage, when it came to feelings of well-being and control was—yes!—middle age. "On balance, the sense we all have is that midlife is the best place to be," one of the researchers told the *Times*. The sweet spot came between 40 and 60.

Most people, the study found, never did have a midlife crisis. Less than a quarter of those surveyed felt they'd gone through one, and most of the people who did reported that the crisis was about an outside event—death, job loss, divorce—rather than any general reaction to age. Those who did have a genuine midlife crisis, the researchers said, tended to have a high "neuroticism" score and a high level of ... education.

The good news from that MIDUS study was mainly limited to middle age—it found that later in life, women in particular seemed to lose their sense of life purpose. Carol Ryff, the director of the Institute on Aging at the University of Wisconsin, told the *Times* that one of the study's messages to middle-aged Americans was to "be mindful of what's ahead."

But the survey was another blow against the popular conception of menopause as something to be feared and dreaded. Most of the women in the MIDUS research said their only reaction to the end of menstruation was "relief." A measly 2 percent reported feeling "only regret." Half didn't get hot flashes—and only around 13 percent said they had them "almost every day." As we've seen, menopause was getting good press all over the place during the 1990s. "Why is menopause suddenly so fashionable?" *Good Housekeeping* asked—rather rhetorically. The answer was (three guesses): the baby-boom generation. "Their feisty spirit—if not their sheer number—has already redefined femininity, work styles and parenting, and it now promises to revolutionize society's views toward 'the change,'" author Martha King told *GH* readers. The *Times* discovered a menopause support group that called itself Red Hot Mamas.

"SOME OF US MAY NEVER DIE"

As the twenty-first century approached, there was a lot of discussion in the media about what the next millennium might bring. It was a very old tradition: back in the sixteenth century, the French astrologer

Nostradamus announced that sometime around the year 2000—well, actually, in July of 1999; the man was very precise—the King of Terror would arrive from the sky and...do something awful. Edgar Cayce, a predictor known as The Sleeping Prophet, who was very popular until his death in 1945, said there was going to be a wonderful era of peace and brotherhood—but not until the earth's axis shifted, creating all kinds of disasters, including the collapse of California into the Pacific. Some students of the Great Pyramid of Giza claimed a careful examination of its interior showed that the world was going to come to an end on September 17, 2001.

Once we got through relatively unscathed, the predictions for life post-2000 were often more cheery. "The Baby Boom generation, and perhaps its parents, can expect to live healthy, active lives that stretch to between 110 and 120 years," wrote Marvin Cetron and Owen Davies in a much-quoted book called *Cheating Death*. Unsurprisingly, given the title, they also suggested that perhaps "some of us may never die, save by accident or choice." On the other hand, the authors thought all those old people would scarf up all the resources, leading to "an all-out war between generations."

We stop once again to contemplate the fact that the news is never all good, even when it's being made up.

16. Into the Twenty-First Century

"The Great Midlife Lemonade Stand"

In 2006, *Newsweek* retracted its 20-year-old story on how an educated 40-year-old white woman had a better chance of being killed by a terrorist than of getting married. It had already been pretty well debunked—in 2000, *Discover* had named it one of the 20 "Greatest Blunders in Science in the Last 20 Years."

The revised version began with Laurie Aronson, who had been profiled in the original article as a 29-year-old facing a statistically unpromising future. When she reappeared at 49, Aronson had been married for 10 years, was the mother of a three-year-old boy, and was "ecstatic" about her life. She was among 8 of the 11 women *Newsweek* managed to locate who had gotten married, though it wasn't clear that they were all equally euphoric. None of the interviewees had been killed by a terrorist. "Those odds-she'll-marry statistics turned out to be too pessimistic," the magazine admitted.

As the world moved into the twenty-first century, Americans had expanded their vision of age. Even if it wasn't necessarily common for a woman to marry in her 40s, make ambitious career changes in her 50s and 60s, continue working (or skiing or skydiving) in her 70s, and take pleasure in an excellent sex life in her 80s, those things were generally seen as desirable rather than weird or shocking. Menopause was getting a makeover as the media became super-enthusiastic about what *Time* called "The Great Midlife Lemonade Stand," where American women were happily "taking the bitter taste of aging and making it sweet, satisfying."

Yeah, it was possible to get carried away.

There were stories everywhere celebrating women who quit their humdrum jobs to start something more exciting—the real estate appraiser who was running food tours or a former consultant on asbestos removal now selling "bright jewelry crafted from gemstones and pearls." An editor at the *Harvard Business Review* reported that she went into "career menopause" and cut back on her regular job so she'd have time to dive "into new undertakings—volunteering in a hospice, songwriting and catching up on the part of me that's been ignored for a very long while." The old catchphrase about going through "change of life" did seem to be getting interpreted in a whole new way.

"Those of us who worked on this knew nothing was coming to us"

At the start of the twenty-first century, looking back over American history, you could see a transformation in the way society regarded older women. Okay, an imperfect transformation—we'll get back to the inevitable downside later. But the rocking-chair-in-the-corner image had been pretty thoroughly squashed. Women were working more, getting better positions—including a majority of the nearly 4.5 million new jobs in management that were created between 1980 and 2010—and staying on the job longer. Nearly 1 million women, most of them 50 or older, had assets of $2 million or more.

If there's one ringing message in American history it's that if you're important economically, you're important. Obsessed as advertisers and entertainment programmers had always been with youthful audiences, they were starting to realize they could sell a ton of tickets and cable subscriptions to older women. Young people were still eager to run the world, but they tended to lend a careful ear toward their elders if said elders controlled a lot of cash.

Who do we thank for all this? The women's rights movement had created job opportunities that offered more money, more satisfaction, and more ability to keep moving forward at work. And the soldiers leading the way were those heroines who had filed suits all across the country, taking advantage of that last-minute change to the Civil Rights Act of 1964 that banned employment discrimination on the basis of sex. They were often older employees—after all, they were the ones who had been around long enough to see that they were being passed over for raises and promotions. But when they made their stands and won their fights, they weren't necessarily the ones who got the benefits. Bosses who agreed to improve the sexual balance in their workplaces preferred to bestow the benefits on younger, newer employees who had not had the opportunity to give them grief. "Those of us who worked on this knew nothing was coming to us. That's what they do when you sue them," said Betsy Wade, who led a legal battle by the women at the *New York Times* in 1974 for equal wage and job opportunities. The unrewarded crusaders weren't just the women who fought to equalize promotions. Alice Muller, a 51-year-old clerk at the Los Angeles Department of Water and Power, led a fight against the DWP's policy of requiring women to contribute 15 percent more to their pension plan than men, under the theory that the women would live longer. While the case was wending its way through court, the state changed the rule to make pension contributions sex-neutral. New hires wouldn't ever be penalized. But Muller and the other older women got no payback for all the years they had contributed extra. Their appeals, which went all the way to the Supreme Court, fell on deaf ears.

"FIFTY IS THE NEW . . ."

The general idea of age-related life crises had hardly gone out of style in the new millennium. There were just way more of them. Suddenly there was discussion of the "quarter life crisis," arriving in the mid-20s to early 30s and sending victims into a whirlpool of insecurity over careers and relationships. And the good old midlife crisis might not have been eliminated so much as restructured. A much-quoted *Atlantic* article suggested there was a "happiness U-curve" that began with a depressive dip through early adulthood, bottomed out in your 40s, then started to rise so that sometime in your 50s "you look at your life again and think, *Actually, this is pretty good.*"

Middle age was turning into a very long middle. Writing a 30th anniversary introduction to *Passages,* Gail Sheehy calculated that a woman in good health at 50 could expect to live to age 92. It was a figure, she said, that made her audiences "gasp, even groan.... Who ever prepared us for the possibility that we might live long enough to forget the name of our first husband!"

In her updated version, written when she was in her 60s, Sheehy announced that there was "a hidden cultural phenomenon taking place under our very noses—a surge of vitality in women's sex, love, and working lives that is taking place *after 50.*" And, in fact, she had written another book about it: *Sex and the Seasoned Woman.* The idea of being sexy in midlife had turned from a fantasy to an expectation, at least for the celebrity class. In 2008, Madonna turned 50. She celebrated with a party for friends, employees, kids, and husband Guy Ritchie. "Although the party went late into the night, that didn't stop this fit fifty-year-old from getting up and hitting the gym the following morning—she does have a tour to prepare for after all," said one celebrity site. In real life, a tour was the least of Madonna's upcoming adventures. Soon she'd be divorcing Ritchie and going out with baseball bad boy Alex Rodriguez, 33. Not all that surprising—since everybody was talking about how 40 was the new 30, 50 was obviously the new 40.

Being in your 50s did seem to be very trendy. The great hero of 2009 was Sully Sullenberger, the 57-year-old hero pilot who brought his crippled plane safely down in the Hudson River after it struck a herd of geese. The flight attendants who calmly led the passengers onto the wing to wait for rescue were Donna Dent, 51, Sheila Dail, 57, and Doreen Welsh, 58, and after the story became a sensation, you couldn't blame travelers if they felt more secure when their flight crew had a lot of wrinkles. A Harris poll announced that America's favorite age was 50. It was interactive and conducted among volunteers, so there wasn't much science involved. However, it was interesting that men, on average, wanted to be younger. They thought the ideal age was 47, while women came in at around 53.

A psychologist commenting on the favorite-age poll on *Today* said the 50s were all about opportunity. You could start an organic farm if you felt so inspired. But if you were tired on the way home from work, you could ask a young man on the bus to give you his seat. Anyway, she added, "I really think fifty is the new thirty to thirty-five."

Going down already.

"I'm over seventy but I feel like I'm fifty," Jane Fonda told Oprah Winfrey in an interview. "I enjoy getting old!" It was a balancing act popular with some of the role models of the boomer generation. You can happily acknowledge your age, as long as you don't look it or feel it. You can even acknowledge that every day isn't physical perfection. On another talk show, Fonda reported that in 2005 she had needed a hip replacement: "That's not my self-image but it's genetic. My dad did. My brother did."

If the nation was beginning to accept the idea of 70 as the new something younger, that was undoubtedly because the baby boomers were hitting the barrier and reassessing their view. Paul McCartney, who wrote "When I'm Sixty-Four" when he was in his 20s, actually turned 64 in 2006. He developed a habit of calling up celebrities on their 64th birthdays and singing them the song. Cyndi Lauper was still belting out "Girls Just Want to Have Fun" at 65. Mick Jagger, who sang "What a drag it is getting old" in the 1960s, had vowed he would "never tour when I'm 50," so the fact that he celebrated his 70th birthday just after the completion of the Rolling Stones' 50th anniversary tour was perhaps a little ironic. Or inspiring: when Cher was in her 50s and being warned she was too old to sing rock and roll, she reportedly told critics: "You'd better check with Mick Jagger." She was still performing at 72, when she had a big part in a *Mamma Mia!* sequel. We will not go into the fact that she played the mother of 69-year-old Meryl Streep.

"THE YEAR OF THE COUGAR"

Newsweek, having revisited the fate of educated women past 40 who wanted to get married, was apparently still looking for an age-sex angle in 2006, when the magazine announced it was "The Year of the Cougar." The nation was indeed talking about women who dated younger men, and the fact that they were nicknamed after a predatory animal suggests that public approval of the act was not exactly ringing. It wasn't clear how old you had to be to qualify for cougar-dom. The reference website ThoughtCo. posted articles declaring that in general "the woman is 35 years or older, the man is more than eight years her junior."

This is not to be confused with a puma, "a woman in her 30s who prefers dating younger men."

Yeah, we've got rules for everything.

Americans had gotten interested in the cougar idea when *Sex and the City* was a TV hit, celebrating the lives and loves of four New York women, the oldest of whom, Samantha, announced she's "forty fucking five" in the final season. Samantha had a long-running affair with a much younger man named Smith, who had to be one of the most sympathetic partners in the history of half-hour entertainment. (When she got breast cancer, he shaved his head during her chemo treatments.) But after the series ended and moved into movie-sequel territory, she decided she wanted to stick with singlehood.

A large crop of May-December movies and TV series followed in which the women, for once, were getting the December role. "This season marks the summer of hot cougar love," Alessandra Stanley of the *New York Times* announced, reviewing television shows in 2007 that starred over-40 actresses like Glenn Close, Holly Hunter, and Kyra Sedgwick, who was returning for her third season as "the sexy and single-minded detective on *The Closer.*" Unfortunately, most were not exactly ratings sensations. *Newsweek* didn't make the situation better by suggesting that "as plastic surgery and Botox have gone mainstream, women are able to look younger, making some of these romances seem marginally believable."

On the more traditional and predictable comedy front there was *Cougar Town,* in which Courteney Cox of *Friends* fame played a recently divorced 40-something mother who "decides to find some excitement in her dating life." There was even a reality show called *Age of Love* that divided women into two teams—the Cougars (39 to 48) and the Kittens (in their 20s). They vied for a 30-year-old Australian tennis player. In the end, a 25-year-old hockey team dancer won. The relationship didn't last. More crucially, the series didn't get renewed.

Cougarism as an entertainment phenomenon didn't last long, either. Cox's series was very successful but quickly dropped the original theme in favor of a more traditional gang-of-crazy-but-supportive-friends motif. Still, the word had made its way into the vocabulary—in 2017, the *New York Times* ran a wedding story in which the 94-year-old groom said that when he began seeing his 98-year-old fiancée, "I kept getting teased about dating a cougar." And celebrities helped make the whole thing seem normal. Courteney Cox herself was married to an actor seven years her junior. Actress Demi Moore, 42, married 27-year-old actor Ashton Kutcher in 2005 (it didn't last). Madonna kept on spinning, spending part of her early 50s dating dancer Brahim Zaibat, who was less than half her age.

But the non-famous population wasn't sold on the concept. A Pew Research Center study found that only 3 percent of women who were getting married for the first time wed a man who was more than five years younger. Things changed a bit with remarriage, when the proportion of much younger grooms rose to 11 percent. But men still led the junior-mate race — one in five who remarried had a new spouse at least ten years younger. (The *Washington Post*, reporting on the findings, illustrated the story with a 2014 picture of reality TV celebrity Donald Trump, 68, and his 44-year-old wife Melania.) Paula England, a professor of sociology at New York University who studied the matter, said her research suggests "that men are judging women by beauty more than women are judging men by looks. And the standard of beauty is a youth-based beauty."

Okay, not a total surprise. Men who sign up at dating sites, England said, tend to "click down in age so much, it's really a problem for a lot of women who'd prefer someone their own age." She did some personal research when she was fifty-five and signed up at Match.com. One of the questions was "desired age for a significant other," and while England answered fifty to sixty, she got responses from "lots of guys over sixty and in their seventies." (This story had a happy ending, and she wound up with a partner four years her junior.)

"A SHOCK TO THE MEDICAL SYSTEM"

You may remember how, in the 1990s, women were simultaneously being encouraged to take hormone replacement therapy and warned that it wasn't quite clear whether it was totally safe. But then there was that big study, launched in 1993, of more than 16,000 women — half on hormones and half taking placebos — that was going to have all the answers. While everyone waited for the results, it was easy to be persuaded to stick with the hormonal program — what with the talk about reducing the chances of dementia. Or tooth loss. Or skin wrinkles. Or colon cancer. And odds were that your doctor was urging hormone treatments on you: one survey of gynecologists showed the vast majority prescribed hormone replacement therapy for long-term use by their postmenopausal patients.

"Obviously, the women on the hormones will be living longer," one doctor friend told Barbara Seaman, the co-founder of the National Women's Health Network. "It's unethical to leave volunteers on the placebos for the full eight and a half years of the trial. At some point they'll have to stop the study and offer hormones to everyone."

The study, by the National Institutes of Health, was a whopper. As fiscal conservatives complained, it cost more than $625 million. The goal was to determine if the popular estrogen-progestin combination — which 6 million women were taking — really prevented heart disease. But it was halted prematurely before its scheduled completion, on July 9, 2002, when a monitoring board decided it was too dangerous to the participants to let it continue. While the women taking hormones did seem to lower their risk of some ailments connected to age — like hip fracture — they also showed a higher than normal tendency to develop breast cancer, plus there was an apparent jump in strokes and coronary disease.

It was more than a shock. It was possibly the biggest rupture of patient confidence in modern medicine. "I tell you — women gotta go insane today," said anchor Paula Zahn on CNN.

There had been earlier warnings. A group of researchers who were funded by Wyeth-Ayerst, the manufacturer of estrogen drugs, had discovered that women with heart disease were not protected against heart attacks by estrogen therapy, and that their chances of having a blood clot increased. But the treatment was regarded so highly that the results weren't taken all that seriously. The *Journal of the American Medical Association* urged physicians not to get carried away, editorializing "there is no emergency." But the news that the NIH results were looking so bad the project had been discontinued created a sort of tsunami of media reporting. "Hormone Replacement Study a Shock to the Medical System," announced a *New York Times* headline. The use of hormone therapy plummeted from 6 million women to about 3.3 million.

Critics of the hormone replacement movement, like the National Women's Health Network, were relieved. Executive Director Cindy Pearson saw it as a double victory—a vindication of those who had health concerns about the long-term effects of estrogen, and a rethinking of that old vision of menopause as a disease or disability rather than a normal progression of life. "It felt to me that we changed, in an important way, the perception of older women and our hormones," she said. "There's nothing we lose in menopause that has to be replaced in order to age healthily." Pearson couldn't help recalling the experts who had argued that hormone replacement was crucial—because how else would the medical community deal with the fact that women were getting so old? "We'd sit and listen to physicians say—they weren't meant to live this long without their hormones."

It wasn't just doctors who had trouble adjusting to the new reality. "Do I prefer a shorter but more active life span, or longevity with possibly more disabilities?" one HRT user wrote to the *New York Times.* "No contest! For me, quality of life wins, even though it may not be quite so long."

"AND HER FACE FALLS APART"

Hormone replacement therapy may have suffered a setback, but cosmetic surgery's popularity never waned. At a time when the nation had generally stopped thinking of women in their 30s as "aging," the surgical makeover specialists stepped in to re-ring the alarm bells. "Even in our early 30s, you can have little tiny signs of aging," a Texas plastic surgeon told the *Dallas Morning News,* describing his efforts to rejuvenate a "30-something" patient: "Someone as young as Jodi can do a lot for herself before she gets older and her face falls apart." In the same article, another surgeon talked about the "competitive work environment" in Dallas that left 30-year-olds requesting "Botox and fillers for premature wrinkling." A specialist in Beverly Hills told *New York* magazine that he warned patients that removing all signs of aging could leave their foreheads looking like blank slates, unable to move or show emotion. Some women, he said, didn't care: "They're more concerned about wrinkles than about the five seconds of emotion people might not notice anyway."

There did not appear to be any way for doctors to discuss these topics without being sort of depressing.

Happily for women who were considering some kind of intervention, the options were increasing. Botox and fillers, along with laser treatments, made facial improvements both more available and less drastic. Surgeons performed 60 percent fewer forehead lifts and 30 percent fewer eyelid surgeries in the post-2000 era. Face-lifts were about as common as they had been in the 1990s, but Botox treatments were up 800 percent. As the procedures became more common, the commentary on what celebrities were doing with their aging faces became increasingly catty. In 2010, an online awards-show watcher complimented Glenn Close for being "one of the few women-of-a-certain-age at the Golden Globes last night that didn't have skin that looked like it had been extruded from the Play-Doh fun factory."

"LIFTED UP OUR BLOUSES AND SHOWED HER OUR HEALED CHESTS"

The openness about breast cancer that Betty Ford had pioneered continued. In 2007, Betty Rollin, who had written about her breast cancer in the 1970s, celebrated the fact that "everyone is talking about breast cancer — even men. But let's face it, women are the talking champions.... How many times have I — have we all — met a scared newcomer and pulled her into the nearest restroom, lifted up our blouses and showed her our healed chests.... Or offered a look at our implant."

Breast cancer was no longer regarded as a death sentence. In just seven years, between 2000 and 2007, the mortality rate dropped by around 2 percent each year. A woman who got the diagnosis — and at some point in their lives, about 12 percent of American women got that news — had, on average, a 90 percent chance of surviving over the next five years. And a great many would get treatment that would lead to permanent remission.

It's the American way, to focus on success stories. But even when we're cheering, it's a good idea to remind ourselves that things don't always work out. Rollin, in her praise for openness, took particular note of the way the wife of presidential candidate John Edwards had spoken up about her case. Elizabeth Edwards was diagnosed in 2004—the day after her husband lost his chance to be vice president when John Kerry's Democratic ticket was defeated by George W. Bush and Dick Cheney. For a while her next chapter seemed to follow the familiar pattern of triumph against adversity. She wrote a bestselling memoir about her fight against the disease, and the Edwardses prepared for his next career step: a presidential campaign against other would-be Democratic nominees that included Barack Obama and Hillary Clinton.

A few years later, Elizabeth revealed that her cancer had not only returned, it had spread into her ribs, hips, and lungs. She kept on campaigning. Nobody could accuse Elizabeth Edwards of not pulling her weight—or, in fact, her luggage, which she carried while traveling through long days and nights of appearances. Despite her illness, she said, "I don't expect my life to be significantly different."

Nothing went well. John Edwards was revealed to have carried on an affair with an aide, and then lied about how long it had gone on, and whether he was the father of the aide's child. He lost the race ignominiously and the marriage broke up. Elizabeth wrote another memoir, *Resilience*, but at the end of 2010, doctors told her the cancer had spread to her liver and there was no point in further treatment. She died at 61.

YOGA TURNS BACK THE CLOCK

Death at 61 had come to be seen as tragically early. But higher life expectancy often came with unpleasant baggage. More than a quarter of people over 65 had diabetes, which hit older minority women particularly hard. About half of Americans 65 and over had arthritis, and it was more common in women than in men. In 1985, the number of people affected had been around 35 million. Twenty years later, it was 66 million. Nearly 30 percent of adults with arthritis were so crippled they had difficulty walking, dressing, or bathing themselves.

Americans who weren't suffering from serious medical problems had come to realize that the ideal recipe for healthy older age involved exercise. Only about 15 percent of women between the ages of 50 and 79 reported being physically active. But they were definitely buying a lot of stuff that would come in handy when they got around to it. The exercise video market was booming, including not only new offers from Jane Fonda but also chair exercises and "BoneJuvenate," which was aimed at preventing osteoporosis. There were many, many variations on yoga for seniors and how-to books with titles like *The Yoga Face: Eliminate Wrinkles with the Ultimate Natural Facelift* or *Yoga for Weight Loss* or *Yoga Turns Back the Clock*.

And—in the department of feeling better even if you're a little battered—in 2017, the *New York Times* reported on a "new growth industry": "older women and medical marijuana." The star of the story was Jeanine Moss, 62, who was suffering after hip replacement surgery and found that the opiates prescribed for her recovery left her disoriented. She switched to medical marijuana, liked it a lot, and started a business that included "pot-related accessories" and travel guides aimed at women who were looking for a medical marijuana source. Another featured entrepreneur was the 66-year-old former owner of a real estate title company who went to care for her mother after a stroke, found medical marijuana was a big help, and eventually applied for a license to open a dispensary. "I thought, for the last stage of my life, I'd like to do something to give back," she told the *Times*. "How much of a glow can you get from a real estate transaction?" It was yet another way women were reinventing themselves. "It's definitely a trend," said the head of an investment firm that specializes in cannabis-related businesses. "A lot of women have this family recipe, or they were making a certain kind of tincture for a loved one who was suffering. Now that pot is legal, they're like, 'Wow, that thing you were making for Grandma could be a real product.'" Think of them as the historic descendants of those older women in the eighteenth century who were revered for passing down family bread-making recipes.

"THE FIRST TIME IN MORE THAN 130 YEARS"

In a surprising shift, multigenerational families were getting more popular. The parents-and-kids-only model had reigned for decades, and by the 1980s, only about 12 percent of American households contained more than one adult generation. By 2000, it was up to 15 percent. After the recession hit in late 2007, the numbers really started climbing, and by 2016, 64 million households — 20 percent of the population — were multigenerational. Partly it was a matter of changing ethnicity — black, Hispanic, and Asian American families were more likely to welcome in grandparents, aunts, or uncles. But there was also another reason about a third of all young adults were living at home with their parents: for "the first time in more than 130 years," the Pew Research Center reported. People were waiting longer to get married, settle down, and start a family of their own. In fact, marriage was, overall, becoming less and less popular. Today, only a little over half of Americans are married — down from 72 percent in 1960. And, of course, there was the matter of home prices. The more expensive it became to rent or buy your own place, the more attractive your childhood bedroom looked. Finally, it would be nice to think that the generations were living together longer just because they were getting along better. Parents tended toward the let's-work-together model of child-rearing, and young people had dropped that thing about not trusting anybody over 30.

But the image of adult children hanging around in the bedroom or the basement haunted the middle class. Some people called it "failure to launch." That became the title of a 2006 film starring Sarah Jessica Parker as an expert in getting adult children to leave home, hired by Matthew McConaughey's parents to work her magic on their son. You will not be startled to learn that love ensues, the new couple relocates, and the happy ending includes the parents singing "Hit the Road Jack."

"CHANGES HAVE COME TO HOLLYWOOD"

Remember the story of the 30-something writer who pretended to be a teenager so she could sell her scripts in Hollywood? Ageism in the entertainment industry did not abate after Riley Weston was outed as a non-teenager. In 2002, 165 writers tried a more direct approach and filed an age discrimination suit against the major TV networks, studios, and talent agencies. In 2010, it was settled, with industry bigwigs shelling out $70 million to the plaintiffs and their attorneys.

During the years the suit was pending, the Writers Guild of America reported the percentage of working TV writers under 31 had fallen by about a third, while the percentage of writers over 50 grew by about 10 percent. A Guild lawyer warned that "there is still a sharp decline in employment rates as writers get older, into their 60s and 70s." But the story was still...better than it had been. The *New York Times,* reporting the news, warned that while no one should expect miracles, "changes have come to Hollywood that appear to have made the bias against older writers less pervasive."

One of the reasons was the change in audience. Television might still regard the 18-to-34-year-old demographic as the perfect target. But the entertainment industry was beginning to face the fact that the younger generation wasn't likely to be viewing regularly scheduled network TV shows in mass numbers, no matter what attractions advertisers tried to scatter about for them. One 2015 survey showed the average age of a prime-time viewer on NBC, ABC, and CBS was 57. A Nielsen report showed Americans over 65 watched an average of 223 hours per month of traditional TV. For teenagers, it was about 84 hours a month.

Hard to say if the same story was true of movies. Older filmgoers weren't much more likely to buy tickets than the general public, but when a film had heroes they identified with, they showed up in droves. *Woman in Gold,* a 2015 drama starring 70-year-old Helen Mirren, got 82 percent of its audience from the 50-and-over crowd. They were also the folks who made *Sully,* the Tom Hanks movie about that plane landing on the Hudson, a big hit. Without them, every art film house in the country would go out of business, and the independent films would lose more than half their ticket sales.

Yet very few studios seemed to get the message. A study of the top 100 films in 2015 found that only about 11 percent of the speaking characters were 60 or older—and of those, women were outnumbered by men more than 3 to 1. It was age prejudice compounded by the Guy Thing. Writer-director Nancy Meyers reported that when she made her 2003 comedy *Something's Gotta Give,* one studio executive fretted about a scene that showed Diane Keaton, 57, carrying on an affair with Jack Nicholson, because he felt audiences did not want to see older women in bed. Fortunately, she said, having a star like Nicholson on board "made [the studio] feel safe." The fact that he was nine years older than Keaton didn't seem to unnerve anybody. The movie, which was about a man who always dated very young women suddenly realizing he wanted to be with someone near his own age, made a ton of money.

17. Onward and Upward

"PULLING THE PLUG ON GRANDMA"

In 2014, *The Atlantic* asked, "What Happens When We All Live to 100?" (The magazine acknowledged it wasn't an immediate worry.) But the nation was wrestling with health care costs, and one of the easiest targets was expensive medical treatments for patients who were going to die soon under any circumstances. "We spend an incredible amount of money on that last year and month," warned a writer in *Forbes*. It was a touchy subject. But even people who had no particular interest in Medicare financing worried about the possibility that doctors might prolong their lives — or the lives of their loved ones — when they were in terrible pain and unable to communicate. When Barack Obama's administration proposed its health care plan, it included a provision that allowed Medicare to pay for doctors to talk with their patients about living wills and other decisions they could make about how much treatment they wanted, under what circumstances.

That became the famous "death panel" controversy. "We should not have a government program that determines you're gonna pull the plug on Grandma," warned Iowa Republican senator Chuck Grassley. The image resonated so hard and long that Obama was soon complaining about "the notion that somehow I ran for public office or members of Congress are in this so that they can go around pulling the plug on Grandma."

The provision made it into law on January 1, 2016, and paid for about 22,000 such conversations that year. Grandma survived fine.

"6 WAYS TO BE A SEXY GRANDMA"

While the plug-pulling controversy was raging on the one hand, there was another debate going on about who to call a "grandmother." There always had been something about the word that begged headline writers to tack it on to every woman whose children had had children—whether she was the victim of a mugging or the newest member of a court of appeals. Things had improved, and news stories were less likely to apply "grandmother" to a woman when they'd never use "grandfather" for a man.

A bigger problem was all in the family. American women became grandmothers at an average age of under 50, which a lot of people regarded as part of their prime. Some weren't comfortable answering to "Grandma" even at home. Yanick Rice Lamb made her sentiments crystal clear on Blackamericaweb.com. "My name is Nini, and I'm a proud, new grandmother. Just don't call me Grandma. Why? I can't really say. Maybe it's because I think I'm too young—or young at heart. I'm not alone."

Enter "Glam-ma."

The word cropped up around 2006, after Goldie Hawn published a memoir in which she gave her son credit for coining the word. Pretty soon it was everywhere. Urban Dictionary defined it as part of "the new generation of grandmas, who are stylish in the way they live and dress. These women do not fit the typical cardigan-wearing, permed hair granny stereotype, they are glamorous."

There were two reactions. One was appalled. "Glamma, to me, sounds fake, pretentious and desperate. It smacks of someone who is terrified of aging, of being old enough to have grandchildren. A panicked, desperate grab for some semblance of youth," wrote Melissa Charles in the *Huffington Post*. In the other corner: Lois Joy Johnson, in an article for AARP on "6 Ways to Be a Sexy Grandma," suggested its female readers look to role models like Hawn or Kris Jenner. "We new Glammas bake kale, wear Lululemon and neon Nikes, dance like Beyoncé, sing along to Katy Perry and Skype when we need a major grannie fix from far away," Johnson declared.

Take your pick. But not everybody likes kale.

Lots of women were happy to have the world know they'd become just-plain-grandmothers. When Hillary Clinton's second grandchild was born, it felt like she mentioned Aidan and Charlotte in her speeches at least as much as "middle-class income" or "free community college tuition." If the name "Grandma" didn't work, there were lots of equivalents. Some women just asked the kids to use their first names. Actress Blythe Danner went for Woof. "My mom's hot and she didn't want to be called Grandma, so she kept trying to make the Woof thing stick. It's even her email address," explained Danner's daughter, Gwyneth Paltrow.

Things have certainly changed from the grandmothers of colonial days to the world of Woof. Being the senior woman in a family used to be a critical role. You were the teacher, passing on important household-ing skills to the next generations, and also the caretaker, looking after the children while their mother and father were out in the fields or off in the factories. The first job sort of faded away—along with the idea that it was necessary for young women to enter adulthood armed with detailed knowledge of how to bake bread and mend the family clothes. The second is still very much alive—there are about 2.7 million grand-parents raising children because their parents aren't around, for reasons ranging from serving in the military to serving time in jail. And, of course, there are the countless women taking care of their grandchildren while the parents are off at work. For low-income families in particular, the burden can be intense. One Harvard study found a 55 percent greater risk of heart disease among grandmothers who cared for their children's children. "We hypothesize that stress may be the main reason," said author Sunmin Lee.

Even in wealthier families, the degree to which grandmothers become de facto babysitters turned out to be a little more than some Woofs had bargained for. The *New York Times,* refusing to give up on That Word, reported that "so-called glam-mas" felt they'd already done their day-to-day childcare duties. Many of them wistfully remembered the postwar world when grandparents came by on special occasions and provided fun outings rather than round-the-clock supervision. One of the grandmothers the *Times* interviewed thought the model of Michelle Obama's mother moving into the White House was wonderful, as long as you could also "hire someone to look after the kids."

"Way Too Much Fun"

In the twenty-first century, women are still complaining about preju-dice against anybody who looks as if they're over 40, but nevertheless a lot of them are planning their lives as if the deadline for retiring to a rocking chair is somewhere around 110. "It seems that old is a moving target," wrote Anna Quindlen. "Some gerontologists divide us into the young-old, ages fifty-five to seventy-four, and the old-old, over seventy-five. In a survey done by the Pew Research Center, most people said old age begins at sixty-eight. But most people over the age of sixty-five thought it began at seventy-five."

In real numbers, the normal life expectancy of an American woman is about 81. (Men are lower, at around 76.) And the older you get, the higher the expectancy. A 50-year-old woman can, on average, expect to live to 83, while the figure for a 70-year-old is a little past 86. And if you make it to 80, you can reasonably hope to make 90. The projections are lower for black women, but the older women grow, the closer the numbers come. At 75, an African American woman has a 50-50 chance of making it to 88. And if she does, people will very possibly be complimenting her on her youthful look. A study led by Harvard researchers discovered a "Methuselah gene" that keeps skin from aging, and it's found in about a fifth of black Americans compared to around a tenth of whites.

If you presume middle age comes around, say, the middle of adult life, a woman in 2018 would figure she'd be living it between 40 and 60. People who want a little more liberal interpretation could consult the *Oxford English Dictionary*, which sets the dates at ages 45 to 65. One way or another, it is a milestone you reach sometime in your 40s. The next big turning point would be in your 60s, when you became . . . older. But that's hardly an end. You've already heard the new estimates. "Seventy is the new fifty. That's not just a cliché. It really is a reasonable statement these days," said Steven Austad, an expert on aging at the University of Alabama at Birmingham.

Still moving upward. We have not yet heard a whole lot about 90 being the new 70, but it's definitely coming. Over in Britain, the Oxford Institute of Population Ageing recommended that people in their 70s and 80s be called "active adults" rather than "old." If it ever catches on, the 90-year-olds will begin complaining about being tossed into an "inactive" pen.

One big change does involve the age of 65, which used to broadcast "retirement time." Now, not so much. In 2017, the *New York Times* reported that two Harvard economists had found that women in their 60s and 70s were having " 'Way Too Much Fun' to Retire." A study by Claudia Goldin and Lawrence Katz estimated that nearly 30 percent of women 65 to 69 were working—twice the percentage as in the late 1980s. And 18 percent of women 70 to 74 had jobs, compared to 8 percent back in the day. The big news was that most of them seemed to be working because they wanted to. Goldin, a 72-year-old professor of economics, said later that she felt the same way: "I wouldn't be doing this if it weren't fun."

And if the current trends continue, Goldin said, "it's quite possible the fraction of women working will exceed men." Back after World War II, more than 70 percent of men over 55 worked, compared to about 17 percent of women. Not all of those men were thrilled about their opportunities—once Social Security benefits rose and Medicare came along, a lot of them jumped at the chance to retire earlier.

There's another reason Goldin believes more women want to keep working longer besides the money and their enjoyment of the job itself. "There's sociability," she said. When it comes to a place where women can go to see friends, talk about life, and just enjoy being with other people, the workplace has taken the space that used to be filled with volunteer organizations and clubs. As they said in an old TV show, it's where "everybody knows your name."

Okay, that show was about a bar. But honestly, hanging out at work is better.

When we're looking at all the good news about older women working, it's important to remember that some of them still don't have a choice. Experts estimate as many as half of American women 65 and older are economically insecure, with 16 percent at or below the poverty line. They tend to make less money over their working lives than men do—for reasons ranging from child care responsibilities to glass ceilings. Then, when it comes time to receive Social Security, they're still on the losing end—the average benefit for a woman is $13,891 a year, compared to $17,663 a year for men. Ruby Oakley, 74, wound up working as a Tulsa school crossing guard when she couldn't live on her Social Security income. The job, she said, only "pays some chump change—

$7 an hour" for work that involves standing in traffic trying to stay between the cars and the children. But, she concluded, "the people at the city think they're doing the senior citizens a favor by letting them work like this." Roberta Gordon, a resident of a senior apartment complex in California, told *The Atlantic* she didn't even expect to be alive at 76, let alone working. But there she was, handing out samples at a local grocery store, trying to make enough to cover her $1,040 monthly rent.

"LIKE HERDING HIPPOS"

Whether women want to work longer for satisfaction or subsistence, they can run into the roadblock of age discrimination. Employers who pride themselves on workplace diversity when the issue is race or gender are often less enthusiastic when it comes to protecting older workers from being denied opportunities for advancement or being particularly targeted when it comes to cutbacks. Although these days they've generally learned a little discretion when it comes to expressing their feelings with terms like "old cow." In 2010, an administrator at Ohio State University forgot that rule — or at least he presumed that he was communicating in private when he said, in an email, that dealing with his older staff members was "like herding hippos." But the email went astray. Later, two teachers of English as a second language got to see what their boss had written, and they weren't surprised. Julianne Taaffe and Kathryn Moon had been in their 50s when the new program director arrived on the scene and began dropping hints that he'd like his older employees to go away. When Taaffe went into her annual performance review, she said the first question she got was "How long have you been around here, anyway?"

The older teachers were moved out of their offices and forced to share computers. They were passed over for promotions and good assignments, and found themselves referred to as "dead wood." Truly, it didn't take a detective. Feeling forced out, Taaffe and Moon left their jobs before they were eligible for full retirement benefits. Then they filed age discrimination suits. After years of painful, expensive, and stressful litigation, the Equal Employment Opportunity Commission decided they were right. Ohio State agreed to rehire Taaffe and Moon and pay them retroactive benefits and attorney's fees. Plus train human resources staff to prevent such cases in the future.

It was about as good a decision as they could get, given that—thanks to a Supreme Court ruling in 2000—state employers do not have to pay damages to people they've discriminated against on the basis of age. Taaffe and Moon said their biggest goal was to make things better for older workers who came later, and pronounced themselves satisfied. But age discrimination cases continue to be tough to pursue, even when the beleaguered employees are blessed with a boss who is careless about his emails.

"Age is treated as a second-class civil right," said Dan Kohrman, an attorney for AARP who supervises national litigation and worked on the Ohio State case. Women continue to have the most problems and the hardest cases to litigate. Some employers—particularly in office situations—prefer female underlings who are young and attractive, and try to get rid of them as they age. Thanks to previous Supreme Court decisions, if they're charged with age bias, they can point to their good record with older men. And if gender comes up, they can point to their large supply of younger women.

"UP THESE STEPS, THEN JUMP OFF"

After Meryl Streep spent her 40s avoiding those witch roles, she decided to play one after all in 2014, when she was 65. It was in a musical, *Into the Woods*, with a complicated character who struggles to regain her youthful beauty and disappears into a vat of boiling tar. She liked the experience so much that she accepted a part in director Rob Marshall's next film, *Mary Poppins Returns*, playing an eccentric supporting character named Topsy. On her first day of shooting, the 67-year-old Streep walked in "and Rob pointed to the chandelier and said, 'up these steps, then jump off, then you'll twirl around on that.'"

Pleased with the chandelier-twirling assignment, Streep said she was "very fortunate" to be working in the entertainment industry at just the point when it seems to be getting more open to older actresses. In 2009, she had starred in a romantic comedy, *It's Complicated*, the story of a 60-year-old woman caught between the attentions of her ex-husband and a new suitor. And in 2019, she joined the cast of *Big Little Lies*, a popular

TV series about a group of mostly middle-aged women in Monterey who try to solve a murder. Streep was playing the role of Nicole Kidman's mother-in-law. In 2018, when Kidman, 50, received a Screen Actors Guild award for her performance in the series, she thanked the older female actresses who had gone before and told the audience "how wonderful it is that our careers today can go beyond 40 years old."

Well, not everybody's. Remember that study that found only 11 percent of the speaking parts in the top 100 films of 2015 were for characters sixty or older. "Most of the jobs go to people in their twenties and thirties," said a spokesman for the Screen Actors Guild–American Federation of Television and Radio Artists. After that, things started to get tougher for everybody — "but men have a longer shelf life into their forties." Opportunities for female actors tend to evaporate when they are in their forties or fifties, he added. "And then they come back a bit — but while you're waiting all those years, men have a better chance of making a living."

So the bottom line is that for women in Hollywood young is good. Old is reasonably well stacked with character parts, but middle age is a desert. Things are somewhat better if you want acting roles on television. In 2016, *Forbes* determined that the highest-paid women on TV were on average five years older than the ones in movies. "In fact, not a single woman over 50 made the film list," *W* magazine pointed out. "Four entrants on the TV list have all reached the half-century mark." It was not the kind of news that would trigger dancing in the streets, but it was still a move in the right direction. TV is, after all, where most of the jobs are popping up. "Now, movie stars who make the move to television are like European aristocrats emigrating to America after World War II — there are so many opportunities in the new world and so little left back home to reclaim," wrote Alessandra Stanley in the *Times*.

And maybe sometime soon Hollywood will figure out how to make an *Avengers* sequel with aging female superheroes.

"I WANT TO BE YOU WHEN I GROW UP!"

As First Ladies go, Michelle Obama was on the younger end of the scale. She came on the job at 45, almost exactly the same age as Hillary Clinton had been and a year younger than Melania Trump. She was, depending on how you counted, either the last First Lady of the baby-boom era or the first Gen Xer in the White House. (Boomers are generally defined as people born between the end of World War II and 1964. Michelle arrived on the scene on January 17, 1964.)

Given her focus on healthy eating and exercise — remember that White House vegetable garden? — it was pretty clear Michelle was going to be one of the fittest First Ladies in history. "When I was at the White House, I often hosted bootcamp weekends for my close girlfriends," she wrote on Instagram. "It didn't matter that we were all at varying fitness levels. Our bootcamp weekends were a reminder that if we want to keep taking care of others, we need to take care of ourselves first." She didn't share many thoughts about aging until she turned 50 and the media started asking her how that felt. The answer was "fabulous."

"Every event I go to, every rope line, women are looking better with every passing year," she told *People* in a birthday interview. "I run into women all the time who will just happen to mention, 'Oh, I'm going to be 60,' and it's like 'You're kidding me!' I just went to see Cicely Tyson on Broadway. She is in her 80s and did a two-hour play with stamina and passion. I told her, 'I want to be you when I grow up!' And there's Jane Fonda..."

Michelle Obama is a wildly popular former First Lady — her autobiography, *Becoming*, sold 1.4 million copies the week it was released in 2018. She was, of course, succeeded in the job by Melania Trump, a 46-year-old former model. Melania steered pretty clear of the press, but Americans who were interested in her health routine could pick up some details, like her fondness for Pilates and habit of eating seven pieces of fruit a day. At one point in 2018 she disappeared from public events for about a month, during which time the administration said she was recovering from a kidney condition. We know there were rumors that she'd had cosmetic surgery because her husband tweeted about them:

The Fake News Media has been so unfair, and vicious, to my wife and our great First Lady, Melania. During her recovery from surgery they reported everything from near death, to facelift, to left the W.H. (and me) for N.Y. or Virginia, to abuse. All Fake, she is doing really well!

Truly, by that point the nation had so much else to think about that Melania's antiaging strategies were really not a major point of consideration.

"LOOK AT THAT FACE! WOULD ANYONE VOTE FOR THAT?"

There was possibly no other woman on the planet as famous as Hillary Clinton. We were with her in her 40s, during a rocky career as First Lady, when she fought endlessly and unsuccessfully for health care reform while living through the humiliation of the Intern in the Oval Office. But then—even before her tenure in the White House had run out—she got herself elected to the Senate by a state she'd never really lived in. And she became a fine lawmaker, great at working across the aisle on projects that were important and wonky, obsessive in her struggle to bring economic development to towns in upstate New York. She ran for president, lost the nomination to Barack Obama, and became his secretary of state. Then she ran again in 2016, becoming the first woman ever to get a major party's nomination. She wore a pantsuit to make her acceptance speech. It was white, in honor of the suffragists.

Early in the campaign it looked as if Clinton's age might be an issue. She was 67, and Republican candidates seemed to enjoy mentioning it. Marco Rubio, 43, kept talking about a "generational choice" between the politics of the future and people who were "promising to take us back to yesterday." Rand Paul, 51, stressed that running for president was "a rigorous physical ordeal." Scott Walker, 47, pointed out that he could wait another 20 years to make the run and "still be about the same age as the former secretary of state."

Some of this sounded silly even when it was being articulated—Scott Walker could have waited 100 years and he still wouldn't have been a viable candidate. And, as a *Chicago Tribune* critic pointed out, while Obama had been described as "a young man on the rise" when he ran for president at 46, the media's description of Clinton supporters of the same age was "white older women."

The discussion pretty much evaporated when the Republicans nominated Donald Trump, who was 69. Still, it was not as if Trump recognized that age in a woman was the same thing as age in a man. During the primary campaigns, he had mocked Republican opponent Carly Fiorina by saying, "*Look* at that face! Would anyone *vote* for that?" Fiorina, 61, retorted that she was "proud of every year and every wrinkle."

And when the choice came down to Trump or Clinton, Trump began claiming that Clinton, who suffered from a bout of pneumonia late in the campaign, didn't "have the stamina" for the job.

"To be president of this country, you need tremendous stamina," he said during a debate. "You have to be able to negotiate our trade deals. You have to be able to negotiate, that's right, with Japan, with Saudi Arabia." Clinton, whose tenure as secretary of state had been nothing if not stamina testing, responded that Trump could make that argument "as soon as he travels to 112 countries and negotiates a peace deal, a cease-fire, a release of dissidents and opening of new opportunities in nations around the world."

Still, the talk about her physical endurance worried her. In September, when she got pneumonia, she kept it secret for fear it would become a campaign issue. Pushing on with her schedule, she weakened and had to be helped into her van after an appearance at the 9/11 memorial. While she was at the ceremony, she recalled later, she ran into Senator Chuck Schumer. Knowing nothing about her condition, Schumer told her he had come down with pneumonia and spent a week at home on doctor's orders. "Looking back, I should have done the same," she wrote.

Clinton's supporters are still debating whether she lost because she was a woman. Or because she was a 69-year-old woman. All we know for sure is that in the end, Trump got elected and went on to become the president who was driven around a gathering of international leaders in a golf cart while the other heads of state walked together to their meetings. And Clinton left the center stage, crushed. It'll be a while before Americans can assign her a proper place in American history. But when we do, people will remember that she was the pioneer who made a woman running for president seem normal.

"She works harder than any human being I've ever known"

In January of 2019, Nancy Pelosi, 78, became the Speaker of the House of Representatives. Getting there had not exactly been a stroll in the park. The *Wall Street Journal* estimated that during the 2018 congressional elections, Republicans had run more than 135,000 ads that mentioned her "in an entirely negative context." Pelosi was a natural target, having been the Democrats' leader in the House since 2007, including four prior years as Speaker. But you couldn't help wondering about the woman angle. In 2010, when the Democrats controlled the Senate but not the House, Pelosi was subjected to seven times more attack ads than Harry Reid, the Senate majority leader.

A lot of rank-and-file House Democrats were grumbling that somebody else deserved a shot at their top job. Pelosi's supporters pointed out that she was a skilled negotiator who was great at rounding up votes in her balky caucus, and a tireless fund-raiser who got a big chunk of credit for the Democrats' sweeping House victories in the 2018 elections. (Like Hillary Clinton, Pelosi has a genius for falling asleep at will while she's flying around the country.) "She works harder than any human being I've ever known," said one of Pelosi's predecessors, Richard Gephardt. In 2018, Pelosi broke a record for longest speech ever given in the House of Representatives when she talked for more than eight hours without a break, recounting stories of young Americans who had been brought into the country illegally as children and were known as the Dreamers.

But still. Rep. Kathleen Rice of New York, 53, told reporters Americans wanted "a next generation of Democrats to lead the way." Among the other rebels were Linda Sánchez of California, 48, who'd been saying for a while that it was time for Pelosi to "pass the torch." She was hardly the only one dropping metaphors about torch passing. Pelosi put the rebellion down rather quickly, but in order to keep her job, she also agreed to a self-imposed term limit—four more years and out.

Complaints about Pelosi came to a screeching halt when the Speaker led her party through a 2019 government shutdown in the battle over Donald Trump's border wall. But the story of the House rebellion is a very high-profile example of a larger generational dilemma. The American women who fought for a place at the table in the 1970s and 1980s not only showed the country how to win; they also demonstrated that they could keep winning and producing great results when they reached their later years. But at the same time, some restive younger women began to wonder whether their seniors were ever going to step down, go away, and give them a chance to lead. When women fought for a future in which age didn't matter, nobody talked much about whether there would be enough room at the top for everybody who deserved to be there.

While Pelosi was reclaiming the Speaker's job, the House Democrats did bow to the younger generation by electing 48-year-old Hakeem Jeffries of New York to the important post of caucus chair. Jeffries beat Barbara Lee of California in a 123–113 vote. Both lawmakers were black, both were regarded as party stars. But Lee was 72, and she blamed ageism for her loss. "That's something that women, especially women of color, African American women, have to face," she told reporters.

"Bubbe, you were sleeping at the State of the Union!"

For a long time, when Ruth Bader Ginsburg was asked whether she was going to step down from the Supreme Court, she would remind her questioners that Louis Brandeis didn't retire until he was 82. When she hit 81, it was clear she was going to need another example, and as Ginsburg progressed on into her late 80s she was telling people that "John Paul Stevens didn't step down until he was 90."

Ginsburg had always been a heroine to American liberals, but after Donald Trump was elected president, her health became something of an obsession. People who might not even be able to name John Roberts, the chief justice, were keenly aware that Justice Ginsburg worked out several times a week with a personal trainer. She became a cult figure. Young women collected RBG T-shirts and coffee mugs. Some even had her initials tattooed on their arms. (If reports of the breadth of this phenomenon were possibly exaggerated, remember that there's probably nobody walking around sporting a John Roberts tattoo.)

Ginsburg is unique in many ways, including for her health history; she is notable for making big comebacks. She was treated for colon cancer in 1999 and for pancreatic cancer in 2009. She had a heart problem in 2014 that first showed itself while she was working out. None of it seemed to slow her down, but in 2015 she did nod off during Barack Obama's final State of the Union speech. She explained later that she was possibly just the slightest bit tipsy. At a meal the justices had before the event, she said, she had "vowed this year, just sparkling water, stay away from the wine. But in the end, the dinner was so delicious it needed wine to accompany it."

She heard about it. One of her grandchildren called her after the event and said: "Bubbe, you were sleeping at the State of the Union!"

Ginsburg also broke two ribs in a fall in 2018, and doctors treating her discovered cancerous growths on one lung. They removed them, and she appeared to be ready for another year on the bench. Her admirers didn't want to see her retire while Donald Trump was in the position to appoint a successor, but some of them couldn't help regretting that she had ignored suggestions that she ought to step down while there was a Democratic president in office. "Who do you think Obama could have nominated and got confirmed that you'd rather see on the court?" she demanded.

She was also probably more than a little fearful of what life would be like without the job. Her friend Sandra Day O'Connor had retired in 2006 to be with her husband, John, who was suffering from Alzheimer's. The loss of O'Connor, a Republican moderate, left Ginsburg voting in the minority in decisions she felt would have gone her way 5–4 if O'Connor had stayed around. And those retirement plans fell through. Ginsburg remembered her friend talking about all the activities she and her husband would do together, but his condition deteriorated quickly. "John was in such bad shape she couldn't keep him at home," Ginsburg recalled.

The story got even worse. John O'Connor, who no longer even recognized Sandra, was moved to an assisted-living center, where he fell in love with another Alzheimer's patient. Their son said his mother was "thrilled" that he had at least found some happiness. But it had to be painful, visiting her husband while he sat on a swing holding hands with his new partner, totally unaware he was chatting with his wife of 55 years. O'Connor devoted her retirement years to working for Alzheimer's research and a personal crusade to get young people more interested in civics. In 2018, at 88, she announced that she had been diagnosed with dementia — probably Alzheimer's — and dropped out of public life entirely.

Ginsburg's husband, Marty, whom she married in 1954, died in 2010. When she wasn't serving as a justice on the nation's most powerful court, or working out with her trainer, or visiting with her grandchildren, she was constantly on the move: giving speeches, sitting on panels, introducing friends when *they* were giving speeches. And occasionally going on working vacations. Once, she and her improbable friend the very conservative justice Antonin Scalia had joint gigs teaching in France. They were taking some time off on the Riviera when Ginsburg stunned Scalia by going parasailing. "This skinny little thing, you'd think she'd never come down," Scalia said.

Which, metaphorically, was exactly Ginsburg's plan.

"JUST TO SEE IF I HAD ANOTHER CHAPTER"

In 2011, when ABC was promoting its coverage of the 10th anniversary of the 9/11 terrorist attacks, the news talent it featured included Katie Couric, 54, Diane Sawyer, 65, Christiane Amanpour, 53, Barbara Walters, 81, Elizabeth Vargas, 49, and Robin Roberts, 50. Things had changed. TV news was a good example of how quickly the nation adapted to seeing women in positions of power once people were given the opportunity to regard it as normal. In 2006, CBS made Couric the first national news sitting-there-all-alone anchor and it was a huge story. Three years later, when Sawyer got the same job at ABC, it was pretty much business as usual.

Sawyer stepped down from the anchor job in 2014, when she was 68, and there were no longer any women at the head of any of the nightly news shows. But the evening news itself had slid in popularity — it had been a long time since families gathered around the TV after dinner to see what had been going on in the world that day. Women were starring in other network TV news programs, and the age barrier seemed to be cracking. In the years immediately following Sawyer's departure, Robin Roberts of ABC's *Good Morning America* was in her late 50s and Rachel

Maddow, who had her own evening talk show on MSNBC, was in her mid-40s. There was also Mika Brzezinski, 50, the co-host of *Morning Joe,* an NBC talk show named after her husband, Joe Scarborough. The couple courted and married while they were working on-air together, and had a famous falling-out with Donald Trump, a former pal who alienated them as his politics went increasingly right wing. By June of Trump's first year in office he sent out an enraged tweet claiming Brzezinski and Scarborough had tried to wrangle a New Year's Eve invitation to Mar-a-Lago: "She was bleeding badly from a face-lift. I said no!" Trump's attitude toward plastic surgery was more along the line of catty gossip than disapproval. In 2014, he tweeted, "Kim should sue her plastic surgeon," after 81-year-old Kim Novak presented an Academy Award on TV. Novak was traumatized and went into seclusion.

Back on the local news scene, viewers were getting a mixed message. The media company Meredith, which owns 15 local television stations, was being sued by female former news anchors from Kansas City and Nashville, who were dismissed and replaced with younger people. One of them, Demetria Kalodimos, then 58, discovered her walking papers in a package that was left at the station's front desk. "The face of WSMV in Nashville for three decades, she is one of the most decorated reporters in the city.... Her departure was a farce," wrote journalist Steve Cavendish, in an op-ed for the *New York Times* called "The Fight to Be a Middle-Aged Female News Anchor."

On a brighter note, Jean Enersen, anchor at Seattle's KING-TV, was still at her desk in 2016, when she was 72. No one, she said, had ever tried to force her out the door over the years. But when the station offered buyouts to its higher-salaried staff, Enersen "took it just to see if I had another chapter." The departure, she said, was "cordial," if not the rousing farewell tribute you might have expected for a 50-year employee.

Enersen did have another chapter, which involved building a children's health clinic. When the station became interested in promoting the project, too, she was invited to come back and do some programs about it. Then, when President Trump's attacks on the media ratcheted up, KING asked Enersen to return as an editorial spokesperson. "I couldn't be happier—I've gone from anchor to advocate," she said.

"The nation is facing a clown shortage"

Enersen's pleasure was partly about her TV work but also very much about that clinic project. "I think it's going to be a shining star on the hill that other communities are going to look to," she predicted. All in all, that new chapter was turning into the equivalent of at least a novelette. "I love it. I absolutely love it," she said. "I feel more jet-propelled than ever because I really want this thing to fly."

It is a story that Lydia Maria Child would have applauded in the nineteenth century—finding extra meaning in later life by serving your community. Given her passion for political reform, Child would probably also have appreciated the idea of coupling volunteer work with editorials denouncing Donald Trump. But in general, the twenty-first century hasn't been working out the way Child might have hoped. Older women are becoming less inclined to volunteerism. It is true for older Americans in general—only about 28 percent of people 55 to 64 report having done nonpaying work for their church, school, or charity. The rate is less than 25 percent for people 65 and over. And those who still put in some time aren't exactly devoting their lives to it. Most of the older volunteers are spending less than 100 hours a year, which boils down to an average of about two hours a week.

"It's not what it used to be for many different reasons," said Anna Quindlen, the novelist and opinion columnist whose work with Planned Parenthood included a stint on the board of directors. "One is that women have jobs now—some jobs that last into their seventies and even beyond. And women who are retired more and more find themselves acting as caregivers for their grandchildren." These days, she said, a prime source for volunteers is "kids who just graduated from college and are given unpaid internships" that count as doing good while also enhancing the résumé.

It is certainly true that retirees have plenty of other options: travel, sports, exercise, relationships. And, of course, there is work. Close to a third of women 55 and over are employed, and others are being encouraged to think about it—even if reality isn't always as enticing as the media suggests. When *Southern Living* published "12 of the Best, Dreamiest and Most Unusual Jobs for When You Retire," the list included everything from cruise staff to Uber driver to clown. ("The nation is facing a clown shortage.")

"OLDER MODELS ARE LIKE SO *IN*"

Or you might be busy online. For most pre-millennials, life on the web is a learning process. At a White House correspondents' dinner during Hillary Clinton's presidential campaign, President Obama compared her to an elderly relative who couldn't get a grip on Facebook: "Did you get my poke? Is it appearing on your wall? I'm not sure I'm using this right. Love, Aunt Hillary." But a great many women who never looked a cellphone in the eye until they were in their 50s or 60s are figuring out how to master the new media and use it for everything from posting on Facebook to doing the accounting for their businesses to organizing political campaigns.

Aging-fabulously blogs are popping up all over. Judith Boyd, a retired psychiatric nurse, started Style Crone in 2005 to document the over-the-top outfits she donned as distraction for her husband when he was undergoing chemotherapy. Helen Ruth Elam Van Winkle, better known as Baddie Winkle, has been constantly referred to in the media as "an internet sensation at the age of 85." A *Times* report on the older women bloggers—after noting that they are "often grandmothers"—pointed out that many stars of this new world are able to monetize their work, collecting advertising contracts. Baddie Winkle, the story said, "has millions of followers and is paid to tout brands like göt2b hair products and Smirnoff on her account and has made personal appearances at Sephora."

The idea that older women can attract advertisers has been kind of revolutionary. Many makers of consumer products had shunned them because they believed older readers/viewers didn't buy anything—or at least wouldn't buy anything new. That is obviously untrue, and a Nielsen survey found that consumers over 55 aren't more attached to their brands than younger people.

The baby-boom generation, which dominated national culture and conversation for half a century, is moving into its 60s and 70s, and it did seem for a while as if the economy was losing interest in them. Nielsen, the global information company, bemoaned the way boomer-targeted ads appeared to be confined in large part to stair lifts and diabetes medication. ("They do not think of themselves as broken and neither should marketers.") It wasn't as if the money was missing. Boomer women have a median income of $795 a week compared to $516 for the much-sought-after male in his early 20s, "but they remain invisible to advertisers," noted the American Marketing Association. Even Jane Fonda felt neglected—at least on television, where her character Grace on *Grace and Frankie* is ignored by the staff at a store where she's shopping. "Do you not see me?" she demands. "Do I not exist?"

But this is still America, and wherever there's money, there's eventually going to be attention. The glossy fashion magazines realized that many young women simply couldn't afford the products in their ads. "We exist in a post-recessionary world and the millennial generation is more challenged in terms of its buying ability," *Times* fashion critic Vanessa Friedman told *Adweek* in 2015. Somewhere during the second decade of the twenty-first century, things evolved. "All hail the rise of the over-70 campaign star," decreed the style magazine *Dazed*, when the luxury brand Céline announced that 80-year-old Joan Didion was going to be the face of its spring line. Saint Laurent gave the honor to Joni Mitchell, 72. "Older models are like so *in* right now, so it makes total sense that Marc Jacobs wants to jump on that trend," *Elle* magazine enthused, when the fashion brand picked Jessica Lange, 64, as the face of its 2014 campaign.

It's largely true that to be featured in a big consumer campaign when you're over 60, you already have to be internationally famous for doing something else. But still, companies were trying to appeal to what they had seen—rather suddenly—as a new market.

Models in their 60s and 70s—even some who never had been famous singers or actresses—were appearing more frequently in magazine fashion spreads. In 2008, the *Los Angeles Times* had quoted Ginni Conquest of Wilhelmina Models as saying that older models were "our fastest-growing area." She was co-director of the "sophisticated women's division" at Wilhelmina, a group that included anybody 25 or over. While the outside world was no longer used to attaching the age of 25 to "older," this was obviously a big deal for the fashion industry.

"IF SHE NO LONGER LOOKS LIKE HERSELF"

During the older-women-models boom in 2014, Julia Roberts, 46, became a face of Lancôme, where she was named the main perfume model. She told a British magazine she had "taken a big risk" in not preparing for her assignment by having a face-lift: "I've told Lancôme that I want to be an ageing model, so they have to keep me for at least five more years until I'm over 50." Her secret to looking young while getting older, she said, was about "non-grasping, non-hoarding, cleaning out your closet, dusting out your mind and letting go of the things that weigh you down mentally and emotionally." It was yet another version of Lillian Russell's Think Beautiful Thoughts dictum. As time went on, not everyone who viewed Roberts's completely seamless face was convinced she had never had work done. But only the true cynics cared. Audiences were used to seeing their favorite stars looking... improved upon. Unless things became really stiff and scary, average viewers seldom complained.

In 2016, a film critic, Owen Gleiberman of *Variety*, wrote a reasonably thoughtful piece about actress Renée Zellweger, asking, "If She No Longer Looks Like Herself, Has She Become a Different Actress?" Gleiberman didn't definitively say he thought Zellweger had had cosmetic surgery—a rather dicey topic unless the celebrity herself acknowledges it. And he didn't criticize her appearance. It was just that he felt she looked attractive in a different way than the *Bridget Jones* star, who looked beautiful, but "in the way an ordinary person is." If Zellweger was going to make sequels, Gleiberman said, he wanted the future Bridget Jones to look the way the old one did. The piece drew a superscathing response from the actress Rose McGowan, who claimed Gleiberman was "an active endorser of what is tantamount to harassment and abuse of actresses and women." If Gleiberman didn't like the way Zellweger was aging, she suggested he shut up: "What you are doing is vile, damaging, stupid and cruel." McGowan would go on to become a central figure in the #MeToo movement against sexual harassment, which everybody can probably agree was a much more critical problem for women than gossiping about face-lifts.

Zellweger had in fact caused quite a stir a year or two earlier when she appeared at an event looking—very much younger. But by the time she wandered into Gleiberman's crosshairs she had "actively returned to her old look," noted writer Caroline Siede in *Quartz*, who felt Zellweger had become "a walking metaphor for the shameful way we treat aging women in Hollywood." Siede then launched into an update of complaints made by every generation of women since the invention of motion pictures. Angelina Jolie had, at 29, been cast as the mother of 28-year-old Colin Farrell in the movie *Alexander*. Maggie Gyllenhaal, 37, had reported being told she was "too old" to play opposite an unnamed 55-year-old actor.

"Put another way," Siede continued, "Robert Downey Jr. is currently playing one of the world's most popular superheroes, while Marisa Tomei and Diane Lane are playing the mother figures of superheroes. All three actors are 51 years old."

Zellweger herself wrote that the whole thing was "deeply troubling."

"Aging and My Beauty Dilemma"

The country's 7,000 cosmetic surgeons performed more than 17 million procedures in 2017, most of them minimally invasive procedures like Botox injections and chemical peels. But 1.8 million patients—the vast majority of them women—underwent surgery. This wasn't all a story about resisting aging. The most common procedures were liposuction and nose reshaping. And more than a million involved women under 30. Still, the biggest clump of patients were 40 to 54, followed by those 55 and over.

Having gotten this far, we ought to discuss whether or not all this is a bad thing. For some actresses, cosmetic surgery is part of the work agenda—one of the burdens of movie stardom is having your every nip and tuck noticed and gossiped about by large numbers of complete strangers. A lot of ordinary people wanted to look a little younger, too, yet felt some angst about having a doctor cut into their face or shove chemical compounds under the skin. And there was also that sense of guilt, the questions about whether having work done meant caving in to the wrong values.

In 2016, Debora Spar, at the time president of Barnard College, published "Aging and My Beauty Dilemma" in the *New York Times*. Like most women in her "liberal, feminist-leaning, highly educated peer group," she said, "I am ideologically opposed to intervening in such a natural and inevitable process as getting on in years. But," she continued, "like many of my peers I am also a two-faced hypocrite, at least when it comes to parts of myself that may well benefit from a twinge of not-quite-so-natural intervention." After all, almost everybody colors their hair, she pointed out, and these days "many women will quietly confess to a shot of Botox from time to time, or a dose of filler to soften their smiles. It's after that point that things become dodgy."

We've been down a long, historic path on the fixing-your-face front. Remember the colonial debate about whether it should be illegal for women to trick men by wearing cosmetics? American women spent a couple of centuries agonizing about hair color—an argument that finally ended when the answer to "Does she or doesn't she?" was "Almost everybody does." Now Spar was saying we'd pretty much passed the point—at least in places like Manhattan or Los Angeles—when having a physician inject chemicals into your face to fill out wrinkles was anything but standard operating procedure. The debate had moved on to the next level, she continued: "Brow lifts. Estrogen. Tummy tucks. Cellfina cellulite treatment....Does a little face-lift along the way constitute treason, or just reasonable accommodation? I don't know."

What she did know, she wrote, was that for women at the top—in business or entertainment or society—the physical appearance bar kept rising, and it was becoming harder and harder to turn down intervention. Women "facing the onslaught of middle age are armed with an arsenal of age-fighting implements and, for many, a feminist inspired philosophy that disdains using them." It was pretty clear the philosophy was on the losing end. Spar recalled a party she had been to in Manhattan that featured "women of a certain age, mostly from the news media and politics," in which everybody looked great but suspiciously similar. "Everyone (at least in certain high-profile or professional circles) is doing it, and very few are confessing," she concluded.

Spar's piece triggered a lot of responses, ranging from outrage

("Vintage faces, like fashion, should be worn proudly") to agreement ("so happy I went under the knife"). But even some of the support letters were tinged with regret. "Although Ms. Spar invokes the need of high-powered women to conform to 'professional standards' all women face the same pressure," wrote one correspondent. "Not all risk losing high-paying jobs, but they face losing a spouse, or a salary, which can mean the difference between home and homelessness."

It always got back to those bag ladies.

"I'M BAAACK!"

In Hollywood, insiders had been reporting for ages — really, ever since they began talking about such things in public — that one standard demand from male directors, producers, and other authority figures was that actresses be young enough to look "fuckable." In 2015, comedian-writer Amy Schumer took the whole thing on in a skit called "Last F**kable Day." In it, she stumbles on Tina Fey, 45, Julia Louis-Dreyfus, 54, and actress Patricia Arquette, 47, celebrating Julia's arrival at that marker. The partygoers burst into laughter when Schumer asks whether men run into similar deadlines. "You know how Sally Field was Tom Hanks's love interest in *Punchline* and then like twenty minutes later she was his mom in *Forrest Gump*?" asks Fey.

In the non-entertainment world, women were discovering that as long as they didn't have to prove it by having an affair with Tom Hanks, their sexual life span could go on pretty much forever. On *Saturday Night Live*, comedian Leslie Jones announced that, since she was 51, she was giving up sex: "No one wants to have sex with an old bitch." She bantered with 36-year-old Colin Jost ("you sexy, full-headed, Old Navy–wearing millennial"), who finally noted that he had just read that "your sexual peak actually starts at age 54."

"I'm baaack!" Jones announced.

Women have, of course, been having sex in their later years forever. But there is definitely a twenty-first-century tendency to talk more about it. "At 80, I met a man. . . . David is the great love of my life," says Frances, 87, in the documentary *Still Doing It*, which chronicles the sex lives of women like Frances — who met her lover in a home for the aged—and Betty, 73, whose partner, Eric, is 47 years her junior. "When she was 67 she had a hip replacement," he explains. "If I'd have come too early, I'd have run into that. And it wouldn't have worked. If I'd come later probably someone else would have been here by now."

"Yep," Betty retorts.

To stay in the game, women have found all sorts of helpful aids, from lubricants to special pillows designed to elevate their hips. And then there's estrogen. Hormone therapy had dropped like a stone after that report by the Women's Health Initiative in 2002. Doctors were worried about prescribing it for their menopausal patients, and women themselves were afraid to take it. Use was down about 80 percent. But the wheel was going around again, and medical experts were beginning to take another look. It was paradoxical, wrote Dr. JoAnn Manson in the *New England Journal of Medicine,* that "FDA-approved hormone treatments for menopausal symptoms are being used so infrequently even though our understanding of their benefits and risks has never been clearer." Feel free to object that we've been down this road before. But HRT was back on the table, with many doctors recommending it for short-term use. The Mayo Clinic announced that the bottom line was— drum roll, please—"Hormone therapy isn't all good or all bad."

"I hate hearing about the U-curve"

As the twenty-first century moves along, Generation X is approaching middle age and looking beyond. They're the women who were born, roughly, in the '60s and '70s, post–baby boom, and their nickname is a good sign of what they've been up against. Google "Gen X" and you may find some kind of addendum along the lines of "often perceived to be disaffected and directionless." If you're squashed between the booming boomers and the moaning millennials, it's easy to be ignored. As the oldest Gen Xers pass 50, they find themselves facing aging issues that had always seemed reserved for their parents or older siblings.

"While studying my face in a well-lit elevator, my daughter describes it bluntly: 'Mommy, you're not old, but you're definitely not young,'" wrote Pamela Druckerman, who was living in Paris and unnerved by the way waiters began calling her "madame" instead of "mademoiselle" at around the time she turned 40. Another Gen Xer, Ada Calhoun, said it felt a little strange to be complaining about a midlife crisis. After all, her generation got fairer wages and more equal rights than women ever had before in history. Plus their spouses knew they were supposed to help with the housework. "Insert your Reason Why We Don't Deserve to Feel Lousy here," she invited her peers.

Boomers had lived out the women's revolution — they might well have been the first in their family to go to college, have a career, or combine work and family. Just having come through their era was a sort of achievement. The Xers, having grown up in a world where trying to have it all was a given, may have had more pangs of unmet goals. "Nearly 60 percent of Gen Xers describe themselves as stressed out," wrote Calhoun. "An awful lot of middle-aged women are furious and overwhelmed." There was, she added, that famous "U-curve" they were supposed to look forward to, when happiness that dipped in midlife went shooting back upward later. "But I hate hearing about the U-curve. That U-curve isn't necessarily a guarantee of future performance. What if ours is the first generation in history with no curve at all, just a diagonal line pointed straight to the lower right-hand corner?" Many felt stalled in their careers, she said, stuck behind the boomers who don't want to retire, with the millennials breathing down their necks.

Plus there was the pressure to have cosmetic surgery. Gen Xers, Calhoun noted, had to compete against not only younger women but also the very large number of women their own age and older who *looked* younger because they'd already had work done. "Midlife is when we need to take care of everyone else while we are most tired, to trust ourselves when we're most filled with doubt," she concluded. "What makes it worse is that many of our midlife fears are well founded. We may, in fact, die alone. Our marriages may never improve. We may never get the number of kids we hoped for. We may never save enough money to make the retirement calculators stop screaming. We may never do a fraction of what we thought we would do in our career."

Okay, that was not encouraging. Ten million surveys showing middle-aged people generally enjoyed being middle-aged are not going to make you feel better if you're the one with an unsatisfying job and a failing marriage. So I am not going to give you a list of quotes from Gen

Xers who are happy with their stage in life. Well, okay. One. "I'm pretty damn thrilled to be 40," announced actress Katherine Heigl, in a 2018 Instagram birthday post that celebrated her freedom "from all the self doubt, insecurities, self loathing, uncertainties and anxieties of my 20's and 30's." We'll draw a veil over the commenters who told her not to worry because "soon you'll be 50 and then you'll feel really old."

"U.S. LIFE EXPECTANCY DECLINES"

As America moves toward the 2020s, the 60-somethings do seem to be taking over. "During the twentieth century the number of persons in the United States under age 65 has tripled," the U.S. Census Bureau reported. "At the same time, the number aged 65 and over has jumped by a factor of 11!" By 2050, it projected, "the elderly population will more than double" to 80 million. Most of the growth, the experts said, would happen between 2010 and 2030, when "the 'baby boom' generation enters their elderly years." No matter how many experts announce that 70 is the new 50, you'll notice that as far as the Census Bureau is concerned, once you're 65 you're elderly.

This isn't a story of longevity-ever-longer for all Americans. In 2016, a *Washington Post* headline announced "U.S. Life Expectancy Declines for the First Time Since 1993." But the big drop involves white men, who are falling victim to the opioid crisis and alcoholism. A woman who is 65 can expect, on average, to live into her 80s. That isn't all that terrific by international standards. Japan, France, Italy, and Hong Kong all have higher life expectancy. The United States is about on par with Vietnam, Uruguay, and Lebanon. But it is still quite a leap from the beginning of the century, and about five years longer than in 1950.

And the chances of reaching 90 are getting better and better. There were about 720,000 American nonagenarians in 1980, but by 2010 the number was closing in on 2 million—two-thirds of them women. Because we're Americans, we're going to be assigning tasks to this new generation aged 80 to 100. Most of them will have left behind their traditional jobs or careers, may have lost their partners, and will need to figure out what new opportunities and challenges there are for them as they march toward the triple digits. It's not irrational to say: "Well, good grief, just take a rest." But if you're pushing 95 and in good health, somebody is going to point out to you that there's a 96-year-old visiting patients at the local hospital, or read you the story of a 97-year-old woman employed by the National Park Service.

Yes! We've got career triumphs for 90-somethings. Our 97-year-old park ranger, Betty Reid Soskin, got her job at 85, giving popular history talks to park visitors in Richmond, California. Soskin, who's African American, made sure to give attention to the non-white side of the story. She received a presidential medal for her work. It was later stolen from her home, and although Soskin wasn't able to stop the burglar, she did manage to tackle him and give his genitals a painful squeeze. Barack Obama sent her a replacement.

This was, of course, the twenty-first-century version of those articles celebrating the 100-year-old female race-car driver or the little old lady lighthouse keeper who kept rowing out to rescue drowning sailors. It was not what you'd call normal. But it was one of many signs that there's not necessarily any fixed stopping point to an American woman's life in our era. Betty White made one of her innumerable comebacks in 2010 when she was 88, playing touch football in a Superbowl ad. That led to a hosting gig on *Saturday Night Live* and a role in a new TV comedy series. At 96, White was still appearing at parties and awards shows, usually to get another prize herself. Pressed for the secret to a long, happy life, she generally recommended positive thinking, and threw in an occasional plug for vodka and hot dogs, "probably in that order."

"This is what eighty looks like"

In 2014, Gloria Steinem had a "This is what eighty looks like" party at a benefit for the Shalom Center in Philadelphia. "Fifty was a shock because it was the end of the center of my life," she recalled. "But once I got over that, 60 was great. Seventy was great. And I loved aging. I found myself thinking things like: 'I don't want anything I don't have.' How great is that?" But 80 was giving her pause. "Eighty is about mortality, not aging. Or not just aging." She quickly bounced back — after the birthday celebration, she was off to ride elephants in Botswana.

Before she left, Steinem listed the good things about moving into her ninth decade. One of them, she said, was a dwindling libido. She always had been a woman with an extremely active romantic life. But looking at it from 80, Steinem couldn't help thinking of what she might have accomplished if she hadn't been distracted by sex. Finally, she decided, she was free to just focus on her priorities. And when she met a new man, she wouldn't have to wonder whether an interesting conversation was going to morph into an assignation. "The brain cells that used to be obsessed are now free for all kinds of great things," she declared. None of the younger women she knew bought into this theory, Steinem admitted. "When I was young I wouldn't have believed it either."

A few years after Steinem celebrated 80, she went to the 90th birthday party of Muriel Fox, a co-founder of the National Organization for Women. They had been in the trenches together since the 1960s. Most of the guests were activists, organizers, and educators, and, except for Fox's daughter and granddaughters, all 70 and beyond. There was toasting, and talking about stages of life, along with quite a bit of moaning about Donald Trump. Afterward, Fox saw everyone off to their many appointed rounds and happily returned herself to Kendal on Hudson, a retirement community in Sleepy Hollow, New York.

Fox's husband, a physician who once served as the president of the New York chapter of NOW, died in 2003. She heard about Kendal and put herself on a waiting list. It took four years to get an apartment. About two-thirds of the 330 residents are 86 or older. They're engaged in all sorts of group projects, from counseling undocumented immigrants in nearby communities to holiday entertainments. One of Fox's assignments was the Fourth of July show — a favorite memory was the time residents celebrated Independence Day by voting on what the national anthem should be. Woody Guthrie's "This Land Is Your Land" demolished "The Star-Spangled Banner."

"There are a bunch of lefties here," she said, quoting Gloria Steinem's theory on how women get more radical with age. But Fox parts company with her old friend on the desirability of giving up on sex. "Since Shep died I've had three really lovely romances," Fox mused. "All the men died. But it was great." She and her female friends at Kendal frequently lament the shortage of single men: "My guess is the ratio is eight to one."

We've come a long way from the era when smart, independent women dreaded an old age filled with well-meaning helpers, forcing them to weave potholders or take classes on how to name the 13 colonies. With luck and money (yes, sometimes a lot of money), people can wind up in retirement communities where they're able to live their own lives in their own homes, supported by some services and surrounded by neighbors like themselves who probably would invite them over for barbecue or golf or a book club. Fox's place is typical of the latest models, which offer a progressive care program. She simply gets housekeeping help now, and the ability to eat in the communal dining room if she chooses: "There are lots of dinner parties, which are pretty easy, given that you can just reserve seats in the dining room." Later, if she needs it, there will be a home health-care attendant, and then maybe all the services of a regular nursing home.

"I still don't feel old," Fox observed. "Except when I have spinal stenosis, which practically everyone here has." An avid tennis player, she had to give up the game due to knee problems, "so I started a ping-pong group."

"Energy — coarse and rich"

This is a good time to remember that less than a century ago *Ladies' Home Journal* was informing its readers that it was the job of older Americans "to adjust themselves to conditions made for them by people who belong to a later generation in a new world." Getting older, the magazine decreed, was to become "obsolete, like fine old words erased from the epic of living." Fair to say that things have improved. True, Lydia Maria Child would be unnerved by all the dermabrasions and the blogs from senior hotties. But it's easy to imagine women from the past looking at our era and finding things pretty darned good. Well, at least on the aging front. Can't say they'd all envy us Donald Trump.

Aging is the one part of life that every human being shares, and it's never an easy territory to navigate. A couple of centuries ago, American women had so few options for how to make the journey that it was natural most of them simply settled for pious acceptance. Then, thanks to modern medicine — and those geniuses who figured out that it was a good idea to separate the sewage from the water—life spans lengthened and people thought a lot more about how to make their later years as full as possible. And now, for the first time in human history, great numbers of women are moving into old age after lives that have been jam-packed with careers, family life, and adventures of their own choosing. The nation is just beginning to appreciate what economic powerhouses they are. They're in the world and they can change the world. Can't wait to see how it works out.

If you're lucky and healthy, there are, as we've seen, a lot of options. You can fight every wrinkle and try to make time stand still at 37. You can re-create yourself at 65—go back to college or move to Cambodia or start a commune. (Okay, we have noticed, over the course of this history, that communes hardly ever work. But you never can tell...) If you always keep your options open, maybe you'll find yourself wearing a park ranger uniform at 97.

While we're teaching ourselves how to get old in the best way possible, we can be grateful for the way the deadlines keep getting pushed back. Forty isn't really seen as middle age anymore—unless, God help you, you're trying to get a job in tech. Fifty is, but so is 60. This is the time when a lot of decisions are made about how long you intend to work and where you want to live in the next stage of your life—presuming the kids have genuinely left home. And for most women, it's the time when friends are going to begin to die. Not the elderly lady you used to talk with at the library. Real friends. Mortality is approaching.

Yet quite a few people feel the best is still ahead. "I wouldn't be twenty-five again on a bet, or even forty," wrote Anna Quindlen. "And when I say this to a group of women at lunch, everyone around the table nods." Quindlen's hitting-sixty book, *Lots of Candles, Plenty of Cake,* chronicled her two-year quest to learn how to do a headstand. It wasn't your typical life goal, but to her it was "about the determination not to give up and give in, the refusal to see 'older' as synonymous with 'less.' " And darned if she didn't make the grade.

Or, on the other hand, you could listen to Nora Ephron, who complained about reading books in which the author "says it's great to be old.... it's great to be at the point where you understand just what matters in life. I can't stand people who say things like this. What can they be thinking? Don't they have necks?" The way a woman's neck changes with age was Ephron's metaphor for the downside of growing older. In fact, she wrote a book about it: *I Feel Bad About My Neck*.

"According to my dermatologist, the neck starts to go at forty-three and that's that," Ephron mused. "Our faces are lies and our necks are the truth."

Actually, Ephron — the one who concluded that everything changed for women when the use of hair coloring became nearly universal — had a very American, very twenty-first-century vision of women and aging. She was diagnosed with leukemia in her 60s, and she had a very keen sense that she was facing the end of life. But she was also still having a great career — writing and directing a movie about the cookbook author Julia Child that would win Meryl Streep another Academy Award nomination. She was very happily married to writer Nick Pileggi; she knew everyone in the New York literary/media circles, and she was busy all the time. She wanted to keep watching and writing about all the things that amused her, warmed her, irritated her, and... tasted good. (In her last book, Ephron concluded a list of "Things I Will Miss" with "pie.") She wanted to keep doing everything, and also talk, very ironically and very realistically, about the day-to-day experience of getting old.

Remember the hair-color motto about "You're not getting older, you're getting better"? Opinions differ. And these days we even have debates about how you define "older." Advertising guru Faith Popcorn calls 60 to 68 "the childhood of old age," and then moves on to 68 to 78 ("the adolescence of old age"), followed by "the adulthood of old age," which lasts until the mid-80s. Then, by Popcorn's reckoning, you spend your late 80s and 90s in "early late old age." Finally, it's time for genuine "old age," which runs, in her mind, from 92 to 110.

Wise women do seem to agree that you've got to find a way to embrace the whole adventure. (Calling it an adventure isn't self-deluding if you acknowledge right off the bat that this one may involve hip replacements.) Essayist Vivian Gornick recounted how "turning sixty was like being told I had six months to live," until she discovered the advantages that came with realizing she could no longer retreat from the problems of today by taking refuge in "a fantasized tomorrow." Gornick stopped daydreaming about what she might do later; when she walked familiar New York streets, she tried to pay attention to what was really happening around her and interact as much as possible with the people she met. "Energy—coarse and rich—began to swell inside the cavity of my chest. Time quickened, the air glowed, the colors of the day grew vivid; my mouth felt fresh. A surprising tenderness pressed against my heart with such strength it seemed very nearly like joy; and with unexpected sharpness I became alert not to the meaning but to the astonishment of human existence."

ACKNOWLEDGMENTS

⇥ ⇤

I don't know anyone who describes the experience of book writing as a total picnic, but for those of us who deal in nonfiction, there's always the pleasure of getting to know new people and reconnecting with old friends.

On the first-time side, I have to give special thanks to Janet Byrne, who not only led me through the fact-checking like a general but also offered invaluable editing suggestions as I staggered through the last phases of this project. Her terrific troops included fact-checkers Sameen Gauhar, Pat McDaniel, Julie Tate, Barbara Clark, and Diana D'Abruzzo. Laboring away on the endnotes were Leah Zinker, Penelope Lin, Barbara Clark, and Allegra Huston.

Before Janet took over the final act, I had the great fortune of spending four years working with Veronica Cassidy, my senior researcher, who kept the information flowing via 1,238 emails as she made her way from New York academia to a career in the French food scene. Leading food tours of Paris is probably a more pleasant occupation than scouring the web for information on menopause during the Civil War, but Veronica, ever cheerful and productive, never let me know it.

Thanks also to researchers Andrew Baker, Laura Bult, Rhaina Cohen, Madison Darbyshire, Mara Heneghan, Katharine Maller, Caitlin Reilly, Kathryn Ryan, Jessica Celeste Ross Salley, Karen Savage, Madeleine Schwartz, Natalie Shutler, and Kate Sinclair. And if you enjoy the pictures here, they were all discovered by photo editor Ruth Mandel.

I had a wonderful time talking with amazing, friendly, and informative people on this trip, and I'm apologizing in advance for not fitting them all into this little thank-you. Muriel Fox, one of the founders of NOW, really helped get me launched with an invitation to her 90th birthday party. Bettina Aptheker, Cora Weiss, Jean Enersen, and Gloria Steinem were awesome interviewees. Thanks to Joseph Reckford for telling me all about his grandmother, Millicent Fenwick; to Sala Elise Patterson for interviewing her mother, Elizabeth Hayes Patterson; and to Senator Ron Wyden, for revisiting his adventures as a young Gray Panther. Meryl Streep, Anna Quindlen, and Gina Kolata generously took time out of schedules that are way more packed than mine to talk.

Also — and I'm going to stop, I promise, even though I could go on for pages — thanks to Cindy Pearson, of the National Women's Health Network; Faith Popcorn; Claudia Goldin, of Harvard; Judith Shapiro, of Barnard; and Paula England, of New York University.

Trish Hall has been reading and editing my work since our days together covering the state legislature in Hartford, and once again she came through as my reader-in-chief. Much gratitude to all my colleagues at the *New York Times* for putting up with me while I kept wandering around moaning about book deadlines. That includes editorial page editor James Bennet, all the ungodly smart editorial board members, editors, researchers, and my co-columnists. Being part of the *Times* has been the greatest privilege of my writing life, and this gives me another chance to thank Arthur Sulzberger, who hired me, and our publisher, A. G. Sulzberger, for keeping the ship so proudly afloat.

I would not be thanking anybody if it weren't for Reagan Arthur of Little, Brown, who's been a champion from the beginning, and the wonderful team at Hachette — particularly Karen Landry, Dianna Stirpe, and Sareena Kamath. And of course, my indefatigable agent, Alice Martell. My family has been a wonderful support, and my sisters — Mary Ann, Patti, Laura — are the best women in the world to get older along with.

I always save the last thanks for my husband, Dan Collins, and point out that without him nothing would be any fun at all. Still true, after all these years.

NOTES

＋> -<+-

INTRODUCTION

3 "In this youth-made world": Advertisement for Loving Care, *Ebony*, October 1972, 19.

3 "There's a reason why forty": Nora Ephron, *I Feel Bad About My Neck* (New York: Alfred A. Knopf, 2006), 35.

4 the 7,000 or so cosmetic surgeons: This was the number of "board-certified" surgeons in 2016, according to the American Society of Plastic Surgeons, which reported some 8,000 worldwide in 2018.

4 "Herodotus tells us of some tribes": David Hackett Fischer, *Growing Old in America* (New York: Oxford Univ. Press, 1978), 6.

5 "super-exaltation": Carroll Smith-Rosenberg, *Disorderly Conduct: Visions of Gender in Victorian America* (New York: Oxford Univ. Press, 1985), 67–68.

5 "Don't trust anyone over 30": "Don't Trust Anyone over 30, Unless It's Jack Weinberg," *Berkeley Daily Planet*, April 6, 2000.

I. THE COLONIES

9 "romping girl": Maurice J. Pollard, *The History of the Pollard Family of America*, vol. 1 (Dover, NH: self-pub., 1960), 273. Although sculptor John F. Paramino portrayed Anne Pollard "as a child, she was fully grown when settling in Boston," notes the 2019 Boston City Walking Guide to the Founders Memorial.

9 at the age of 104: Pollard, *History of the Pollard Family*, says that she died in her "105th year" (p. 273). The Massachusetts Historical Society and all other sources agree that her birth date is not known.

9 "social pipe": Ibid., xxviii.

9 Of the women who managed: John Demos, "Notes on Life in Plymouth Colony," *William and Mary Quarterly* 22 (April 1965): 271.

9 In 1632, the 19-year-old: Thomas R. Cole, *The Journey of Life: A Cultural History of Aging in America* (New York: Cambridge Univ. Press, 1992), 37. The poem has been rendered in several different ways over time, with changing line breaks and punctuation. See, for example, Helen Campbell, *Anne Bradstreet and Her Time* (Boston: D. Lothrop Co., 1891), 72; and Anne Bradstreet, *To My Husband and Other Poems*, ed. Robert Hutchinson (New York: Dover Publications/Dover Thrift Editions, 2000).

10 mortality rates before 1624 ran as high as 37 percent: Carville Earle, "Environment, Disease and Mortality in Early Virginia," *Journal of Historical Geography* 5, no. 4 (1979): 365–90. Earle, citing Darrett B. Rutman and Anita H. Rutman, "Of Agues and Fevers: Malaria in the Early Chesapeake," *William and Mary Quarterly* 33 (January 1976): 31–60, notes that even as the population generally developed various immunities, morbidity still disproportionately affected pregnant women. See also Lois Green Carr and Lorena S. Walsh, "The Planter's Wife: The Experience of White Women in Seventeenth-Century Maryland," *William and Mary Quarterly* 34 (October 1977): 542–71.

10 "If any Maid": Julia Cherry Spruill, *Women's Life and Work in the Southern Colonies* (New York: W. W. Norton, 1972), 15; and Bartholomew Rivers Carroll, comp., *Historical Collections of South Carolina; Embracing Many Rare and Valuable Pamphlets, and Other Documents, Relating to the History of That State, from Its First Discovery to Its Independence, in the Year 1776*, vol. 2 (New York: Harper & Bros., 1836), 17.

10 This open attitude: Carol Berkin, *First Generations: Women in Colonial America* (New York: Hill and Wang, 1996), 6.

10 If you were Margaret Brent: Mary Beth Norton, *Founding Mothers & Fathers: Gendered Power and the Forming of American Society* (New York: Vintage, 1997), 281–87; and Spruill, *Women's Life and Work*, 240.

11 "in any man[']s": Spruill, *Women's Life and Work*, 240.

11 Frances Culpeper: Mary Beth Norton, *Separated by Their Sex: Women in Public and Private in the Colonial Atlantic World* (Ithaca, NY: Cornell Univ. Press, 2011), 9–36.

11 "I have often thought": Elaine Forman Crane, ed., *The Diary of Elizabeth Drinker: The Life Cycle of an Eighteenth-Century Woman*, abridged ed. (Philadelphia: Univ. of Pennsylvania Press, 2010), 175.

12 made her way to Valley Forge in 1778: Historical Society of Montgomery County, Pennsylvania, *Historical Sketches: A Collection of Papers Prepared for the Historical Society of Montgomery County, Pennsylvania*, vol. 4 (Norristown, PA: Herald Printing and Binding Rooms, 1910), 203.

12 "If a man is favored": Carole Haber, *Beyond Sixty-Five: The Dilemma of Old Age in America's Past* (New York: Cambridge Univ. Press, 1983), 8.

12 One Massachusetts congregation: David Hackett Fischer, *Growing Old in America* (New York: Oxford Univ. Press, 1978), 38–39.

13 "old Women to young ones": Leonard W. Labaree, ed., *The Papers of Benjamin Franklin*, vol. 3 (New Haven, CT: Yale Univ. Press, 1961), 31.

13 average housewife was 63: Haber, *Beyond Sixty-Five*, 10.

13 "The patient was safe delivered": Laurel Thatcher Ulrich, *A Midwife's Tale: The Life of Martha Ballard, Based on Her Diary, 1785–1812* (New York: Vintage, 1991), 340.

13 On Long Island: Kathleen Waters Sander, *Mary Elizabeth Garrett: Society and Philanthropy in the Gilded Age* (Baltimore: Johns Hopkins Univ. Press, 2008), 150.

13 "I believe I never had": Crane, *Diary of Elizabeth Drinker*, 137.

14 Ministers urged: Terri L. Premo, *Winter Friends: Women Growing Old in the New Republic, 1785–1835* (Urbana: Univ. of Illinois Press, 1990), 108.

14 "in rapture": Ibid., 161.

14 In Boston, Rev. Benjamin Colman: Vivian Bruce Conger, *The Widows' Might: Widowhood and Gender in Early British America* (New York: New York Univ. Press, 2009), 112.

15 faces floating in the dark: See, for example, *Portrait of the Ege-Galt Family*, Abby Aldrich Rockefeller Folk Art Museum, 1976.100.1, gift of Mrs. V. Lee Kirby.

15 Maria and Harriet Trumbull: Eric Homberger, *Mrs. Astor's New York: Money and Social Power in a Gilded Age* (New Haven, CT: Yale Univ. Press, 2002), 39.

15 "impose upon, seduce or betray": William T. Shore, *John Woolman, His Life and Our Times* (London: Macmillan, 1913), 49; and Albert Gibson, Arthur Weldon, and Robert McLean, eds., *Law Notes: A Monthly Magazine for Students and Practitioners,* vol. 8 (London: "Law Notes" Publishing Offices, 1889), 165.

15 "Hoops and Heels" laws: Thanks to Amy Denholtz, senior research analyst, New Jersey Office of Legislative Services, and assistant librarian Dana Combs.

15 practiced a little dental work: New England Historical Society, "Paul Revere, America's First Forensic Dentist," last modified 2017, accessed March 14, 2019, http://www.newenglandhistoricalsociety.com/paul-revere-americas-first-forensic-dentist/.

15 The toothbrush: Dorothy and Thomas Hobbler, *Vanity Rules: A History of American Fashion and Beauty* (Brookfield, CT: Twenty-First Century Books, 2000), 17.

16 Researchers excavating the site: William Kelso, *Jamestown, the Truth Revealed* (Charlottesville: Univ. of Virginia Press, 2017), 140.

16 Jamestown was notoriously: Spruill, *Women's Life and Work*, 5.

16 "The women are pitifully tooth-shaken": Daniel Freeman Hawke, *Everyday Life in Early America* (New York: Harper and Row, 1988), 72.

16 Martha seemed: Patricia Brady, *Martha Washington* (New York: Penguin, 2005), 177.

16 it must have worked: Carl Sferrazza Anthony, *First Ladies,* vol. 1 (New York: Quill, 1990), 44.

16 But when Dolley: Catherine Allgor, *A Perfect Union* (New York: Henry Holt, 2006), 357.

16 "To be old": Fischer, *Growing Old*, 67.

16 subject to fainting spells: Helen Campbell, *Anne Bradstreet and Her Time* (Teddington, Middlesex, UK: Echo Library, 2007), 210.

16 "giddiness in my head": Crane, *Diary of Elizabeth Drinker*, 82, 157, 167.

17 "peevishness, doubts, fears": Benjamin Waterhouse, "Lecture: Dyspepsia or Indigestion," Autumn 1796, OnView: Digital Collections and Exhibits, Center for the History of Medicine, Countway Library of Medicine, Harvard University, accessed March 24, 2019, http://collections.countway.harvard.edu/onview/items/show/17141.

17 "Venice Treacle": Crane, *Diary of Elizabeth Drinker*, 35.

17 Bleeding was: J. S. Moore, "Prelude to Chiropractic: Doctor Books, Anodynes, and Back Pain in Nineteenth-Century America," *Chiropractic History* 29, no. 2 (2009): 51.

17 Drinker, when she: Crane, *Diary of Elizabeth Drinker*, 214.

17 life "tolerable": Fischer, *Growing Old*, 67.

17 "shattered incurably": Gerda Lerner, *The Grimké Sisters from South Carolina* (Chapel Hill: Univ. of North Carolina Press, 2004), 204.

18 In 1664 in Massachusetts: Ulrich, *A Midwife's Tale*, 98.

18 "professional immunity": Ibid., 99.

18 Esther Lewis: Joan Jensen, *Loosening the Bonds: Mid-Atlantic Farm Women 1750–1850* (New Haven, CT: Yale Univ. Press, 1988), 133–36.

19 That was the story for Jenny Slew: Ben Z. Rose, *Mother of Freedom: Mum Bett and the Roots of Abolition* (Waverley, MA: TreeLine Press, 2009), 17–18, 51, 90.

19 "Attended Court": Ibid., 18, quoting John Adams's diary entry of November 5, 1765.

20 "She could neither read nor write": Ibid., 110.

20 "preaches better Gospell": Norton, *Founding Mothers & Fathers*, 368.

20 A more optimistic example: Mary Maples Dunn, "Saints and Sinners: Congregational and Quaker Women in the Early Colonial Period," *American Quarterly* (Winter 1978): 582–601.

21 Ann Powell kept a diary: Berkin, *First Generations*, 43, 62; and Frank H. Severance, ed., *Studies of the Niagara Frontier*, vol. 15, *Publications of the Buffalo Historical Society* (Buffalo, NY: Buffalo Historical Society, 1911), 230.

21 "Nothing is more real": Berkin, *First Generations*, 62.

21 Missionaries were uncomfortable: Anthony Wallace, *The Death and Rebirth of the Seneca* (New York: Vintage, 1972), 226.

22 "The Creator is sad": Ibid., 212, 241.

22 "with a wrinkled face": Malcolm Gaskill, "Witchcraft in Early Modern Kent: Stereotypes and the Background to Accusation," in *Witchcraft in Early Modern Europe: Studies in Culture and Belief*, eds. Jonathan Barry and Marianne Hester (Cambridge, UK: Cambridge Univ. Press, 1996), 260; and *Fraser's Magazine for Town and Country*, vol. 79, March 1869 issue (London: Longmans, Green, and Co., [1869?]), 378.

22 as many as 200 people: John Demos, *Entertaining Satan: Witchcraft and the Culture of Early New England* (New York: Oxford Univ. Press, 1982), 11, 87; and Stacy Schiff, *The Witches: Suspicion, Betrayal, and Hysteria in 1692 Salem* (New York: Alfred A. Knopf, 2012), 424n4. Schiff cites figures ranging from 141 to 204, noting that while most sources—including at least one contemporaneous source—say "more than two hundred," the number is unknowable.

22 Ann Hibbins: William F. Poole, "Witchcraft in Boston," in *The Memorial History of Boston*, ed. Justin Winsor, vol. 2 (Boston: James R. Osgood and Co., 1882), 138–41.

22 Rebecca Nurse: Rebecca Beatrice Brooks, "The Witchcraft Trial of Rebecca Nurse," *History of Massachusetts* (blog), November 5, 2012, https://historyofmassachusetts.org/the-trial-of-rebecca-nurse/.

22 "Must the younger Women": John Demos, "Underlying Themes in the Witchcraft of Seventeenth-Century New England," *American Historical Review* (June 1970): 1,311–26.

22 no short-term prejudice: Jack Larkin, *The Reshaping of Everyday Life: 1790–1840* (New York: Harper Perennial, 1989), 11–12.

23 wanted to avoid solitude: Daniel Freeman Hawke, *Everyday Life in Early America* (New York: Harper and Row, 1988), 55–57.

23 "passed my night in rolling down hill": Elizabeth Donaghy Garrett, *At Home: The American Family, 1750–1870* (New York: Harry N. Abrams, 1990), 111.

23 "one of the most cranky": Spruill, *Women's Life and Work*, 138; and *In Search of Early America: The William and Mary Quarterly, 1943–1993* (Williamsburg, VA: Institute of Early American History and Culture, 1993), 288.

23 "putrid abomination": *New-York Weekly Museum*, June 19, 1790. The paper was published out of 3 Peck Slip, New York, NY, by John Harrisson and Stephen Purdy, whose all-purpose printing shop also put out chapbooks and books of poetry.

24 widows outnumbering widowers seven to one: Conger, *The Widows' Might*, 4.

24 "poor, helpless" widows: Mary Beth Norton, *Liberty's Daughters* (Ithaca, NY: Cornell Univ. Press, 1980), 117.

24 The distinctly nonpathetic writer Judith Sargent Murray: Judith Sargent Murray, *The Gleaner: A Miscellaneous Production, In Three Volumes*, vol. 3 (Boston: I. Thomas and E. T. Andrews, 1798), 220. Cathy N. Davison notes that Murray used the male pseudonym Mentor when the essays in this collection were first published and a female pen name, Constantia, for book publication (*Revolution and the Word: The Rise of the Novel in America* [New York: Oxford Univ. Press, 2004], 419).

24 British jurist William Blackstone famously: William Blackstone, *Commentaries on the Laws of England*, vol. 1 (Chicago: Univ. of Chicago Press, 1978 [originally published 1765]), 442–45, accessed June 23, 2019, http://www.kentlaw.edu/faculty/fbatlan/classes/BatlanGender&LawS2007/CourseDocs/coursedoc07/Blackstone.pdf.

24 Ann Franklin…Lydia Bailey: Gay Walker, "Women Printers in Early American Printing History," *Yale University Library Gazette* 61, nos. 3–4 (April 1987): 116–24.

24 Some male colonists complained: Conger, *The Widows' Might*, 5.

25 "And now her Husband": Paula A. Treckel, *To Comfort the Heart: Women in Seventeenth-Century America* (New York: Twayne Publishers, 1996), 126.

25 estimated that 20 percent: Conger, *The Widows' Might*, 3.

25 If a husband failed to leave a will: Norton, *Liberty's Daughters*, 137.

25 "the East End": John Demos, *A Little Commonwealth: Family Life in Plymouth Colony* (New York: Oxford Univ. Press, 2000 [originally published in 1970]), 75.

25 "the new room": Carol Berkin and Leslie Horowitz, eds., *Women's Voices, Women's Lives* (Boston: Northeastern Univ. Press, 1998), 81–82.

25 "old persons": Fischer, *Growing Old*, 61.

25 "to me a cave": Premo, *Winter Friends*, 134.

25 "last resort": Berkin and Horowitz, *Women's Voices*, 110–11.

26 "a prudent speech": Brady, *Martha Washington*, 32.

26 Martha was a widow: Dorothy Schneider and Carl J. Schneider, *First Ladies: A Biographical Dictionary*, 3rd ed. (New York: Facts on File, 2010), 2.

26 "to keep all your matters": Norton, *Liberty's Daughters*, 146.

26 "wrached": Ibid.

26 "Washy" and "Tub": Brady, *Martha Washington*, 147.

26 "like a Spartan mother": Brady, *Martha Washington*, 152; and Anne Hollingsworth Wharton, *Martha Washington* (New York: Charles Scribner's Sons, 1899), 82.

27 "a sociable pretty kind": Crane, *Diary of Elizabeth Drinker*, 75.

27 "rather weak": Ibid., 182.

27 "it will make you very ugly": Catherine Clinton, *The Plantation Mistress: Woman's World in the Old South* (New York: Pantheon, 1982), 100.

27 "the honor of drinking coffee": Anthony, *First Ladies*, vol. 1, 43; and John Austin Stevens et al., eds., *The Magazine of American History with Notes and Queries: Volume 1* (New York and Chicago: A. S. Barnes & Co., 1877), 388.

27 "If I live much longer": Brady, *Martha Washington*, 169.

28 "younger and gayer": Wharton, *Martha Washington*, 203.

28 "She speaks": "The Deaths of George and Martha," Mount Vernon website, accessed March 14, 2019, https://www.mountvernon.org/george-washington /martha-washington/the-deaths-of-george-martha/.

28 "The fewer women": Bernard Bailyn, *Voyagers to the West: A Passage in the Peopling of America on the Eve of the Revolution* (New York: Alfred A. Knopf, 1986), 258.

28 While in the pre-revolutionary era: Fischer, *Growing Old*, 84.

28 "Your mother, or your husband's mother": Haber, *Beyond Sixty-Five*, 22; and Rev. John Wesley, *Sermons on Several Occasions*, vol. 2, ed. T. Jackson (London: J. Kershaw, 1825), 500.

29 the best seats: Fischer, *Growing Old*, 79.

2. THE 1800S ARRIVE

30 "through the long half-opened": Julie Delafaye-Brehier, "Fifteen Years Difference," *Godey's Lady's Book*, August 1837, available in M. L. B., "Fifteen Years Difference: From the French of Madame J. Delafaye-Brehier," in *New Monthly Belle Assemblée: A Magazine of Literature and Fashion*, vol. 6 (London: Printed by Joseph Rogerson, 1837[?]), 237.

30 But in the decades between: David Hackett Fischer, *Growing Old in America* (New York: Oxford Univ. Press, 1978), 101.

30 A Currier & Ives lithograph: Currier & Ives, *The Life & Age of Woman: Stages of Woman's Life from the Cradle to the Grave. Depiction of Women at Various Life Stages, from Infancy to 100, Ascending and Descending a Set of Stairs*, 1850, lithograph, Schlesinger Library on the History of Women in America, Radcliffe Institute, Cambridge, MA.

31 "There is no fame": Sara Agnes Pryor, *The Mother of Washington and Her Times* (n.p.: Ulan Press, 2012), 355–56.

31 Washington had found: "Case 5—Family Background, Part I," *George Washington: Getting to Know the Man Behind the Image*, exhibit, William L. Clements Library, University of Michigan, http://clements.umich.edu/exhibits/past/g.wa shington/case.05/case05.html.

32 averaged around seven children: Heather J. Gibson and Jerome F. Singleton, eds., *Leisure and Aging: Theory and Practice* (Champaign, IL: Human Kinetics, 2012), 5.

32 "grandmothers took to caps": "The Passing of the Old Lady," Contributors' Club, *Atlantic Monthly*, vol. 99 (Boston and New York: Houghton Mifflin, 1907), 874.

32 "with the aged": Carole Haber, *Beyond Sixty-Five: The Dilemma of Old Age in America's Past* (New York: St. Martin's Press, 1983), 97.

32 "Mary Had a Little Lamb": Norma Fryatt, *Sarah Josepha Hale: The Life and Times of a Nineteenth-Century Career Woman* (New York: Hawthorn Books, 1975), 16, 114.

32 "enjoy the luxuries": Nancy Woloch, *Women and the American Experience* (New York: McGraw-Hill, 2000), 109.

32 delivering lectures about women's rights: Sarah Josepha Hale, *The Lecturess, or, Woman's Sphere* (Boston: Whipple and Damrell, 1839). For a summary and discussion of the

novel, see James Perrin Warren, *Culture of Eloquence: Oratory and Reform in Antebellum America* (University Park: Pennsylvania State Univ. Press, 1999), 87–89.

33 "It is only on emergencies": Woloch, *Women and the American Experience*, 104. The original "on emergencies" is sometimes silently corrected to "in emergencies."

33 listened to about 7,000 sermons: Thomas R. Cole, *The Journey of Life: A Cultural History of Aging in America* (New York: Cambridge Univ. Press, 1992), 35.

33 new printing technologies: Woloch, *Women and the American Experience*, 136.

34 Susan Warner: Helen Waite Papashvily, *All the Happy Endings* (New York: Harper & Bros., 1956), 11–13.

34 Catharine Sedgwick got: Catharine Maria Sedgwick, *A New England Tale* (New York: Penguin Classics, 2003).

34 *Two Pictures:* Zsuzsa Berend, "'The Best or None!' Spinsterhood in Nineteenth-Century New England," *Journal of Social History* 33 (Summer 2000): 949.

34 "She was always beautiful": Mrs. Wilson Woodrow (Nancy Woodrow), "The Woman of Fifty," *Cosmopolitan,* March 1903; and punctuation per Mrs. Wilson Woodrow, *The Bird of Time: Being Conversations with Egeria* (New York: McClure, Phillips & Co., 1907), 10.

35 "sylph-like figure": Lydia Maria Child, *Hobomok: A Tale of Early Times* (Boston: Cummings, Hilliard & Co., 1824), 20.

35 Mary weds Hobomok: Ibid., 168–88.

35 *The Frugal Housewife:* Carolyn Karcher, *The First Woman in the Republic: A Cultural Biography of Lydia Maria Child* (Durham, NC: Duke Univ. Press, 1994), 131.

35 "earning or saving money": Ibid., 133.

35 "Let us keep our women": Ibid.

35 *A Treatise on Domestic Economy:* Catharine Beecher, *A Treatise on Domestic Economy* (New York: Harper & Bros., 1848). Beecher's first name is spelled "Catherine" on the title page of this edition. The spelling "Catherine" was also used by the *New York Times* in its obituary of Beecher (May 13, 1878). Kathryn Kish Sklar's *Catharine Beecher: A Study in American Domesticity* (see following note) primarily uses "Catharine," although both spelling variants appear in the text and in the index.

35 "wandering like a trunk without a label": Kathryn Kish Sklar, *Catharine Beecher: A Study in American Domesticity* (New York: W. W. Norton, 1976), 272.

36 14,000 unmarried women: Dana Goldstein, *The Teacher Wars* (New York: Anchor Books, 2015), 19.

36 "we raise our voice": Catharine Maria Sedgwick, *Married or Single?* (New York: Harper & Bros., Sabin Americana Print Editions, 1857), vi.

37 "No devices to give": Robert Tomes, *The Bazar Book of Decorum* (New York: Harper & Bros., 1870), 111–12.

37 bismuth, spermaceti, and hog lard: Annie Randall White, *Polite Society at Home and Abroad* (Chicago: Monarch Book Co., 1891), 412.

37 "young lady...not twenty-eight": Sean Tranior, "Dyeing to Impress: Hair Products and Beauty Culture in Nineteenth-Century America," The Recipes Project, posted January 1, 2015, by Jess Clark, https://recipes.hypotheses.org/4742.

37 "Whatever is false or artificial": Mrs. Merrifield, "How Far Should the Fashions Be Followed?," *Godey's Lady's Book and Magazine* 52, January 1856, 30.

37 universally accepted way: Lois W. Banner, *In Full Flower: Aging Women, Power, and Sexuality* (New York: Alfred A. Knopf, 1992), 252.

37 Dolley Madison, a social star: Richard N. Côté, *Strength and Honor: The Life of Dolley Madison* (Mount Pleasant, SC: Corinthian Books, 2004), 342.

37 "I was one day walking": Virginia Cary, *Letters on Female Character, Addressed to a Young Lady, on the Death of Her Mother* (Richmond, VA: Ariel Works, 1830), 142.

38 "You must dismiss": "Sketches of American Society," *Fraser's Magazine for Town and Country*, vol. 41, May 1850 (London: John W. Parker, 1850[?]), 526.

38 "only adapted to the young": Mary Kelley, ed., *The Power of Her Sympathy: The Autobiography and Journal of Catharine Maria Sedgwick* (Boston: Massachusetts Historical Society, 1993), 135.

38 "To dress cheerfully": Mrs. C. M. [Caroline Matilda] Kirkland, "Growing Old Gracefully," *Home Journal*, May 17, 1851, in *Sartain's Union Magazine of Literature and Art*, vol. 8, eds. Prof. John S. Hart and Mrs. C. M. Kirkland (Philadelphia: John Sartain & Co., 1851), 258.

39 "No sooner are they married": Francis J. Grund, *The Americans in Their Moral, Social and Political Relations* (London: Longman, Rees, Orme, Brown, Green, and Longman, 1837), 35.

39 "The elderly part": Terri Premo, *Winter Friends: Women Growing Old in the New Republic, 1785–1835* (Urbana: Univ. of Illinois Press, 1990), 112.

39 "in the form of a coffin": Ralph Waldo Emerson, "Mary Moody Emerson," in Ralph Waldo Emerson, *The Works of Ralph Waldo Emerson: Lectures and Biographical Sketches*, vol. 10, ed. James Elliot Cabot (Boston and New York: Houghton Mifflin, 1883), 400.

39 "always to church": Currier & Ives, *The Life & Age of Woman*.

40 "Col. Burr is an old man": *Hartford Review*, July 7, 1833. Margaret Oppenheimer, in *The Remarkable Rise of Eliza Jumel: A Story of Marriage and Money in the Early Republic* (Chicago: Chicago Review Press, 2016), notes that this piece on Burr and Jumel also appeared subsequently on July 19, 1833, in the *Newburyport Herald* (Massachusetts); and she suspects that the otherwise obscure and untraceable *Hartford Review* was actually the *New-England Daily Review* or the *New-England Weekly Review*.

40 "seems to enjoy": "Madame Jumel, Widow of Aaron Burr," *Wisconsin Daily Patriot*, October 4, 1859, 3.

40 "Mrs. H. an invalid": Sklar, *Catharine Beecher*, 204; and Catharine Esther Beecher, *Woman's Profession as Mother and Educator: With Views in Opposition to Woman Suffrage* (Philadelphia and Boston: Geo. Maclean; New York: Maclean, Gibson & Co., 1872), 215.

41 People who moved: Donald A. Yerxa, "The Invention of the American Meal: An Interview with Abigail Carroll," *Historically Speaking: The Bulletin of the Historical Society* 14, no. 5 (November 2013): 28.

41 Working women undoubtedly: Christine Stansell, *City of Women: Sex and Class in New York, 1789–1860* (Chicago: Univ. of Illinois Press, 1987), 113–14.

41 "It was a thrilling game": Josephine DeMott Robinson, *The Circus Lady* (New York: Thomas Y. Crowell Co., 1926), 56.

41 "is sufficient to disorder": Carroll Smith-Rosenberg, *Disorderly Conduct: Visions of Gender in Victorian America* (New York: Oxford Univ. Press, 1985), 192.

42 "steam-power, the periodical press": Joan D. Hedrick, *Harriet Beecher Stowe: A Life* (New York: Oxford Univ. Press, 1994), 141.

42 "the various painful face": Tomes, *The Bazar Book,* 56.

42 "WASTE OF TIME!": Dorothy Sterling, ed., *We Are Your Sisters: Black Women in the Nineteenth Century* (New York: W. W. Norton, 1984), 92.

42 "I knit five pairs of stockings!": Ibid.

42 "voluntarily leave home": Sharon Harley and Rosalyn Terborg-Penn, eds., *The Afro-American Woman: Struggles and Images* (Baltimore: Black Classic Press, 1978), 12, quoting Martin Delany, *The Condition, Elevation, Emigration and Destiny of the Colored People of the United States* (Philadelphia: printed by the author, 1852), 43.

42 "old 'omans": Deborah Gray White, *Ar'n't I a Woman? Female Slaves in the Plantation South,* rev. ed. (New York: W. W. Norton, 1999), 135–36.

42 "Yes, she was": Ibid.

43 "sent to live": Fischer, *Growing Old,* 64–65.

43 "seamed with wrinkles": Frances Kemble, *Journal of a Residence on a Georgia Plantation* (New York: Cambridge Univ. Press, 2009), 239.

43 "needy gentlewomen": Fischer, *Growing Old,* 150.

43 Philadelphia's Indigent Widows': Haber, *Beyond Sixty-Five,* 96–97.

44 "to contribute by": Ibid.

44 "children of mature growth": Ibid., 104; and G. F. Richings, *Evidences of Progress Among Colored People* (Philadelphia: George S. Ferguson Co., 1902), 405.

44 "There is absolutely no class": Haber, *Beyond Sixty-Five,* 100.

3. BEFORE THE CIVIL WAR

45 "See a common woman": Margaret Fuller, *Woman in the Nineteenth Century, and Kindred Papers Relating to the Sphere, Condition, and Duties of Woman* (Boston: Roberts Bros., 1893), 99.

45 "care-worn face": Ibid.

45 "the topic of jest": Ibid., 258–59.

46 "Courage Susan": Elisabeth Griffith, *In Her Own Right: The Life of Elizabeth Cady Stanton* (New York: Oxford Univ. Press, 1984), 93.

46 "Two years more": Ibid.

47 "long since past": Carroll Smith-Rosenberg, *Disorderly Conduct: Visions of Gender in Victorian America* (New York: Oxford Univ. Press, 1985), 195. See also Carroll Smith-Rosenberg, "Puberty to Menopause: The Cycle of Femininity in Nineteenth-Century America," *Feminist Studies* 1, nos. 3–4 (Spring 1973): 68.

47 "The Great Red Harlot of Infidelity": Sharon Harley, "Northern Black Female Workers: Jacksonian Era," in *The Afro-American Woman: Struggles and Images,* eds. Sharon Harley and Rosalyn Terborg-Penn (Baltimore: Black Classic Press, 1978), 14.

47 "I find it is no use": Karlyn Kohrs Campbell, *Women Public Speakers in the United States, 1800–1925* (Westport, CT: Greenwood Press, 1993), 340.

48 "kindly, generous, peaceful and benevolent": Kathryn Kish Sklar, *Catharine Beecher: A Study in American Domesticity* (New York: W. W. Norton, 1976), 315.

48 "nature recoiled": Gerda Lerner, *The Grimké Sisters from South Carolina* (Chapel Hill: Univ. of North Carolina Press, 2004), 167.

48 "Alas!! Alas!!!!": Griffith, *In Her Own Right*, 96.

48 "the same woman may have": Corinne Field, *The Struggle for Equal Adulthood: Gender, Race, Age, and the Fight for Citizenship in Antebellum America* (Chapel Hill: Univ. of North Carolina Press, 2014), 113.

49 "married early in life": Ibid.; and see Elizabeth Cady Stanton et al., *History of Woman Suffrage* (New York: Fowler and Wells, 1881), accessed March 23, 2019, http://utc.iath.virginia.edu/abolitn/abwmct.html.

49 "I go straight to my rooms": Lynn Sherr, ed., *Failure Is Impossible: Susan B. Anthony in Her Own Words* (New York: Times Books, 1996), 242.

49 "Susan is lean, cadaverous and intellectual": Alma Lutz, "Susan B. Anthony," in *Notable American Women, 1607–1950: A Biographical Dictionary*, vol. 1, eds. Edward T. James, Janet Wilson James, and Paul S. Boyer (Cambridge, MA: Belknap Press of Harvard Univ. Press, 1971), 52. See also Elizabeth Cady Stanton, Susan B. Anthony, Harriot Stanton Blatch, and Matilda Gage, *History of Women's Suffrage Trilogy, Part 1* (n.p.: E-artnow, 2017), ebook.

49 "That ancient daughter of Methuselah": Elizabeth Cady Stanton, *Eighty Years and More: Reminiscences, 1815–1897* (New York: European Publishing, 1898), 306.

49 "Miss Anthony's love-life": Ibid., 172.

50 "loved with sufficient devotion": Lois W. Banner, *Elizabeth Cady Stanton: A Radical for Woman's Rights* (Boston: Little, Brown, 1980), 128.

50 "comments of the leading journals": Stanton, *Eighty Years and More*, 173.

50 "vital forces": Griffith, *In Her Own Right*, 110.

50 Journalists compared her: Ibid., 161.

51 "Two months more": Ibid., 169.

51 She recalled speaking: Stanton, *Eighty Years and More*, 246.

51 "all the wonders": Ibid., 293.

51 "The next day": Ibid.

51 Stanton killed the boredom: Banner, *Elizabeth Cady Stanton*, 122.

51 Anthony once delivered: Sherr, *Failure Is Impossible*, 132.

52 "a fearful snowstorm": Griffith, *In Her Own Right*, 162.

52 "an old waterman, astride": Dorothy Clarke Wilson, *Stranger and Traveler: The Story of Dorothea Dix, American Reformer* (Boston and New York: Little, Brown, 1975), 144.

52 "thirty miles to Downingtown": Jarena Lee, *Religious Experience and Journal of Mrs. Jarena Lee* (London: Forgotten Books, 2012), 29.

52 "discovered in time": Julie Roy Jeffrey, *The Great Silent Army of Abolitionism* (Chapel Hill: Univ. of North Carolina Press, 1998), 208.

52 "Then I will speak upon the ashes": Dorothy Sterling, ed., *We Are Your Sisters: Black Women in the Nineteenth Century* (New York: W. W. Norton, 1984), 251.

53 "her breasts had suckled": Nell Irvin Painter, *Sojourner Truth: A Life, A Symbol* (New York: W. W. Norton, 1996), 139.

53 It took four men to move her: Catherine Clinton, *Harriet Tubman: The Road to Freedom* (New York: Little, Brown, 2004), 189.

53 During the war: Ibid., 166.

53 "under the guidance of a black woman": Sterling, *We Are Your Sisters*, 259.

53 Henrietta Duterte: Euell A. Nielsen, "Henrietta S. Bowers Duterte (1817–1903)," Blackpast.org, April 28, 2015, https://www.blackpast.org/african-american-history/duterte-henrietta-s-bowers-1817-1903/.

53 One elderly woman: Jeffrey, *The Great Silent Army*, 179.

54 "I am a very old woman": Julie Roy Jeffrey, *Frontier Women*, rev. ed. (New York: Hill and Wang, 1998), 91.

54 she instantly took: Jean M. Ward, "Tabitha Moffat Brown (1780–1858)," Oregon Encyclopedia, Oregon Historical Society, last modified March 17, 2018, https://oregonencyclopedia.org/articles/brown_tabitha_moffat_1780_1858_/#.XMEp2UyZPXE.

54 "The Mother of Oregon": Ibid. See also Jeffrey, *Frontier Women*, 111.

54 "Stagecoach" Mary Fields: William Loren Katz, *Black Women of the Old West* (New York: Atheneum Books, 1995), 76–77.

54 "His laundry bill is paid": Ibid.

55 broke her hip: Celia Morris, *Fanny Wright: Rebel in America*, rev. ed. (Urbana and Chicago: Univ. of Illinois Press, 1992), 293–94.

55 Stowe made $10,000: Joan D. Hedrick, *Harriet Beecher Stowe: A Life* (New York: Oxford Univ. Press, 1994), 223. The figure would be about $327,000 today.

55 "a little bit of a woman": Ibid., 239. Her admirer was Eliza Lee Cabot Follen, a Bostonian residing in London.

56 read her remarks: Ibid., 238.

56 "So far my health": Ibid., 386.

56 "so utterly used up": Ibid., 387.

4. THE MID-1800S

57 "Oh, Uncle Tommy": Lydia Maria Child, *Looking Toward Sunset: From Sources Old and New, Original and Selected* (Boston: Ticknor and Fields: 1865), 373.

57 "Never step from your bed": Ibid., 433.

57 "Travel cheerfully": Ibid., 222.

57 "take an interest": Ibid., 175.

58 "All my dreams have settled": Carolyn Karcher, *The First Woman in the Republic: A Cultural Biography of Lydia Maria Child* (Durham: Duke Univ. Press, 1994), 386.

58 "never live my own life": Martha Saxton, *Louisa May: A Modern Biography of Louisa May Alcott* (Boston: Houghton Mifflin, 1977), 366.

59 Child used the profits: Deborah Pickman Clifford, *Crusader for Freedom: A Life of Lydia Maria Child* (Boston: Beacon Press, 1992), 272.

59 "Her dress is usually plain": Edgar Allan Poe, *The Literati — Minor Contemporaries, Etc.*, vol. 3, eds. Edmund Clarence Stedman and George Edward Woodberry (New York: Charles Scribner's Sons, 1914), 140–41.

59 almost all the women who worked: Theodora Penny Martin, *The Sound of Our Own Voices: Women's Study Clubs, 1860–1910* (Boston: Beacon Press, 1987), 20.

60 "Between [caring for] old *people*": Victoria E. Bynum, *Unruly Women: The Politics of Social & Sexual Control in the Old South* (Chapel Hill: Univ. of North Carolina Press, 1992), 44–45.

60 "no very extensive sphere": Kathryn Kish Sklar, *Catharine Beecher: A Study in American Domesticity* (New York: W. W. Norton, 1976), 52. See also Lyman Beecher, *Autobiography, Correspondence, &c., of Lyman Beecher,* vol. 1, ed. Charles Beecher (London: Sampson Low, Son, and Marston, 1863), 451.

60 "To make education universal": Sklar, *Catharine Beecher,* 182.

60 view of a teacher, Milly: Helen Wall Pierson, "Tom's Education," *Harper's New Monthly* 30, January 1865, 188–93.

61 when the supervisor retired: Dana Goldstein, *The Teacher Wars* (New York: Anchor Books, 2015), 34.

61 Western Female Institute: "Catherine Beecher," in *An American Family: The Beecher Tradition,* online exhibit, curated by Sandra Roff, William and Anita Newman Library, Baruch College, City University of New York, 2001; the spelling variant "Catherine" was used here. See also Debra Michals, "Catharine Esther Beecher (1800–1878)," National Women's History Museum, 2015, https://www.womenshistory.org/education-resources/biographies/catharine-esther-beecher.

61 "The school numbers over 40": Dorothy Sterling, ed., *We Are Your Sisters: Black Women in the Nineteenth Century* (New York: W. W. Norton, 1984), 128.

61 But in 1838: Ibid.

61 Clara Barton opened: "Clara's Life: Miss Clarissa H. Barton, Instructor and Teacher," Clara Barton Birthplace Museum, North Oxford, MA, 2017, http://www.clarabartonbirthplace.org/claras-life/.

62 Underground Railroad skills: Catherine Clinton, *Harriet Tubman: The Road to Freedom* (Boston and New York: Little, Brown, 2004), 203–4.

62 Tubman had returned: Ibid., 198–99.

62 "You wouldn't think": Ibid., 207.

62 "I want to ride!": Nell Irvin Painter, *Sojourner Truth: A Life, A Symbol* (New York: W. W. Norton, 1996), 210–11.

62 "I have been hoping": Ibid., 240. See also "Letter from Sojourner Truth—Land for the Freed People, Florence, MA, February 18, 1871," in *Friends' Intelligencer,* vol. 28, edited and published by An Association of Friends (Philadelphia: John Comly, 1871–72), 93.

63 "if colored men get their rights": Sterling, *We Are Your Sisters,* 411.

63 "ignorant negroes and foreigners": Ibid., 415.

63 societies convened in New York in 1837: Sharon Harley and Rosalyn Terborg-Penn, eds., *The Afro-American Woman: Struggles and Images* (Baltimore: Black Classic Press, 1978), 18.

63 man named Archibald Grimké: Gerda Lerner, *The Grimké Sisters from South Carolina* (Chapel Hill: Univ. of North Carolina Press, 2004), 257.

63 "the name of Grimké": Ibid., 258–59.

63 Grimké biographer Gerda Lerner: Ibid., 258–61.

64 "a liberal in religion": Ibid., 261.

64 "far exceed in talents": Ibid.

64 their regimen often consisted: Ibid., 179–90.

64 "Many seem to have no idea": Mary S. Gove, *Lectures to Women on Anatomy and Physiology* (New York: Harper & Bros., 1846), 20.

65 "accidents and the evil influences": Thomas R. Cole, *The Journey of Life: A Cultural History of Aging in America* (New York: Cambridge Univ. Press, 1992), 100.

65 a child who was a good Christian: Ibid., 98.

65 "You may sin at one end": Ibid., 134.

66 an adulterous affair: Barbara Goldsmith, *Other Powers: The Age of Suffrage, Spiritualism and the Scandalous Victoria Woodhull* (New York: Alfred A. Knopf, 1998), 100, 120. See also Richard Wightman Fox, *Trials of Intimacy: Love and Loss in the Beecher-Tilton Scandal* (Chicago: Univ. of Chicago Press, 1999), 155–57, 159.

66 "more like a school-girl of 18": Fox, *Trials of Intimacy*, 64.

66 Catharine and Harriet took: Goldsmith, *Other Powers*, 426–37.

67 "dear guileless simple-hearted": Fox, *Trials of Intimacy*, 69.

67 "she would not live a day": *The Inter Ocean* (Chicago), May 14, 1875, 4.

67 "used to pour": Fox, *Trials of Intimacy*, 68–69.

67 "[A]nd there she remains": *St. Louis Globe-Democrat*, July 1, 1875, 4.

67 "A Remarkable Woman": Ibid.

68 "If CLEANLINESS is next to GODLINESS": Richard L. Bushman and Claudia L. Bushman, "The Early History of Cleanliness in America," *Journal of American History* 74 (March 1988): 1,218. See also Advertisement for Pears' Soap, "Henry Ward Beecher's Opinion of Pears' Soap," *Life*, March 14, 1889, 162.

68 "the water cure": Sklar, *Catharine Beecher*, 206.

68 Harriet's husband, Calvin: Joan D. Hedrick, *Harriet Beecher Stowe: A Life* (New York: Oxford Univ. Press, 1994), 178.

68 treatment included brandy: Ibid., 174.

68 some of the ailments: Ibid., 174–75.

68 Union Hotel Hospital: Saxton, *Louisa May*, 253.

69 "The hospital experience": Ibid., 369.

69 still using leeches: Hedrick, *Harriet Beecher Stowe*, 174.

69 popular cough medication: Elizabeth Pendergast Carlisle, *Earthbound and Heavenbent: Elizabeth Porter Phelps and Life at Forty Acres, 1747–1817* (New York: Scribner, 2004), 20–21.

69 "small box": Mrs. John A. Logan, *The Home Manual: Everybody's Guide in Social, Domestic, and Business Life* (Philadelphia: H. J. Smith & Co., 1889), 221.

69 Abby Hopper Gibbons regarded herself: Lori D. Ginzberg, *Women and the Work of Benevolence: Morality, Politics, and Class in the 19th-Century United States* (New Haven, CT: Yale Univ. Press, 1990), 13.

69 "There's a face that haunts": Sarah Stage, *Female Complaints: Lydia Pinkham and the Business of Women's Medicine* (New York: W. W. Norton, 1979), 41. See also "Pebbles," *The Independent* 51, no. 2620, February 16, 1899 (New York: S. W. Benedict, 130 Fulton St., [1899?]), 519.

70 "That pulmonary disease": Lydia H. Sigourney, *Letters to Young Ladies*, 2nd ed. (Hartford, CT: William Watson, 1835), 44. See also Ellen M. Plante, *Women at Home in Victorian America: A Social History* (New York: Facts on File, 1997), 126.

70 Critics did tend: Edward Shorter, *Women's Bodies: A Social History of Women's Encounter with Health, Ill-Health, and Medicine* (New York: Taylor & Francis, 1984), 28–30.

70 his wife's collie: Richard W. Schwarz, *John Harvey Kellogg, MD: Pioneering Health Reformer* (Hagerstown, MD: Review and Herald Publishing Association, 2006), 60–61. See also Colleen Ruby Gau, "Historic Medical Perspectives of Corseting and Two Physiologic Studies with Reenactors" (PhD diss., Iowa State Univ., 1998), 108.

70 "Does it make any sense": Lois W. Banner, *American Beauty* (New York: Alfred A. Knopf, 1983), 95.

71 visiting reporter revealed: Jean Silver-Isenstadt, *Shameless: The Visionary Life of Mary Gove Nichols* (Baltimore: Johns Hopkins Univ. Press, 2002), 170.

71 had been sure: Lois W. Banner, *Elizabeth Cady Stanton: A Radical for Woman's Rights* (Boston: Little, Brown, 1980), 56–57.

71 "fair, fat and forty buxom widow": "Malicious Conduct of Major Rucker," *Macon Telegraph*, December 5, 1862, 4.

72 "Nobody, except some ancient female": City Items, *New-York Daily Tribune*, August 7, 1862.

72 report to New York City's Board of Health: "Poisonous Cosmetics: Report of Prof. C. F. Chandler to the Metropolitan Board of Health," in *The Manufacturer and Builder: A Practical Journal of Industrial Progress*, vol. 2 (New York: Western & Co., 1870), 202.

72 "lady in Fauquier county": "Brevities and Levities," *Albany Argus*, May 29, 1868.

72 death of one Dr. J. M. Witherwax: "Poisoned by Hair Dye," in S. W. Butler, MD, and D. G. Brinton, MD, eds., *Medical and Surgical Reporter* 21 (July–December 1869): 224, accessed March 29, 2019, https://archive.org/stream/medicalsurgical1869phil/medicalsurgical1869phil_djvu.txt.

72 fixing breakfast: Jack D. Welsh, *Medical Histories of Union Generals* (Kent, OH, and London: Kent State Univ. Press, 1996), 128; and William L. Richter, *Historical Dictionary of the Civil War and Reconstruction*, 2nd ed. (Lanham, MD; Toronto; and Plymouth, UK: Scarecrow Press/Rowman and Littlefield, 2012), 275.

72 "to dye or not to dye": "A Matter of Taste," *American Journal of Education* 7, no. 1 (January 1874): 13.

72 "If his wife will love": "Beecher on Hair Dye," *Weekly Clarion* (Jackson, MS), May 13, 1869.

72 "if her happiness": Ibid.

72 "Ladies who are so unscrupulous": "Dyed Plumage," *Boston Daily Advertiser*, December 13, 1871; and *The Pall Mall Budget: Being a Weekly Collection of Articles Printed in the Pall Mall Gazette from Day to Day*, vol. 7, December 1, 1871 (London: printed at 2 Northumberland Street, Strand, W.C., 1872), 18.

73 "Growing old!": Mrs. Lucy E. Sanford, "Mrs. Sarah J. Hale," *Granite Monthly*, March 1880.

73 beginning to regard death: Carole Haber, *Beyond Sixty-Five: The Dilemma of Old Age in America's Past* (New York: Cambridge Univ. Press, 1983), 66.

5. THE NINETEENTH-CENTURY FINALE

74 try to vote: Elisabeth Griffith, *In Her Own Right: The Life of Elizabeth Cady Stanton* (New York: Oxford Univ. Press, 1984), 171.

74 "at that time she was a woman": "United States v. Anthony," a segment of *Not for Ourselves Alone: The Story of Elizabeth Cady Stanton and Susan B. Anthony*, a film by Ken Burns and Paul Barnes, aired November 7, 1999, on PBS.

74 "Stately Mrs. Stanton": Griffith, *In Her Own Right*, 196.

75 "I have one melancholy fact": Ibid., 197.

75 "to think them up": Elizabeth Cady Stanton, *Eighty Years and More: Reminiscences, 1815–1897* (New York: European Publishing, 1898), 387.

75 "perhaps one may find": Elizabeth Cady Stanton, *Elizabeth Cady Stanton Papers: Speeches and Writings, 1848–1902; Speeches; 1885, 12 Nov., "The Pleasures of Age," an Address Delivered on Her Seventieth Birthday*, 1885, images of manuscript, Library of Congress, https://www.loc.gov/resource/mss41210.mss41210-004 _ 00195 _ 00202/?st=gallery. See also Ann D. Gordon, ed., *The Selected Papers of Elizabeth Cady Stanton and Susan B. Anthony*, vol. 4 of *When Clowns Make Laws for Queens 1880 to 1887* (New Brunswick, NJ: Rutgers Univ. Press, 2006), 452.

75 "inspiring sentiments in prose and verse": Gordon, *The Selected Papers*, 454.

76 "surely each of us": Stanton, *Elizabeth Cady Stanton Papers*, https://www.loc.gov/resource/mss41210.mss41210-004 _ 00195 _ 00202/?st=gallery.

76 "a pioneer in the anti-slavery": *Cincinnati Enquirer*, October 28, 1879, 4.

76 under the headline: "Sensible to the Last," *Weekly Times*, November 20, 1879, 6, accessed March 22, 2019, https://chroniclingamerica.loc.gov/lccn/sn84027691/1879-11-20/ed-1/seq-6/.

76 "50,000 words if still living": Kathleen Barry, *Susan B. Anthony: A Biography of a Singular Feminist* (New York: New York Univ. Press, 1988), 308.

76 "From being the most": Stanton, *Eighty Years and More*, 174.

76 "I plunge again": Elizabeth Cazden, *Antoinette Brown Blackwell* (Old Westbury, NY: Feminist Press, 1983), 235.

77 vigorous hoeing in the garden: Ibid., 255.

77 "the most remarkable woman": Ibid., 261.

77 "In fact, I prefer": Kathryn Kish Sklar, *Catharine Beecher: A Study in American Domesticity* (New York: W. W. Norton, 1976), 258.

77 "I have been for many": Ibid., 269.

77 "and still more to those": Catharine Esther Beecher and Harriet Beecher Stowe, *The American Woman's Home: Or, Principles of Domestic Science* (New York: J. B. Ford and Co., 1869), 304.

77 "courteous attention": Ibid., 304–5.

78 "beautiful in itself": Margaret White, *After Noontide* (Boston: Houghton Mifflin, 1888), 112.

78 "repulsively ugly in person": Lydia Maria Child, *Looking Toward Sunset: From Sources Old and New, Original and Selected* (Boston: Ticknor and Fields, 1865), 326.

78 "We put bright colors": Ellen Plante, *Women at Home in Victorian America* (New York: Facts on File, 1997), 188.

78 "mothers and gray-haired grandmothers": Dorothy Sterling, ed., *We Are Your Sisters: Black Women in the Nineteenth Century* (New York: W. W. Norton, 1984), 412.

78 Hairdressers who fitted: John Woodforde, *The Strange Story of False Hair* (New York: Drake Publishers, 1972), 89–91.

78 "The hygienically furnished": Madame Millefleurs, "Physical Beauty Scenes," *The Woman Beautiful*, December 1909, 46.

79 "Madame Yale": "Madame Yale's Beauty Talk," *Pittsburg Press*, April 28, 1905, 23. The newspaper's name was not spelled with an *h* until 1921.

79 "It would be hard to describe": Ibid.

79 "Perfectly fitting false teeth": "The Growing Youthfulness of Age," *Harper's Bazar*, January 3, 1885, 2.

79 "Women's reproductive organs": John Wiltbank, *Introductory Letter for the Session, 1853–54* (Philadelphia: Edward Grattan, 1854), 7.

80 "a morbid impulse": Carroll Smith-Rosenberg, "Puberty to Menopause: The Cycle of Femininity in Nineteenth-Century America," *Feminist Studies* 1, nos. 3–4 (Spring 1973): 66.

80 "ovarian manic": Patricia Vertinsky, "Stereotypes of Aging Women and Exercise," *Journal of Aging and Physical Activity* 3 (1995): 106n59.

80 "Sexual life begins": John Harvey Kellogg, *Plain Facts for Old and Young* (Burlington, IA: Segner & Condit, 1881), 123.

80 "Females in whom": Ibid., 78.

80 "We insist that every woman": Smith-Rosenberg, "Puberty to Menopause," 66. The date of publication is misstated as 1872 in Smith-Rosenberg; see Walter C. Taylor, *A Physician's Counsels to Woman* (Springfield, MA: W. J. Holland & Co., 1871), where the quote is on p. 93.

81 "ripe age of fifty-three": Frances Willard, *A Wheel Within a Wheel*, 2nd ed. (Bedford, MA: Applewood Books, 1997), 9.

81 Chicago in 1897: Karen Pastorello, *The Progressives: Activism and Reform in American Society, 1893–1917* (Malden, MA: Wiley-Blackwell, 2014), 22.

81 "would affect future": Kathleen Waters Sander, *Mary Elizabeth Garrett: Society and Philanthropy in the Gilded Age* (Baltimore: Johns Hopkins Univ. Press, 2008), 145.

82 "the most remarkable": Willard, *A Wheel*, 75.

82 "the more interests"; "acquiring this new"; "Last but not least": Ibid., 73.

6. TURN OF THE CENTURY

83 Sarah Bernhardt: Felicia Hardison Londré, *The History of World Theater: From the English Restoration to the Present* (New York: Continuum, 1991), 321. As the author notes, whether there were four or five farewell tours is uncertain.

83 "fifty lady sharpshooters": Letter from Annie Oakley to President William McKinley, April 5, 1898, National Archives, Records of the Adjutant General's Office, 1780s–1917, Record Group 94.

83 "One of the most remarkable": Jane Addams, "Need a Woman over Fifty Feel Old?," *Ladies' Home Journal*, October 1914, 7.

83 "never has time": "The Growing Youthfulness of Age," *Harper's Bazar*, January 3, 1885, 2.

83 "[t]he woman who to-day": Mrs. Wilson Woodrow (Nancy Woodrow), "The Woman of Fifty," *The Cosmopolitan*, March 1903, 505.

84 By 1890, more than 90 percent: Carole Haber, *Beyond Sixty-Five: The Dilemma of Old Age in America's Past* (New York: Cambridge Univ. Press, 1983), 31.

84 By 1905, virtually all: David Tyack and Elisabeth Hansot, *The Dream Deferred: A Golden Age for Women School Administrators* (Stanford, CA: Institute for Research on Educational Finance and Governance, 1981), 16, found in Kathleen Weiler, "Women's History and the History of Women Teachers," *Journal of Education* 171, no. 3 (1989): 20.

84 teaching was beginning to pay: Mary Cookingham, "Bluestockings, Spinsters and Pedagogues: Women College Graduates, 1865–1910," *Population Studies: A Journal of Demography* 38, no. 3 (1984): 357.

84 Older women were seeing: Ibid., 359.

84 "When I want *good* work": Marion Harland, *Eve's Daughters: Or, Common Sense for Maid, Wife, and Mother* (New York: John R. Anderson & Henry S. Allen, 1882), 318.

84 "clamber up and down": Elisabeth Griffith, *In Her Own Right: The Life of Elizabeth Cady Stanton* (New York: Oxford Univ. Press, 1984), 206–7.

85 "a slur on all natural": Elizabeth Cady Stanton et al., *The Woman's Bible* (Mineola, NY: Dover, 2002), 114: "I think that the doctrine of the Virgin birth as something higher, sweeter, nobler than ordinary motherhood, is a slur on all the natural motherhood of the world." The comment is sometimes attributed to one of the two dozen or more women with whom Stanton produced the book rather than to Stanton herself.

85 "the so-called Woman's Bible": "Discuss the Woman's Bible: A Difference of Opinion Among Leading Members of the National Suffrage Association," *New York Times*, January 24, 1896.

85 "now generally recognized": Lois W. Banner, *In Full Flower: Aging Women, Power, and Sexuality* (New York: Alfred A. Knopf, 1992), 277.

85 "speeded on to heaven"; "was mentally making": Lois W. Banner, *Elizabeth Cady Stanton: A Radical for Woman's Rights* (Boston: Little, Brown, 1980), 173.

85 "It is seldom": Kathleen Waters Sander, *Mary Elizabeth Garrett: Society and Philanthropy in the Gilded Age* (Baltimore: Johns Hopkins Univ. Press, 2008), 243–44.

86 "I wish the men": Ken Burns and Geoffrey Ward, *Not for Ourselves Alone: The Story of Elizabeth Cady Stanton and Susan B. Anthony* (New York: Alfred A. Knopf, 1999), 211–12.

86 "are not such a queer lot": Sander, *Mary Elizabeth Garrett*, 247.

86 Her Hull House settlement: Louise W. Knight, *Jane Addams: Spirit in Action* (New York: W. W. Norton, 2010), 97.

86 Amelia Earhart, who generated: Susan Butler, *East to the Dawn: The Life of Amelia Earhart* (Philadelphia: Da Capo Press, 1997); and Edward T. James, Janet Wilson James, and Paul S. Boyer, eds., *Notable American Women, 1607–1950: A Biographical Dictionary*, vol. 1 (Cambridge, MA: Belknap Press of Harvard Univ. Press, 1971), 539.

86 *Chicago Tribune* named Addams: "Best Woman in Chicago," *Chicago Tribune*, November 4, 1906, 60.

87 "The modern 'old maid' ": Fanny Fern, *Ginger-Snaps* (New York: Carleton, 1870), 146, 147.

87 "bachelor girl" or "bachelor woman": Banner, *In Full Flower*, 276–77.

87 "a woman of thirty-five": Grace Johnston, "The New Old Maid," *The Woman Beautiful*, May 1909, 68.

87 "I fear you think": Burns and Ward, *Not for Ourselves Alone*, 7.

88 "to write papers": Addams, "Need a Woman over Fifty Feel Old?," 7.

88 She named it Sorosis: Theodora Penny Martin, *The Sound of Our Own Voices: Women's Study Clubs, 1860–1910* (Boston: Beacon Press, 1987), 49.

89 "better class": Shirley Yee, *Black Women Abolitionists: A Study in Activism, 1828–1860* (Knoxville: Univ. of Tennessee Press, 1992), 13.

89 "The undersigned feeling": Martin, *The Sound of Our Own Voices*, 11.

90 "Homes will be ruined": Louise L. Stevenson, *The Victorian Homefront: American Thought and Culture, 1860–1880* (Ithaca, NY: Cornell Univ. Press, 1991), 55.

90 "[n]o club with": Jacqueline Van Voris, *Carrie Chapman Catt: A Public Life* (New York: Feminist Press at the City University of New York, 1987), 121.

90 "Ladies, you have chosen": Martin, *The Sound of Our Own Voices*, 172.

90 purpose of "mental development": Susan J. Eck, "Harriet Townsend and the Women's Union," Western New York History, accessed March 23, 2019, http://www.wnyhistory.org/portfolios/women/harriet_townsend/harriet_townsend.html.

90 "association of benevolent": Ibid.

91 project became so successful: Ibid.

91 Rochester Women's Educational and Industrial Union: Maria Soscia, "Guide to the Rochester Women's Educational and Industrial Union Records, 2014.005," finding aid, Local History & Genealogy Division, Central Library of Rochester and Monroe County, NY, February 13, 2015, 5.

91 "One woman of sixty": Addams, "Need a Woman over Fifty Feel Old?" See also Jean Bethke Elshtain, ed., *The Jane Addams Reader* (New York: Basic Books, 2002), 434.

91 General Federation of Women's Clubs: Rosalyn Terborg-Penn, "Discrimination Against Afro-American Women in the Woman's Movement, 1830–1920," in *The Afro-American Woman: Struggles and Images*, eds. Sharon Harley and Rosalyn Terborg-Penn (Baltimore: Black Classic Press, 1978), 23.

92 there was a rich world: Dorothy Sterling, ed., *We Are Your Sisters: Black Women in the Nineteenth Century* (New York: W. W. Norton, 1984), 105–10.

92 "Clubs make women read": Josephine St. P. Ruffin and Florida R. Ridley, "Club News: News from the Clubs," *The Woman's Era* 1 (1894), Emory Women Writers Resource Project.

92 "Mental Feasts": Yee, *Black Women Abolitionists*, 63.

92 "Mrs. Bruce's toilette": Sterling, *We Are Your Sisters*, 427–28.

92 When her son went: Otis Graham, *The Senator and the Socialite: The True Story of America's First Black Dynasty* (New York: Harper Perennial, 2006), 185.

92 job there as a principal: Her title was "Lady Principal" (see William B. Gatewood, *Aristocrats of Color: The Black Elite, 1880–1920* [Fayetteville: Univ. of Arkansas Press, 2000], 37) and then dean of women (Bruce Glasrud, "Josephine Beall Willson Bruce [1853–1923]," Blackpast.org, September 17, 2007, accessed March 23, 2019, https://www.blackpast.org/african-american-history/bruce-josephine -beall-willson-1853-1923/).

92 Baby of the Association: Sterling, *We Are Your Sisters*, 399.

93 "no lodgings which would": Catherine Clinton, *Harriet Tubman: The Road to Freedom* (New York: Little, Brown, 2004), 212.

93 "the Moses of her race": "Tubman Home Open," *Auburn Citizen,* June 24, 1908. See also Jean M. Humez, *Harriet Tubman: The Life and the Life Stories* (Madison: Univ. of Wisconsin Press, 2003), 105–7.

93 "I go to prepare": Clinton, *Harriet Tubman,* 210–15.

93 "a walking chandelier": Greg King, *A Season of Splendor: The Court of Mrs. Astor in Gilded Age New York* (Hoboken, NJ: John Wiley & Sons, 2009), 228–29.

93 "people who came": Ibid., 400.

94 Vanderbilt's daughter-in-law: Lois W. Banner, *American Beauty* (New York: Alfred A. Knopf, 1983), 191–94.

94 an estimated $250,000: Susannah Broyles, "Vanderbilt Ball: How a Costume Party Changed New York Elite Society," Museum of the City of New York blog, August 6, 2013, https://blog.mcny.org/2013/08/06/vanderbilt-ball-how-a-costume-ball -changed-new-york-elite-society/.

94 "Amid the rush": Ibid.

94 On the evening of: Ibid.

94 "Failure Is Impossible!"; "Votes for Women!"; "Brace up, dear": King, *A Season of Splendor,* 442.

94 "the Mrs. Astor of the Middle West": Edward T. James, Janet Wilson James, and Paul S. Boyer, eds., *Notable American Women, 1607–1950: A Biographical Dictionary,* vol. 1 (Cambridge, MA: Belknap Press of Harvard Univ. Press, 1971), 8–10.

95 "Ants Ruin Part of House": Sander, *Mary Elizabeth Garrett,* 230.

95 "Miss Mary Garrett": Ibid., 232.

95 the first American: "Graduate Education in a Liberal Arts Environment," Graduate School of Arts and Sciences, Bryn Mawr College website, brynmawr.edu/gsas.

95 "Old Maids of Wealth": Sander, *Mary Elizabeth Garrett,* 214–15.

95 theater sensation Lillian Russell: Armond Fields, *Lillian Russell: A Biography of "America's Beauty"* (Jefferson, IA: McFarland, 1999), 58.

95 Or Belle Boyd: See Louis A. Sigaud, *Belle Boyd: Confederate Spy* (Richmond, VA: Dietz Press, 1944).

95 Madeline Pollard: Patricia Miller, "The Author of *Bringing Down the Colonel* Finally Meets Her Subject," Roundtable: Lost and Found, *Lapham's Quarterly,* November 15, 2018, https://www.laphamsquarterly.org/roundtable/lost-and-found; and Gail Collins, "A Predatory Congressman, His Jilted Lover and a Gilded Age Lawsuit That Foreshadowed #MeToo," review of *Bringing Down the Colonel: A Sex Scandal of the Gilded Age and the "Powerless" Woman Who Took on Washington* by Patricia Miller, *New York Times,* Book Review, December 19, 2018.

96 "in life's midsummer": Fields, *Lillian Russell,* 161.

96 Everyone admired her: Ibid., 51.

96 famous eating contests: Ibid., 85.

96 "Corpulency is the most": Banner, *American Beauty,* 59.

97 actress Eileen Karl: Ibid., 114.

97 "a pair of ponderous legs": "Big Legs and Chests Now the Rage," *New York World,* October 15, 1893, 26.

97 "sagging breasts": Banner, *In Full Flower*, 281.

97 "It is no longer considered": Margaret Hubbard Ayer, "The Pursuit of Personal Beauty," chap. 11 in Ella Wheeler Wilcox et al., *Correct Social Usage*, vol. 1 (New York: New York Society of Self-Culture, 1906), 153–54. See also Ellen M. Plante, *Women at Home in Victorian America* (New York: Facts on File, 1997), 212.

97 "No woman under 95": Julia B. Foraker, *I Would Live It Again: Memories of a Vivid Life* (New York: Harper & Bros., 1932), quoted in Banner, *American Beauty*, 208.

98 "I began my career": "Lillian Russell Dies of Injuries," *New York Times*, June 6, 1922.

98 the lovely soul: Albert Auster, *Actresses and Suffragists: Women in the American Theater, 1890–1920* (Westport, CT: Praeger, 1984), 96.

98 Lillie Langtry credited: "Advertisement for Pears' Soap," 1891, online gallery, British Library, http://www.bl.uk/onlinegallery/onlineex/evancoll/a/014eva00000000000u 07536000.html.

98 getting in shape: Banner, *American Beauty*, 203.

7. THE TWENTIETH CENTURY ARRIVES

99 "There is another question": Amelia Huddleston Barr, *Three Score and Ten: A Book for the Aged* (New York: D. Appleton & Co., 1915), 59.

99 "vigorous old age": Ibid., 229–34. Barr also spoke about sleeping, resting, and being solitary for 10 hours each day.

99 "author of nearly 80 books": "Amelia Barr Is 88 [*sic*]: Event Quietly Celebrated by Authoress in Home," *Richmond Hill Record*, April 5, 1918. The newspaper misstates Barr's age in its headline but correctly uses 87 in the text of the article.

99 Parts of her *Remember the Alamo*: Barbara Leah Harman and Susan Meyer, *The New Nineteenth Century: Feminist Readings of Underread Victorian Fiction* (New York: Garland Publishing, 1996), xv.

99 "a good thing for America": "Amelia Barr Is 88."

99 "are coming back from battle": Ibid.

100 "I was not afraid": Nellie Bly, *Around the World in Seventy-Two Days and Other Writings* (New York: Penguin, 2014), 290.

100 "My God! Nellie Bly!": Nellie Bly, "American Woman Imprisoned in Austria; Liberated When Identified by Doctor Friedman," *Los Angeles Evening Herald*, January 12, 1915; and Brooke Kroeger, *Nellie Bly: Daredevil, Reporter, Feminist* (New York: Times Books, 1994), 405.

100 "born May 4, 1877": Kroeger, *Nellie Bly*, 427.

100 "I am a daughter of adventure": Ken and Lisa Marks, *Molly Brown from Hannibal, Missouri* (Charleston, SC: History Press, 2013), 81–83, 125.

101 "between the ages of fifty and seventy": Jane Addams, "Need a Woman over Fifty Feel Old?," *Ladies' Home Journal*, October 1914, 7.

101 "the whiteheads of the modern age": Lucy Jerome, "Some Grand Old Women," *World Today*, July 11, 1911.

101 the "old lady" of 1907: "The Passing of the Old Lady," *Atlantic Monthly*, June 1907, 874.

101 "on a dozen visiting committees": "In an Editorial Way," *Ladies' Home Journal*, July 1907, 6.

101 "that magnetism": Ibid.

101 Mother Jones: Jerome, "Some Grand Old Women."

102 "My address is like my shoes": Elliott Gorn, *Mother Jones: The Most Dangerous Woman in America* (New York: Hill and Wang, 2001), 4.

102 "She came into the mine": Ibid., 73.

102 "an army of strong mining women": Ibid., 83.

102 "If you should kill a rat": Ibid., 256.

102 "You are surprised": Ibid., 104.

102 "I had to slide down": Ibid., 92.

102 when she was 92: Ibid., 290–91.

102 "If you are too cowardly to fight": Ibid., 178.

103 "Whatever I have done in West Virginia": Ibid., 188.

103 "My fault was the irreparable one": An Elderly Woman, "The Land of Old Age," *Harper's Bazar*, August 1906, 2A.

104 "If they only sat": Barr, *Three Score and Ten*, 112.

104 "Aside from the sentimental reasons": Carole Haber, *Beyond Sixty-Five: The Dilemma of Old Age in America's Past* (New York: Cambridge Univ. Press, 1983), 86.

104 "Here we are": Elizabeth Cazden, *Antoinette Brown Blackwell* (Old Westbury, NY: Feminist Press, 1983), 254–55.

105 "The History of the Standard Oil Company": Ida M. Tarbell, "The History of the Standard Oil Company," *McClure's*, November 1902–October 1904.

105 "the most popular woman in America": Kathleen Brady, *Ida Tarbell: Portrait of a Muckraker* (Pittsburgh: Univ. of Pittsburgh Press, 1989), 150.

105 "very bad taste": Louise W. Knight, *Jane Addams: Spirit in Action* (New York: W. W. Norton, 2010), 180.

106 "silly, vain, impertinent old maid": Ibid., 204.

106 "56 campaigns of referenda": Janet Zollinger Giele, *Two Paths to Women's Equality* (New York: Twayne Publishers, 1995), 112.

106 "talking of the time": Ken Butigan, "Alice Paul's Enduring Legacy of Nonviolent Action," *Waging Nonviolence*, November 15, 2012, https://wagingnonviolence .org/feature/alice-pauls-enduring-legacy-of-nonviolent-action/; and Dianne G. Bystrom and Barbara Burrell, eds., *Women in the American Political System: An Encyclopedia of Women as Voters, Candidates, and Office Holders*, vol. 2 (Santa Barbara, CA: ABC-CLIO, 2019), 387.

106 the vote would be long since won: Jacqueline Van Voris, *Carrie Chapman Catt: A Public Life* (New York: Feminist Press, 1987), 131.

107 "those of us who really want": Ibid., 120.

107 "for the purpose of creating": Edna K. Wooley, "Mere Man Opposes Woman's Vanities," *Milady Beautiful*, July 1915, 27.

107 "physical care in beauty shops": *The Woman Beautiful*, 1908, cited in Lois W. Banner, *Elizabeth Cady Stanton: A Radical for Woman's Rights* (Boston: Little, Brown, 1980), 217.

107 "Dr. Olga Schiller's Gray Hair Restorer": Advertisement for Dr. Olga Schiller's Gray Hair Restorer, *Milady Beautiful,* vol. 8, no. 7, April 1919, 47, in bound collection of *Milady Beautiful* issues (Chicago: NYPL Research Libraries).

108 Helena Rubinstein: Lindy Woodhead, *War Paint: Madame Helena Rubinstein & Miss Elizabeth Arden* (Hoboken, NJ: John Wiley & Sons, 2003), 25ff. See also Rubinstein's autobiography, Helena Rubinstein, *My Life for Beauty* (New York: Simon & Schuster, 1966).

108 "World's Richest Negress in Delta": A'Lelia Bundles, *On Her Own Ground: The Life and Times of Madam C. J. Walker* (New York: Scribner, 2001), 195.

108 "a degree of elegance and extravagance": Ibid., 233; and "Wealthiest Negro Woman's Suburban Mansion," *New York Times,* November 4, 1917.

108 her hair began to fall out: Bundles, *On Her Own Ground,* 59.

108 "a big black man appeared": Ibid., 60.

108 "a Walker parlor on every corner": Ibid., 249.

108 "scrub floors or pick up baby": Robert L. [Latou] Dickinson, "Toleration of the Corset: Prescribing Where One Cannot Proscribe," *American Journal of Obstetrics and Diseases of Women and Children* 63 (January–June 1911): 1,055.

109 "an ill-advised experiment": Martha Cutler, "How to Remain Young," *Harper's Bazar,* November 1909.

109 "as straight and yielding": Jean V. Matthews, *The Rise of the New Woman: The Women's Movement in America, 1875–1930* (Chicago: Ivan R. Dee, 2003), 116.

8. THE 1920S

110 "Our Wages Highest": "Our Wages Highest in World's History, Hoover Declares," *New York Times,* December 2, 1927. The subhead: "Sees Lasting Prosperity."

110 a third of American families: Office of Highway Information Management, Federal Highway Administration, "State Motor Vehicle Registrations, by Years, 1900–1995," in *Highway Statistics Summary to 1995* (Washington, DC: U.S. Dept. of Transportation, 1997).

110 moving to the cities in droves: Gerald Leinwand, *1927: High Tide of the 1920s* (New York: Four Walls Eight Windows, 2002), 6.

110 "If we get married": Ibid., 177. See also Roland Marchand, *Advertising the American Dream: Making Way for Modernity, 1920–1940* (New York: Basic Books, 2002), where the ad is represented slightly differently.

111 "a great, hulking": The piece appeared in papers throughout the world, including, for instance, on the front page of the *Christchurch Star* (New Zealand), October 13, 1913.

111 The New Woman: David Kyvig, *Daily Life in the United States, 1920–1940* (Chicago: Ivan R. Dee, 2004), 120.

111 "fat lady": Lois W. Banner, *Elizabeth Cady Stanton: A Radical for Woman's Rights* (Boston: Little, Brown, 1980), 153.

111 "reach to that part of the foot": Frederick Lewis Allen, *Only Yesterday: An Informal History of the 1920s* (New York: Harper Perennial, 2000; first published 1931 by Harper & Bros. [New York]), 77.

111 "fine and imprisonment": Ibid.

111 "three inches": Ibid.

111 "Repressions have been released": V. F. Calverton, "The Jazz Age," in *The Bank-ruptcy of Marriage* (New York: Macaulay Co., 1928), 11–20. V. F. Calverton was the pseudonym of George Goetz.

111 "My candle burns": Edna St. Vincent Millay, "First Fig," in *A Few Figs from Thistles* (New York: F. Shay, 1921), 9. Millay won the Pulitzer Prize for poetry in 1923.

112 "awoke from her lethargy": Zelda Sayre Fitzgerald, "Eulogy on the Flapper," *Metropolitan Magazine,* June 1922.

112 average of 800 feature films: Tim Dirks, "The History of Film: The 1920s—The Pre-Talkies and the Silent Era, Part 1," AMC Filmsite, accessed March 14, 2019, https://www.filmsite.org/20sintro.html.

112 all-American city of Muncie, Indiana: Kyvig, *Daily Life in the United States,* 96.

113 the first Miss America Pageant: Susan Faludi, "American Electra," *Harper's,* October 2010, 38. At the time, it was called the Atlantic City Pageant. It wasn't until 1922 that the winner was referred to as "Miss America": see Samir Mezrahi, "This Was the First Miss America Pageant, Held in 1921," *BuzzFeed,* May 28, 2012, https://www.buzzfeed.com/samir/this-was-the-first-miss-america-pageant-held-in-1.

113 "To say that Ma holds her own": "In Old Kaysee," *Chicago Defender,* January 21, 1928, 7.

113 "keeping the modern woman slim": Lynn Dumenil, *The Modern Temper* (New York: Hill and Wang, 1995), 142.

113 "the young girl who isn't built": Advertisement for Gossard Corsets, *Ladies' Home Journal,* March 1922, 170.

114 "Mother, you're looking younger every day!": Kathy Peiss, *Hope in a Jar: The Making of America's Beauty Culture* (New York: Metropolitan Books, 1998), 141.

114 "broken on the wheel": Barton W. Currie, "Human Junk," *Ladies' Home Journal,* September 1921, 24.

114 "The alleged joys of old age": Serge Voronoff, *How to Restore Youth and Live Longer* (New York: Falstaff Press, 1928), 73, quoted in Carole Haber, "Anti-Aging Medicine: Life Extension and History: The Continual Search for the Fountain of Youth," *Journals of Gerontology: Series A* 59, no. 6 (June 2004): B515–22.

115 "on a large scale": Serge Voronoff, *The Study of Old Age and My Method of Rejuvenation* (London: Gill Publishing, 1926), 110, quoted in Haber, "Anti-Aging Medicine."

115 "Immortal life"; "grossness, coarseness": Thomas R. Cole, *The Journey of Life: A Cultural History of Aging in America* (New York: Cambridge Univ. Press, 1992), 13, quoting Charles Asbury Stephens, *Natural Salvation: The Message of Science—Outlining the First Principle of Immortal Life on Earth* (Norway Lake, ME: The Laboratory, 1906; first published 1903), 126–27; and Charles Asbury Stephens, *Immortal Life: How to Achieve It* (Norway Lake, ME: The Laboratory; Boston: Colonial Press/C. H. Simonds Co., 1920), 235. See also Haber, "Anti-Aging Medicine."

115 "hipped on Freud": F. Scott Fitzgerald, *This Side of Paradise* (New York: Charles Scribner's Sons, 1920), 255.

115 "It is a well-known fact": Sigmund Freud, "The Disposition to Obsessional Neurosis," in *The Standard Edition of the Complete Psychological Works of Sigmund Freud,* vol. 12, trans. James Strachey (New York: Vintage, 2001), 317–26.

115 pathetically stripped of all sexuality: Banner, *Elizabeth Cady Stanton*, 287ff.

115 "It's been in the background": Gertrude Atherton, *Black Oxen* (New York: Boni & Liveright, 1923), 175.

116 "withered"; "condemned for prejudice": Ibid., 11, 95.

116 "The senile female": Norman Haire, *Rejuvenation: The Work of Steinach, Voronoff, and Others* (New York: Macmillan, 1925), 32, quoted in Haber, "Anti-Aging Medicine," 518. Haire practiced in England.

116 "it soon will not be necessary": Ethel Lloyd Patterson, "Why Grow Old?: Face Value," *Ladies' Home Journal*, September 1922, 28. Ethel Lloyd Patterson was also, in or around 1922, the editor of the magazine.

116 lose weight without "table restraint": Leinwand, *1927*, 223.

117 19¼ yards to 7: Allen, *Only Yesterday*, 86–87.

117 "lipsticks, perfumes": David Porter, *Mary Norton of New Jersey, Congressional Trailblazer* (Madison, NJ: Fairleigh Dickinson Univ. Press, 2013), 36.

117 netting $7.3 million: Lindy Woodhead, *War Paint: Madame Helena Rubinstein and Miss Elizabeth Arden: Their Lives, Their Times, Their Rivalry* (Hoboken, NJ: John Wiley & Sons, 2003), 456.

117 "She retires, a reigning beauty": Advertisement for Brownatone hair color, 1924, in "You Cannot Afford to be Gray in the Day of Youth: 1920s Ads for Hair Coloring," Witness2fashion.com, June 27, 2014, accessed March 14, 2019, https://witness 2fashion.wordpress.com/2014/06/27/you-cannot-afford-to-be-gray-in-the-day-of -youth-1920s-ads-for-hair-coloring/.

118 "Causes sweep by them unheeded": Margaret Culkin Banning, "The Lazy Thirties," *Harper's*, February 1927, 357.

118 "the old school of fighting feminists": Dorothy Dunbar Bromley, "Feminist— New Style," *Harper's*, October 1927.

119 rewarded by their new constituents: Kyvig, *Daily Life in the United States*, 4.

119 "ladies who have not had babies": Dorothy M. Brown, *Setting a Course: American Women in the 1920s* (Boston: Twayne Publishers, 1987), 53.

119 "old maids are voting now": Jan Doolittle Wilson, *The Women's Joint Congressional Committee and the Politics of Maternalism, 1920–30* (Champaign: Univ. of Illinois Press, 2007), 47.

119 violation of liquor laws: Kyvig, *Daily Life in the United States*, 3.

120 close-ups of their fleshy ankles: Mary Ryan, "The Projection of a New Womanhood: The Movie Moderns in the 1920s," in *Decades of Discontent: The Women's Movement, 1920–1940*, eds. Lois Scharf and Joan Jensen (Westport, CT: Greenwood Press, 1983), 124.

120 Older women's reactions: Allen, *Only Yesterday*, 91.

120 Nearly 300 movies: Ryan, "The Projection of a New Womanhood," 124.

120 "Go ahead, he's right over there": Tim Lussier, "*Dancing Mothers:* Synopsis, Commentary," Silentsaregolden.com, March 2, 2008, http://www.silentsaregolden .com/featurefolder9/DMcommentary.html.

121 "'married men' are no longer taboo": Helen Bullitt Lowry, "The Evolution of a New Social Technique: Or How to Keep a Husband," *Harper's Bazar*, May 1922, 54.

121 male "lounge lizards": Banner, *Elizabeth Cady Stanton*, 289ff.

121 ad in the *Chicago Tribune:* Dumenil, *Modern Temper,* 129.

122 "considered overindulgence": Lillian Symes, "Still a Man's Game: Reflections of a Slightly Tired Feminist," *Harper's Monthly,* May 1929, 678–79.

122 Vida Scudder, a prominent reformer: Patricia Ann Palmieri, *In Adamless Eden: The Community of Women Faculty at Wellesley* (New Haven, CT: Yale Univ. Press, 1995), 212.

122 "yearns for the trapeze": Margaret Sherwood, "The Ideal of a College," *Wellesley Magazine* 15, no. 2, November 1906, 47.

122 "remembered as comrades and not as mentors": Louise W. Knight, *Jane Addams: Spirit in Action* (New York: W. W. Norton, 2010), 248.

122 Edith Hull: E. M. [Edith Maude] Hull, *The Sheik* (Philadelphia: Pine St. Books/ Univ. of Pennsylvania Press, 2001; first published 1919 by E. Nash & Grayson [London]), 57. The dialogue is repeated later in the book: "Why have I brought you here? You ask me? *Mon Dieu!* Are you not woman enough to know? No! I will not spare you. Give me what I want willingly and I will be kind to you, but fight me, and by Allah! you shall pay the cost" (p. 239). E. M. Hull was the pseudonym of Edith Maude Winstanley, according to the University of Pennsylvania Press. The British National Archives uses the spelling "Maud" and notes that she was born Edith Maud Henderson and that her husband, Percy Winstanley, was a "gentleman pig farmer" (from "Papers of Edith Maud Hill," 1875–1956, Women's Library, London School of Economics, London University, accessed March 24, 2019, National Archives online, https://discovery.nationalarchives.gov.uk/details/r/ 610F43D4-bf92-4ACA-99ED-6869447E9068).

123 "Repose, dignity, independence": Ellen Glasgow, *Barren Ground* (Garden City, NY: Doubleday, Page, and Co., 1925), pt. 2, chap. 18.

123 "Within the space of a single day": Miriam Simons Leuck, quoted in Leinwand, *1927,* 48–49.

123 number of women professionals: Brown, *Setting a Course,* 151.

124 "the useful maiden aunt": Robert Lynd and Helen Lynd, *Middletown: A Study in Contemporary American Culture* (New York: Harcourt, Brace, 1929), 25.

124 During World War I: Dumenil, *Modern Temper,* 120.

124 recruiting their faculty: Leinwand, *1927,* 227.

124 "intense dreariness": Rhoda Broughton, "Girls Past and Present," *Ladies' Home Journal,* September 1920.

124 about 10 percent of married women: Karen Pastorello, *The Progressives: Activism and Reform in American Society, 1893–1917* (Malden, MA: Wiley-Blackwell, 2014), 49.

125 "She can if she has brains": "Can a Woman Run a Home and a Job, Too?," *Literary Digest,* November 11, 1922, 40, 44.

125 survey of white-collar men: Dumenil, *Modern Temper,* 122.

125 "children of gainfully employed mothers": David Snedden, "Some Probable Social Consequences of the Out-Working of Well-Endowed Married Women," *Annals of the American Academy of Political and Social Science* 143, no. 1 (May 1929): 354.

126 a sideline like "typing, sewing": Lorene Pruette (1929 essay), quoted in Dumenil, *Modern Temper,* 125.

126 "What is a woman 35 years of age to do?": Johanna Lobsenz, *The Older Woman in Industry* (New York: Charles Scribner's Sons, 1929), 103.

126 "either unsuitable or dangerous": Gwen Kay, *Dying to Be Beautiful: The Fight for Safe Cosmetics* (Columbus: Ohio State Univ. Press, 2005), 60.

126 "less moody and irritable": Lobsenz, *Older Woman in Industry,* 94.

126 "supplying of domestic help": Ibid., 92.

126 the population of maids, cooks: In 1910, 42 percent, and in 1930, 63 percent, according to the U.S. Department of Commerce, Bureau of the Census, *The Social and Economic Status of the Black Population of the United States: An Historical View, 1790–1978* (Washington, DC: U.S. Government Printing Office, 1978), 72, table 51. Jacqueline Jones, in *Labor of Love, Labor of Sorrow: Black Women, Work, and the Family from Slavery to the Present* (New York: Basic Books, 1985), 206, says that by 1937, 81 percent of black women worked in domestic service.

127 a friendly voice calling: M. M. Manring, *Slave in a Box: The Strange Career of Aunt Jemima* (Charlottesville: Univ. Press of Virginia, 1998), 118.

127 "How happy she had been": Ibid., 120.

127 mixed the actual facts of her life: Ibid., 77.

127 a former happy plantation cook: Dave Tabler, "Nancy Green, the First 'Aunt Jemima,'" Appalachianhistory.net, March 1, 2017, http://www.appalachianhistory.net/2017/03/nancy-green-first-aunt-jemima.html.

127 "There is no good reason why": A. L. Jackson, "The Onlooker," *Chicago Defender,* September 29, 1923, 12.

127 Rebecca Latimer Felton: David B. Parker, "Rebecca Latimer Felton (1835–1930)," New Georgia Encyclopedia, May 14, 2003, https://www.georgiaencyclopedia.org/articles/history-archaeology/rebecca-latimer-felton-1835-1930.

128 Winnifred Huck: "Huck, Winnifred Sprague Mason," History, Art, & Archives, United States House of Representatives, accessed March 15, 2019, https://history.house.gov/People/Detail/15397.

128 Katherine Langley: "Langley, Katherine Gudger," History, Art, & Archives, United States House of Representatives, accessed March 15, 2019, https://history.house.gov/People/Detail/16680.

128 Edith Nourse Rogers: "Rogers, Edith Nourse," History, Art & Archives online project, United States House of Representatives, accessed March 15, 2019, https://history.house.gov/People/Detail/20569.

128 a protégé of Frank Hague: Porter, *Mary Norton of New Jersey,* 11.

129 "I was starting a…career": Ibid., 56.

129 lost her only child: Ibid., 36.

129 "How very, very fortunate": Ibid., 15.

129 "controlled by a woman": "Norton, Mary Teresa," History, Art & Archives online project, United States House of Representatives, accessed March 15, 2019, https://history.house.gov/People/Listing/N/NORTON,-Mary-Teresa-(N000153)/.

130 Belmont's actual testimonial: Jennifer Scanlon, *Inarticulate Longings: The Ladies' Home Journal, Gender and the Promise of Consumer Culture* (London: Routledge, 1995), 132.

130 "the most marvelous mattress": Leinwand, *1927,* 177.

9. THE 1930S

131 "nearly one billion hours": Hadley Cantril and Gordon Allport, *The Psychology of Radio* (New York: Harper & Bros., 1935), 219, quoted in Susan Douglas, *Listening In: Radio and the American Imagination* (New York: Times Books, 1999), 131.

131 the generic name of "soap operas": Michele Hilmes, *Radio Voices: American Broadcasting, 1922–1952* (Minneapolis: Univ. of Minnesota Press, 1997), 151.

131 "the real-life drama of Helen Trent": Hilmes, *Radio Voices*, 159.

131 her 28 suitors: "The Romance of Helen Trent," National Radio Hall of Fame website, last modified 2018, accessed March 24, 2019, https://web.archive.org/web/20180408070657/http://www.radiohof.org:80/helen_trent.htm.

131 *The Story of Mary Marlin:* "The Story of Mary Marlin: Famous Soap-Opera Heroine Survives a New Crisis," *Life*, September 11, 1944, 70.

131 *Stella Dallas:* Robert LaGuardia, *From Ma Perkins to Mary Hartman: The Illustrated History of Soap Operas* (New York: Ballantine, 1977), 9.

132 a quarter of the working population: Daniel Béland, *Social Security: History and Politics from the New Deal to the Privatization Debate* (Lawrence: Univ. Press of Kansas, 2005), 64.

132 family income dropped 40 percent: Steven Mintz and Susan Kellogg, *Domestic Revolutions: A Social History of American Family Life* (New York: Free Press, 1988), 134.

132 popular comic strip *Blondie:* Dean Young and John Marshall, "The Blondie Story," Comics Kingdom website, accessed March 16, 2019, http://blondie.com/the_blondie_story/.

132 sale of glass jars: Ruth Milkman, "Women's Work and the Economic Crisis: Some Lessons of the Great Depression," *Review of Radical Political Economics* 8, no. 1 (April 1976): 82.

132 "Grandmother made the opportune purchase": "Grandmother Had Horse Sense," *Harper's Bazaar*, March 1931, 39.

133 "You Can Have My Job": Poppy Cannon, "Pin-Money Slaves," in *The American New Woman Revisited: A Reader, 1894–1930*, ed. Martha Patterson (New Brunswick, NJ: Rutgers Univ. Press, 2008), 203.

133 "flimsy pay envelope": Ibid., 206.

133 "sin and hay fever": Susan Ware, *Holding Their Own: American Women in the 1930s* (Boston: Twayne Publishers, 1982), 27.

133 "married women whose husbands"; 1936 Gallup poll: Ruth Milkman, *On Gender, Labor, and Inequality* (Champaign: Univ. of Illinois Press, 2016), 23; and Sandra Stencel, "Women in the Work Force," *Editorial Research Reports* 1 (February 18, 1977), accessed online March 24, 2019, http://library.cqpress.com/cqresearcher/cqresrre1977021800.

133 "may be supporting a family": Mrs. F. D. Roosevelt, "Too Old for the Job," *Woman's Home Companion*, February 1934.

134 grabbing up the clerical openings: Bernard Sternsher and Judith Sealander, eds., *Women of Valor: The Struggle Against the Great Depression as Told in Their Own Life Stories* (Chicago: Ivan R. Dee, 1990), 6.

134 about $1,600 a year during the Depression: See, for instance, Floyd J. Doering, *A History of Vocational Agriculture/Agribusiness in Wisconsin Secondary Schools, 1900–1976* (n.p.: Department of Public Instruction, Bureau for Career and Manpower Development, [1976?]), 40.

134 "As professionals...paid or not": Studs Terkel, *Hard Times: An Oral History of the Great Depression* (New York: Pantheon/Random House, 1970), 442.

134 mutter about younger workers: David R. Craig, "The Problem of the Superannuated Worker," *Bulletin of the National Retail Dry Goods Association* 12 (March 1930): 143–44, quoted in Susan Porter Benson, *Counter Cultures: Saleswomen, Managers, and Customers in American Department Stores, 1890–1940* (Urbana: Univ. of Illinois Press, 1988), 203, 223n44.

134 "needle trades, beauty culture": Dorothy Dunbar Bromley, "Women Victims of Depression Present a Huge New Problem," *New York Times*, January 14, 1934.

134 Over half of black female workers: Nancy Woloch, *Women and the American Experience* (New York: McGraw-Hill, 2000), 461.

134 reported 68 percent of the job availabilities: Elaine S. Abelson, "'Women Who Have No Men to Work for Them': Gender and Homelessness in the Great Depression, 1930–1934," *Feminist Studies* 29, no. 1 (Spring 2003): 106.

134 first luxury to go: Christopher Klein, "Last Hired, First Fired: How the Great Depression Affected African Americans," History.com, April 18, 2018, https://www.history.com/news/last-hired-first-fired-how-the-great-depression-affected-african-americans.

135 "we divided whatever we had": Terkel, *Hard Times*, 458.

135 "We called her Ma Kuntz": Ibid., 456–57.

135 "optimism was expressed": Kathleen McLaughlin, "Maturity Held Aid to Women over 40; Those of That Age Should Not Be on Defensive, Business Federation Hears," *New York Times*, July 21, 1937, 23.

135 "I am now daily confronted": Frank Crowninshield, introduction to *Live Alone and Like It: A Guide for the Extra Woman*, by Marjorie Hillis (New York: Bobbs-Merrill, 1936), 4.

136 A 1936 survey of single women on relief: Harriet Byrne and Cecile Hillyer, *Unattached Women on Relief in Chicago, 1937* (Washington, DC: U.S. Government Printing Office, 1938), 7–8.

136 Maude, a 51-year-old widow: Lois Rita Hembold, "Beyond the Family Economy: Black and White Working-Class During the Great Depression," *Feminist Studies* 13, no. 3 (Autumn 1987): 647.

136 Mary, a 53-year-old widow: Ibid., 631.

136 "the kind of widows": Terkel, *Hard Times*, 278.

137 "Doctors will have to be warned": "A Modest Proposal," *The Nation*, April 10, 1935, 404.

137 "I Am the Mother-in-Law": "I Am the Mother-in-Law in the Home," *Saturday Evening Post*, September 18, 1937.

137 "better to be brazen than neglected": Hillis, *Live Alone and Like It*, 101.

138 "A reputation for good cuisine": Ibid., 40.

138 focus on "friends, hobbies, parties": Ibid., 39.

138 "standing on her head": Ibid., 69.

138 "colored-maid-in-for-the-afternoon": Ibid., 91.

138 Mrs. O, a middle-aged divorcée: Ibid., 94.

140 "the best-loved star of her time": Matthew Kennedy, *Marie Dressler: A Biography with a Listing of Major Stage Performances, a Filmography, and a Discography* (Jefferson, NC: McFarland, 1999), 3.

140 "That's all me!"; "old mud hen": Ibid., 172–73, 176.

140 "buxom blonde": George Eells and Stanley Musgrove, *Mae West: The Lies, the Legends, the Truth* (London: Robson Books, 1989; first published 1984), 104.

140 "stole everything but the cameras": Ibid., 107.

141 "You forget": "Mae West: Timing," *Mae West* (blog), July 28, 2007, posted by NYC Mae West, accessed April 4, 2019, http://maewest.blogspot.com/2007/07/.

141 "the gal with the hourglass figure": Eells and Musgrove, *Mae West*, 114, 115.

141 "Why should I complain": *Root* staff, "75 Years Ago, Hattie McDaniel Made History by Winning an Oscar," *The Root*, February 22, 2015; Robin Washington, "A Hattie McDaniel U.S. Mail Stamp?," *News & Notes*, National Public Radio, March 28, 2006; and Julie Salamon, "The Courage to Rise Above Mammyness," *New York Times*, August 6, 2001.

141 "I sincerely hope": Oscars, "Hattie McDaniel Winning Best Supporting Actress," 12th Academy Awards acceptance speech, following the presentation of the Oscar by Fay Bainter, YouTube video, 1:40, posted September 27, 2011, accessed April 4, 2019, https://www.youtube.com/watch?v=e7t4pTNZshA.

142 asexual, middle-aged devoted slave: Catherine Clinton, *The Plantation Mistress: Woman's World in the Old South* (New York: Pantheon, 1982), 202.

142 Mammy loved her white charges: David Pilgrim, "The Mammy Caricature," Jim Crow Museum of Racist Memorabilia, Ferris State University, last modified 2012, https://www.ferris.edu/jimcrow/mammies/.

142 black maid in West's movies: Pilgrim, "Mammy Caricature."

142 Utah provided the last: Frederick Lewis Allen, *Only Yesterday: An Informal History of the 1920s* (New York: Harper Perennial, 2000; first published 1931 by Harper & Bros. [New York]), 140–41.

142 A study by *Fortune* in 1937: Ibid., 145.

142 "I have found it impossible": Edward, Duke of Windsor, "A King's Story," *Life*, June 12, 1950, 125.

143 "a new anatomical species": Ware, *Holding Their Own*, xvii.

143 " 'Try one' ": Paula Reed, *Fifty Fashion Looks That Changed the 1950s* (London: Conran Octopus, 2012), 16.

143 law against women wearing slacks: Sally Keil, *Those Wonderful Women in their Flying Machines: The Unknown Heroines of World War II* (New York: Four Directions Press, 1990), 259.

144 "the pitiless hand of Time": Advertisement for Dorothy Gray skin products, *Harper's Bazaar*, March 1930, 10.

144 " 'The One Woman in the World' ": Advertisement for Edna Wallace Hopper's Special Restorative Cream, *Woman's Home Companion*, February 1934.

144 "smile indulgently at the mad struggle": Thurman B. [Brooks] Rice, "Sex Education: Sex in Middle and Advanced Life," *Hygeia* 12 (March 1934): 242–45. For

more on Rice, see Angela Bowen Potter, "Thurman Rice's Sex Education Campaigns, 1933–1948," in Potter's "From Social Hygiene to Social Health: Indiana and the United States Adolescent Sex Education Movement, 1907–1975" (master's thesis, Indiana University, 2015).

145 rediscovering the middle-aged market: W. Andrew Achenbaum, *Old Age in the New Land: The American Experience Since 1790* (Baltimore: Johns Hopkins Univ. Press, 1978), 118.

145 *Life Begins at Forty:* Walter Pitkin, *Life Begins at Forty* (New York: McGraw-Hill, 1932), 115.

145 "Here is a woman of seventy-five": Frances Fenton, "Old Age Is What You Make It," *Independent Woman*, November 1939.

145 "Instead of slowing down": Mary Church Terrell, *A Colored Woman in a White World* (Amherst, NY: Humanity Books, 2005; first published 1940 by Ransdell [Washington, DC]), 451.

146 "understands more"; "frontline trenches": Louise W. Knight, *Jane Addams: Spirit in Action* (New York: W. W. Norton, 2010), 261, 267.

146 "a holy discontent": Ibid., 269.

146 fought against segregated housing: Ibid., 255.

146 almost as long as Addams herself: Ibid., 250.

146 gave most of the award money: Ibid., 257.

147 "Jane grieved every day": Ibid., 265.

147 "I know I'll go on living": Louise DeKoven Bowen, *Open Windows: Stories of People and Places* (Chicago: R. F. Seymour, 1946), 272, quoted in Blanche Wiesen Cook, *Eleanor Roosevelt: The Defining Years*, vol. 2, *1933–1938* (New York: Viking, 1999), 263.

148 "A wonderful power": Elliott Gorn, *Mother Jones: The Most Dangerous Woman in America* (New York: Hill and Wang, 2001), 291–93.

148 an earlier requiem Mass: Ibid., 292–93.

148 "could not believe human beings": *American Experience*, "Eleanor Roosevelt," written and directed by Sue Williams, aired January 10, 2000, on PBS, transcript, https://www.pbs.org/wgbh/americanexperience/films/eleanor/#transcript.

148 "Eleanor was better known to politicians": Woloch, *Women and the American Experience*, 437.

149 nicknamed her "Granny": Blanche Wiesen Cook, *Eleanor Roosevelt: The Early Years*, vol. 1, *1884–1933* (New York: Viking, 1992), 71.

149 wearing her yellow bathing suit: Cook, *Eleanor Roosevelt*, vol. 2, 36.

149 "In prison, Mr. President": Susan Ware, *Letter to the World: Seven Women Who Shaped the American Century* (New York: W. W. Norton, 1998), 15–16.

149 led them in a round: Woloch, *Women and the American Experience*, 439.

149 "glad to take two old things": Robert McElvaine, *The Great Depression: America, 1929–1941* (New York: Times Books, 1984), 175.

149 "what I want most out of life": Woloch, *Women and the American Experience*, 438.

150 "only bore you": Doris Kearns Goodwin, *No Ordinary Time: Franklin and Eleanor Roosevelt: The Home Front in World War II* (New York: Simon & Schuster, 1994), 179.

150 denounced as a "Jezebel": Cook, *Eleanor Roosevelt,* vol. 2, 12.

150 gave up wearing her black hairnet: Goodwin, *No Ordinary Time,* 204.

150 "if you haven't any chin": Ware, *Letter to the World,* 5.

150 take the family dogs: Cook, *Eleanor Roosevelt,* vol. 2, 13.

150 agreed to travel with a revolver: Sternsher and Sealander, *Women of Valor,* 51. See also David Kopel, "A Chance to Fight Back," *New York Times,* last modified December 6, 2012, which has a photograph of Eleanor shooting.

150 became godmother to his daughter: Cook, *Eleanor Roosevelt,* vol. 2, 93.

151 "collection of statesmen": Susan Ware, *Beyond Suffrage: Women in the New Deal* (Cambridge, MA: Harvard Univ. Press, 1981), 4.

151 Mary McLeod Bethune: Woloch, *Women and the American Experience,* 467.

151 "My name is Mrs. Bethune": "Interview with Virginia Foster Durr, October 16, 1975. Interview G-0023-3. Southern Oral History Program Collection (#4007)," interview by Sue Thrasher, *Documenting the American South,* University Library at Univ. of North Carolina at Chapel Hill, accessed March 17, 2019, https://docsouth.unc.edu/sohp/G-0023-3/G-0023-3.html.

151 "The friendships that were formed": Ware, *Beyond Suffrage,* 31.

152 Governor Roosevelt named her: Leah W. Sprague, "Her Life: The Woman Behind the New Deal," Frances Perkins Center website, June 1, 2014, http://francesperkinscenter.org/life-new/.

152 "Don't be such a baby": Ware, *Beyond Suffrage,* 47.

153 "How fine it is . . . finished our soup": Ibid., 13, 10.

153 got little or nothing at all: Béland, *Social Security,* 65–66.

153 "thought it was such a nice idea": Frances Perkins, "The Roots of Social Security," radio address delivered at Social Security Administration Headquarters, Baltimore, MD, October 23, 1962, transcript at Virginia Commonwealth University Libraries, https://socialwelfare.library.vcu.edu/social-security/the-roots-of-social-security-by-frances-perkins/.

154 "Oh no; terrible": Ibid.

154 "as though anybody hadn't": Ibid.

154 "come to the worker as a right": Béland, *Social Security,* 77.

154 "carry a dependent child": Perkins, "The Roots of Social Security."

154 "red-upholstered, high-back chair": Ibid.

155 a princely $22.60: This was the average benefit. See Lars Osberg, ed., *Economic Inequality and Poverty: International Perspectives* (Armonk, NY: M. E. Sharpe, 1991), 199, table 7.1: "Percentage of Work Force Covered, Average Retired Worker Benefit, Average Wages, Selected Years 1940–87."

155 the First Lady nagging her: Sternsher and Sealander, *Women of Valor,* 139.

155 "task may well prove insuperable": Béland, *Social Security,* 88.

155 "let them take out one group": Perkins, "The Roots of Social Security."

155 it was still a start: David Hackett Fischer, *Growing Old in America* (New York: Oxford Univ. Press, 1978), 184.

156 "It wasn't that I expected anything": Social Security Administration, "Social Security History," accessed March 28, 2019, https://www.ssa.gov/history/imf.html.

10. THE WAR

157 "She's making history": "Rosie the Riveter," 1943, written by Redd Evans and John Jacob Loeb.

157 "building a plane to bomb Hitler": "Confederate General's Widow," *Life*, December 27, 1943, 37.

157 nearly 16 million American men: Barrie Barber, "For Those Who Fought, Memories Never Fade," *Dayton Daily News*, August 14, 2015, https://www.daytondaily news.com/news/for-those-who-fought-memories-never-fade/ FmtI5WSOE3NrESL8nIoFUP/.

157 not to mention 350,000 women: "Research Starters: U.S. Military by the Numbers," National WWII Museum website, accessed May 15, 2019, https://www .nationalww2museum.org/students-teachers/student-resources/research -starters/research-starters-us-military-numbers.

157 no more unmarried women: Emily Yellin, *Our Mothers' War: American Women at Home and at the Front During World War II* (New York: Free Press, 2004), 44.

157 no fan of the draft even for men: J. Garry Clifford and Samuel Spencer Jr., *The First Peacetime Draft* (Lawrence: Univ. Press of Kansas, 1996), 1–5. The Selective Training and Service Act, the first peacetime draft, which Roosevelt signed into law on October 30, 1940, originated not with the president or the White House but from a small group of private citizens who lobbied a Republican.

157 "Women, women, women": Mary Kelly, "Calling All Women," *Christian Science Monitor*, May 27, 1944.

158 between 45 and 65: Carrie Brown, *Rosie's Mom: Forgotten Women Workers of the First World War* (Boston: Northeastern Univ. Press, 2002), 195.

158 "As a woman I can't go to war": "Rankin, Jeannette," History, Art & Archives online project, United States House of Representatives, accessed March 18, 2019, https:// history.house.gov/People/Listing/R/RANKIN,-Jeannette-(R000055)/.

158 lock herself in a phone booth: Yellin, *Our Mothers' War*, 282.

158 "so many things I'd like to do": David Porter, *Mary Norton of New Jersey, Congressional Trailblazer* (Madison, NJ: Fairleigh Dickinson Univ. Press, 2013), 118.

159 One of Rogers's top priorities: Matthew Wasniewski, ed., *Women in Congress, 1917– 2006*, prepared under the direction of the Committee on House Administration of the U.S. House of Representatives, by the Office of History and Preservation, Office of the Clerk, U.S. House of Representatives (Washington, DC: U.S. Government Printing Office, 2006), 143.

159 "enlisted men to perform tedious duties": Susan Hartmann, "Women in the Military Service," in Mabel Deutrich and Virginia Purdy, eds., *Clio Was a Woman: Studies in the History of American Women* (Washington, DC: Howard Univ. Press, 1980), 196.

159 "a better postwar wife": Leisa Meyer, *Creating GI Jane: Sexuality and Power in the Women's Army Corps during World War II* (New York: Columbia Univ. Press, 1996), 55.

159 "Who will then do the cooking": Judith Bellafaire, *The Women's Army Corps: A Commemoration of World War II Service* (Washington, DC: U.S. Army Center of Military History, 1993), 3.

159 Esther McGowin Blake: Lisa Tendrich Frank, ed., "Blake, Esther McGowin, (1897–1979)," in *An Encyclopedia of American Women at War: From the Home Front to the Battlefields,* vol. 1 (Santa Barbara: ABC-CLIO, 2013), 82; and Robert Kane, "Blake Paved Way for Thousands of Air Force Women," U.S. Air Force website, March 10, 2015, https://www.af.mil/News/Article-Display/Article/580077/blake -paved-way-for-thousands-of-air-force-women/.

160 Ruth Cheney Streeter: Patricia Chappine, *New Jersey Women in World War II* (Charleston, SC: History Press, 2015), 55; and *Dames in Uniform* (Washington, DC: National Society of the Colonial Dames of America, 1996), published in conjunction with the exhibition of the same name, shown from June 23, 1995, to November 11, 1996, at Dumbarton House, headquarters of the National Society of the Colonial Dames of America, in Washington, DC.

160 "have no home ties": Lorena Hermance, quoted in Kathryn Dobie and Eleanor Lang, eds., *Her War: American Women in WWII* (Lincoln, NE: iUniverse, 2003), 82.

160 "how 'Grandma' received word": Ibid., 86.

161 "things got so bad": Eleanor "Bumpy" Stevenson and Pete Martin, *I Knew Your Soldier* (Washington, DC: Infantry Journal, [1945], 41–54), in *American Women in a World at War: Contemporary Accounts from World War II,* eds. Judy Litoff and David Smith (Wilmington, DE: Scholarly Resources, 1997), 110–12.

161 military overalls and pearls: Elizabeth Norman, *We Band of Angels: The Untold Story of the American Women Trapped on Bataan* (New York: Random House, 2013), 125.

161 maternal sympathy; "Admittedly, I tired": Ibid., 45.

162 from 156 pounds to 80: Evelyn Monahan and Rosemary Neidel-Greenlee, *All This Hell: U.S. Nurses Imprisoned by the Japanese* (Lexington: Univ. Press of Kentucky, 2000), 190, appendix F.

162 "With meager equipment": Norman, *We Band of Angels,* 236.

162 "not considered a position of great responsibility": Alice Booher, "Celebrating Angel Maude Davison," American Ex-Prisoners of War website, 2002, accessed May 15, 2019, http://web.archive.org/web/20160829055943/http://www.axpow .org/celebratingangelmaudedavison.htm.

162 record number over 35: Yellin, *Our Mothers' War,* 47.

162 "Granny has gone to work": Melissa McEuen, *Making War, Making Women: Femininity and Duty on the American Home Front, 1941–1945* (Athens: Univ. of Georgia Press, 2010), 183.

162 Ah Yoke Gee, a middle-aged welder: Xiaojian Zhao, "World War II and Chinese American Women Defense Workers," in Lon Kurashige and Alice Yang, eds., *Major Problems in Asian American History: Documents and Essays* (Boston: Cengage Learning, 2017), 291.

162 "mythical thirty-year-old woman": Doris Weatherford, *American Women and World War II* (New York: Facts on File, 1990), 152.

163 "no employer wanted 'old women'": Ibid., 181.

163 "A health record"; "weird and wonderful": "More Comments on 'Womanpower 4F,'" letters to the editor, *Independent Woman,* December 1943.

163 "specter of age": Louise Fillebrown, "I Helped Build Fighter Planes," *Independent Woman,* November 1943.

164 only 74 open to hiring: Karen Anderson, *Wartime Women: Sex Roles, Family Relations, and the Status of Women During World War II* (Westport, CT: Greenwood Press, 1981), 84.

164 "indulge in such prejudice": Yellin, *Our Mothers' War,* 39.

164 dropped to 15 percent: Sherna Gluck, *Rosie the Riveter Revisited: Women, the War, and Social Change* (Boston: Twayne Publishers, 1987), 24.

164 "Eleanor Clubs": Doris Kearns Goodwin, *No Ordinary Time: Franklin and Eleanor Roosevelt: The Home Front in World War II* (New York: Simon & Schuster, 1994), 370–71.

164 "free hardier men and women": "Seeks 100,000 Women for Jobs in Detroit," *New York Times,* February 12, 1943, 17.

164 "the ideal woman clerk": "Grocers Open Door to Women Clerks," *New York Times,* June 19, 1941, 17.

165 "wanted, not to work in war plants": "Women Cautioned About War Jobs," *New York Times,* December 13, 1942, 63.

165 "pride in their bright eyes": Quoted in Weatherford, *American Women and World War II,* 141.

165 a total mental blank: "Rosemary," Old Time Radio Catalog online, last modified February 3, 2011, https://www.otrcat.com/p/rosemary.

165 Women's Land Army: Judy B. Litoff and David C. Smith, "'To the Rescue of the Crops': The Women's Land Army During World War II," *Prologue* 25, no. 4 (Winter 1993), accessed March 18, 2019, National Archives website, https://www.archives.gov/publications/prologue/1993/winter/landarmy.html.

165 "might as well be working on a farm": "Women Enrolled in New Land Army," *New York Times,* May 26, 1943, 20.

166 "one noble purpose": Lisa Ossian, *The Home Fronts of Iowa, 1939–1945* (Columbia: Univ. of Missouri Press, 2009), 141.

166 "Mrs. America": Ibid., 124, 146.

166 "Uncle Sam certainly does not want": Marion Dixon, "Fitting the Feminine Form," *Hygeia,* August 1942, bound in vol. 20 (Chicago: American Medical Association, [1942]), 624.

166 Eventually the government would promote: Kathryn M. Brown, "Patriotic Support: The Girdle Pin-Up of World War II" (master's thesis, University of Akron, December 2010), 15.

166 all in the military service: J. Tomney, "Sons of the Commander in Chief: The Roosevelt Boys in World War II," *Forward with Roosevelt* (blog), Franklin D. Roosevelt Library and Museum, National Archives, January 31, 2018, https://fdr.blogs.archives.gov/2018/01/31/sons-of-the-commander-in-chief-the-roosevelt-boys-in-world-war-ii/.

166 accept more Jewish refugees: "First Lady Biography: Eleanor Roosevelt," National First Ladies' Library website, accessed March 18, 2019, http://www.firstladies.org/biographies/firstladies.aspx?biography=33.

167 "blood on your hands": Goodwin, *No Ordinary Time,* 446; and Angela Beauchamp, "Suffering Saint, Asexual Victorian Woman, or Queer Icon? Cinematic Representations of Eleanor Roosevelt" (master's thesis, Skidmore College, May 16, 2015),

60–61, https://creativematter.skidmore.edu/cgi/viewcontent.cgi?referer=https:// www.google.com/&httpsredir=1&article=1106&context=mals_stu_schol.

167 if he minded her speaking out: Ibid., 164.

167 Admiral Halsey: His full title was commander, South Pacific Forces and South Pacific Area.

167 "I marveled at her hardihood": *American Experience*, "Eleanor Roosevelt," written and directed by Sue Williams, aired January 10, 2000, on PBS, transcript, https:// www.pbs.org/wgbh/americanexperience/films/eleanor/#transcript.

167 wasting taxpayer money on "junkets": Goodwin, *No Ordinary Time*, 467.

167 Half of the American public: Ibid., 397.

167 "This is no ordinary time": Ibid., 13; and "July 1940: U.S. and World Events plus Additional Resources," Franklin D. Roosevelt Day by Day project, Pare Lorentz Center at the Franklin D. Roosevelt Presidential Library, last modified 2011, http://www.fdrlibrary.marist.edu/daybyday/resource/july-1940/.

168 Eleanor took a shine to Lash: David Pitt, "Joseph P. Lash Is Dead; Reporter and Biographer," *New York Times*, August 23, 1987.

168 "When I was testifying": *American Experience*, "Eleanor Roosevelt," transcript, Joe Lash 1972 interview, https://www.pbs.org/wgbh/americanexperience/films/ eleanor/#transcript.

168 grew to twenty rooms: Goodwin, *No Ordinary Time*, 209.

168 "she feared she would dry up and die": Joseph Lash, *Eleanor Roosevelt: A Friend's Memoir* (Garden City, NY: Doubleday, 1964), 141, quoted in Goodwin, *No Ordinary Time*, 123.

169 "reunion always like a new discovery": Goodwin, *No Ordinary Time*, 421.

169 Lash was shipped overseas: Ibid.

169 "share your evening after the wedding": Ibid., 560.

11. THE 1950S

170 summoning her back to the White House: Trevor Hammond, "Death of FDR: April 12, 1945," *Fishwrap* (blog), Newspapers.com, April 1, 2016, https://blog .newspapers.com/death-of-fdr-april-12-1945/.

170 the charity musicale in progress: "Mrs. Roosevelt was attending a meeting of the Thrift Club near Dupont Circle when Stephen Early, the President's secretary, telephoned her to come to the White House as soon as possible," from Arthur Krock, "End Comes Suddenly at Warm Springs," *New York Times*, April 13, 1945, https:// archive.nytimes.com/www.nytimes.com/learning/general/onthisday/ big/0412.html. See also Phyllis Theroux, "Roosevelt Revised," *Washington Post*, January 31, 1982; and Steven Lomazow and Eric Fettmann, "As It Really Happened: April 12, 1945," *FDR's Deadly Secret* (blog), March 13, 2014, http:// fdrsdeadlysecret.blogspot.com/2014/03/how-it-really-happened-april-12th -1945.html.

170 "leaving before this delightful concert": Doris Kearns Goodwin, *No Ordinary Time: Franklin and Eleanor Roosevelt: The Home Front in World War II* (New York: Simon & Schuster, 1994), 693.

170 widows by the age of 70: Tamara Hareven and Peter Uhlenberg, "Transition to Widowhood and Family Support Systems in the Twentieth Century, Northeastern United States," in *Aging in the Past: Demography, Society, and Old Age*, eds. David Kertzer and Peter Laslett (Berkeley: Univ. of California Press, 1995), 275; and U.S. Census Bureau, "Characteristics by Age: Marital Status, Relationship, Education, and Citizenship, by States," *Sixteenth Census of the United States: 1940* (Washington, DC: U.S. Government Printing Office, 1943).

170 a diplomat who sent his condolences: The letter was to New Zealand's finance minister.

170 affair with Franklin had crushed Eleanor: Although the affair began in 1916, Eleanor Roosevelt did not discover it until 1918. Charles McGrath, "No End of the Affair," review of *Franklin & Lucy: President Roosevelt, Mrs. Rutherfurd and the Other Remarkable Women in His Life* by Joseph Persico, *New York Times*, Book Review, April 20, 2008.

170 Eleanor returned to Hyde Park: Joseph Lash, *Eleanor: The Years Alone* (New York: W. W. Norton, 1972), 1.

171 mainly there as The Widow: *American Experience*, "Eleanor Roosevelt," written and directed by Sue Williams, aired January 10, 2000, on PBS, transcript, Margaret Bruce interview, https://www.pbs.org/wgbh/americanexperience/films/elea nor/#transcript.

171 there would "never be another woman": *American Experience*, "Eleanor Roosevelt," transcript, https://www.pbs.org/wgbh/americanexperience/films/eleanor/ #transcript.

171 sent birthday and Christmas cards: Elizabeth Hanink, "Josephine Nesbit and the WWII Angels of Bataan: Fighting for Their Patients in the Filipino Jungle," Working Nurse, September 23, 2009, https://www.workingnurse.com/articles/ Josephine-Nesbit-and-the-WWII-Angels-of-Bataan.

171 number of working women: Mary Elizabeth Pidgeon, "Employment of Women in the Early Postwar Period: With Background of Prewar and War Data," *Women's Bureau Bulletin* 211 (Washington, DC: U.S. Government Printing Office, 1946), 2.

172 wanted to remain in the workforce: Ruth Milkman, "Women's Work and the Economic Crisis: Some Lessons of the Great Depression," *Review of Radical Political Economics* 8, no. 1 (April 1976): 88.

172 average female worker was in her 40s: Howard Fullerton Jr., "Labor Force Participation: 75 Years of Change, 1950–98 and 1998–2025," *Monthly Labor Review* 122, no. 12 (December 1999): 3–12; and Susan Ware, *Beyond Suffrage: Women in the New Deal* (Cambridge, MA: Harvard Univ. Press, 1981), 24.

172 "A girl who hasn't a man": Sidonie Gruenberg, "Why They Are Marrying Younger," *New York Times Magazine*, January 30, 1955.

172 just a little more than half: Andrew Cherlin, "The 50's Family and Today's," *New York Times*, November 18, 1981, 31.

173 a quarter of all families: Becky Nicolaides and Andrew Wiese, "Suburbanization in the United States after 1945," published online April 2017, in *Oxford Research Encyclopedias*, https://oxfordre.com/americanhistory/view/10.1093/acrefore/97 80199329175.001.0001/acrefore-9780199329175-e-64.

173 "We are usually not good": Eleanor Roosevelt, response to reader comment, If You Ask Me, *Ladies' Home Journal*, December 1946, 48.

173 "Susan's catalogue of grievances": Agnes Rogers, "My Mother Lives with Us," *Harper's*, November 1952, 34–39.

173 "in forgetting our elders": "Adding Life to Their Years," *Ladies' Home Journal*, October 1946, 6.

173 clubs where "oldsters" could get together: Margaret Hickey, "Elder-Agers—Recreation in Philadelphia—Longer and Happier Lives," *Ladies' Home Journal*, November 1948, 23, 241–44.

174 "assume that we are lonely": Hannah Trimble, "An Old Lady Refuses to be Aged," *New York Times*, November 12, 1950, 178.

174 speaker at the American Home Economics Association: Isabel LaFollette, "Making the Most of Our Maturity," *Journal of Home Economics* 48, no. 7 (September 1956): 513–16.

174 "indulgent to illness in the female": Alexander Simon, "Psychological Problems of Aging," *California Medicine* 75, no. 2 (August 1951): 73–80.

174 "Age is a matter of the mind": Eleanor Roosevelt, response to reader comment, If You Ask Me, *Ladies' Home Journal*, December 1947, 51.

174 "Business Now Holds Women": "Business Now Holds Women 'Old' at 35, Expert Says in Plea for a Liberal Policy," *New York Times*, April 11, 1950, 34.

175 "on the road toward a gerontomatriarchy": "U.S. Found on Way to Matriarchal Rule," *New York Times*, May 9, 1955, 48.

175 "cluttering up the continent": Catherine Drinker Bowen, "The Magnificence of Age," *Harper's*, April 1953, 58–62.

175 "a middle-aged puffin": Philip Wylie, *Generation of Vipers* (New York: Rinehart, 1942), 189.

175 "medicine's neglected stepchild": C. Lester Walker, "Arthritis: The Unseen Enemy," *Harper's*, April 1943, 473–78.

175 "the most chronic malady": "Fighting Arthritis," *New York Times*, October 23, 1958, 30.

175 "Today there is hope": "The No. 1 Crippler," *New York Times*, September 14, 1959, 28.

175 cortisone, a new medication: William L. Laurence, "Discovery of Cortisone-Yielding Plant Adds to the Great Advances Against Arthritis," *New York Times*, August 21, 1949, 7.

175 *"arthritis cases can be greatly helped":* Advertisement for Metropolitan Life Insurance Company, *Ladies' Home Journal*, November 1952, 72.

176 "walk, run and even dance": Laurence, "Discovery of Cortisone-Yielding Plant," *New York Times*.

176 red-hot mama: "Keep Women in Line with Geritol 1960 Iron Poor Blood," television advertisement for Geritol, Dailymotion video, 1:13, posted by "Kenney Olie," accessed March 20, 2019, https://www.dailymotion.com/video/x2soqeo.

176 injected female prison inmates: Waldemar Kaempffert, "Aging Processes Are Arrested by the Injection of Male and Female Sex Hormones," *New York Times*, August 30, 1953, 9.

177 "fulfilled their destiny as seed-pods": E. K. Shelton, "Hormone Advice Given; 50-and 60-Year-Old Women Encouraged on Use," *New York Times,* June 18, 1954, 16.

177 as a pill instead of an injection: Lois W. Banner, *In Full Flower: Aging Women, Power, and Sexuality* (New York: Alfred A. Knopf, 1992), 291ff.

177 her Estrogenic Hormone Cream: Helena Rubinstein, "How Women over 35 Can Look Younger; Your Skin Looks Young Again, a Thrilling Experience," *New York Times,* November 11, 1951, 29.

177 brought on castration anxiety: Banner, *In Full Flower,* 301ff.

177 prevention of nymphomania: Ibid., 300ff.

178 divided the vote . . . "worship of youth": Banner, *In Full Flower,* 40ff.

179 "I hate old-lady clothes": Karal Ann Marling, *As Seen on TV: The Visual Culture of Everyday Life in the 1950s* (Cambridge, MA: Harvard Univ. Press, 1994), 24, 26.

180 "give a lift to the fashion industry": "Taste in Garb Shown by Next First Lady," *New York Times,* November 12, 1952, 20.

180 regularly yell, "Where's Mamie?": Carl Sferrazza Anthony, *First Ladies: The Saga of the Presidents' Wives and Their Power, 1789–1961* (New York: Quill, 1990), 546–47.

180 her inaugural ball gown: Marling, *As Seen on TV,* 34–35.

180 Mamie figurines; "pretty neck": Ibid., 35–36.

180 frequently kissed and hugged: Anthony, *First Ladies,* 559.

180 a pink toilet seat: Ibid., 571.

180 political mini scandal in 1958: Ibid., 584–85.

181 "stay in bed until noon": Ibid., 551.

181 Mamie liked to play canasta: Ibid., 552–59.

181 appear on the cover of *Time:* Biography.com editors, "Elizabeth Arden Biography," Biography.com, April 2, 2014, https://www.biography.com/people/elizabeth-arden-9187777.

181 earned more money than any woman: Lindy Woodhead, *War Paint: Madame Helena Rubinstein and Miss Elizabeth Arden: Their Lives, Their Times, Their Rivalry* (Hoboken, NJ: John Wiley & Sons, 2003), 22.

182 "pass them on to Negroes everywhere": Mary McLeod Bethune, quoted by Kwekudee, "Mary MacLeod [*sic*] Bethune: The Only Black Woman Present at the Formation of United Nation and the Great African-American Educator of All Time," *Trip Down Memory Lane* (blog), September 15, 2012, http://kwekudee-tripdownmemorylane.blogspot.com/2012/09/mary-macleod-bethune-only-black-woman.html.

182 "messed with the wrong one now": Rosa Parks, *Rosa Parks: My Story* (New York: Puffin Books, 1999), 133.

183 "too much like my mother": Lynne Olson, *Freedom's Daughters: The Unsung Heroines of the Civil Rights Movement from 1830 to 1970* (New York: Scribner, 2001), 152.

183 "After all, who was I?": Barbara Ransby, *Ella Baker and the Black Freedom Movement: A Radical Democratic Vision* (Chapel Hill: Univ. of North Carolina Press, 2003), 173.

183 "women do not organize": David Porter, *Mary Norton of New Jersey, Congressional Trailblazer* (Madison, NJ: Fairleigh Dickinson Univ. Press, 2013), 178.

184 "a more entertaining companion": Ibid., 179.

184 Margaret Chase had grown up: Janann Sherman, *No Place for a Woman: A Life of Senator Margaret Chase Smith* (New Brunswick, NJ: Rutgers Univ. Press, 1999), 15–18.

185 Smith fathered a baby girl: Ellen Fitzpatrick, *The Highest Glass Ceiling: Women's Quest for the American Presidency* (Cambridge, MA: Harvard Univ. Press, 2016), 75.

185 "gave me many heartaches": Sherman, *No Place for a Woman*, 31.

185 apparently advanced syphilis: Ibid., 41.

185 replaced him in a special election: Ibid., 42–43.

185 a "question of sex": Fitzpatrick, *Highest Glass Ceiling*, 82.

186 monthly payments to the illegitimate daughter: Ibid., 86.

186 an after-dinner walk: Sherman, *No Place for a Woman*, 61.

186 "made more time for love": Ibid., 89.

186 muffin recipe: Teri Finneman, *Press Portrayals of Women Politicians, 1870s–2000s: From "Lunatic" Woodhull to "Polarizing" Palin* (Lanham, MD: Lexington Books, 2015), 106.

187 "don't know how she stays single": Ibid., 78.

187 she was definitely spunky: Ibid., 82.

187 "Declaration of Conscience": 87 Cong. Rec. S20,626 (Sept. 23, 1961) (statement of Sen. Smith).

187 succeeded in getting Smith thrown off: Lorraine Boissoneault, "The Senator Who Stood Up to Joseph McCarthy When No One Else Would," Smithsonian.com, September 13, 2018.

188 "I have not slackened my pace": Lash, *Eleanor: The Years Alone*, 238.

188 "changed during her years alone": "Mrs. R.," *Time*, April 7, 1952, as quoted in Lash, *Eleanor: The Years Alone*, 171, 360n14. She was 67 at the time of the interview.

189 "At 70"; "what I had to do": Lash, *Eleanor: The Years Alone*, 238, 239.

189 "Ack — regret no time": Ibid., 167.

189 deaf in her right ear: Ibid., 48.

189 "a good old-fashioned shake": Ibid., 329.

189 Adlai Stevenson: Ibid., 246.

189 went out alone after dark: Goodwin, *No Ordinary Time*, 71.

189 kept a picture of him; "platonic union": Ibid., 39, 41.

190 "I like young men": Anthony, *First Ladies*, 319.

12. THE 1960s

191 "cast off the black guard of defeatism": "Senior Citizens Get Advice on Fashions," *New York Times*, May 3, 1957.

192 "What would become of Gina": Karal Ann Marling, *As Seen on TV: The Visual Culture of Everyday Life in the 1950s* (Cambridge, MA: Harvard Univ. Press, 1994), 43.

192 A *Ladies' Home Journal* poll in 1962: Barbara Ehrenreich, Elizabeth Hess, and Gloria Jacobs, *Re-making Love: The Feminization of Sex* (New York: Anchor Books,

1986); and Ken Gelder and Sarah Thornton, eds., *The Subcultures Reader* (London: Routledge, 1997), 530.

192 Because of the low birth rate in the 1930s: "N.A.M. Forecasts Job Gain for Aging in Next 10 Years," *New York Times*, August 15, 1959.

192 The number of women 45 and older: "American Women: Report of the President's Commission on the Status of Women" (Washington, DC: U.S. Dept. of Labor, 1963), 66. Digital version available at Hathitrust.org.

192 "If your interviewer persists": Mabel Kingston Green, "When You're Job Hunting, Think Young," *Chicago Tribune*, May 31, 1964.

193 "The American Medical Assn. has estimated": Ray Kovitz, "Loneliness—the Aged's Reward," *Los Angeles Times*, April 16, 1961.

193 antibiotics and other "miracle" drugs: David Cutler and Ellen Meara, "Changes in the Age Distribution of Mortality over the Twentieth Century," NBER working paper 8556 (Cambridge, MA: National Bureau of Economic Research, October 2001), 13–14. Digital version available at NBER.org.

193 Smoking, which had been on the rise: Cutler and Meara, "Changes in the Age Distribution," 16–17.

193 The suicide rate among the elderly: Ibid., 20.

193 One *Chicago Tribune* columnist: Mary Merryfield, "Old Age Isn't that Bad!," *Chicago Tribune*, August 25, 1968.

194 "A woman of 83": Bernadine Bailey, "Around the World at 80," *New York Times*, October 14, 1956.

194 *Ebony* celebrated; "The oldsters": "Why Great-Grandma Dances," *Ebony*, March 1957, 55–57; and "Golden Age Club: Oldsters Visit Canada," *Ebony*, October 1, 1958, 104–6.

194 Dr. Joseph Peck: Dr. Joseph Peck, "Dr. Peck Tells How to Live After 65," *Chicago Tribune*, June 17, 1963.

194 "[s]he, however, can survive her boredom": Dr. Joseph Peck, "The Gals Have Retirement Woes, Too," *Chicago Tribune*, August 11, 1963.

194 Describing the way "an apparently healthy woman": Paul J. Poinsard, "Psychiatric Aspects of the Woman over Sixty-Five," *Clinical Obstetrics and Gynecology* 10, no. 3 (September 1967): 533, 535.

194 "You must be interested in your life": Anita Colby, "Be Your Age and Look Great," This Week, *Los Angeles Times*, February 4, 1962, 14.

194 At a symposium on "The Emotional Basis of Illness": "Balanced Woman Takes Menopause Calmly," *Daytona Beach Morning Journal*, May 23, 1968; and "Emotionally Balanced Women Take Menopause in Stride," *Hutchinson News*, May 10, 1968.

195 In 1961, Dagmar Wilson: Amy Swerdlow, *Women Strike for Peace: Traditional Motherhood and Radical Politics in the 1960s* (Chicago: Univ. of Chicago Press, 1993), 17.

195 "We wanted to look nice": Swerdlow, *Women Strike for Peace*, 73.

195 "As mothers, we cannot help but be": Dennis Hevesi, "Dagmar Wilson, Anti-Nuclear Leader, Dies at 94," *New York Times*, January 23, 2011.

196 "I arrived at one Fifth Avenue": Cora Weiss, interview by author, August 28, 2016.

196 their supporters filled the hearing room: Cora Weiss, "Remembering Dagmar Wilson," *The Nation,* January 28, 2011, 86.

196 "I had the opportunity not only to confront": Emma Brown, "Dagmar Wilson, Founder of Women's Peace Group, Dies at 94," *Washington Post,* January 23, 2011.

196 "Peace March Gals": Brown, "Dagmar Wilson"; and Russell Baker, "Peace March Gals Make Red Hunters Look Silly," *Pittsburgh Post-Gazette,* December 18, 1962.

197 George Dixon, a columnist: Quoted in Ellen Fitzpatrick, *The Highest Glass Ceiling: Women's Quest for the American Presidency* (Cambridge, MA: Harvard Univ. Press, 2016), 121.

197 "I am only thinking of": Ibid., 124.

197 Nellie Tayloe Ross: Ibid., 125.

197 She complained that "almost every news story": "66-Year-Old Sen. Smith Hits Age Talk," *Los Angeles Times,* February 7, 1964.

197 Smith announced she was running: Fitzpatrick, *Highest Glass Ceiling,* 130; and Ellen Fitzpatrick, "The Unfavored Daughter: When Margaret Chase Smith Ran in the New Hampshire Primary," Page-Turner, *The New Yorker* online, February 6, 2016.

198 Richard Wilson, a columnist: Richard Wilson, "Obstacles in Sen. Smith's Path," *Los Angeles Times,* February 4, 1964.

198 Smith attempted to relate: Janann Sherman, *No Place for a Woman: A Life of Senator Margaret Chase Smith* (New Brunswick, NJ: Rutgers Univ. Press, 1999), 186; and Cyndy Bittinger, "Madam President: The Struggle to Break the Last Glass Ceiling," *Vermont Woman,* November/December 2016.

199 She told her readers: Betty Friedan, *The Feminine Mystique* (New York: W. W. Norton, 2013), 420.

199 And Friedan did cannily note: Ibid., 411.

199 Back in the day, Friedan wrote: Ibid., 433.

199 "certain institutions concerned with the mentally retarded": Quoted in Stephanie Coontz, *A Strange Stirring: The Feminine Mystique and American Women at the Dawn of the 1960s* (New York: Basic Books, 2011), 33–34.

199 "They seem to get younger": Friedan, *Feminine Mystique,* 418.

200 "And now for the $64,000 question": Judith Hillman Paterson, *Be Somebody: A Biography of Marguerite Rawalt* (Austin, TX: Eakin Press, 1986), 122–23.

200 "the woman with the tight hairdo": Esther Peterson with Winifred Conkling, *Restless: The Memoirs of Labor and Consumer Activist Esther Peterson* (Washington, DC: Caring Publishing, 1995), 123.

200 "Men have to be reminded": Gail Collins, "Girls and Boys Together," *New York Times,* March 2, 2011.

201 Pauli Murray said her own work was: Pauli Murray, *Pauli Murray: The Autobiography of a Black Activist, Feminist, Lawyer, Priest, and Poet* (Knoxville: Univ. of Tennessee Press, 1989), 351.

201 Eleanor spent her last years: Edna P. Gurewitsch, *Kindred Souls: The Friendship of Eleanor Roosevelt and David Gurewitsch* (New York: St. Martin's Press, 2002), 186–87.

202 working with the Commission on the Status of Women: Lynne Olson, *Freedom's Daughters: The Unsung Heroines of the Civil Rights Movement from 1830 to 1970* (New York: Scribner, 2001), 194.

202 "Marie has left bread": Gurewitsch, *Kindred Souls*, 196.

202 But her niece remembered: *American Experience*, "Eleanor Roosevelt," written and directed by Sue Williams, aired January 10, 2000, on PBS, transcript, https://www.pbs.org/wgbh/americanexperience/films/eleanor/#transcript.

203 "I seem to lose myself": Paterson, *Be Somebody*, 152.

203 "an airline or a whorehouse?": "Griffiths, Martha Wright," History, Art & Archives online project, United States House of Representatives, accessed June 23, 2019, https://history.house.gov/people/Detail/14160.

203 Two years after that law: Marie Smith, "HEW 'Age Limit' Under Fire," *Washington Post*, March 4, 1969.

203 When age came up: Sabrina F. Crocette, "Considering Hybrid Sex and Age Discrimination Claims by Women: Examining Approaches to Pleading and Analysis—A Pragmatic Model," *Golden Gate University Law Review* 28, no. 2 (January 1998): 115–75.

203 Decades later, women would still: Mary Ann Crawford v. Medina General Hospital, Darla Kermendy, Kenneth Milligan, and Rex Slee, 96 F.3d 830 (6th Cir. 1996).

204 She would say later that she sympathized: Katherine A. Towle, interview by Harriet Nathan, Online Archive of California, University History Series, Administration and Leadership (1967), https://oac.cdlib.org/view?docId=kt0000000gm&brand=oac4&doc.view=entire_text.

204 Jack Weinberg, an environmental activist: Paul Galloway, "Radical Redux," *Chicago Tribune*, November 16, 1990.

204 Aptheker has a vivid memory: Bettina Aptheker, interview by author, August 29, 2016.

204 fond memories of: Ibid.

205 Emily Taylor, the 49-year-old: Kelly C. Sartorius, *Deans of Women and the Feminist Movement: Emily Taylor's Activism*, Historical Studies in Education (New York: Palgrave Macmillan, 2014), 166.

205 "Hippie women over thirty": Rosalyn Baxandall and Linda Gordon, eds., *Dear Sisters: Dispatches from the Women's Liberation Movement* (New York: Basic Books, 2000), 225.

205 "A world like this deserves contempt": M. A. Farber, "High School Graduates Express Disenchantment," *New York Times*, June 28, 1968.

205 in the words of Hillary Rodham: Katie Reilly, "Read Hillary Clinton's 1969 Wellesley Commencement Speech," *Time*, June 7, 2016.

206 "What we found": Swerdlow, *Women Strike for Peace*, 140.

206 "liberal mother-daughter conflict": Swerdlow, *Women Strike for Peace*, 139.

207 "Women's Lib girls": "Leading Feminist Puts Hairdo Before Strike," *New York Times*, August 27, 1970.

207 When Friedan wound up: Rachel Blau DuPlessis and Ann Snitow, eds., *The Feminist Memoir Project: Voices from Women's Liberation* (New Brunswick, NJ: Rutgers Univ. Press, 2007), 105.

207 "She misrepresents the case for feminism": Paul Wilkes, "Mother Superior to Women's Lib," *New York Times Magazine*, November 29, 1970, 150.

207 Later she would recant: "Feminist Pioneer Betty Friedan Dies at 85," Obituaries, National Public Radio, February 4, 2006.

208 "Feminists all over the country": Gwen Gibson, "Liberation Does an About-Face," *Los Angeles Times*, May 6, 1979.

208 NOW co-founder Muriel Fox: Martha Weinman Lear, "The Second Feminist Wave," *New York Times Magazine,* March 10, 1968, 24.

208 *Ebony* contended: "Five Plans for Retirement," *Ebony* 13, June 1958, 50–56.

208 *Chicago Daily Defender:* F. L. B., "This Is Life: Old Woman," *Chicago Daily Defender,* March 3, 1960, A13.

209 "Lord have mercy!...I did worry": Elizabeth Hayes Patterson, interview by Sala Elise Patterson, January 12, 2017.

209 Septuagenarian Florence Price: Ayana D. Byrd and Lori L. Tharps, *Hair Story: Untangling the Roots of Black Hair in America* (New York: St. Martin's Press, 2001), 61.

209 "Around 1965 there began": Joanne Grant, *Ella Baker: Freedom Bound* (Hoboken, NJ: John Wiley & Sons, 1998), 229.

210 "our Gandhi": Gail Collins, *When Everything Changed: The Amazing Journey of American Women from 1960 to the Present* (New York: Little, Brown, 2009), 121.

210 One former SNCC member: Charles Payne, *I've Got the Light of Freedom: The Organizing Tradition and the Mississippi Freedom Struggle* (Berkeley: Univ. of California Press, 1995), 97.

210 Baker was, Nash recalled: Barbara Ransby, *Ella Baker and the Black Freedom Movement: A Radical Democratic Vision* (Chapel Hill: Univ. of North Carolina Press, 2003), 259.

210 he denied the quote: Ibid., 310.

210 To make the chasm clear: Diane White, "Liberation Movement Building in Strength," *Boston Sunday Globe,* February 22, 1970.

211 "the newest glamour girl": Helen Gurley Brown, *Sex and the Single Girl* (New York: Bernard Geis Associates, 1962), 5.

211 Marriage, she decreed: Ibid., 4.

211 Brown herself had married: Collins, *When Everything Changed,* 156; and Harriet Sigerman, ed., *The Columbia Documentary History of American Women Since 1941* (New York: Columbia Univ. Press, 2003), 171.

211 She told one associate: Gerri Hirshey, *Not Pretty Enough: The Unlikely Triumph of Helen Gurley Brown* (New York: Farrar, Straus and Giroux, 2016), 279.

211 "She looked at me very strangely": Ibid., 262.

212 "my girls": Ibid., 276.

212 Neugarten, one of the nation's foremost: Ruth Moss, "Dispelling Fears of the Menopause," *Chicago Tribune,* March 4, 1970.

213 Robert Wilson, a New York gynecologist: "Damaging News for Hormone Therapy," National Public Radio, August 8, 2002.

213 "It shows how women": Nancy Sommers and James Ridgeway, "Can a Woman Be Feminine Forever?," *New Republic* 154, no. 12, March 1966, 15.

213 "gynecologist on the staff": Faye Marley, "Sex and the Older Woman," *Science News,* April 29, 1967, 413.

213 Ayerst Laboratories produced a film: Joe Neel, "Damaging News for Hormone Therapy," *All Things Considered,* National Public Radio, August 8, 2002, accessed May 12, 2019, https://www.npr.org/news/specials/hrt/. The film was called *Physiologic and Emotional Basis of Menopause,* notes Neel, in a segment subtitled "The Marketing of Menopause: Historically, Hormone Therapy Heavy on Promotion, Light on Science—Popularizing Estrogen."

213 "castrates": Robert Wilson, *Feminine Forever* (New York: M. Evans & Co., 1966), 18.

214 had once been visited: Robert Bazell, "The Cruel Irony of Trying to Be 'Feminine Forever,'" NBCNews.com, January 2, 2007.

214 "Since recent medical progress": Robert Wilson, "Which Hormones to Take When," *Vogue*, June 1966.

214 He provided charts to illustrate: Ibid.

214 *New Republic* would obtain: Judith A. Houck, *Hot and Bothered: Women, Medicine, and Menopause in Modern America* (Cambridge, MA: Harvard Univ. Press, 2006), 155.

214 Wilson's son eventually said: Gina Kolata with Melody Petersen, "Hormone Replacement Study a Shock to the Medical System," *New York Times*, July 10, 2002.

214 Her long-suffering personal secretary: Lindy Woodhead, *War Paint: Madame Helena Rubinstein and Miss Elizabeth Arden — Their Lives, Their Times, Their Rivalry* (Hoboken, NJ: John Wiley & Sons, 2003), 402.

214 weathered a break-in: Ibid., 404–5.

215 When Rubinstein died: Ibid., 406.

215 eight years younger: This presupposes that we are using the most reliable birth dates we have for each of the women: Rubinstein, December 25, 1872; Arden, January 31, 1881 (for Arden: Woodhead, *War Paint*, citing "birth records and census data on file in Thunder Bay, Ontario"). Arden's *New York Times* obituary gives the date offered by a company spokesman, December 31, 1884: "Elizabeth Arden Is Dead at 81; Made Beauty a Global Business," *New York Times*, October 19, 1966.

215 "Death...was a subject Miss Arden": Woodhead, *War Paint*, 362.

215 real estate shopping in Ireland: Ibid., 390.

215 "There's no middle age anymore": Karen Peterson, "Growing Old with the Youth Cult," *Chicago Tribune Magazine*, May 14, 1967, 14.

215 According to an ad in *Vogue*: Advertisement for Youth Cosmetics cream, *Vogue*, March 1967.

215 "Plastic surgery is admittedly": Quoted in Hirshey, *Not Pretty Enough*, 200.

215 Her husband declared: Hirshey, *Not Pretty Enough*, 386.

216 "[S]omeday women and men will enter": Dr. T. R. Van Dellen, "Aids for Aging Skin," *Chicago Tribune*, April 12, 1969.

216 "Twenty years ago women started": Mary Lou Loper, "Splashing in the Fountain of Youth," *Los Angeles Times*, March 28, 1968.

216 "My hair's gray": Advertisement for Come Alive Gray rinse, *New York Times*, April 8, 1962.

216 "The crucial question": Marylin Bender, "Beautiful Women Prove Gray Hair Can Be Chic," *New York Times*, December 13, 1963.

216 "A feeling of smugness": Bender, "Beautiful Women."

217 Shirley Polykoff: Robert McG. Thomas Jr., "Shirley Polykoff, 90, Ad Writer Whose Query Colored a Nation," *New York Times*, June 8, 1998.

217 When the '60s began: Victoria Sherrow, *Encyclopedia of Hair: A Cultural History* (Westport, CT: Greenwood Press, 2006), 159.

217 "This historian observed": David Hackett Fischer, *Growing Old in America* (New York: Oxford Univ. Press, 1977), 132–33.

217 "It's not really what you'd call a figure": Giselle Benatar, "Skinny Supermodel," *Entertainment Weekly* (EW.com), March 19, 1993.

217 "Skinny is sacred": "Helen Gurley Brown," Obituaries, *The Telegraph*, August 14, 2012.

218 "dressed up to go to the store": Robert Klara, "How Clairol Went from Taboo to New You," *Adweek*, February 28, 2013.

218 "To sum up": Giuseppe Cardinal Siri, "Notification Concerning Men's Dress Worn by Women," June 12, 1960.

218 Levi's discovered: "Concern Unveils Levi's Made Just for Women," *Wall Street Journal*, January 3, 1968.

218 In 1969, she became: Nancy L. Ross, "Rep. Reid in a Pantsuit," *Washington Post*, December 24, 1969.

219 "Mother of three—10, 11 & 15": Keith Uhlich, "Behind Hollywood's Biggest Feud," BBC.com, March 6, 2017.

219 It was, she claimed later, a joke: Sheila O'Malley, "'Feud: Bette and Joan' Episode 4 Recap: Aftermath," *New York Times*, March 26, 2017.

13. THE 1970S

221 Geritol, which had faded a bit: "I Think I'll Keep Her," YouTube video, 0:29, posted by "Michael Chiu," June 3, 2017, https://www.youtube.com/watch?v =_lNfpQ_8tEw.

221 It may have been a comfort: Caryl Rivers, "Why Can't Hollywood See That 35 Is Beautiful, Too?," *New York Times*, April 1, 1973, https://timesmachine.nytimes .com/timesmachine/1973/04/01/97123306.pdf.

221 Garry Trudeau's popular *Doonesbury:* Garry Trudeau, *Doonesbury,* September 12, 1972, GoComics online catalogue, https://www.gocomics.com/doonesbury/ 1972/09/12.

222 She got so many letters: Chris Lamb, *Drawn to Extremes: The Use and Abuse of Editorial Cartoons* (New York: Columbia Univ. Press, 2004), 37.

222 "And they put a mortarboard": "Trudeau Reflects on Four Decades of 'Doonesbury,'" *Morning Edition*, National Public Radio, October 26, 2010.

222 Her grandson Joseph Reckford remembers: Joseph Reckford, interview by author, October 25, 2016. All further quotations from Reckford in this chapter come from this conversation.

223 A reformed cigarette chain-smoker: Amy Schapiro, *Millicent Fenwick: Her Way* (New Brunswick, NJ: Rutgers Univ. Press, 2003), 124.

223 Fenwick said later that she might have complied: Ibid., 136.

223 During the race, her driver-assistant: Ibid., 139.

223 "I'd be glad to stay": Ibid., 141.

223 Her election was described: "Fenwick, Millicent Hammond," History, Art & Archives online project, United States House of Representatives, accessed May 15, 2019,

https://history.house.gov/People/Listing/F/FENWICK,-Millicent-Hammond -(F000078)/.

224 Early on, Fenwick found the idea: Schapiro, *Millicent Fenwick*, 189.

224 She had an impressive attendance: Ibid., 191.

224 "I always like style": Ibid., 154.

225 They got into an intense fight: Ibid., 155.

225 seemed to feel a black man deserved to be first: Jackson Landers, "'Unbought and Unbossed': When a Black Woman Ran for the White House," *Smithsonian*, April 25, 2016, quoting attorney Robert Gottlieb, at 21 her student campaign coordinator. See also Barbara Winslow, *Shirley Chisholm: Catalyst for Change*, Lives of American Women series, ed. Carol Berkin (New York: Westview Press/Perseus Books Group, 2014), 110.

225 "far more discrimination being a woman than being black": Walter Ray Watson, "A Look Back on Shirley Chisholm's Historic 1968 House Victory," from *1968: How We Got Here*, Special Series, *Morning Edition*, National Public Radio, November 6, 2018, quoting a February 20, 2003, conversation between Chisholm and Tavis Smiley.

225 a leader in organizing a congresswomen's caucus: Gerrie Schipske, "The End of the Beginning," *Washington Post*, September 30, 2016. Holtzman, Chisholm, and Barbara Mikulski were the others.

226 Bill Lewis, her companion: Janann Sherman, *No Place for a Woman: A Life of Senator Margaret Chase Smith* (New Brunswick, NJ: Rutgers Univ. Press, 1999), 213–14.

226 Lewis did recover: Ibid., 213–14.

226 "In polite society": Berkeley Rice, "Is the Great Lady from Maine Out of Touch?," *New York Times*, June 11, 1972.

226 Lewis read her brief concession: Sherman, *No Place for a Woman*, 218.

226 The president of the Maine chapter: Susan J. Carroll, ed., *The Impact of Women in Public Office* (Bloomington: Indiana Univ. Press, 2001), 111.

226 "Here I was": Sherman, *No Place for a Woman*, 216.

227 Paul, who had undergone: Susan Brownmiller, *In Our Time: Memoir of a Revolution* (New York: Dial Press, 1999), 55.

227 "a few people came over": Jeannette Smyth, "A Day for Celebration: Scene," *Washington Post*, March 4, 1972.

228 "tired, preoccupied domestic servants": Andrea Dworkin, *Right Wing Women* (New York: TarcherPerigee, 1983), 15.

228 The 1970s was the decade when: "Divorce Epidemic," editorial, *New York Times*, June 15, 1976.

228 In 1983, the federal government: National Center for Health Statistics, *Monthly Vital Statistics Report* 32, no. 3, suppl. (June 27, 1983).

228 Phyllis Schlafly, the leading force: Phyllis Schlafly, *The Power of the Positive Woman* (New York: Arlington House, 1977), 27.

228 The Hays story became even more: Marion Clark and Rudy Maxa, "Closed Session Romance on the Hill," *Washington Post*, May 23, 1976.

228 "I can't type": Ibid.

229   It had never really existed: Laurie Shields, *Displaced Homemakers: Organizing for a New Life* (New York: McGraw-Hill, 1981), 15; and Lenore J. Weitzman and Ruth B. Dixon, "The Alimony Myth: Does No-Fault Divorce Make a Difference?," *Family Law Quarterly* 14, no. 3 (Fall 1980): 141–85.

229   about 14 percent of wives: Shields, *Displaced Homemakers*, 15.

229   "We're a minority": Glenda Daniel, "Putting 'Little Old Ladies' Back on the Job," *Chicago Tribune*, January 21, 1976.

229   "If a town had a lunch program": Ron Wyden, interview by author, August 23, 2018. All further comments from Wyden in this chapter come from this interview.

230   Tish Sommers, an organizer for NOW: Patricia Huckle, *Tish Sommers, Activist: And the Founding of the Older Women's League* (Knoxville: Univ. of Tennessee Press, 1991), 191.

230   She'd been a dancer: Ibid., 88–89.

230   once had an affair: Ibid., 86.

230   They divorced: Ibid., 167.

230   In 1976, *Ladies' Home Journal:* Cynthia Gorney, "The Discarding of Mrs. Hill," *Ladies' Home Journal* 93, February 1976, 58–64.

231   Age, Kuhn argued: Roger Sanjek, *Gray Panthers* (Philadelphia: Univ. of Pennsylvania Press, 2009), 101–2.

232   For the first time more than half: "Women at Work: A Visual Essay," *Monthly Labor Review* 126, no. 10 (October 2003): 45–50.

232   *Los Angeles Times* reported: Mary Barber, "Women's Clubs: Some Beginning to Show Age," *Los Angeles Times*, October 6, 1974.

232   "I came out in 1976": Tita Caldwell, "Age Limit for OLOC," Old Lesbians Organizing for Change, June 2009, http://www.oloc.org/about/articles/TitaWhyOld.pdf.

233   when Audrey's neighbors: "SAGE in the Beginning," SAGEUSA.org, posted May 21, 2018, https://www.sageusa.org/sage-in-the-beginning/.

233   In March of 1974: "Gloria Steinem: First Feminist," interview by Susan Dominus, *New York*, April 6, 1998, accessed March 28, 2019, http://nymag.com/nymetro/news/people/features/2438/.

234   "We've been ignored so long": Judy Klemesrud, " 'If Your Face Isn't Young': Women Confront Problems of Aging," *New York Times*, October 10, 1980.

234   Sheehy told her readers: Gail Sheehy, *Passages: Predictable Crises of Adult Life*, 30th anniversary ed. (New York: Ballantine, 2006), 407.

234   Susan Sontag wrote a diatribe: Susan Sontag, "The Double Standard of Aging," *Saturday Review*, September 23, 1972, 29–38.

234   rocking, with a white cap: Klemesrud, " 'If Your Face Isn't Young.' "

235   but 16 percent of the marriages: Lois W. Banner, *In Full Flower: Aging Women, Power, and Sexuality* (New York: Alfred A. Knopf, 1992), 330.

235   "They're finding, like men": Helen Van Slyke, "Older Women, Younger Men— Why Not?," *Saturday Evening Post*, vol. 247, no. 5, July/August 1975, 16.

235   there were 2,000 American women over 55: Ibid.

235   "the next tee": Ibid., 101.

236   "Never before": Sandra Pesmen, "Being a Mother to Your Parents," *Los Angeles Times*, October 19, 1977.

236 "If we don't do something now": Nancy Baltad, "Who Gives a Hoot About Older Women? The OWLs!," *Los Angeles Times,* October 9, 1977.

237 Maggie Kuhn: Judy Klemesrud, "Gray Panther Founder and a Family of Choice," *New York Times,* June 22, 1981.

237 The vast majority of nursing home residents: John Gorman, " 'There Is No Pressure to Treat the Old People Better,' " *Chicago Tribune,* September 25, 1978.

238 By the 1970s there were 23,000: Walter Rugaber, "Senate Unit Finds Bigotry on Aged," *New York Times,* December 17, 1974.

238 A *Chicago Tribune* investigation: Ellen Soeteber, "Nursing Home Horror," *Chicago Tribune,* October 19, 1975.

238 One Senate subcommittee: Linda Charlton, "Misuse of Drugs Reported in Nation's Nursing Homes," *New York Times,* January 17, 1975.

238 Another subcommittee reported: Ray Moseley, "The Nursing Homes: 'A Place to Wait for the End,' " *Chicago Tribune,* September 25, 1978.

238 four-year national study: Hugh J. Parry, "Use of Psychotropic Drugs by U.S. Adults," *Public Health Reports* 83, no. 10 (October 1968): 799–810.

238 By the '70s, one in five American women: David T. Courtwright, *Dark Paradise: A History of Opiate Addiction in America* (Cambridge, MA: Harvard Univ. Press, 2001), 146–47, citing Richard Hughes and Robert Brewin, *The Tranquilizing of America: Pill Popping and the American Way of Life* (New York: Harcourt Brace Jovanovich, 1979), 62–66, 191–210.

239 "Where they wouldn't": Andrea Tone, *The Age of Anxiety: A History of America's Turbulent Affair with Tranquilizers* (New York: Basic Books, 2009), 45.

239 "What the world really needs": Ibid., 52.

239 comedian Milton Berle: Ibid., 64.

239 A 1957 time capsule: Ibid., 103.

239 "problem that has no name": Quoted in Tone, *Age of Anxiety,* 178.

239 newspapers and magazines in the early 1970s: "Housewife Is a Junkie," *Atlanta Journal and Constitution,* May 10, 1970.

239 one such ad recommended: Morton Mintz, "These Doctors Were in Bad Moods Because Too Many Housewives, in Bad Moods, Listen to Too Much Drug Advertising," *Washington Post,* July 24, 1971.

239 An ad for a tranquilizer-antidepressant: Jean Dietz, "Women and Drug Ads," *Boston Sunday Globe,* August 5, 1973.

240 "When they told me I had to be operated on": Marjorie Hunter, "A Fresh Start and No Tears for Betty Ford," *New York Times,* January 25, 1977.

241 "Some people didn't even tell": Quoted in Schapiro, *Millicent Fenwick,* 94.

241 Breast cancer was a major cause: "New Attitudes Ushered in by Betty Ford," *New York Times,* October 17, 1987.

241 "There had been so much cover-up": "Betty Ford Today: Still Speaking Out," interview by Gloria Steinem, *Ms.,* April 1984, 41; and Nancy Gibbs, "Betty Ford, 1918–2011," *Time,* July 8, 2011, accessed March 28, 2019, http://content.time.com/time/nation/article/0,8599,2082229,00.html.

241 "I'm sure I've saved at least": "Breast Cancer: Fear and Facts," *Time,* November 4, 1974.

241 In part because detections: Stephanie E. King and David Schottenfeld, "The 'Epidemic' of Breast Cancer in the U.S.—Determining the Factors," *Oncology* 10, no. 4 (April 1996): 453–72.

241 Like Ford, Black was: Judy Klemesrud, "New Voice in Debate on Breast Surgery," *New York Times*, December 12, 1972.

241 "The doctor will make the incision": Lynne Olson, *Freedom's Daughters: The Unsung Heroines of the Civil Rights Movement from 1830 to 1970* (New York: Scribner, 2001), 127.

242 As Ford's daughter Susan observed: John Robert Greene, *Betty Ford: Candor and Courage in the White House*, Modern First Ladies (Lawrence: Univ. Press of Kansas, 2004), 50.

242 In 1972, the *New York Times* profiled: Klemesrud, "New Voice."

242 She told the press that she'd heard: Hunter, "A Fresh Start."

242 Nancy Brinker, who founded: Nicole C. Brambila, "Cancer Fight Eased National Stigma," *Desert Sun*, July 9, 2011, 62.

242 fell in love: Greene, *Betty Ford*, 18.

243 When Jerry Ford became president: Ibid., 29.

243 Betty was quietly in treatment: Ibid., 32.

243 "You just cost me 10 million votes"; the White House was deluged with: Ibid., 78–79.

243 In 1969, 68 percent of Americans: Elaine Tyler May, *Homeward Bound: American Families in the Cold War Era* (New York: Basic Books, 1988), 198–99.

243 "No woman can be her glowing best": Catherine Lanham Miller, "What? At My Age?," *Harper's Bazaar*, March 1970, 182–83.

244 When she told a Washington columnist: Gibbs, "Betty Ford."

244 She pushed her unsuspecting: Caitlin Johnson, "Ford Photographer Remembers His Friend," CBSNews.com, January 2, 2007.

244 Susan and a friend: Greene, *Betty Ford*, 86–87.

244 The president had lost his voice: Greene, *Betty Ford*, 99.

244 She was supposed to be writing her memoirs: Greene, *Betty Ford*, 102.

244 "The reverberations from her latest": Ronald Kotulak, "Betty Ford Beacon to Drinking Women," *Chicago Tribune*, May 28, 1978.

245 Experts said the number of women: Judy Klemesrud, "Helping Troubled Women in an Era of Change," *New York Times*, May 21, 1979.

245 a few years later she was honored: "Betty Ford's 'Awakening,'" *St. Louis Post-Dispatch*, May 6, 1987.

245 One writer described: Miller, "What? At My Age?"

245 Margaret Chase Smith tried that method: Sherman, *No Place for a Woman*, 208–13.

246 There would be between 20,000: Harry Schwartz, "Arthritis: Surgery for a Crippling Disease," *New York Times*, June 11, 1972.

246 "Four weeks ago an elderly": Schwartz, "Arthritis."

246 "It is a gradual process": Advertisement for Zeigler Facial Care, *Harper's Bazaar*, April 1970, 185.

246 "The brilliance of intellect": Bettie Wysor, "Cosmetic Surgery," *Harper's Bazaar*, July 1970, 94–95.

247 "Isn't it wonderful?": Greene, *Betty Ford*, 107.

247 A lot of male politicians: Ibid.

247 "Hypnotize yourself into thinking": Miller, "What? At My Age?"

247 In another very different article: "Twenty Years of Looking Thirty," *Harper's Bazaar*, April 1971, 67.

247 When asked why she was starring: Marybeth Hamilton, *The Queen of Camp: Mae West, Sex, and Popular Culture* (London: Pandora, 1996), 207.

247 "One eye sometimes sags": Vincent Canby, "Mae West, 87, Does an Encore: Trying for 6th Marriage," *New York Times*, June 8, 1979.

247 one Chicago reviewer: Jonathan Rosenbaum, "Sextette," *Chicago Reader*, September 29, 1988.

248 When she died, in 1980: Ted O. Thackrey and Kevin Thomas, "Mae West, Epitome of Witty Sexuality, Dies," *Los Angeles Times*, November 23, 1980.

249 *The Mary Tyler Moore Show* first arrived: Jennifer Keishin Armstrong, *Mary and Lou and Rhoda and Ted: And All the Brilliant Minds Who Made* The Mary Tyler Moore Show *a Classic* (New York: Simon & Schuster, 2013), 148.

249 "the Joan of Arc": Ibid., 175.

249 In a *New York Times* essay: Rivers, "Why Can't Hollywood See."

250 In 1972, a reader wrote: Thomas Collins, "Woman Dislikes New Pantsuits," *Hartford Courant*, November 27, 1972.

250 "I'm 45, and I've been working too long": Julie Hatfield, "Who'll Wear the Pants at the Office?," *Boston Globe*, September 8, 1988.

250 Older women were showing up: Bernadine Morris, "Pants: They're Going to Any Lengths," *New York Times*, November 26, 1975.

251 Jack Winter: Leonard Sloane, "Advertising: Pants (Girls') in the Office," *New York Times*, August 10, 1971.

251 "The beginning of the new spirit": Margie Albert, "Something New in the Women's Movement," *New York Times*, December 12, 1973.

251 In 1973, at a bill signing: Erving Goffman, *Forms of Talk* (Philadelphia: Univ. of Pennsylvania Press, 1981), 125.

251 a few weeks later, the White House: "White House Lifts Ban on Women in Pants," *New York Times*, November 26, 1973.

251 "In the past, women after 25": Lance Morrow, "In Praise of Older Women," *Time*, April 24, 1978.

252 It was a good day, and Ford: Sanjek, *Gray Panthers*, 53, 55; and Maggie Kuhn with Christina Long and Laura Quinn, *No Stone Unturned: The Life and Times of Maggie Kuhn* (New York: Ballantine, 1991), 140–41.

252 "Twelve of us—I almost said girls": Gerri Hirshey, *Not Pretty Enough: The Unlikely Triumph of Helen Gurley Brown* (New York: Farrar, Straus and Giroux, 2016), 317.

252 During the student occupation of a building: Jerry L. Avorn, *Up Against the Ivy Wall: A History of the Columbia Crisis* (New York: Atheneum, 1969), 130; and Clara Bingham, "'The Whole World Is Watching': An Oral History of the 1968 Columbia Uprising," *Vanity Fair*, March 26, 2018, 118–27, 130–31.

252 Madeleine Kunin, a state legislator: Madeleine M. Kunin, *Living a Political Life: One of America's First Woman Governors Tells Her Story* (New York: Alfred A. Knopf, 1994), 182.

253 The *Chicago Tribune*'s positive report: "'Tough Old Gal' Rose Kennedy OK After Surgery," *Chicago Tribune*, September 27, 1979.

253 A *Los Angeles Times* celebration: Tom Gorman, "Postscript: Reflections on Being a College Queen at 72," *Los Angeles Times*, March 12, 1979, 17.

253 *Washington Post* editor Ben Bradlee: "The Press: Grandmothers Die Hard," *Time*, August 24, 1970, accessed March 28, 2019, http://content.time.com/time/magazine/article/0,9171,902664,00.html.

253 "grandmother making her first bid": Robert Pisor, "Romney Victory Narrow: Candidate Must Now Win Conservatives," *Washington Post*, August 6, 1970.

14. THE 1980S

254 She arrived at the Waldorf-Astoria: Georgia Dullea, "Birthday Celebration: Gloria Steinem at 50," *New York Times*, May 24, 1984.

255 In 1986, *Newsweek:* Eloise Salholz with Renee Michael, Mark Starr, Shawn Doherty, Pamela Abramson, and Pat Wingert, "Too Late for Prince Charming?," *Newsweek*, June 2, 1986.

255 even less promising: Ibid. According to *Newsweek*, "Black women face an even larger gap, since there are far fewer black, college-educated males than females."

255 *Newsweek* eventually retracted it: "Marriage by the Numbers," *Newsweek*, June 4, 2006.

255 In Nora Ephron's *Sleepless in Seattle:* Megan Garber, "When *Newsweek* 'Struck Terror in the Hearts of Single Women,'" *The Atlantic*, June 2, 2016.

255 Tish Sommers frequently pointed out: Judy Klemesrud, "Conference on Aging Views Older Women," *New York Times*, December 1, 1981.

255 Multigenerational families — home to a quarter of Americans: Pew Research Center, "The Return of the Multi-Generational Family Household," March 18, 2010.

255 Betty Friedan couldn't understand: Betty Friedan, *The Fountain of Age* (New York: Simon & Schuster, 1993), 59.

255 Charles Longino, a director of social research: Fred Ferretti, "Elderly Choose Retirement Community Living," *New York Times*, April 5, 1984.

256 "Older people who live in communities": Tamar Lewin, "Children as Neighbors? Elderly Are Worried," *New York Times*, November 28, 1989.

256 To make it clear they meant business: Marc Lacey, "Retirement Haven Hunts Youthful Violators," *New York Times*, August 28, 2010.

256 In 1980, the Census Bureau counted: Robert Lindsey, "A Premium on Men in Retirement Life," *New York Times*, June 18, 1981.

257 "Twenty years ago, 'midlife crisis'": Roberta Grant, "Women and the New Midlife Crisis," *Ladies' Home Journal*, August 1987, 87.

258 When Jane Fonda, who was one of: Patricia Bosworth, *Jane Fonda: The Private Life of a Public Woman* (New York: Houghton Mifflin Harcourt, 2011), 505.

258 Fonda flew to Milan: Ibid., 506.

258 Fonda married Turner in December: Ibid., 512.

258 "I'm getting lines and gray hairs": Ibid., 484.

258 She published a famous workout book: Ibid., 478.

258 That was followed by the release of: Ibid., 477, 479.

258 and the creation of a workout empire: Ibid., 479.

259 Fonda theorized in her autobiography: Jane Fonda, *My Life So Far* (New York: Random House, 2005), 419–20.

259 "I went out and I bought all these other tapes": Debbie Reynolds, *Do It Debbie's Way*, video clip, 3:36, in Lauren Wiegle, "Richard Hamlett, Debbie Reynolds' Third Ex-Husband: 5 Fast Facts You Need to Know," Heavy.com, December 28, 2016.

259 Besides the exercises, it included: Andy Wickstrom, "'Angela Lansbury's Positive Moves,'" *Boston Globe*, November 13, 1988.

260 The *Chicago Tribune* described Letney as: Bob Greene, "Pat Boone Works Out for the Mellow Set," *Chicago Tribune*, September 14, 1986.

260 The scriptwriter, Joe Eszterhas: Bosworth, *Jane Fonda*, 489.

260 "After that, we were able to send": Garin Pirnia, "13 Enchanting Facts About *Moonstruck*," Mental Floss, December 16, 2017.

260 "I've had my day": Homer Dickens, *The Films of Katharine Hepburn*, revised and updated by Lawrence J. Quirk (New York: Citadel Press, 1990; first published 1971 by Carol Publishing Group [New York]), 31.

262 "The networks seem to be chasing": Bernard Weinraub, "Angela Lansbury Has a Hit. She Wants Respect," *New York Times*, December 1, 1991.

262 "Shows that can generate heat": Ibid.

262 "I was as shocked as everybody else": Samantha Miller, "Legend of the Fall," *People*, February 7, 2000.

262 In 1981, Christine Craft, the 36-year-old: Sue Ellen Jares, "TV Anchor Christine Craft Was Dropped for Not Being Just Another Pretty Face," *People*, November 15, 1982; and Frank Prial, "Christine Craft: Reporter or Symbol or Both?," *New York Times*, September 7, 1983.

263 "too old, too unattractive": Jares, "TV Anchor Christine Craft."

263 A *New York Times* editorial noted: "'Is She a Mutt?,'" editorial, *New York Times*, August 11, 1983.

263 Claims that good-looking women: Sally Bedell Smith, "TV Newswoman's Suit Stirs Debate on Values in Hiring," *New York Times*, August 6, 1983.

263 There were approximately 1,200: Patti Buchman, "Title VII Limits on Discrimination Against Television Anchorwomen on the Basis of Age-Related Appearance," *Columbia Law Review* 85, no. 1 (January 1985): 190–215.

263 Fuldheim would, in fact: Cary O'Dell, *Women Pioneers in Television: Biographies of Fifteen Industry Leaders* (Jefferson, NC: McFarland & Co., 1997), 113.

263 "I remember reaching toward him": Barbara Walters, "Ms. Walters Reflects," *Vanity Fair*, June 2008.

264 "Other than being turned down": Jean Enersen, interview by author, August 27, 2018.

264 But the Kansas City judge tossed: Leslie S. Gielow, "Sex Discrimination in Newscasting," *Michigan Law Review* 84, no. 3 (December 1985): 443–74.

264 Craft worked for a while in California: "On Air Staff: Christine Craft," KGO-AM 810 archives, September 3, 2012, accessed March 28, 2019, https://web.archive .org/web/20120903053831/http://www.kgoam810.com/showdj.asp?DJID =12850.

264 "A miniskirt doesn't suit you": Mary Rourke, "The Mini: Why They Will (or Won't) Wear It," *Los Angeles Times,* July 1, 1987.

265 "I didn't ever wear pants": Pat Wingert, "Geraldine Ferraro: Women Candidates Still Face Sexism," *Newsweek,* September 14, 2008.

265 "I guess I can understand how some older women": Bella Stumbo, "Feminist Advances Spawn a New 'Generation Gap,'" *Los Angeles Times,* September 17, 1984.

266 "I don't know if I feel vindicated": Wolfgang Saxon, "Martha Griffiths, 91, Dies; Fighter for Women's Rights," *New York Times,* April 25, 2003.

266 "This old-fashioned lady is also": Transcript of *60 Minutes,* June 21, 1981, 16–17, quoted in Amy Schapiro, *Millicent Fenwick: Her Way* (New Brunswick, NJ: Rutgers Univ. Press, 2003), 189.

266 The *Wall Street Journal* claimed that Fenwick: Albert R. Hunt, "Millicent Fenwick Is Rich, Feisty, Candid, 72, and Smokes a Pipe," *Wall Street Journal,* May 21, 1982, quoted in Schapiro, *Millicent Fenwick,* 203–4.

266 On Thanksgiving of 1981, in bed: Schapiro, *Millicent Fenwick,* 198.

266 she spent $776,000: Joseph F. Sullivan, "Jersey Democrat, in First Contest, Upsets Rep. Fenwick for the Senate," *New York Times,* November 3, 1982. The figure includes the general-election campaign and the June primary, as the *Times* notes.

266 "She had never raised money": Joseph Reckford, interview by author, October 25, 2016. All further quotations from Reckford in this chapter come from this conversation.

266 One of her eccentricities was: Schapiro, *Millicent Fenwick,* 206.

266 "The last thing I wanted to do was assault her": Schapiro, *Millicent Fenwick,* 208.

267 He ran his own final campaign: Karen Sparks, "Frank Raleigh Lautenberg," Britannica.com, June 18, 2013.

267 "I am accredited to an organization": Andrew Nagorsky, "Millicent Fenwick: A Maverick in Rome," *Newsweek,* November 7, 1983, quoted in Schapiro, *Millicent Fenwick,* 219.

267 By the end, one biographer jibed: Steven Krage, "Nancy Reagan Turns 90, and Biographer Kitty Kelley Reflects on the Special Day," *Chicago Now,* July 6, 2011.

267 A slightly catty *Chicago Tribune* writer: Michael Kilian, "Dutch's Duchess," *Chicago Tribune,* December 6, 1989.

268 "My life began with Ronnie": "Nancy Reagan: A Life Spent Caring for 'Ronnie' as Protector, Caregiver, First Lady," *The Oregonian,* March 6, 2016.

268 Critics sniped about her $200,000: Lou Cannon, "Nancy Reagan, an Influential and Protective First Lady, Dies at 94," *New York Times,* March 6, 2016.

268 Nancy was open about the mastectomy: Ibid.

268 While polls showed natural public sympathy: Shelby Grad and David Colker, "Nancy Reagan Turned to Astrology in White House to Protect Her Husband," *Los Angeles Times,* March 6, 2016.

268 "Later, in her long goodbye": Cannon, "Nancy Reagan."

268 The government's contributions soared: Jesse F. Ballenger, *Self, Senility, and Alzheimer's Disease in Modern America: A History* (Baltimore: Johns Hopkins Univ. Press, 2006), 113–14.

269 "We have a classic notion": Ibid., 122–24.

269 "They steal. They shoplift": Ibid., 136.

269 The bag lady legend might have begun: Lee A. Daniels, "Murdered 'Shopping-Bag Lady' Cremated, a Mystery to the End," *New York Times*, April 30, 1979.

269 Oprah Winfrey said she once rejected: Patricia Sellers, "The Business of Being Oprah," *Fortune*, April 1, 2002.

269 Sherry Lansing, the former chair: Geraldine Fabrikant, "Talking Money with Sherry Lansing: Under a Mattress Will Be Fine, Thanks," *New York Times*, December 3, 1995.

270 Adrienne Arsht, the chairwoman of TotalBank: Vanessa Small, "Helping Out: Adrienne Arsht," *Washington Post*, April 14, 2011.

270 Alexandra Penney, a former bestselling author: Alexandra Penney, "The Bag Lady Papers," *Daily Beast*, December 17, 2008.

15. THE 1990s

271 "It's over": Vicki Woods, "Meryl Streep: Force of Nature," *Vogue*, December 12, 2011.

271 "an old drunk of indeterminate age": Meryl Streep, interview by author, September 18, 2018. Unless otherwise noted, all further quotes from Streep in the chapter are from this interview.

272 "she was the first woman to understand": Nora Ephron, quoted in Bernard Weinraub, "Dawn Steel, Studio Chief and Producer, Dies at 51," *New York Times*, December 22, 1997.

272 "I don't know how to tell you this, babe": Charles Roven, quoted in Weinraub, "Dawn Steel."

272 "In a business fraught with age bias": Edward Wyatt, "After 10 Years, Age-Bias Suit Ends in Changed Hollywood," *New York Times*, January 27, 2010.

273 In 1950, less than a quarter: Frank Hobbs with Bonnie L. Damon, *65+ in the United States*, Current Population Reports, Special Studies, P23-190, U.S. Bureau of the Census (Washington, DC: U.S. Government Printing Office, 1996), vi, https://www.census.gov/prod/1/pop/p23-190/p23-190.pdf.

273 One survey of women 55 and older: Beth Sherman, "Older Women Overcome Obstacles to Enter Job Market," *St. Petersburg Times* (Florida), October 6, 1993. See also William H. Crown, Phyllis H. Mutschler, James H. Schulz, and Rebecca M. Loew, *The Economic Status of Divorced Older Women* (Waltham, MA: Brandeis Univ. Policy Center of Aging, Heller School, 1993); Rebecca M. Loew, "Determinants of Divorced Older Women's Labor Supply," *Research on Aging* 17, no. 4 (December 1, 1995): 27; Rebecca M. Loew, "The Economic Situation of Divorced Older Women and Its Relationship to Older Divorcées' Labor Force Participation"

(portion of research paper, Adelphi University, n.d.), https://kb.osu.edu/bitstream/handle/1811/36813/1/7_Loew_paper.pdf; and Steven J. Haider, Alison Jacknowitz, and Robert F. Schoeni, "The Economic Status of Divorced Elderly Women" (MRRC working paper 2003-046, Univ. of Michigan Retirement Research Center, Ann Arbor, MI, May 2003).

273 average monthly Social Security check: Social Security Administration, Social Security Office of Policy, "Fast Facts & Figures About Social Security, 2001," accessed March 31, 2019, https://www.ssa.gov/policy/docs/chartbooks/fast_facts/2001/fast_facts01.html.

273 a 1998 White House panel: Robert A. Rosenblatt, "White House Points Out Women's Reliance on Social Security," *Los Angeles Times*, October 28, 1998.

273 average one-bedroom apartment cost about $1,500 a month: Mervyn Rothstein, "New York Apartment Rents Moving Up," *New York Times*, February 27, 1994.

273 "That convinced me not to retire": Louis Uchitelle, "She's Wound Up in Her Career but He's Ready to Wind Down," *New York Times*, December 14, 1997.

274 "What would I do?": Dennis McLellan, "New Lease on Work Life," *Los Angeles Times*, July 18, 1993.

274 "are starting to talk about the likelihood": Jeffrey Kluger, "Can We Stay Young?," *Time*, November 25, 1996.

274 "to reset your aging clock": *Newsweek* staff, "Melatonin Mania," *Newsweek*, November 5, 1995.

275 everything from prevent cancer to burn fat: Marian Burros, "Eating Well," *New York Times*, April 23, 1997.

275 "Some enthusiasts say": Jane E. Brody, "Behind the Hoopla over a Hormone," *New York Times*, February 3, 1998.

275 "Our data provide no evidence": Rob Stein, "DHEA's Fountain of Youth May Be Dry," *Washington Post*, October 19, 2006.

275 "In a few decades, the traditional"; "reasonably believe": Ronald Klatz with Carol Kahn, *Grow Young with HGH: The Amazing Medically Proven Plan to Reverse Aging* (New York: HarperCollins, 1997), 28, quoted in Carole Haber, "Anti-Aging Medicine: Life Extension and History: The Continual Search for the Fountain of Youth," *Journals of Gerontology: Series A* 59, no. 6 (2004): B 515–22.

275 using it regularly: Marcia L. Stefanick, "Estrogens and Progestins: Background and History, Trends in Use, and Guidelines and Regimens Approved by the U.S. Food and Drug Administration," *American Journal of Medicine* 118 (December 2005): 64S, citing Adam L. Hersh, Marcia L. Stefanick, and Randall S. Stafford, "National Use of Postmenopausal Hormone Therapy: Annual Trends and Response to Recent Evidence," *Journal of the American Medical Association* 291, no. 1 (2004): 47–53; and D. K. Wysowski, L. Golden, and L. Burke, "Use of Menopausal Estrogens and Medroxyprogesterone in the United States, 1982–1992," *Obstetrics and Gynecology* 85, no. 1 (January 1995): 6–10. See also Jennifer Kelsey and Robert Marcus, "Prevention Trials in Perimenopausal and Postmenopausal Women," in *Menopause: Biology and Pathology*, eds. Rogerio A. Lobo, Jennifer Kelsey, and Robert Marcus (San Diego: Academic Press/Harcourt, 2000), 405–17; and James

Woods and Elizabeth Warner, "The History of Estrogen," *Obstetrics & Gynecology: menoPAUSE* (blog), February 17, 2016, Univ. of Rochester Medical Center, accessed April 1, 2019, https://www.urmc.rochester.edu/ob-gyn/gynecology/menopause-blog/february-2016/the-history-of-estrogen.aspx.

275 Senate subcommittee on aging: U.S. Senate, 102nd Congress, *The Role of Menopause and Gender Difference in Aging on the Development of Disease in Mid-Life and Older Women: Hearing Before the Subcommittee on Aging of the Committee on Labor and Human Resources [...] April 19, 1991* (Washington, DC: U.S. Government Printing Office, 1992), 33, https://babel.hathitrust.org/cgi/pt?id=mdp.39015042563877;view=1up;seq=37.

276 "She's Elizabeth Cady Stanton": Patricia Cronin Marcello, *Gloria Steinem: A Biography* (Westport, CT: Greenwood, 2004), 156.

276 "see what this country will be like": Gloria Steinem, *Doing Sixty and Seventy* (Oakland, CA: Elders Academy Press, 2006), 6.

276 "When my friends threw a surprise party": Ursula Vils, "Betty Friedan Emerges from 'The Fountain of Age,'" *Los Angeles Times*, March 3, 1986.

277 "distancing me": Betty Friedan, *The Fountain of Age* (New York: Simon & Schuster, 2006), 13.

277 "a musical comedy"; "the new 'in' disco": Vils, "Betty Friedan Emerges."

277 "there was a curious *absence*": Friedan, *Fountain of Age*, 35.

277 attempts to portray older people: Ibid., 57–58.

278 "Our Foremothers": Ibid., 63.

278 When the National Women's Political Caucus: Myrna Lewis and Robert Butler, "Why Is Women's Lib Ignoring Old Women," *Aging and Human Development* 3, no. 3 (1972): 223–31.

278 "[T]he message has gone out": Barbara Macdonald, "Outside the Sisterhood: Ageism in Women's Studies," *Women's Studies Quarterly* 25, nos. 1–2 (Spring–Summer 1997): 47–52, quoted in Lois W. Banner, *Elizabeth Cady Stanton: A Radical for Woman's Rights* (Boston: Little, Brown, 1980), 333.

278 "You have to be a good sport": Amy Schapiro, *Millicent Fenwick: Her Way* (New Brunswick, NJ: Rutgers Univ. Press, 2003), 228–29.

279 "We all admired her": Joseph Reckford, interview by author, October 25, 2016. All further remarks by Reckford in this chapter are from this interview.

279 Fenwick alter ego Lacey Davenport: Gerald Renner, "Lacey Faces Death in Comic Vein," *Hartford Courant*, July 26, 2013.

279 "Must be wonderful, like a long sleep": *Katharine Hepburn: All About Me*, directed by David Heeley, produced by Tophat Productions and Turner Pictures, originally aired January 18, 1993, on TNT.

280 "Smith was gradually transformed": Janann Sherman, *No Place for a Woman: A Life of Senator Margaret Chase Smith* (New Brunswick, NJ: Rutgers Univ. Press, 1999), 220.

280 "I have this possibly benighted idea": Helen Gurley Brown, *I'm Wild Again: Snippets from My Life and a Few Brazen Thoughts* (New York: St. Martin's Press, 1982), 375.

280 "They had to tell *me*": Ibid., 390.

280 young woman offered her a seat: Helen Gurley Brown, *The Late Show: Having It All* (New York: Morrow, 1993), 12.

281 *The Late Show* was about everything: Ibid., 56.

281 "as wide as Sunset Boulevard": Ibid., 56.

281 discovered Brown doing sit-ups: Eve Ensler, "Helen Gurley Brown: Author and Pioneering Editor of *Cosmopolitan* Magazine," in Ensler's *The Good Body* (New York: Dramatists Play Service, 2010), 8.

281 "He's feisty": Ibid., 9.

281 "Now that dear old dad": Barbara Mathias, "The Sexes," *Washington Post*, April 3, 1992.

282 "more knowledge of the world": Linda Burstyn, "Words of Love," *Washington Post*, February 13, 1996.

282 "They're showing up at movie theaters en masse": Elizabeth Gleick, "Hell Hath No Fury," *Time*, October 7, 1996.

282 "The public thinks": Ibid.

283 "because they were afraid": Alison Beard, "Life's Work: Goldie Hawn," *Harvard Business Review*, March 2015.

283 "I just really wanted": Erica Euse, "The Revolutionary History of the Pantsuit," *Vice*, March 21, 2016.

283 "I might be short": Perry Stein, "Sen. Barbara Mikulski's Most Colorful Moments," *Washington Post*, March 2, 2015.

283 "pushed her to take the purse": Nadine Brozan, "Chronicle," *New York Times*, October 6, 1995.

284 "You would have thought": Euse, "Revolutionary History."

284 "We've heard from women staff": "The Evolution of the Pantsuit: A Debate That Continues, One Leg at a Time," *Washington Post*, June 5, 2002.

284 Once Braun and Mikulski: Robin Givhan, "Moseley Braun: Lady in Red," *Washington Post*, January 21, 2004.

284 "Mrs. Clinton believes": Nora Caplan-Bricker, "Women Who Wear Pants Somehow Still Controversial," *Slate*, February 16, 2016.

284 "Why must she dress that way?": Alex Steinman, "Tim Gunn: Hillary Clinton Dresses Like She's 'Confused About Her Gender,'" *New York Daily News*, July 29, 2011.

284 "And sixty-two counties": Senate victory speech, quoted in Dan Amira, "A History of Hillary Clinton Making Pantsuit Jokes," *New York*, June 4, 2013.

284 "Middle Age Is Prime of Life": Erica Goode, "New Study Finds Middle Age Is Prime of Life," *New York Times*, February 16, 1999.

285 "Why is menopause suddenly so fashionable?": Martha King, "The Baby Boom Meets Menopause," *Good Housekeeping*, January 1992, 46, 48, 50.

285 Red Hot Mamas: Camille Sweeney, "Seeking Natural Remedies for Hot Flashes," *New York Times*, July 1, 2009.

286 "The Baby Boom generation": Marvin J. Cetron and Owen Davies, *Cheating Death: The Promise and the Future Impact of Trying to Live Forever* (New York: St. Martin's Press, 2013), 5, 39.

16. INTO THE TWENTY-FIRST CENTURY

287 "Those odds-she'll-marry statistics": Daniel McGinn, "Marriage by the Numbers," *Newsweek,* June 4, 2006.

287 "taking the bitter taste of aging": Nancy Gibbs, "Midlife Crisis? Bring It On!," *Time,* May 16, 2005.

288 "bright jewelry crafted from gemstones and pearls": Stephanie Chen, "From Lawyer to Comedian? Making a Midlife Career Change," CNN.com, January 14, 2011.

288 "career menopause": Bronwyn Fryer, "Coping with 'Career Menopause,'" *Harvard Business Review,* October 28, 2009.

288 assets of $2 million or more: Internal Revenue Service, *SOI Bulletin: A Quarterly Statistics of Income Report* 31, no. 3 (Winter 2012), https://www.irs.gov/pub/irs-soi/12winbul.pdf.

289 "Those of us who worked on this": Betsy Wade, interview by author for *When Everything Changed* (New York: Little, Brown, 2014).

289 Alice Muller, a 51-year-old clerk: Gillian Thomas, *Because of Sex: One Law, Ten Cases, and Fifty Years That Changed American Women's Lives at Work* (New York: Picador/Macmillan, 2016), 62–65, 255n4.

289 "quarter life crisis": Blair Decembrele, "Encountering a Quarter Life Crisis? You're Not Alone...," LinkedIn Official Blog, November 15, 2017, https://blog.linkedin.com/2017/november/15/encountering-a-quarter-life-crisis-you-are-not-alone.

289 "happiness U-curve": Jonathan Rauch, "The Real Roots of Midlife Crisis," *The Atlantic,* December 2014.

289 Sheehy calculated: Gail Sheehy, *Passages,* 30th anniversary ed. (New York: Ballantine, 2006), xxi.

290 "a hidden cultural phenomenon": Ibid., xxii.

290 "Although the party went late into the night": Celebrity, "Madonna's 50th Birthday Bash Before the Gym," PopSugar, August 18, 2008, https://www.popsugar.com/celebrity/Photos-Madonna-her-50th-Birthday-Party-1872684.

290 A Harris poll announced: The Harris Poll, "Is Fifty the Perfect Age?," September 12, 2013, https://theharrispoll.com/new-york-n-y-september-12-2013-no-pun-intended-but-its-the-age-old-question-what-is-the-perfect-age-is-there-a-perfect-age-overall-a-perfect-age-for-having-children-or-getting-married-o/.

290 A psychologist commenting on the favorite-age poll: Diane Mapes, "America's Favorite Age?," *Today,* September 15, 2013.

291 "I'm over seventy but I feel like I'm fifty": Patricia Bosworth, *Jane Fonda: The Private Life of a Public Woman* (New York: Houghton Mifflin Harcourt, 2011), 532.

291 "That's not my self-image": TheEllenShow, "Jane Fonda Battles a Bear," YouTube video, 2:49, posted December 10, 2010, https://www.youtube.com/watch?v=mItsiyC4xvQ. Transcript of the show: Andrea Reiher, "Jane Fonda on Breast Cancer, Hip Replacement on 'Ellen,'" *Screener,* December 10, 2010, http://screenertv.com/news-features/jane-fonda-on-breast-cancer-hip-replacement-on-ellen/.

291 "When I'm Sixty-Four": Barry Miles, *Paul McCartney: Many Years from Now* (New York: Holt, 1998), 23, 319. Although McCartney wrote the melody even earlier (as

a teenager), the song was completed when he was in his 20s, for the Beatles' *Sgt. Pepper's Lonely Hearts Club Band* album (May 1967).

291   "never tour when I'm 50": Mick Jagger to Johnny Kay, backstage at Wembley Stadium, London; story told by Ryan Cormier, "Wilmington's Johnny Kay on His Days with Bill Haley…and The Beatles…and Mick Jagger," Delawareonline .com, May 11, 2009, http://blogs.delawareonline.com/pulpculture/2009/05/11/ wilmingtons-johnny-kay-on-his-days-with-bill-haley-and-the-beatles-and -mick-jagger/.

291   "check with Mick Jagger": Tim Askew, "Looking for Entrepreneurship in All the Wrong Places," *Inc.*, February 12, 2018.

291   "the woman is 35 years or older": Linda Lowen, "What Does It Mean When a Woman Is Called a Cougar?," ThoughtCo., January 21, 2019.

292   "woman in her 30s who prefers": Linda Lowen, "What Is a Puma as Compared to a Cougar in Regards to Dating?," ThoughtCo., January 10, 2019.

292   "This season marks the summer": Alessandra Stanley, "In the Prime of Their Time," *New York Times*, June 17, 2007.

292   "as plastic surgery and Botox have gone mainstream": Ramin Setoodeh, "Why 2009 Is the Year of the Cougar," *Newsweek*, June 17, 2009.

292   "decides to find some excitement in her dating life": Helen Zhao, quoting IMDb, "Now It Really IS a Cougar Town! Courteney Cox, 50, Shows Off Her Toned Legs in LBD as She Grabs Lunch with Girlfriends in Beverly Hills," *Daily Mail Online*, November 8, 2014.

293   "I kept getting teased about dating a cougar": Vincent Mallozzi, "She's 98. He's 94. They Met at the Gym," *New York Times*, August 11, 2017.

293   only 3 percent of women: Christopher Ingraham, "Study: Men Who Remarry Really Do Prefer Younger Women," *Washington Post*, December 8, 2014.

293   "that men are judging women by beauty": Paula England, interview by author, July 24, 2018. Unless otherwise noted, all further remarks by England are from this source.

293   that big study, launched in 1993: Women's Health Initiative, "About WHI," accessed March 24, 2019, https://www.whi.org/about/SitePages/About%20WHI .aspx. See also National Heart, Lung, and Blood Institute, "Clinical Alert: NHLBI Stops Trial of Estrogen Plus Progestin Due to Increased Breast Cancer Risk, Lack of Overall Benefit," NIH U.S. National Library of Medicine website, July 9, 2002, https://www.nlm.nih.gov/databases/alerts/estrogen_progestin.html.

294   one survey of gynecologists: Elizabeth Siegel Watkins, *The Estrogen Elixir: A History of Hormone Replacement Therapy in America* (Baltimore: Johns Hopkins Univ. Press, 2010), 244. Watkins cites Boris Kaplan et al., "Gynecologists' Trends and Attitudes Toward Prescribing Hormone Replacement Therapy During Menopause," *Menopause* 9 (September–October 2002): 354.

294   "Obviously, the women on the hormones": Barbara Seaman, *The Greatest Experiment Ever Performed on Women* (New York: Seven Stories Press, 2003), 1.

294   "I tell you—women gotta go insane today": Ibid., 4.

294   funded by Wyeth-Ayerst: Watkins, *Estrogen Elixir*, 267. See also 334n69, where Watkins writes, of the corporate history of Ayerst at the time her book was completed,

"Wyeth-Ayerst, now simply Wyeth, is the manufacturer of the Premarin brand of estrogen replacement therapy and the Prempro brand of combined estrogen-progestin replacement therapy." In October 2009, Wyeth was bought by Pfizer, of which it is now a subsidiary. Much earlier, in the 1940s, when Premarin was first being developed for and sold to consumers, Ayerst was owned by American Home Products.

294 "there is no emergency": Diana B. Petitti, MD, "Hormone Replacement Therapy and Heart Disease Prevention: Experimentation Trumps Observation," *Journal of the American Medical Association* 280, no. 7 (August 19, 1998): 650–52, quoted in Watkins, *Estrogen Elixir*, 267. Watkins slightly misstates the title of the paper.

294 tsunami of media reporting: See, for instance, Gina Kolata with Melody Peterson, "Hormone Replacement Therapy a Shock to the Medical System," *New York Times*, July 10, 2002.

295 "It felt to me that we changed": Cindy Pearson, interview by author, July 20, 2018. Unless otherwise noted, all remarks by Pearson are from this interview.

295 "Do I prefer a shorter but more active life span": Letter to the editor, *New York Times*, July 22, 2002, quoted in Watkins, *Estrogen Elixir*, 275.

295 "little tiny signs of aging": Sherry Jacobson, "More Dallas-Area Women Going for the 'Lunch-Hour Face-Lift,'" *Dallas News*, March 9, 2013.

296 "They're more concerned about wrinkles": Amanda Fortini, "Lines, Please," *New York*, March 7, 2010.

296 "one of the few women-of-a-certain-age": Vicki Hyman, "Golden Globes: Sophia Loren, Cher, Jessica Lange, and Other Things That Give Us Nightmares," NJ.com, January 18, 2010, https://www.nj.com/entertainment/celebrities/index .ssf/2010/01/golden_globes_sophia_loren_che.html.

296 "everyone is talking about breast cancer": Betty Rollin, "Talk for the Cure," *New York Times*, April 1, 2007.

296 mortality rate dropped by around 2 percent: Department of Defense Breast Cancer Research Program, *The Breast Cancer Landscape* (February 2016), 3, fig. 3, https:// cdmrp.army.mil/bcrp/pdfs/bc_landscape.pdf; and National Cancer Institute, "SEER Cancer Statistics Review 1975–2010," table 1.8, accessed April 5, 2019, https://seer.cancer.gov/archive/csr/1975_2010/results_single/sect_01_table .08_2pgs.pdf.

296 about 12 percent of American women: "U.S. Breast Cancer Statistics," Breastcancer .org, last modified February 13, 2019; and DOD Breast Cancer Research Program, *Breast Cancer Landscape*, 1.

296 a 90 percent chance of surviving: National Cancer Institute, "SEER Cancer Statistics Review 1975–2010," table 4.14, accessed April 5, 2019, https://seer.cancer .gov/archive/csr/1975_2010/results_merged/sect_04_breast.pdf.

297 Elizabeth Edwards: Robert D. McFadden, "A Political Life Filled with Cruel Reversals," *New York Times*, December 7, 2010.

297 More than a quarter of people over 65: Centers for Disease Control and Prevention, *National Diabetes Fact Sheet: National Estimates and General Information on Diabetes and Prediabetes in the United States, 2011* (Atlanta, GA: U.S. Dept. of Health and Human Services, Centers for Disease Control and Prevention, 2011), https:// www.cdc.gov/diabetes/pubs/pdf/ndfs_2011.pdf.

297 About half of Americans 65 and over: Centers for Disease Control and Prevention, National Center for Chronic Disease Prevention and Health Promotion, Division of Population Health, "Arthritis-Related Statistics," last modified July 18, 2018, accessed March 25, 2019, https://www.cdc.gov/arthritis/data_statistics/arthritis -related-stats.htm.

297 so crippled they had difficulty walking: Kamil E. Barbour et al., "Geographic Variations in Arthritis Prevalence, Health-Related Characteristics, and Management— United States, 2015," *Morbidity and Mortality Weekly Report* 67, no. SS-4 (Summer 2018): 1–28.

298 about 15 percent of women: RoperASW, *Exercise Attitudes and Behaviors: A Survey of Adults Age 50–79*, AARP, May 2002, 39. See also Deborah Jordan Brooks, "Ms. Couch Potato? Gender and Exercise," *Gallup News*, January 28, 2003.

298 "older women and medical marijuana": Abby Ellin, "Older Women and Medical Marijuana: A New Growth Industry," *New York Times*, May 25, 2017.

298 multigenerational families were getting more popular: D'Vera Cohn and Jeffrey S. Passel, "A Record 64 Million Americans Live in Multigenerational Households," Pew Research Center, April 5, 2018, http://www.pewresearch.org/fact-tank/2018/04/05/ a-record-64-million-americans-live-in-multigenerational-households/.

299 only a little over half of Americans are married: Kim Parker and Renee Stepler, "As U.S. Marriage Rate Hovers at 50%, Education Gap in Marital Status Widens," Pew Research Center, September 14, 2017, http://www.pewresearch.org/fact-tank/ 2017/09/14/as-u-s-marriage-rate-hovers-at-50-education-gap-in-marital -status-widens/.

300 "sharp decline in employment rates": Edward Wyatt, "After 10 Years, Age-Bias Suit Ends in Changed Hollywood," *New York Times*, January 27, 2010.

300 "changes have come to Hollywood": Ibid.

300 One 2015 survey: Steve Steinberg, "Will All TV Median Ages Soon Be over 50?," *Media Daily News*, April 30, 2015.

300 A Nielsen report: Molly Soat, "Aging Prime TV Demographics Forcing Advertisers to Adapt," *Marketing News Weekly*, May 5, 2015.

300 A study of the top 100 films in 2015: Stacy L. Smith, Marc Choueiti, and Katherine Pieper, *Over Sixty, Underestimated: A Look at Aging on the "Silver" Screen in Best Picture Nominated Films*, USC Annenberg School for Communication and Journalism, February 2017, https://annenberg.usc.edu/sites/default/files/Over_Sixty _Underestimated_Report_2_14_17_Final.pdf.

301 "made [the studio] feel safe": Donna Freydkin and William Keck, "Five Actresses Face Down the Big 40," *USA Today*, February 18, 2005. The words "the studio" were Freydkin and Keck's interpolation.

17. ONWARD AND UPWARD

302 *The Atlantic* asked: Gregg Easterbrook, "What Happens When We All Live to 100?," *The Atlantic*, October 2014.

302 "We spend an incredible amount of money": Michael Bell, "Why 5% of Patients Create 50% of Health Care Costs," *Forbes*, January 10, 2013.

302 "We should not have a government program": Sam Stein, "Grassley Endorses 'Death Panel' Rumor: 'You Have Every Right to Fear,'" *Huffington Post*, September 12, 2009.

302 "the notion that somehow I ran for public office": Don Gonyea, "From the Start, Obama Struggled with Fallout from a Kind of Fake News," as heard on *All Things Considered*, National Public Radio, January 10, 2017.

302 about 22,000 such conversations: "Medicare Now Covers Conversations About End-of-Life Care," ElderLawAnswers, last modified November 30, 2017, accessed April 5, 2019, https://www.elderlawanswers.com/medicare-now-covers-conversations -about-end-of-life-care--15454; and Carin van Zyl and Dawn M. Gross, "For People Dying to Talk, It Finally Pays to Listen with Reimbursable Advance Care Planning," *AMA Journal of Ethics* 20, no. 8 (2018): E750–56, citing Marian Grant, "Use of Billing Codes for Advance Care Planning Exceeds Projections," *B-TAC: The Blog to Transform Advanced Care*, August 10, 2017, accessed April 5, 2019, https:// www.thectac.org/2017/08/use-billing-codes-advance-care-planning-exceeds -projections/.

303 "My name is Nini": Yanick Rice Lamb, "The 'G' Word: Grandmas Who Don't Want to Be Called Grandma," Blackamericaweb.com, September 7, 2012, https:// blackamericaweb.com/2012/09/07/the-g-word-grandmas-who-dont-want-to-be -called-grandma/.

303 gave her son credit: Goldie Hawn, *A Lotus Grows in the Mud* (New York: G. P. Putnam's Sons, 2005), 445. Hawn styles it "Glam-Ma."

303 "Glamma, to me, sounds fake": Melissa Charles, "The Problem with 'Glamma,'" *Huffington Post*, May 20, 2015, https://www.huffingtonpost.com/melissa-charles/ the-problem-with-glamma_b_7315096.html.

303 "We new Glam-mas bake kale": Lois Joy Johnson, "6 Ways to Be a Sexy Grandma," *AARP Bulletin*, last modified September 2015, https://www.aarp.org/home -family/friends-family/info-2014/6-ways-to-be-a-sexy-grandma.html.

303 When Hillary Clinton's second grandchild: Nikki Schwab, "Clinton Gushes About Being a Grandma Again: 'We Are Just Truly over the Moon,'" *Daily Mail*, June 21, 2016.

304 "My mom's hot": Alexandra Zissu, "Who Are You Calling Grandma?," *New York Times*, May 11, 2011.

304 about 2.7 million grandparents raising children: Sarah Jones, "The Grandparenting Generation," *New Republic*, January 8, 2018.

304 "We hypothesize that stress": Laura Johannes, "Baby-sitting May Be Hazardous to Grandmother's Health," *Wall Street Journal*, last modified October 31, 2003.

304 "so-called glam-mas": Joanne Kaufman, "When Grandma Can't Be Bothered," *New York Times*, March 4, 2009.

305 "It seems that old is a moving target": Anna Quindlen, *Lots of Candles, Plenty of Cake* (New York: Random House, 2012), 105.

305 50-50 chance of making it to 88: Centers for Disease Control, "Table 22: Life Expectancy at Birth, at 65 Years of Age, and at 75 Years of Age, by Race and Sex: United States, Selected Years 1900–2007," accessed March 21, 2019, https:// www.cdc.gov/nchs/data/hus/2010/022.pdf.

305 "Methuselah gene": Melissa Malamut, "Harvard Scientists Have Discovered Why Some People Look Like They Don't Age," *Boston Magazine,* June 10, 2015.

305 "Seventy is the new fifty": Gail Collins, "Who's Really Older, Trump or Clinton?," *New York Times,* September 29, 2016; and Steven Austad, "A Biologist's Perspective: Whence Come We, Where Are We, Where Go We?," in *Enduring Questions and Changing Perspectives in Gerontology,* eds. D. J. Sheets, D. B. Bradley, and J. Hendricks (New York: Springer, 2005). Austad writes, "As a *New Yorker* cartoon aptly put it, 'Good news, honey — seventy is the new fifty.'"

305 Oxford Institute of Population Ageing: Alexandra Preston, "90 Is the New 70: Old Age Just Isn't Old Age Anymore," *Natural Society,* August 24, 2017.

306 nearly 30 percent of women 65 to 69: Claire Cain Miller, "More Women in Their 50s and 60s Are Having 'Way Too Much Fun' to Retire," *New York Times,* February 11, 2017.

306 "if it weren't fun": Claudia Goldin, interview by author, July 25, 2018. Unless otherwise noted, all further remarks from Goldin are from this interview.

306 more than 70 percent of men: Mitra Toossi, "A Century of Change: The U.S. Labor Force, 1950–2050," Bureau of Labor Statistics, accessed March 31, 2019, https://www.bls.gov/opub/mlr/2002/05/art2full.pdf.

306 with 16 percent at or below the poverty line: Amber Christ and Tracey Gronniger, *Older Women & Poverty: Special Report,* Justice in Aging, December 2018, 3, accessed March 21, 2019, http://www.justiceinaging.org/wp-content/uploads/2018/12/Older -Women-and-Poverty.pdf.

306 the average benefit for a woman: Social Security Administration, "Fact Sheet — Social Security: Social Security Is Important to Women," August 2018, accessed March 21, 2019, https://www.ssa.gov/news/press/factsheets/women-alt.pdf; and Sargent Shriver National Center on Poverty Law, "Older Women and Poverty," *WomanView* 19, no. 9 (March 30, 2016).

306 "some chump change — $7 an hour": Peter Whoriskey, "'I Hope I Can Quit Working in a Few Years': A Preview of the U.S. Without Pensions," *Washington Post,* December 23, 2017.

307 Roberta Gordon: Alana Semuels, "This Is What Life Without Retirement Savings Looks Like," *The Atlantic,* February 22, 2018.

307 administrator at Ohio State University: Paula Span, "He Called Older Employees 'Dead Wood.' Two Sued for Age Discrimination," *New York Times,* July 6, 2018.

308 "Age is treated as a second-class civil right": Dan Kohrman, interview by author, July 25, 2018.

308 "and Rob pointed to the chandelier": Zach Johnson, "Why the *Mary Poppins Returns* Cast Thought Meryl Streep Died on Set," E! News, November 9, 2018, accessed March 21, 2019, https://www.eonline.com/news/985624/why-the-mary-poppins -returns-cast-thought-meryl-streep-died-on-set.

309 "how wonderful it is that our careers today": Karma Allen, "Nicole Kidman Slams Ageism in Hollywood, Says Women over 40 Are 'Potent, Powerful and Viable,'" ABC News online, January 22, 2018; and Lynsey Eidell, "Read Every Word of Nicole Kidman's 2018 SAG Awards Speech on Aging in Hollywood," *Glamour,* January 22, 2018.

309 "Most of the jobs go to people in their twenties": Spokesperson for the Screen Actors Guild-American Federation of Television and Radio Artists (SAG-AFTRA), interview by author, late 2018 or early 2019.

309 "not a single woman over 50": Kyle Munzenrieder, "Television's Highest Paid Actress List Is Much More Diverse than Film," *W*, September 14, 2016.

309 "the move to television": Alessandra Stanley, "It's Her Freak Show Right Now," *New York Times*, January 2, 2015.

310 "When I was at the White House": Calin Van Paris, "Michelle Obama Has Never Looked Better and It's Because of This Bootcamp Workout," *Vogue*, June 19, 2017, quoting Obama's Instagram account.

310 "Every event I go to": *People* staff, "Michelle Obama at 50," *People*, January 27, 2014.

310 disappeared from public events: Katie Rogers, "Melania Trump Appears in Public After 'a Little Rough Patch,'" *New York Times*, June 6, 2018.

310 "so unfair, and vicious": Donald Trump (@realDonaldTrump), June 6, 2018, 9:48 a.m., https://twitter.com/realDonaldTrump/status/1004359335399641089.

311 "generational choice": Richard Luscombe, "'Yesterday Is Over': Marco Rubio to Run for President as 'Generational Choice,'" *The Guardian*, April 13, 2015.

311 "a rigorous physical ordeal": Mike Allen, "Rand's Grand Plan," *Politico*, November 9, 2014.

311 "still be about the same age": Sara Fischer, "Scott Walker Talks Presidential Run, Takes Shot at Hillary Clinton's Age," CNN.com, November 18, 2014.

311 "a young man on the rise": Virginia Rohan, "As Women Age, Do They Become Invisible? It Appears So," *Bergen County Record* (New Jersey), September 30, 2008.

312 "*Look* at that face!": Paul Solotaroff, "Trump Seriously: On the Trail with the GOP's Tough Guy," *Rolling Stone*, September 9, 2015.

312 "have the stamina": Chris Cillizza, "Why Donald Trump's Attack on Hillary Clinton's 'Stamina' Fell Flat, in 1 Picture," *Washington Post*, September 27, 2016.

313 "Looking back": Hillary Rodham Clinton, *What Happened* (New York: Simon & Schuster, 2017), 101.

313 Republicans had run more than 135,000 ads: Julie Bykowicz, Brian McGill, and Anthony DeBarros, "Trump and Pelosi Dominate Ads Aimed at Rallying and Repelling Voters," *Wall Street Journal*, October 29, 2018.

313 seven times more attack ads: Data from the Wesleyan Media Project, reported in Robert Draper, "Nancy Pelosi's Last Battle," *New York Times Magazine*, November 19, 2018.

313 "harder than any human being": Mike Debonis and Robert Costa, "'Her Skills Are Real,'" *Washington Post*, December 14, 2018.

313 "pass the torch": Julie Hirschfeld Davis, "Meet the Democrats Who Want Pelosi to Step Aside," *New York Times*, November 21, 2018.

314 "That's something that women": Elise Viebeck, "After Loss, Rep. Barbara Lee Wonders," *Washington Post*, November 29, 2018; and Jim Newell, "A Potential Future Speaker Beats a Progressive Icon in Key House Leadership Election," *Slate*, November 28, 2018.

314 "John Paul Stevens": Gail Collins, "The Unsinkable R.B.G.," *New York Times*, February 20, 2015.

315 "vowed this year, just sparkling water": Ruth Bader Ginsburg, from speaking event at Lisner Auditorium, George Washington University, Washington, DC, February 12, 2015, quoted by Nina Totenberg, "Justices Ginsburg and Scalia: A Perfect Match Except for Their Views on the Law," *All Things Considered,* National Public Radio, February 13, 2015.

315 "Bubbe, you were sleeping": Collins, "The Unsinkable R.B.G."

315 "Who do you think Obama": Ibid.

315 "John was in such bad shape": Ibid.

316 "This skinny little thing": Nina Totenberg, "Notes on a Life," in Scott Dodson, ed., *The Legacy of Ruth Bader Ginsburg* (New York: Cambridge Univ. Press, 2015), 8.

317 "bleeding badly from a face-lift": Donald Trump (@realDonaldTrump), June 29, 2017, 5:58 a.m., https://twitter.com/realDonaldTrump/status/880410114456465 411?ref_src=twsrc%5Etfw%7Ctwcamp%5Etweetembed%7Ctwterm%5E8804101 14456465411&ref_url=https%3A%2F%2F.

317 "Her departure was a farce": Steve Cavendish, "The Fight to Be a Middle-Aged Female News Anchor," *New York Times,* March 11, 2019.

317 "see if I had another chapter": Jean Enersen, interview by author, August 27, 2018. All further comments from Enersen in the chapter are from this interview. Enersen started at KING in 1968, as an on-air reporter and talk show host, and hit the fifty-year mark in 2018, two years after she departed as anchor and began doing editorials for the station.

318 less inclined to volunteerism: U.S. Department of Labor, Bureau of Labor Statistics, "Volunteering in the United States, 2015," news release, February 25, 2016, accessed March 24, 2019, https://www.bls.gov/news.release/volun.nr0.htm.

318 "It's not what it used to be": Anna Quindlen, interview by author, December 17, 2018.

319 "The nation is facing a clown shortage": Melissa Locker, "12 of the Best, Dreamiest, and Most Unusual Jobs for When You Retire," *Southern Living,* May 3, 2017.

319 "Did you get my poke?": Deena Zaru, "Clinton Approves of Obama's WHCD Joke About Her," CNN.com, last modified May 1, 2016.

319 Judith Boyd, a retired psychiatric nurse: Emanuella Grinberg, "Aging Stylishly, Online and in the Streets," CNN.com, last modified April 28, 2012.

319 "an internet sensation at the age of 85": "How Baddie Winkle Became an Internet Sensation at the Age of 85 and Ignored What the Critics Had to Say," *Mirror,* November 26, 2017.

319 "paid to tout brands": Ruth La Ferla, "The Glamorous Grandmothers of Instagram," *New York Times,* June 20, 2018. In the *Times* piece, the brand name göt2b is rendered "Got2b."

320 "They do not think of themselves as broken": Nielsen & BoomAgers, *Introducing Boomers: Marketing's Most Valuable Generation* (2012).

320 "but they remain invisible to advertisers": Quoted in Sarah Steimer, "Baby Boomer Women Remain Invisible to Marketers," *Marketing News,* American Marketing Association, October 1, 2016.

320 "We exist in a post-recessionary world": Emma Bazilian, "Why Older Women Are the New It-Girls of Fashion," *Adweek,* April 6, 2015.

320 "All hail the rise": Zing Tsjeng, "Joni Mitchell Stars in New Saint Laurent Campaign," *Dazed*, January 9, 2015.

320 "like so *in* right now": Sally Holmes, "Jessica Lange Lends Her Face to Marc Jacobs," *Elle*, February 27, 2014.

320 "our fastest-growing area": Monica Corcoran, "Mature Models Increasingly in Demand," *Chicago Tribune*, by way of the *Los Angeles Times* (where the story originally appeared under the headline "Demand for Older Models Grows"), July 16, 2008, accessed March 26, 2019, https://www.chicagotribune.com/news/ct-xpm -2008-07-16-0807140253-story.html.

321 "taken a big risk": Anita Singh, "Julia Roberts: I've Risked My Career by Not Having a Facelift," *Telegraph*, October 26, 2014. The interview appeared originally in *You* magazine.

321 reasonably thoughtful piece: Owen Gleiberman, "Renée Zellweger: If She No Longer Looks Like Herself, Has She Become a Different Actress?," *Variety*, June 30, 2016; and Rose McGowan, "Rose McGowan Pens Response to Critic of Renée Zellweger's Face: 'Vile, Damaging, Stupid, and Cruel,'" *Hollywood Reporter*, July 6, 2016.

322 "actively returned to her old look": Caroline Siede, "Renée Zellweger Is a Walking Metaphor for the Shameful Way We Treat Aging Women in Hollywood," *Quartz*, July 6, 2016.

322 "deeply troubling": Renée Zellweger, "We Can Do Better," *Huffington Post*, August 5, 2016.

322 biggest clump of patients: American Society of Plastic Surgeons, *2017 Plastic Surgery Statistics Report*, https://www.plasticsurgery.org/documents/News/Statistics/2017/ plastic-surgery-statistics-full-report-2017.pdf.

323 "liberal, feminist-leaning, highly educated peer group": Debora L. Spar, "Aging and My Beauty Dilemma," *New York Times*, September 24, 2016.

323 Spar's piece triggered: Bonnie Wertheim, "To Age Naturally or Not? Readers Respond to Debora L. Spar's 'Aging and My Beauty Dilemma,'" *New York Times*, September 29, 2016.

324 took the whole thing on: Comedy Central, "Inside Amy Schumer—Last F**kable Day—Uncensored," YouTube video, 4:57, posted April 22, 2015, https://www .youtube.com/watch?v=XPpsI8mWKmg&list=PLlgI2eKjrAW—IJe7gFmk 5dt75EGVLzJd&index=2&t=0s.

324 Leslie Jones: *Saturday Night Live*, season 44, episode 7, "Weekend Update" featuring Leslie Jones, aired December 1, 2018, on NBC.

324 "David is the great love": *Still Doing It*, directed by Deirdre Fishel (Newburgh, NY: New Day Films, 2008). There is also an accompanying book: Deirdre Fishel and Diana Holtzberg, *Still Doing It: The Intimate Lives of Women over 60* (New York: Avery, 2008).

325 "FDA-approved hormone treatments": JoAnn E. Manson and Andrew M. Kaunitz, "Menopause Management—Getting Clinical Care Back on Track," *New England Journal of Medicine* 374 (2016): 804.

325 "isn't all good or all bad": Mayo Clinic staff, "Hormone Therapy: Is It Right for You?," Mayo Clinic website, May 24, 2018, accessed May 14, 2019, https://www

.mayoclinic.org/diseases-conditions/menopause/in-depth/hormone-therapy/art-20046372.

325 "While studying my face in a well-lit elevator": Pamela Druckerman, "How to Survive Your 40s," *New York Times,* May 4, 2018.

326 "Nearly 60 percent of Gen Xers": Ada Calhoun, "The New Midlife Crisis: Why (and How) It's Hitting Gen X Women," Oprah.com, n.d., http://www.oprah.com/sp/new-midlife-crisis.html.

327 "pretty damn thrilled": Curtis M. Wong, "Katherine Heigl Says Turning 40 Represents 'A Certain Kind of Freedom,'" *Huffington Post,* November 26, 2018.

327 "the number aged 65 and over has jumped": U.S. Census Bureau, "Sixty-Five Plus in the United States," statistical brief of report, May 1995, accessed March 24, 2019, https://www.census.gov/population/socdemo/statbriefs/agebrief.html.

327 "U.S. Life Expectancy Declines": Lenny Bernstein, "U.S. Life Expectancy Declines for the First Time Since 1993," *Washington Post,* December 8, 2016.

327 A woman who is 65: Centers for Disease Control, "Table 22. Life Expectancy," 2010, https://www.cdc.gov/nchs/data/hus/2010/022.pdf.

327 on par with Vietnam: The World Bank, "Life Expectancy at Birth, Female (Years)," 2017, http://data.worldbank.org/indicator/SP.DYN.LE00.FE.IN.

327 chances of reaching 90: Wan He and Mark N. Muenchrath, *90+ in the United States: 2006–2008,* report no. ACS-17, U.S. Census Bureau, November 2011, https://www.census.gov/library/publications/2011/acs/acs-17.html.

328 Our 97-year-old park ranger: Farai Chideya, "The 97-Year-Old Park Ranger Who Doesn't Have Time for Foolishness," *Glamour,* November 2, 2018.

328 secret to a long, happy life: Erin Clements, "Betty White's Secret to a Long, Happy Life: Positivity (Also, Vodka and Hot Dogs)," *Today,* January 5, 2018.

328 "Fifty was a shock": Gail Collins, "This Is What 80 Looks Like," *New York Times,* March 22, 2014.

329 "bunch of lefties here": Muriel Fox, interview by author at Kendal, June 5, 2018.

330 "to adjust themselves to conditions": Corra Harris, "The Borrowed Timers," *Ladies' Home Journal* 43, September 1926, quoted in W. Andrew Achenbaum, *Old Age in the New Land* (Baltimore: Johns Hopkins Univ. Press, 1978), 113.

331 "I wouldn't be twenty-five again": Quindlen, *Lots of Candles,* xii.

331 "says it's great to be old": Nora Ephron, *I Feel Bad About My Neck* (New York: Alfred A. Knopf, 2006), 7.

332 "the childhood of old age": Faith Popcorn, interview by author, July 24, 2018.

332 "like being told I had six months to live": Vivian Gornick, *The Odd Woman and the City* (New York: Farrar, Straus and Giroux, 2016), 131–32.

INDEX

➤➤ ◂◂

Stewart, Maria, 47

Still Doing It (documentary), 324–25

Sting, The (movie), 248

stock market crash, 117, 132

Stonewall riots, 232

Stowe, Calvin, 56, 68

Stowe, Harriet Beecher, 35, 47, 55–56, 66, 68–69, 77

Streep, Meryl, 6, 271, 291, 308–9, 332

Streeter, Ruth Cheney, 160

Student League for International Democracy, 168

Student Nonviolent Coordinating Committee (SNCC), 209–10

suffrage movement: generational gap in, 106–7; history of, 74, 85–87, 151–52; nineteenth-century alliance with racist politicians, 63; twentieth-century campaign strategies of, 106–7, 158. *See also* voting rights

Sullenberger, Sully, 290

Sully (movie), 300

Sumner, Charles, 59

Sunset Boulevard (movie), 113, 178

Susan G. Komen Breast Cancer Foundation, 242

Swanson, Gloria, 113, 178

Swerdlow, Amy, 206

Swett, Susannah, 14

Swift, Jonathan, 137

Symes, Lillian, 121–22

syphilis, 78

Taaffe, Julianne, 307–8

Taft, William Howard, 105

Tarbell, Ida, 105

Taylor, Emily, 205

teaching: as career for married women, 157; as career for single women, 60–61, 84, 123, 124, 157; in 1950s, 191; in 1970s, 250; in postwar era, 172; salaries, 60–61, 124, 134

television: attitudes toward older women in, 178–79, 191, 219–20, 248–50, 260–61; in 1950s, 178–79, 188, 220; in 1960s, 217–18, 219, 220; in 1970s, 249, 263; in 1980s, 260–64; in 1990s, 272, 277; in twenty-first century, 292, 300, 308–9, 316–17

temperance movement, 63, 81

Temple, Shirley. *See* Black, Shirley Temple

Terkel, Studs, 134, 135

Terms of Endearment (movie), 260

Terrell, Mary Church, 91–92, 145, 182

theater, 95, 96, 97, 112

Thomas, Helen, 251

Tilt, Edward, 80

Tilton, Elizabeth, 66–67, 68

Tilton, Theodore, 66–67, 68

Time magazine, 140, 181, 188–89, 251, 274, 282, 287

Tomei, Marisa, 322

Tomes, Robert, 37, 42

Tomlin, Lily, 258

Towle, Katherine, 204

Townsend, Harriet, 90–91

tranquilizers, 238–39

Triangle Shirtwaist Factory, 152

Trimble, Hannah, 174

Trouble with Angels, The (movie), 219

Trudeau, Garry, 221, 222–25, 254, 279

Truman, Harry, 171, 182

Trumbull, Harriet, 15

Trumbull, Maria, 15

Trump, Donald, 293, 310–15, 317, 318, 329, 330

Trump, Melania, 293, 309, 310–11

Truth, Sojourner, 52–53, 62–63, 78

Tubman, Harriet, 53, 62, 92–93

Turner, Ted, 258

twentieth century: attitudes toward older women in, 100–101, 103, 104, 105, 111; defining older women's age in, 126; life span in, 107, 174, 192; older women as celebrities in early twentieth century, 95. *See also* 1920s; 1930s; 1950s; 1960s; 1970s; 1980s; 1990s; World War II

twenty-first century: advertising of, 319–20; attitudes toward aging in, 319–20, 328–33; attitudes toward exercise, 290, 297–98; attitudes toward older women in, 304–7; breast cancer in, 296–97; cougars and, 291–93; defining older women's age in, 305, 331; hormone replacement therapy in, 293–95, 325; life span in, 305, 327–28; middle-aged women in, 289–91; movies of, 299–301, 308; multigenerational families and, 298–99; older women's role in, 4, 287–89, 302–4; plastic surgery in, 292, 295–96; retirement in, 306–7

Twiggy, 217

Tyler, John, 191

ABOUT THE AUTHOR

→ ← ←

Gail Collins is an op-ed columnist for the *New York Times,* where she has worked since 1995. She is the author of six previous books, most recently *When Everything Changed: The Amazing Journey of American Women from 1960 to the Present,* and her numerous honors include the George Polk Award for commentary. Collins lives in New York City.